Microsoft®
# Visual InterDev™ 6.0 Enterprise
## Developer's Workshop

*G. Andrew Duthie, MCSD*

**Microsoft** Press

PUBLISHED BY
Microsoft Press
A Division of Microsoft Corporation
One Microsoft Way
Redmond,Washington 98052-6399

Library of Congress Cataloging-in-Publication Data
Duthie, G. Andrew, 1967-
    Microsoft Visual InterDev 6.0 Enterprise Developer's Workshop / G. Andrew
  Duthie.
       p.  cm.
    Includes index.
    ISBN 0-7356-0568-8
    1. Microsoft Visual InterDev.   2. Web sites--Design.  I. Title.
TK5105.8885.M55D88   1998
005.2'76--dc21                              98-42528
                                             CIP

Printed and bound in the United States of America.

1 2 3 4 5 6 7 8 9  QMQM    4 3 2 1 0 9

Distributed in Canada by ITP Nelson, a division of Thomson Canada Limited.

A CIP catalogue record for this book is available from the British Library.

Microsoft Press books are available through booksellers and distributors worldwide. For further
information about international editions, contact your local Microsoft Corporation office or
contact Microsoft Press International directly at fax (425) 936-7329. Visit our Web site at
mspress.microsoft.com.

**Acquisitions Editor:** Eric Stroo
**Project Editor:** Rebecca McKay
**Production Services:** *TIPS* Technical Publishing

# TABLE OF CONTENTS

## PART I: TERMS, TOOLS, AND TECHNOLOGIES

### CHAPTER ONE

#### What Is Enterprise Web Development? 3

## CHAPTER TWO

# Defining the Web Application Environment  **31**

## CHAPTER THREE

# Challenges Faced in
# Enterprise Web Development        **55**

## CHAPTER FOUR

## Enter Visual InterDev 6.0   **95**

**PART II:** SOLVING CLIENT TIER CHALLENGES

**CHAPTER FIVE**

Features vs. Reach—Cross-Platform Support **131**

**CHAPTER SIX**

Navigation and Content
Design and Management **167**

**PART III:** SOLVING BUSINESS
TIER CHALLENGES

**CHAPTER SEVEN**

Addressing Performance and Scalability  **199**

## CHAPTER TEN

# User
# Authentication and Security   **351**

## PART IV: SOLVING DATA TIER CHALLENGES

**CHAPTER THIRTEEN**

# Response Time   **485**

## APPENDIX B

## Installing the
## Rent-A-Prize Sample Application    **547**

# FOREWORD

When I began with computers, there were two choices available to me at my school: a timeshare mainframe system with both CRT and TTY terminals and a couple of TRS-80s. I rather innocently asked the physics teacher, "What do you do with computers?" He could have said any number of things like accounting, order processing, or games, but instead he said, "You write programs." Looking back now, I realize he was right. Application development is the most serious thing you can do with computers. I used to split my time between the PC and mainframe, saving my programs on cassette tapes and paper tape respectively.

In those days the PC and mainframe seemed miles apart. Since then we've seen a host of new technologies and new architectures. With widespread use of dBase, application development underwent a fundamental change from being process-oriented to being data-oriented. Standalone PC architecture gave way to client/server systems. More recently, the concept of three-tier or component-based development — an intelligent client talking to business processes and rules housed in components that talk to the database — has returned us to a process-oriented paradigm. The move to a three-tier architecture has been closely followed (indeed some would say overtaken) by an Internet/intranet development frenzy. Many of the new features of Visual InterDev 6.0 are designed to facilitate accessing and editing data in a Web-based application with drag-and-drop functionality.

When Andrew first began discussing writing a book on Visual InterDev, we had long discussions about the specific challenges and requirements of enterprise developers. In my opinion, the Web doesn't change the fundamental architecture that makes for good enterprise applications. It simply provides another mechanism to deploy those applications — another way to generate the "user services" layer. What was needed was not a book about Visual InterDev per se but rather about enterprise application development challenges and how to meet them using Visual InterDev 6.0. That is what he and his contributing authors have provided within this book. With its coverage of components, transactions, and accessing legacy data, this book will prove to be an essential resource for the serious enterprise Web developer.

The essential concept to remember is that whether your application is form-based or Web-based, the underlying architecture should remain the same. Fundamentally, you have a services-based architecture made up of user services, business services, and data services. In a Web-based three-tier system, the browser and Web server combine to form the user services provider. The code you write in both of those places governs the user interface and the workflow of the application, *not* its underlying business functionality. For developers who use Microsoft tools, the word for the day is *COM* or Component Object Model. The core business processes should reside in components written to the COM specification and operate under the management of Microsoft Transaction Server. This is the architecture that will ultimately deliver the best performance, scalability, transactional integrity, and user satisfaction in the enterprise space.

We've come a long way in refining the architecture with which we develop PC applications. There's been a lot of code written and a lot of failed projects along the way. We need to be ever wary of taking steps backward when we are confronted with something new. I'm very happy that Andrew and his colleagues here at Spectrum have written a book aimed at the enterprise developer. I'm certain it took great discipline to avoid dwelling on some of the neato-keen new features of the tool that weren't necessarily meant for our use. I encourage you to exercise similar discipline when building your applications, using the new features to solve business problems, rather than just "because they're there." You'll sleep better at night. Good luck and enjoy the book!

*Jonathan Zuck*
Director of Technical Services
Spectrum Technology Group
September 1998

# ACKNOWLEDGMENTS

The road that led to my writing this book was an interesting one. In fact, when I set out, it was not my intention to write a book. I set out with the intention of signing on to a project and writing a chapter or two. My agent, Bob Kern, convinced me that it would be a better idea to put together a proposal for a new book, a book that would discuss a poorly covered subject area, namely enterprise Web development. We put together the proposal, Microsoft Press signed on, and before I knew it I began that months-long journey known as writing a book.

During that journey, there have been many deserving of my thanks and appreciation. They include: Bob Kern, for convincing me to take this crazy trip in the first place. Marty Minner, Jessica Ryan, Russ Mullen, Adam Newton, Manny Rosa, and the rest of the production team for their cogent editing, helpful comments, and patience. Rebecca McKay, Eric Stroo, and John Pierce at Microsoft Press, first and foremost for believing in my ideas, and also for having patience with my implementation (and all of my questions). Members of the Visual InterDev 6.0 development team, Garth Fort, Greg Leake, and especially David Lazar, whose timely answers to my questions helped improve the accuracy and the coverage of this book. Barry Dwyer and Jonathan Zuck at Spectrum Technology Group for believing in the importance of this project (and for giving me time to work on it). All the developers at Spectrum who had a hand in building the sample application, and of course my contributing authors, Susie Adams, Chris Dellinger, Paul Parry, and Geoff Snowman, who added much-needed expertise in those areas where mine was lacking.

I also want to acknowledge a number of the people who were instrumental in convincing me to enter the world of computers professionally and without whom this book would not have been written: John Hodges and Mike Foley, who saw that I was headed for a career in computers more than a year before I did (and told me so). David Rothschild, who convinced me that, yes, I could make a better living working in computers than in theater. And especially my mother, who always taught me that success is in doing what you love, and that if you do what you love, everything else will follow. Right, as always.

I save the most important for last. This project would never have gotten started, much less finished, without the loving and unfailing support of my wife, Jennifer, who, on hearing about the book proposal, told me that she was behind me 100 percent, and never backed down from that, despite my crankiness, tiredness, and general unavailability during this process. Words are not sufficient to express my gratitude to her.

# Introduction

The release of the 6.0 version of Visual InterDev represents a paradigm shift in Web development tools. The new version moves from a world of page-based tools that concentrated on making it easier to write HTML and script to a complete project-based development environment that extends into the realm of project management and organization. Rich tools are now available within the IDE for creating, editing, and managing pages, site structure, database connections, and data objects.

As a result, working with Visual InterDev has become much more like working with a development tool such as Visual Basic, with plenty of drag-and-drop functionality, and features to make developing Web applications faster and more efficient. While the new tools available in Visual InterDev 6.0 make Web development easier and more powerful, with the increased power of the Web development environment comes greater complexity, particularly in enterprise-class applications, which it is now possible to design and build with Visual InterDev (with a little help from some of the other Visual Studio family members).

This book is designed to give the reader unfamiliar with Visual InterDev 6.0 a brief introduction to its new features as well as show the basics of how to use those features. We've also included some background on Web development for client-server application developers just getting started with Web development. The real thrust of this book, however, is in describing the challenges faced by the Web developer creating enterprise-class applications with Visual InterDev, and offering solutions to those challenges.

Because we are working with enterprise applications, it will be necessary at times to discuss issues and technologies outside the immediate world of Visual InterDev, such as Microsoft SNA Server. These discussions should help solidify your understanding of the role Visual InterDev and the various tools of the Windows DNA architecture play in the creation and maintenance of enterprise-class Web applications.

# Who Can Use This Book

This book was written with three groups in mind:

- Visual Basic programmers
- Web developers
- Webmasters

These three groups will likely take different things from the book, but all should gain a more solid understanding of the issues facing Web developers today, as well as the solutions available for those issues. In particular, we'll focus on solutions offered by Visual InterDev and other Visual Studio tools, as well as by the underlying services of the Windows DNA architecture, including Microsoft Transaction Server (MTS), and Microsoft Message Queue Server (MSMQ).

## Visual Basic Programmers

It's clear that for a variety of reasons, the foremost being total cost of ownership (TCO), companies are moving to Web applications for their business solutions at an ever-increasing pace. Given that many of these solutions are implemented using Active Server Pages (ASP) technology, they can and will take advantage of Visual Basic Scripting Edition (VBScript) and Visual Basic COM components. This trend puts Visual Basic developers in a great position to supply these solutions. In order to supply these solutions, however, Visual Basic developers will need to learn and embrace (or at least work with) the differences inherent in a Web development environment (for example, the statelessness inherent in the HTTP protocol used for communications between the browser and Web server).

This book offers Visual Basic developers both background and perspective on the Web development environment as it exists today, as well as solid step-by-step solutions for the challenges they will face in implementing business solutions in a Web-based environment.

## Web Developers

Until now, Web developers have often found themselves working with a variety of tools, from text editors such as Notepad, to WYSIWYG page editors such as that provided by FrontPage 97, to build their Web applications. Visual InterDev 1.0, while offering the ability to manage Web applications as projects, an excellent color-coded text editor, and other features that improved the Web development environment, was still somewhat limited, particularly from the perspective of enterprise development. Web developers and their applications, therefore, were often assumed to be limited to departmental-level applications, or even written off as not being "real" developers.

With Visual InterDev 6.0 Web developers will finally have the tools with which to move their applications fully into the mainstream. This book offers Web developers the solutions necessary to move their applications to the next level, from producing consistent (and efficient) user interfaces, to profiling and optimizing data access within their applications.

## Webmasters

Webmasters are an often overlooked group in the discussions of Web development, perhaps because Webmasters are often thought of more as administrators than developers. This is an inaccurate perception, however, given the fact that as the sites they administer become more and more interactive, Webmasters are often called upon to perform some of the same tasks as developers. The danger, of course, is that for the most part Webmasters are not trained as developers, and that lack of training can lead to a patchwork approach to developing Web applications. Functionality is added piecemeal as it is needed or requested, with little or no planning as far as the overall applications architecture is concerned.

This book offers Webmasters the benefit of a structured approach to Web application development that can help them create unified Web application solutions rather than patchwork Web sites. The background material and solutions provided will combine to give a Webmaster a clearer idea of the process of moving from Web sites to Web applications.

# What's Not Covered

This book covers a lot of material, but obviously it is not possible to completely cover the entire subject of Web development, even limiting oneself to Visual InterDev Web development, in a single book. This is a huge topic that is becoming larger every day. In addition to limiting ourselves to Web application development using Visual InterDev 6.0, we have further limited ourselves to the discussion of using Visual InterDev 6.0 to create enterprise-class applications.

Because Visual InterDev 6.0 is a brand new tool, we'll provide a certain amount of coverage of the basics of using Visual InterDev 6.0. This coverage, however, is limited to getting those who are completely unfamiliar with the tool up to speed, so we can concentrate on issues related to enterprise development. Those looking for more in-depth coverage of the basics of Visual InterDev 6.0 would be better served by *Inside Visual InterDev (2nd Ed.)* by Ken Spencer, Ken

Miller, et. al. (Microsoft Press, 1998), or by some solid study of the product documentation, which is thorough.

It is also assumed that readers have some background in the basics of computer programming. As such, this book provides no explicit discussion of such basic concepts as procedural versus event-driven programming, flow-of-control logic, and the use of variables to represent values within applications, to name a few. Some understanding of these concepts may, however, be gleaned from the code examples included in the various Solutions sections within the book, as well as from the related discussions. Inexperienced developers interested in creating enterprise-class solutions, however, would be well served to invest in a class or book on programming fundamentals, as well as some good hands-on experience, before diving headfirst into developing large-scale Web applications.

## How to Use This Book

Those new to Web development (and those wishing to get the most out of the book) would be best served by going through the book sequentially. While the last three parts do not depend on one another explicitly, they do depend to a certain extent on concepts discussed in Part I, so readers not already intimately familiar with Web development in the Microsoft milieu are encouraged not to skip Part I.

That said, experienced developers looking for specific solutions may choose to use a piecemeal approach, reading just the parts and chapters that are pertinent to their needs, as those needs arise. The division of the book into the tiers of a three-tier solution, and chapters based on the challenges posed by those tiers, facilitates this approach.

## The Organization of This Book

As mentioned above, the organization of this book is based on the tiers of a three-tier Web application, preceded by an introductory section that describes the Web application environment and introduces Visual InterDev 6.0. The last three parts of the book use a goal and solutions framework in which each chapter has a stated goal that is supported by several step-by-step Solutions sections, many of which contain valuable code examples.

Part I, *Terms, Tools, and Technologies* (Chapters 1 through 4), defines and describes the Web application environment, differentiates between Web sites, Web applications, and enterprise Web applications, and introduces and describes the new features of Visual InterDev 6.0. This part also describes the challenges faced by enterprise Web developers, challenges to which the remaining parts will offer solutions.

Part II, *Solving Client Tier Challenges* (Chapters 5 and 6), deals with the issues and challenges involved in creating the user interface for your Web application. These issues include deciding whether to use Active Server Pages for the broadest reach or DHTML for richer interactivity, using Visual InterDev's Site Designer to plan and maintain your site, and providing a consistent look and feel with Visual InterDev themes (or your own custom theme).

Part III, *Solving Business Tier Challenges* (Chapters 7 through 10), discusses challenges faced in the business tier, including how to make your application scaleable and improve its performance, ways to secure your application, and how to improve the reliability of your application with message queuing. Chapter topics cover such complementary technologies as Microsoft Transaction Server (MTS) and Microsoft Message Queue Server (MSMQ).

Part IV, *Solving Data Tier Challenges* (Chapters 11 through 14), describes and offers solutions to the challenges involved in integrating data into your application. Topics covered include using the new Visual Database Tools for rapid development of database queries and objects, using SNA Server to access legacy data, and improving application response time through profiling and optimizing data access and queries.

Finally, Appendix A describes the use of the debugging and team-based development features of the 6.0 release of Visual InterDev, while Appendix B contains instructions for the installation of the Rent-A-Prize sample application.

## Using the Companion CD-ROM

The companion CD-ROM contains:

- Installation files for the Rent-A-Prize sample application and sample SQL Server database creation scripts
- Sample code for the components used in the sample application
- All sample code listings used in the book
- Microsoft Visual InterDev 6.0 Trial Edition

Instructions for installing the sample application can be found in Appendix B at the end of the book. For late-breaking information, please refer to the README.TXT file found in the root directory of the companion CD-ROM.

# Support

Every effort has been made to ensure the accuracy of this book and the contents of the companion CD-ROM. Microsoft Press provides corrections for books through the Web at http://mspress.microsoft.com/mspress/support/

If you have comments, questions, or ideas regarding this book or the companion CD-ROM, please send them to Microsoft Press using postal mail or e-mail:

Microsoft Press
Attn: Microsoft Visual InterDev 6.0 Enterprise Developer's
Workshop Editor
One Microsoft Way
Redmond, WA 98052-6399
MSPINPUT@MICROSOFT.COM

Please note that product support is not offered through the above mail addresses. For support information regarding Microsoft Visual InterDev, you can call the technical support line (425) 635-7012. Microsoft also provides information about Visual InterDev at http://msdn.microsoft.com/vinterdev and about the Microsoft Developer Network at http://msdn.microsoft.com/developer.

# PART I

# TERMS, TOOLS, AND TECHNOLOGIES

## CHAPTER ONE

# What Is Enterprise Web Development?

The World Wide Web and Internet technology have made a profound difference in the way developers build applications. For that matter, these technologies are making an even more profound difference in who is developing these applications.

Until the advent of the Internet and the World Wide Web, applications were traditionally written with a specific number of users in mind. Whether this was tens, hundreds, or even thousands of users, developers usually had a good idea how many users their application needed to support. Thanks to the Internet, Web applications can be made available to a potentially unlimited number of users, which in turn vastly increases the importance of application scalability.

Many client/server applications require installing a portion of the application on each client machine. For clients accessing applications via the World Wide Web, or a corporate intranet, this may not be practical. One of the advantages of Web applications is that they typically require little or no installation to be performed on the client.

Traditional client/server development was the undisputed realm of the experienced developer. Tools such as Visual Basic made client/server development easier and faster; but to develop truly robust applications, knowledge and understanding of how to fulfill business requirements was a must.

Although the Internet and the World Wide Web were initially used primarily for simply linking together static content, it didn't take long before tools became available that rapidly increased the amount of interactivity a Web site could deliver. Soon, tools allowing data access became available, enabling Web sites to take yet another step toward the world of true applications. Within the last year, new technologies have emerged that revolutionized the process of creating interactive, data-driven Web sites. These technologies allowed, for the first time, the creation of what could truly be called *Web applications*. It also opened up Web development to the traditional client/server developer through familiar languages and development environments.

Two of these technologies are Active Server Pages (ASP) and Visual InterDev 1.0. Both technologies helped to simplify the process of creating true Web applications so that just about anyone could successfully create a simple Web application in virtually no time at all. Unfortunately, in most cases, a simple Web application is not sufficient, particularly when that application needs to be supported in the enterprise. This book will guide the reader to and through the processes and examples that will lead to the development of a robust, scalable, and—most important—a successful enterprise Web application using Visual InterDev 6.0 as his or her central development tool. Although this book is aimed primarily at Visual Basic developers, we hope that the information provided will also be useful for site designers and Webmasters wishing to step up to a higher level of development, as well as for C++ and Java programmers who wish to gain a greater understanding of enterprise development in the context of the Microsoft Windows DNA application architecture. To begin our journey, let's talk about how we define enterprise Web development.

# What Enterprise Web Development Is *Not*

Enterprise Web development is different from both traditional application development and Web development in a variety of ways. Let's start by taking a look at what enterprise Web development is *not*.

## It Is *Not* "Building a Web Site"

A Web site and a Web application are, by definition, two different animals, each with its own properties, and each with its own purpose. A Web site is simply a collection of HTML pages designed to provide, or in some cases collect, information. A Web application is a collection of HTML pages and script or components designed to provide services, from document management to online purchasing. An enterprise Web application has the added burden of supporting large numbers of users while maintaining good performance, and often of connecting to and using a wide variety of data sources, including legacy sources, such as mainframe VSAM files. Another difference is that Web sites typically are built by content creators and designers. Web applications, and in particular, enterprise Web applications, must be designed and built by experienced developers in order to stand any chance of success.

## It Is *Not*, Strictly Speaking, Client/Server Development

Web development and traditional client/server development differ in some fundamental ways. These can include, but are not limited to, how they use database connections, how they interact with users, and how they maintain state information (let's not forget that HTTP is a stateless protocol). For example, it is not uncommon for a developer of a client/server application to improve the performance of the application by opening a database connection at the beginning of a user's session and caching that connection for the duration of the session in order to avoid the expense of repeatedly opening the connection. In a Web application, this strategy could backfire. For example, as the number of users increases, the maximum number of connections is reached, and additional users are unable to get a connection. Instead, Web applications typically use some form of connection pooling to reduce the cost of opening connections, while still allowing the largest number of users possible.

Not only do Webmasters or designers need to learn new lessons to successfully make the transition to the role of Web developer, client/server developers will also need to relearn some of their tricks, as well as learn new ones.

## It Is *Not* about "Dancing Baloney"

"Dancing baloney," aka "eye candy," is a term used to describe cute, but mostly useless, fluff such as animated GIFs, and the infamous <BLINK> and <MARQUEE> tags. The truth is that all the ShockWave animations, animated GIFs, and JavaScript mouseover effects in the World Wide Web don't amount to much if they don't fulfill the business requirements of the application. At their core, enterprise Web applications are about retrieving, manipulating, and storing data in an efficient, secure, and cost-effective manner. If a Web application can provide these services and be able to support such functionality to all those who require it, no matter where they are, or how many of them need access to the application at the same time, then we might begin to think about calling it an enterprise Web application. That said, once you have fulfilled your business requirements, there is nothing that says you can't add a little eye candy. Visual InterDev 6.0 provides ample support for inserting images, marquees, and other treats (though you'll have to add your own <BLINK> tags, which is probably just as well).

# What Enterprise Web Development *Is*

Now that we have some idea of what enterprise Web development isn't, let's take a look at what it is. Enterprise Web applications are all about data and services, as we'll discuss in the following sections.

## Enterprise Web Development Is *Enterprise* Development

One of the first things to remember about enterprise Web applications is the word "enterprise," which has some important implications. Enterprise applications in general share several broad characteristics, and enterprise *Web* applications are no exception:

- Enterprise applications are big. Real big. They serve hundreds or even thousands of users. By contrast, Web applications may serve tens or hundreds of thousands of users. They are typically multi-developer projects that employ multiple components, often on many diverse platforms. They access and make use of large amounts of data, frequently from multiple sources, which may include legacy systems.

- Enterprise applications are expected to have a relatively long, useful life. This should be obvious, given that implementing an enterprise application, Web-based or not, is a substantial investment, and it is only reasonable for a company to expect that they will have adequate time to recoup the costs of the system by having it enjoy a substantial lifespan. This does not mean that the application will not be upgraded or have features added during that lifespan. Rather, the application's architecture should be sufficiently well designed that the application need not be completely replaced for a significant length of time.

- Enterprise applications solve business problems. Everything about an enterprise application is business driven. Enterprise applications are not about entertainment or about showing off the coolest and latest technologies (though it's nice if you can do that, too). They are about efficiently and effectively solving your client's business problems.

■ Last, enterprise applications are, by definition, mission critical. They provide the kinds of business services that require 24x7 operation. Enterprise applications must be sufficiently robust to support this kind of continuous use, as well as sufficiently scalable to support both the typical number of users, and peak usage, which can potentially be anywhere from two to ten times the base usage or more, depending on how your application is deployed. If an online bookstore's customers aren't able to order books because of a server outage, or because the server can't handle the demand caused by the release of the latest Stephen King novel, that store is going to lose money. If the outages are prolonged or frequent, it won't be long before that store is out of business. It's our job to prevent that.

## Enabling Enterprise-Wide Access to Mission-Critical Data

One of the advantages of the advent of Internet technology is that since it's based on the same protocols used in most corporate networks today, all of the things that are possible to do over the Internet can also be made available to your in-house network, or intranet, and vice-versa. This means that if you write a Web application that allows access to corporate data, you can make that data available anywhere in the enterprise with just a Web browser, thus avoiding installing and maintaining a custom client application on the desktop of every user of your application.

## Providing Decision Support Systems
## That Can Be Used Around the Corner or Around the World

Another advantage of Internet technology is that with the appropriate security measures, you can make your Web applications available worldwide via the Internet, allowing users anywhere to access and use data and services. A good example of this is Decision Support Systems. Suppose you have a company with offices around the world, and executives in each of those offices need to be able to query and drill down into the sales data that is maintained at the corporate headquarters. By developing a Web application that supports this functionality, you save time and money because much of the development work, including specifying communications protocols, dealing with security issues, and providing user interface services, is taken care of for you. You can also substantially reduce maintenance and upgrade costs, since most upgrades will be done at the server, rather than at the client. Even if you use functionality from Java applets or ActiveX controls, code for those objects is automatically downloaded when the client uses your application, again saving you the trouble of client installations.

## Providing Streamlined Business Processes

The area where Web applications shine is in replacing or supplementing business processes that typically are done on paper, and in providing more efficient access and ability to update data.

### Employee In-Processing and Out-Processing

When an employee is hired there are forms to fill out. These forms are then given to a person who enters the information into a database of some sort, and who then passes the form on to others for further processing. The same process typically occurs at other significant points during an employee's tenure, such as promotions, leaves of absence, and retirement. By implementing these functions in a Web application, the amount of time and paperwork required to attend to these processes can be significantly reduced. For example, by reducing redundancies in data entry, using document routing to reduce the time required to process a particular change, and allowing employees, where appropriate, to take on some of the burden of taking care of their own data. An employee could use an HTML form to enter a change to his or her address online, directly updating his or her employee record, without intervention by human resources personnel. In addition, the page containing the form could incorporate script code to validate some of the address data entered, such as ensuring that the zip code is five or nine digits (see Figure 1-1). You could even use commercially available address information databases to validate that the city and zip code correspond to a real address.

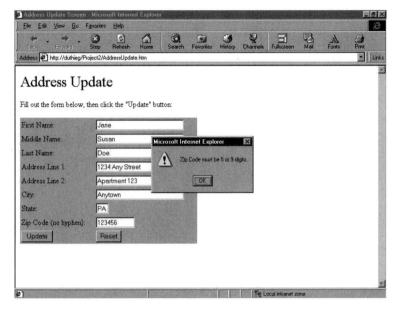

**Figure 1-1.**
*Address Update Form.*

The code for the page shown in Figure 1-1, which was prepared with the help of Visual InterDev 6.0's table editor, HTML Toolbox, and Script Outline, is shown below:

```
<HTML>
<HEAD>
<META NAME="GENERATOR" Content="Microsoft Visual Studio 6.0">
<TITLE>Address Update Screen</TITLE>
<SCRIPT ID=clientEventHandlersJS LANGUAGE=javascript>
<!-- Comment hides script from non-script browsers

function textZip_onblur() {
   var strZip = formAddressUpdate.textZip.value;
   if (strZip.length != 5 && strZip.length != 9) {
   alert ("Zip Code must be 5 or 9 digits.");
   }
}

//-->
</SCRIPT>
</HEAD>
<BODY>
<FONT size=6 style="BACKGROUND-COLOR: #ffffff">Address Update </FONT>

<FORM action="ProcessAddress.asp" method=post id=formAddressUpdate>
```

(continued)

9

```
<P>Fill out the form below, then click the <B>Update</B> button:</P>

<TABLE WIDTH=50% BGCOLOR=silver ALIGN=left BORDER=0 CELLSPACING=1
CELLPADDING=2>
   <TR>
      <TD nowrap>First Name:
      </TD>
      <TD>
         <INPUT id=textFirstName name=textFirstName maxLength=25 size=25>
      </TD>
   </TR>
   <TR>
      <TD nowrap>Middle Name:
      </TD>
      <TD>
         <INPUT id=textMiddleName name=textMiddleName maxLength=25 size=25>
      </TD>
   </TR>
   <TR>
      <TD nowrap>Last Name:

      </TD>
      <TD>
         <INPUT id=textLastName name=textLastName maxLength=25 size=25>
      </TD>
   </TR>
   <TR>
      <TD nowrap>Address Line 1:
      </TD>
      <TD>
         <INPUT id=textAddress1 name=textAddress1 maxLength=25 size=25>
      </TD>
   </TR>
   <TR>
      <TD nowrap>Address Line 2:
      </TD>
      <TD>
```

*(continued)*

```
                   <INPUT id=textAddress2 name=textAddress2 maxLength=25 size=25>

         </TD>
      </TR>
      <TR>
         <TD nowrap>City:
         </TD>
         <TD>
            <INPUT id=textCity name=textCity maxLength=25 size=25>
         </TD>
      </TR>
      <TR>
         <TD nowrap>State:
         </TD>
         <TD>
            <INPUT id=textState name=textState maxLength=2 size=2>
         </TD>
      </TR>
      <TR>
         <TD nowrap>Zip Code (no hyphen):
         </TD>
         <TD>
            <INPUT id=textZip name=textZip maxLength=10 size=10
LANGUAGE=javascript onblur="return textZip_onblur()">
         </TD>
      </TR>
      <TR>
         <TD>
            <INPUT type="submit" value="Update" id=submit1 name=submit1>

         </TD>
         <TD>
            <INPUT type="reset" value="Reset" id=reset1 name=reset1>

         </TD>
      </TR>
   </TABLE>

</FORM>
</BODY>
</HTML>
```

Note that the script for validating the zip code is contained within the <HEAD> tags of the HTML document (which makes your scripts easier to manage), and that the form and all its elements have ID properties (which allows them to be scripted via the Visual InterDev Script Outline). This page submits to an ASP page called ProcessAddress.asp, but you could just as easily make this page an ASP page and have it submit to itself. The page could then update a database with the new values, or call a component to do so.

## Employee Benefits Enrollment

Another example of a way that employees can make business processes more efficient is with a Web application that allows online benefits enrollment. In many companies today the benefits enrollment period is a time of terror, particularly for the human resources and benefits specialists who have to cope with the flood of paperwork and the inevitable questions of employees confused by the myriad choices available to them.

By offering online benefits enrollment, a company can empower employees to find answers through online documentation, and to make their decisions more efficiently and with a minimum of human intervention. By using a Web application for benefits enrollment, an employee can make benefits choices that can be immediately validated against the appropriate business rules, and if successfully validated, can update the employees records with the appropriate changes. This will reduce wait time for employees and improve overall employee satisfaction with benefits. There are probably very few human resources managers who would say no to that idea.

The idea of using online documentation could, for example, be implemented as a series of simple HTML pages explaining the various fields on the enrollment screen. The labels for the fields could then be hyperlinked to the individual pages, allowing an employee to access the required information without having to call their benefits officer. If your application uses Internet Explorer 4, you can take advantage of DHTML to provide inline help, as shown in Figure 1-2. In this case when a user clicks on a field name, hidden text is displayed using dynamic styles. This technique will be discussed in detail in Chapter 5, "Features vs. Reach—Cross-Platform Support."

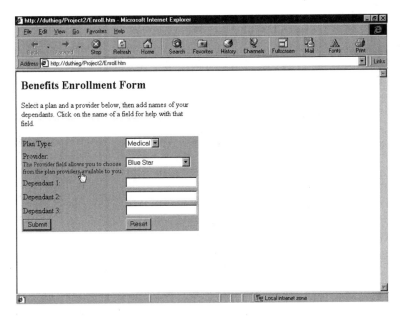

**Figure 1-2.**
*Inline Help with DHTML.*

## Increasing Accuracy

You may have noticed a common thread among the examples above: all of them have the potential to significantly reduce the amount of paperwork that a company has to process. While it is unlikely that companies will ever achieve the much-vaunted "paperless" office, it is certainly true that reducing the load of paper that must be filled out, handed around, approved, keyed in, and filed, is one important way for companies to save money, which is, after all, the goal of automating processes through computerization.

Another important advantage that many of the above Web applications can offer is increased accuracy of data, particularly in areas where employees or customers fill out forms online that were once done on paper. In allowing the user to input the data directly, at least one step in the process is eliminated—since the data does not need to be keyed in at a later time from a paper form. This eliminates potential problems due to forms being filled out incorrectly by the user (since data validation can be done at the time data is entered, as shown above), reduces typos (by providing users with a confirmation of the data they entered for review), and avoids problems of incomplete or conflicting information (by explicitly requiring fields and disallowing certain combinations, or giving only predefined choices). Overall, the power and flexibility of having users fill out forms online far exceeds the development investment required to make such a system a reality.

# Creating a Web Site vs. Developing a Web Application

While it may seem obvious to those experienced in Web development, it's important to point out the differences between creating a Web site and developing a Web application. Attempting to develop an enterprise Web application without understanding the differences will likely result in failure. As noted above, a Web site can have a great deal of interactivity and still not truly be an application in the strictest sense, while a Web application, for obvious reasons, shares a great deal in common with a Web site (hyperlinks, graphics formats and styles, and so on). How then, does one distinguish between the two? One of the best ways of understanding the difference is by looking at what the site does; that is, what purpose does it serve?

Web sites typically focus on delivering content, while Web applications focus on delivering services. In the next section, we'll discuss some examples that illustrate each.

## Web Sites Focus on Delivering Content

As a general rule, Web sites are about content delivery. Whether that content is static and rarely updated, as is the case of many Web-based FAQ (Frequently Asked Questions) lists, or interactive and frequently updated, as is the case with an online stock ticker, the purpose of the sites is the transfer of information. Following are two examples of Web sites you might encounter on your company's intranet or out on the Internet.

### Online Phone Directory

One relatively simple use of a Web site that can be made available both in-house and externally is an online telephone directory. Anyone who's had to put up with incorrect and infrequently updated phone listings knows how useful such a site can be. With very little effort, a single phone listing for a department or even an entire company can be placed online. When the phone listing is updated, anyone looking at the online list automatically gets the updated information, without having to manually send out new phone lists, either as files or on paper.

### Online Job Listings

Another area where a Web site is generally more than adequate is in providing online job listings. Many of you have probably already seen such a site where you can select from a number of job categories, choose a date range for searching, and provide numerous other search criteria, which produce a set of job listings that meet your criteria. Such sites, many of which even allow you to search multiple newspapers' classified sections, clearly illustrate the difference between Web sites (providing information) and Web applications (providing services). To borrow a page from the object-oriented programming world, a Web site is somewhat analogous to a class with only properties, while a Web application has both properties and methods. That is, a Web site allows you to look at information, but not necessarily to manipulate it or make direct use of it, while a Web application allows you to view information and take action based on that information or to manipulate that information.

## Web Applications Focus on Delivering Services

It is those all-important methods that set apart a Web application, allowing its users to accomplish tasks (such as updating databases or performing calculations) that were once solely the purview of custom Visual Basic applications. Applications are about delivering services. In other words, not just giving the user information, but also giving the user tools with which to manipulate and make use of that information. They can also supply information of their own, which is then acted on by the application. The following examples roughly parallel the examples given in the prior section, and illustrate how much further a Web application can take you (and your users).

### Web-based Contact Management

While a Web site can excel at providing information like company phone listings online, imagine how much better it would be to not only have phone listings available online, but also to have information about management chains or customer relationships. Imagine a consulting company with consultants constantly going on new assignments and coming back from completed ones. A Web application could, for example, allow a manager who needs to find a consultant for an upcoming assignment to search a list of consultants with the necessary skills for the assignment, then find out from within the same application who those consultants report to, then send an e-mail to that person regarding the consultant's availability for the assignment. Potentially, the consultant's current assignment status could also be made available in the application. Imagine how much faster that manager could find the consultant he or she needs with the assistance of such an application.

Another possibility for expanding the idea of an online phone directory is an application that allows a corporate field sales force to enter customer and order information through a Web browser, and have that information automatically sent to the corporate database the next time they are connected to the company network. With that information updated, customers could be assigned to a new salesman if the original salesman left the company or was transferred, and customers could be automatically given or offered discounts or special offers based on their purchase history. This type of application can make a company seem much more responsive to customers, and help salesmen manage their customers more effectively.

### Automated Employment
### Application Process with Intelligent Routing

This example builds on the idea of online job listings. If you take a look at the jobs being listed in online classifieds these days, one thing you'll notice is that more and more of them provide an e-mail address to which you can send your resume. Some even provide the URL of their company Web site, allowing you to get more information about the company. Imagine, however, if you could actually apply for the job right there online. A Web application could easily provide that kind of functionality.

Here's how it would work. When a user searches the online classifieds and comes up with your company's ad, the ad provides a URL that links the potential employee to your application. The link would supply the application with the code for the job to which the applicant was responding. With this information, the Web application would provide the applicant with a series of form fields for standard applicant information as well as fields corresponding to the requirements for that particular job. By knowing at this time which job the user was applying for, the application could potentially validate certain data, such as level of education, years of pertinent experience, and so forth, and even potentially inform applicants with inadequate qualifications of that fact up front, reducing the amount of time both parties potentially waste on pursuing unsuitable matches. Next time you talk to someone in your Human Resources department, ask them if they'd be interested in having such an application.

## It's a Fine Line

While it's important to understand the theoretical differences between a Web site and a Web application in order to design better applications, it's not as important to be able to easily decide which is which in reality. In the real world, the line between a Web site and a Web application can be fine, and what was a Web site can become a Web application as functionality is added to it. It is, however, unlikely for an enterprise Web application to be created this way. This is because the greater needs of an enterprise application require that the application's architecture be carefully designed to support the performance and security that these applications demand. In other words, while there may be a fine line between a Web site and a Web application, the line between a Web application and an enterprise Web application is much broader. Enterprise Web applications require careful planning to succeed—a level of planning that is not typically needed for a Web site (though Web sites can certainly benefit from planning).

Clearly, the characteristics and requirements of developing enterprise applications make it a challenging, even daunting, task even for a team of seasoned programmers, but nobody ever said it would be easy. Fortunately, there are lots of tools available to help, although many are somewhat lacking from the perspective of enterprise Web applications. In the next section we'll discuss some of the available tools for Web development, and their respective strengths and weaknesses.

# Available Tools

Until recently, one of the potential obstacles to building successful enterprise Web applications was the fact that the tools available for Web development did not support the kind of functionality and performance required of an application of enterprise scope. In most cases Web applications had to be created piecemeal, with little or no integration between the tools used to create the parts. The user interface would be cobbled together in Notepad, with graphics pulled in from Paint Shop Pro (or if you were at a high-end shop from Photoshop), the interactivity and processing provided by a mix of C++ executables and Perl scripting, and let's not get into data access. The resulting applications neither performed nor scaled particularly well from an enterprise point of view. Here is a brief (and admittedly biased) discussion of the available tools for Web development, and a description of some of the advantages Visual InterDev 6.0 offers over them.

## HTML with CGI

Common Gateway Interface (CGI) is the grand-daddy of Web programming. CGI was developed as a standard way in which user input from HTML forms could be processed on the Web server and could generate HTML dynamically in response. CGI is still widely used for several good reasons. One reason is that in its simplest form, using Perl or other scripting languages, a CGI application can be very easy to create. Another reason is that until recently, there really were no alternatives. In addition, the wide acceptance of CGI has meant that most Web server software supported CGI, and therefore it was fairly easy to find developers with CGI skills.

Unfortunately, CGI also has some downsides, which include:

### Performance Drawbacks

For example, CGI applications written in a scripting language, such as Perl, and those written as compiled C or C++ executables have potential performance drawbacks. Programs written solely in script suffer from performance problems because script languages are substantially slower to execute than compiled code, due to the overhead of interpreting the language at runtime. With CGI executables, the Web server must create a new process or instance of the executable for each user request. This can amount to a substantial burden, particularly for an application with a large user base. This can result in rapid performance degradation as the number of requests increases.

### Lack of Debugging Tools

Although it is possible to a limited degree to debug executables created for CGI, there are no tools available to effectively debug a CGI application from end to end, meaning that development and maintenance of CGI applications can be more time-consuming and costly. CGI also lacks the kind of development environment that has been available to developers using languages such as Visual Basic, in which a developer has numerous supporting tools at hand to make their work more efficient.

Visual InterDev 6.0 offers superior ease-of-use, as well as in many cases superior performance over CGI, as well as support for debugging your applications.

## HTML with ISAPI

The Internet Server Application Programming Interface (ISAPI) was introduced by Microsoft with Internet Information Server (IIS) to address some of the shortcomings of CGI in server programming. Because they are DLLs that run in the process of the Web server, ISAPI programs, known as filters and extensions, are able to handle new client requests using threads IIS creates and passes to the ISAPI DLL to handle the request. Because IIS would have created the thread in any case, there is little or no overhead in calling ISAPI DLLs. This, in turn, means that ISAPI can provide a substantial performance improvement over, and greater scalability than, an equivalent CGI executable.

ISAPI DLLs, since they are written in C++, can also take full advantage of the Win32 API, Open Database Connectivity (ODBC), and other useful Win32 technologies. This can save a developer a substantial amount of time by not requiring him or her to reinvent the wheel with every program.

So what are the downsides for ISAPI? They include:

- **Steep Learning Curve** ISAPI DLLs are written in C++, meaning that for non-C++ programmers, ISAPI filters and extensions are out of reach, or at the very least, a difficult challenge. While this might make for a good excuse to go ahead and start learning C++, it also makes ISAPI less attractive to those of us less familiar with the rarified air of the C++ world.

- **Lack of Debugging Tools** Although ISAPI does provide some improvements in terms of the availability of techniques that can help in partial debugging of ISAPI programs, it still lacks the kind of feature-rich debugging available in the integrated development environments (IDEs) developers are familiar with today.

Visual InterDev 6.0 offers many of the performance advantages of ISAPI applications through support for integration of COM components into your Web application, allowing you to develop your components in any language that supports COM.

## HTML Editors

HTML editors have been introduced over the last couple of years as tools that allow Webmasters, Web developers, or anyone else for that matter, to create Web pages with little or no HTML coding. The guiding principle of HTML editors seems to be to provide the equivalent of a word processor for the Web. While this has allowed whole new groups to joins the ranks of the World Wide Web in terms of creating personal home pages, HTML editors have not as yet had much to offer Web developers, for reasons including:

### Helpful for UI, but Not Great for Programming

HTML editors can be helpful when you need to develop the user interface of a Web application quickly. Unfortunately, even some of the best HTML editors can be frustrating for the experienced developer to use, in part because some of the features provided to make coding simpler serve to limit the flexibility available to more advanced users. Advanced developers need to be able to quickly and easily jump out of the WYSIWYG (or close approximation) view of their page and dive into the code, without having to worry about whether the editor will then come behind them and "correct" their changes (see Figure 1-3). Additionally, support for programmability features, including the use of server programming, is limited at best.

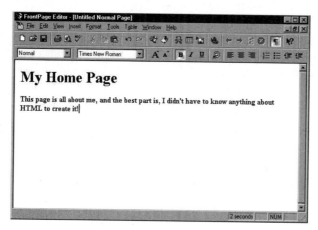

**Figure 1-3.**
*FrontPage 97 HTML Editor.*

By contrast, Visual InterDev 6.0's editor provides easy access to both WYSIWYG and source code views of your pages, as well as access to the attributes of most HTML tags through a properties window, simplifying the task of editing tags. In addition, Visual InterDev 6.0 provides excellent support for server programming, including drag-and-drop access to server objects, including Active Server Page (ASP) intrinsic objects.

### Many Lack Tweaking Ability

Because the goal of many HTML editors is to simplify Web page creation, these tools tend to use a somewhat brute-force approach, reducing the amount of fine control available over certain options, such as font colors, use of forms and tables, and so on. Even if you are able to tweak your use of such options without the editor negating your changes, such a choice usually means giving up some of the benefits of using an editor in the first place. While Visual InterDev 6.0 offers many features that simplify page creation, its editor also allows you, the developer, as much control over customization as you need, from drilling down into the source view of the editor, to changing certain options on a language-by-language basis.

## "Visual" Notepad

Notepad, the simplest text editor on the Windows block is often jokingly referred to as "Visual" notepad, a reference to its tenacity as a development tool in the face of more sophisticated visual tools.

### The De Facto Standard for Many Web Developers

The fact of the matter is that in Web development you ultimately do not need anything other than a text editor to do anything short of compiling an executable. HTML code can be written in Notepad, as can scripting code. You can even write your C++ EXEs and DLLs in Notepad if you really want to. For those who still want to deal directly with their code, Notepad is frequently the chosen tool.

### Makes Up for in Ease-of-Use What It Lacks in Style

Notepad has two things going for it: it is simple, and it is ubiquitous. A Web developer who uses Notepad as their chosen development tool knows that it is available on any Windows machine. This means that if they need to make changes to their code, they don't need to worry about whether or not the machine they have access to has the tool installed. Although it appears that Visual Basic is everywhere (certainly VBA is getting close), it doesn't yet approach the ubiquity of Notepad.

On the other hand, Notepad is lacking in many areas, and code written with it can be substantially less readable (and therefore less maintainable) than code written in a text editor with more advanced features, like customizable tab stops.

Visual InterDev 6.0 offers one of the most advanced editors available, with IntelliSense statement completion (as seen in Visual Basic), syntax color-coding for both HTML and script, and other features that may make the decision to finally abandon Notepad a whole lot easier.

## Site Design and Management Tools

Another category of tools available for developing Web sites are site design and management tools, such as the FrontPage family from Microsoft. These tools provide an environment that simplifies the creation of content.

## Good for Quickly Creating Consistent, Easy-to-Manage Sites

The one thing these types of tools are best at is providing an easy way to create consistent, manageable Web sites. They provide themes for a consistent look and feel, wizards for creating content (see Figure 1-4), and tools for managing site structure and checking the integrity of links within a site. They also frequently offer tools that simplify the task of publishing your site to your Web server, whether to a server on your local network or to a remote server via FTP.

**Figure 1-4.**
*The New FrontPage Web Dialog Box.*

There is, of course, a tradeoff for using these tools. FrontPage, at least, requires that you (and your Web server) use the FrontPage server extensions that allow FrontPage to provide much of its magic. This may not seem like much of a downside, but as anyone who has accidentally deleted a _vti_cnf directory can tell you, if you mess with how FrontPage manages your site, you can end up with a whole heap of problems. The moral: *If you use FrontPage, don't do any site management outside of FrontPage.*

## Not as Good for Providing Programming Support

Because FrontPage and its cousins are designed for content creation and management, support within them for programming is limited. Many can insert client-side script, Java applets, or ActiveX controls, but implementation can be difficult, and debugging tools are almost nonexistent. In addition, there is little or no support for server programming, making these tools unsuitable for developing enterprise Web applications.

With its Site Designer, Themes, and Layouts, Visual InterDev 6.0 offers some of the same powerful site design and management features offered by tools such as FrontPage and then some, while also offering advanced support for development necessities such as data access and debugging.

## Java Applets

Anyone who has not yet heard of Java has probably spent the last several years in a cave. Java, created by Sun Microsystems, is a programming language in which programs are compiled into a generic "p-code," which is then run on what is referred to as a "virtual machine," which, in theory, enables a Java applet or application to run on any platform that has a Java virtual machine available. In practice, this kind of "write-once, run anywhere" nirvana has yet to material-ize anywhere other than in Web browsers. For most purposes, a Java applet written to work in one browser should work in any Java-enabled browser. This is due in part to the fact that Java applets running in a Web browser are severely limited in their access to the system on which they are running.

### Can be Great for Small Utility Programs

Because of their ability to be run in any Java-enabled browser, Java applets can be a great answer to the question of providing advanced services, such as user input forms that can do validation without a round-trip to the server, or applets that provide graphics, animation, or other multimedia support, without sacri-ficing cross-platform availability for your site, or requiring users to download plug-ins to enable functionality.

### Lacks Ability to Access Many OS Services

Unfortunately, Java applets run in a Web browser are unable to access resources of the system on which they are run. This behavior is by design. Java applets are run in what is referred to as the "sandbox" in order to protect the client system from the danger of malicious code. The downside is that without access to system services, such as file access and API access, Java applets are unable to perform some of the most basic functions of applications, such as working with persistent storage (files).

### Relatively Steep Learning Curve

Another potential downside to Java applets is that for those without prior experience in Java or other object-oriented languages, the learning curve can be rather steep. The programming paradigm used by Java, while very powerful and elegant, is very different from that familiar to Visual Basic programmers. For that reason, and because of Java's limitations in accessing system services, ActiveX controls may provide a better answer.

While Java applets may still be useful in Web applications, many of the functions performed by them are more easily accomplished through the use of ASP code or through the use of DHTML. But when you do choose to use Java in your Web application, Visual InterDev 6.0's debugger allows you to debug your applets along with your scripts, saving you the time and headaches of using a separate debugger.

## ActiveX Controls

ActiveX controls are compiled components (OCXs) that may be run in any ActiveX control container. ActiveX control containers include Internet Explorer, the Visual Basic IDE, and the Microsoft Office family of tools, among others.

### Browser Compatibility Issues

One of the first issues to be aware of when using ActiveX controls as a part of a Web application is that they are currently only natively supported by Internet Explorer 3.0 and above. Plug-ins are available that enable the use of ActiveX controls in Netscape browsers, but these may not enable the full range of your control's functionality, and so may be unacceptable. The upshot of this is that the use of ActiveX controls in your Web application constitutes a decision to exclude browsers that do not support ActiveX. This may not be acceptable for an application that is accessible to the Internet. But for applications where it is acceptable, the decision offers a great deal of power. ActiveX controls can do virtually anything any other application can do, thereby allowing a great deal of functionality to be built into controls.

### Vast Array of Controls
### Readily Available for Download or Purchase

One of the things that has made ActiveX controls hugely popular is that they provide a way for developers to package up, or componentize, frequently used functionality in a way that makes that functionality easily reusable. Many of these reusable components can be downloaded for free, or purchased over the Internet. In fact, ActiveX controls are one of the first technologies to truly deliver on the promise of reusable code components.

## Relatively Steep Learning Curve to Develop—Less So with VB5

Until recently, ActiveX controls were the purview of C++ programmers. While tools were provided for Visual C++ that made control creation easier, it was still difficult for VB programmers to build their own controls. With the release of Visual Basic 5.0, it's quite easy to create ActiveX controls from within Visual Basic. There is even a separate category selection available from VB's opening dialog box that sets the IDE up for control creation (see Figure 1-5).

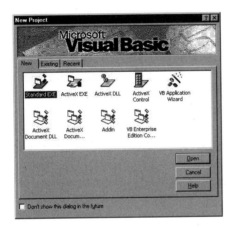

**Figure 1-5.**
*Visual Basic 5.0 New Project Dialog Box.*

## Can Access OS Services, but Only on Win32

One of the distinct advantages of using ActiveX controls is that since they are actually COM DLLs (see Chapter 2, "Defining the Web Application Environment," for a brief history of COM), they can access the full range of functionality available in the Win32 API. Unfortunately, this functionality does not extend to the recent releases of Internet Explorer 4 for non-Windows platforms. Hopefully with the ongoing movement of COM to a number of UNIX platforms, it may not be long before this limitation is overcome.

Visual InterDev provides some of the best support yet for ActiveX controls. In fact, VI 6 has an entire section of its Toolbox devoted to ActiveX controls. You can drag controls from the Toolbox onto your pages, and even add new controls to the Toolbox.

# Client Side Scripting — VBScript, JScript (JavaScript, ECMAScript)

One of the most valuable development tools to come from the world of browsers and the Web is scripting languages like VBScript and JavaScript. Although there have been scripting languages long before the Web, it's only been since the introductions of JavaScript by Netscape and VBScript by Microsoft, that scripting languages have taken off in popularity as well as utility.

## Easy to Learn

Since both VBScript and JavaScript are based at least in part on familiar programming languages (JavaScript shares some of the syntax and primitive data types of Java, while VBScript is a subset of the Visual Basic programming language), the tools they provide are easy for most programmers to learn. Because both VBScript and JavaScript are more limited in scope than full-blown programming languages like Visual Basic, Java, and Visual C++, they are also much easier for less experienced developers to learn.

## Can be Very Powerful

Both VBScript and JavaScript provide features that allow for sophisticated client-side functionality, including validation logic and complex calculations done locally on the client, saving repeated server round-trips.

## VBScript Is IE Only

Like ActiveX controls, VBScript is supported only in Internet Explorer. Also, like ActiveX controls, there are plug-ins available to enable use of the VBScript with Netscape Navigator, but the same caveats apply regarding the availability of VBScript's full functionality.

## JavaScript Has Numerous Versions – Until Now

Until recently, the use of JavaScript has been complicated by the fact that there have been multiple versions and implementations of JavaScript. Netscape has provided different versions of JavaScript with each of their browsers since version 2.0, while Microsoft's implementation, JScript, has attempted to keep pace with the changes being made in JavaScript. The result has been that developers have been forced once again to either choose one over the other (and of course choose the browser that that decision entails), or to limit themselves to functionality that the implementations have in common. ECMAScript, an attempt to address this problem, is an industry-standard implementation of Java/JScript agreed upon by both Microsoft and Netscape. JScript 3.0, the scripting engine included with Internet Explorer 4 and IIS 4.0, fully supports the

ECMAScript standard. Unfortunately, until Netscape releases a browser that fully supports the ECMAScript standard, developers still have to decide which to use.

### Interpreted Languages Lack Speed

Scripting languages share one disadvantage with CGI: because they must be compiled and interpreted at run time, they are relatively slow. For sites with a substantial amount of traffic, this could be a potential bar to scalability.

### Proprietary Business Logic Is Exposed in Pages

One of the most important disadvantages of client-side scripting from the perspective of enterprise development is that client-side script is sent to the client. Though this may seem both obvious and somewhat circular, the upshot is that any business logic embedded in client-side script is, for all intents and purposes, given away. Anyone wanting to use any of the code that makes your application work need only view the source for the pages and cut and paste the code they want to use. This means that client-side scripting is effectively limited to only those parts of your application that do not use proprietary business logic. Fortunately, recent improvements in server-side scripting make the server an excellent choice for processing that requires proprietary business logic.

Visual InterDev 6.0 provides strong support for both VBScript and JavaScript/JScript, including client and server debugging support, statement completion through IntelliSense, and the Script Outline, which provides point-and-click access to events of scriptable client and server elements and events. Where script performance is a concern, Visual InterDev also offers strong support for components, including automatic component registration, and packaging components for use with Microsoft Transaction Server (MTS).

## Internet Information Server (IIS) and Active Server Pages (ASP)

With version 3.0 and later, Microsoft Internet Information Server (IIS) has offered a technology called Active Server Pages (ASP). ASP combines support for server-side scripting with support for component use on the server and a powerful intrinsic object model to provide what is arguably the most powerful, as well as easy-to-use, Web programming platform available today. ASP is compatible with any browser that supports cookies and HTML 3.2.

### ASP Hosts Scripting Engines for Web Server (IIS)

ASP comes with built-in support for both JScript 2.0 and VBScript 2.0, but it also allows for the installation of other scripting engines to enable support for other languages, such as Perl, to be used with IIS. With ASP, IIS refers all pages with the .ASP extension to the ASP.DLL, which calls upon the appropriate script engine to interpret the script(s) in the page, then returns the results to IIS. Note that a given ASP page can use more than one scripting language, although at the obvious expense of the overhead required by multiple scripting engines.

### Win32-Only Technology

At present IIS only runs on Windows NT Server. Fortunately, this is a much smaller concern than client compatibility issues, particularly given that as a general rule, Windows NT Web servers are both easier and less expensive than UNIX servers to set up and maintain.

### Solves Problems Posed by
### Client-Side Scripting, HTTP Statelessness, CGI, and so on.

ASP provides a great many solutions to the disadvantages of the tools mentioned. ASP provides a solution to concerns about exposure of proprietary business logic by moving such logic to the server, where it can be secured. It also provides a solution to the challenge of HTTP statelessness by providing intrinsic objects that allow ASP applications to keep track of both session and application state. It also provides a solution to the problems inherent in CGI by providing for the simple use of COM components in addition to server-side scripting, increasing both the flexibility and performance of Web applications built with ASP.

### ASP Is Useful as "Glue" for Components

ASP scripting, in fact, is at its best when used as "glue" for COM components. ASP scripts are used to instantiate COM components, set properties on the components, and call methods. The components can even be built to return results as HTML, saving the ASP page the trouble of writing the HTML to the browser. This use of ASP can create both extremely powerful as well as highly scalable Web applications.

### ASP Has Simple, Programmable Object Model

The intrinsic objects provided by ASP provide a powerful paradigm for server programming that is remarkably easy to use. By providing services such as session management, user input, browser output, and component creation and management through an object model, much of the complexity of server programming is abstracted, allowing Web developers to concentrate on developing their application, rather than the services required to support it.

## Visual InterDev 1.0

The first version of Visual InterDev brought forth a new paradigm in Web programming, one very similar to the paradigm of Visual Basic and similar tools, in which an application is developed by combining controls and other tools available in the development environment. VI 1.0 provided the first taste of the future of Web application development, including Design-Time Controls (DTCs). DTCs allowed Web progr ammers to insert code into their ASP pages to generate the actual ASP code to be used for such tasks as data access. While their usefulness in VI 1.0 was somewhat limited, it showed the possibilities of the technology. VI 1.0 also provided an HTML editor that provided syntax-based color-coding of HTML and script code, as well as the ability to preview pages within the VI IDE, the next best thing to having a WYSIWYG editor. Visual InterDev 6.0 builds on the best of VI 1.0 and makes a giant leap forward by adding numerous features designed to simplify the task of Web development.

## What's Still Lacking

Although IIS and ASP have provided a great step forward for Web development, and Visual InterDev 1.0 offered for the first time an IDE for Web developers with some real promise, there were still some major issues that have yet to be dealt with adequately, including:

### Debugging

Ask any group of Web developers what their biggest gripe is about Web development, and the chances are pretty good that many will answer, "debugging." With IIS 3.0 and Visual InterDev 1.0, there is still no way to easily do end-to-end debugging of ASP applications. Components must be debugged separately from script, and client script must be debugged separately from server script. This makes developing Web applications much harder than it needs to be, and makes it much more difficult to provide the kind of bullet-proof reliability required of enterprise applications.

### True Drag-and-Drop Development

For years, Visual Basic programmers have had the advantage of a development environment in which they could simply drag-and-drop controls from a toolbox, then write a minimal amount of code to integrate those controls into a powerful application. Web developers are still waiting for an environment that gives them that kind of power, and affords them the ability to be accordingly productive. In other words, a rapid application development environment for Web applications.

As you will see in Chapter 4, "Enter Visual InterDev 6.0," Visual InterDev addresses these and other deficiencies by offering drag-and-drop support for many common Web development tasks (including data access), by adding end-to-end debugging support, and by providing one of the best HTML and script editors available. Although it may not be the only tool you ever use, you will find Visual InterDev 6.0 a strong replacement for many of the tools discussed above.

## Summary

In this chapter, we've discussed what enterprise Web development provides, including:

- Enterprise access to mission-critical data
- Decision-support systems available worldwide
- Streamlined business processes
- Reduced paperwork and increased accuracy

We've also described some examples of the differences between Web sites and Web applications, for example:

- Web sites deliver content
- Web applications deliver services

Finally, we talked about some of the tools available today for doing Web development, and their respective strengths and weaknesses, as well as the ways in which Visual InterDev improves on them.

In the next chapter, we'll take an in-depth look at the Web development environment on the Windows platform. We will also take a brief look at the history of COM, from which you will gain an understanding of its importance to Web developers.

C H A P T E R    T W O

# Defining the Web Application Environment

In the last chapter, we discussed what enterprise Web development is and is not, and looked at the tools available for Web development. In this chapter, we'll take a look at the Web application development environment as it exists for Windows NT Web development, and begin to look at Visual InterDev 6.0's place in that environment. We'll look at many of the choices that make up Web application architecture, and how Visual InterDev 6.0 supports them. Finally, we'll wrap up the chapter with a brief history of Microsoft's Component Object Model (COM), the technology that enables so much of what can be done in Web development today.

## Web Development Technologies

At its simplest, a Web application can consist of only two machines: a server running a Web server and a client running a Web browser. Using some of the technologies described in the last chapter, it's possible to create a Web application with this very simple configuration. To take full advantage of the benefits of a Web application, however, and to create scalable and robust Web applications, often requires using more machines and more technologies. In this section we'll describe some of these technologies—including server software, operating system services, and development tools—and the benefits they bring to Web development.

### Server Software

Since you're reading this book, it's a safe bet you're already committed to developing on the Windows platform. But you may not yet be decided on whether to use Windows 95/98 or Windows NT Server for your servers. In some cases, this may seem like a difficult choice for reasons of cost, and for small

Web applications with a minimal number of users, Windows 95/98 may be an appropriate choice. But for applications requiring high performance and scalability, Windows NT Server should be your choice for a variety of reasons. Windows NT Server provides support services and performance monitoring tools that are not available for Windows 95/98. And of course, Internet Information Server (IIS), which we'll discuss later, only runs on Windows NT Server. In short, for servers supporting enterprise Web applications built on the Microsoft platform, NT Server is the only way to go.

## Internet Information Server (IIS)

Internet Information Server, now in its 4.0 release, is one of the primary reasons to develop and run your Web application on Windows NT Server. In addition to simply serving up Web pages, IIS provides the following features, to name a few:

- Integration with Windows NT Server directory and security services
- Improved Active Server Pages (ASP) object model
- Built-in FTP, Gopher, News (NNTP), SMTP, and Web services
- Application debugging support
- Custom HTTP error messages

IIS 4.0 also makes setting up and configuring Web applications much easier with its integration with the Microsoft Management Console (MMC). The MMC is a framework that accepts modules called *snap-ins* for a host of services including IIS, Microsoft SQL Server, Microsoft Transaction Server (MTS), Microsoft Message Queue Server (MSMQ), and SNA Server, allowing a "one-stop shopping" approach to administering and configuring your Web applications. Some of the features of IIS 4.0, including the newest version of Active Server Pages, are also available in the latest release of the Personal Web Server for Windows 95/98 and Windows NT Workstation.

## Microsoft SQL Server

Choosing database server software is not easy in the best of circumstances. One must balance cost, performance and scalability, compatibility with existing data assets, as well as many other factors when choosing a Database Management System (DBMS) to support your application. Making a choice of this nature is beyond the scope of this book, but you would be well served (pun intended) to take a serious look at Microsoft SQL Server for your Web application needs. SQL Server continues in both its 6.5 version and in the 7.0 version (still in beta at the time of this writing), to break record after record in performance versus cost on the Windows platform. In addition, SQL Server integrates very well with both IIS and Visual InterDev 6.0, as well as with ODBC, OLE DB, and ActiveX Data Objects (ADO), giving you a great deal of power and flexibility in data access, with a minimum of headache.

## Operating System Services

You may not realize it, but some of the most powerful tools for developing enterprise Web applications won't cost you a penny. If you're running Windows NT Server, there are a number of new Windows NT services. These are part of the Windows NT Server 4.0 Option Pack (which is free) that will make your Web applications more powerful and more scalable. These services include Microsoft Transaction Server (MTS), Microsoft Message Queue Server (MSMQ), and one we've already talked about, Internet Information Server (IIS).

### Microsoft Transaction Server (MTS)

Microsoft Transaction Server is a component management tool that manages component resources, database connections, component security, and transaction boundaries. Components developed for MTS can be written in a number of languages, including Visual Basic, Visual C++, and Visual J++. MTS components can be developed as single-user, single-threaded components, simplifying development and reducing development time and costs. MTS supplies the plumbing necessary to make the components scalable, saving the developer time and effort. Visual InterDev 6.0 is integrated with MTS, allowing developers to import components into their projects and package them for use with MTS with just a few mouse clicks.

### Microsoft Message Queue Server (MSMQ)

*Message queuing*, as we'll discuss further in Chapter 9, "Ensuring Reliable Communication," is a process that allows communication between application processes (say, a client process and a component), without a constant, consistent connection between the processes. Microsoft Message Queue Server brings the power of message queuing to the Windows NT platform. MSMQ provides support for asynchronous communication for better scalability, store-and-forward functionality for disconnected users (such as mobile workers with laptops), and guaranteed delivery over unreliable networks. Because of these features, MSMQ can be an important tool for improving the reliability and scalability of an enterprise Web application.

## Development Tools

Development tools are chosen for a wide variety of reasons, including what tools developers are familiar with, the capabilities of various tools, and cost. For the purposes of Web development, the tools available on the Windows platform fall into two basic categories: component development tools and Web development tools.

### Component Development Tools

For developing components for use in your Web applications, there are a wide variety of tools available. It is well beyond the scope of this book to discuss each one. However, there are several things you should look for in a tool for component development. The first is that your development tool must be able to create true COM components, preferably DLLs (for performance reasons). This is not a particularly restrictive requirement, as there are a wide variety of tools available for developing COM components in a number of languages, including C++, Java, and COBOL. The second thing to look for is a tool that supports the development of components for Microsoft Transaction Server for greater component scalability that includes Visual C++, Visual J++, and of course, Visual Basic.

Of the available choices, the one we'll focus on for the component development examples in this book is Visual Basic. We'll use Visual Basic because of its ease-of-use and Rapid Application Development (RAD) features, as well as its familiar interface—it shares many features with Visual InterDev 6.0. Visual Basic makes a string partner to Visual InterDev for enterprise Web development and has the added advantage of having a large pool of experienced developers to draw on, something that any project manager will appreciate.

### Web Development Tools

Clearly, in a book about developing enterprise Web applications with Visual InterDev 6.0, we're not going to suggest that you use any other Web development tool. That said, it would be disingenuous to suggest that there are no other tools available for developing Web applications. Other tools, including NetObject's Fusion and Elemental Software's Drumbeat 2.0, offer features similar to Visual InterDev 6. There are also editors available that provide support for DHTML and scripting. None of these tools, however, can offer the comprehensive features and ease-of-integration that Visual InterDev 6.0 offers.

Visual InterDev is the tool where it all comes together for the Web developer. Client- and server-side script can be joined with COM components, which can be packaged for use within MTS. ASP pages can be written that take advantage of MSMQ to communicate asynchronously with components or other applications. And application navigation and appearance can be managed in a simple and consistent fashion. Visual InterDev 6.0 allows you, the developer, to take advantage of the power of all the technologies discussed above to create a successful enterprise Web application.

So, once you've decided on the tools for your Web application, what's the next step? Designing the architecture of your application, which we'll describe in the next sections.

## Web Application Architecture

Designing a Web application's architecture is probably one of the most crucial steps (or series of steps) in its development. It is during this stage of development that you'll be making decisions that determine how many users your application will support (or can support), where the code will reside that comprises your application, and a myriad of other choices that determine whether your application will succeed or fail. In this section, we'll give you a general blueprint of Web application architecture to help you make those decisions.

Web applications can include (but are not limited to): a Web browser, client- and/or server-side scripts, a Web server, components (which may or may not run on the Web server), and a database (which may service one or perhaps many applications). The database may also host some of the application's code in the form of stored procedures. Notice that in the above description, only one machine is mentioned explicitly, the Web server. The reason for this is that theoretically your application could be hosted entirely on a single machine (although it is not recommended). Ultimately it is up to you, the developer, to determine whether your application requires a separate database server or component server, or possibly even multiple component servers for a particularly high-use site (see Figure 2-1). Other architectural decisions discussed in later chapters include using Microsoft Transaction Server to provide scaling and transactional support, using Microsoft Message Queue Server to provide interapplication communication services, and using the Visual Database Tools to provide data access for your application.

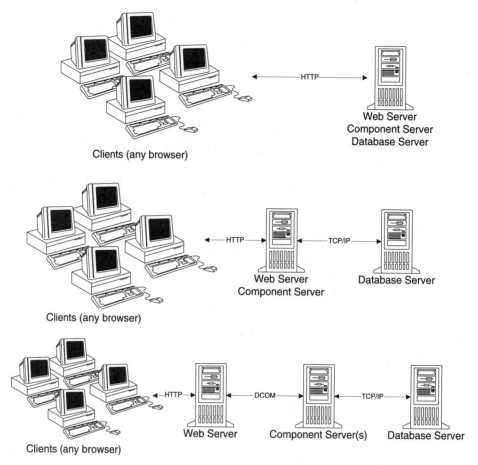

**Figure 2-1.**
*Web Application Architecture Example.*

# Making Architectural Choices

As implied above, an application's architecture, if well designed and thought out, is one of its most important assets, and if poorly designed, can be one of its greatest deficits. But what is an application's architecture? The term *architecture* can refer to the physical platform, that is, the servers, client machines, and network hardware on which the application will be run, as well as the software, operating systems, support services, network protocols, and so forth, that run on those platforms. This is generally referred to as the *physical architecture* of the application. Architecture can also refer to how the application is distributed across the platform(s) or broken up into tiers, such as user services, business services, and data services. This is generally referred to as the *logical architecture* of the application. It can also describe *component* or *implementation architecture*, which determines how an application will be broken up into sections, based on functional and physical requirements.

So how does one sort out the wide variety of issues that shelter under the umbrella of "architecture"? The same way one eats an elephant, as the saying goes, by taking small bites. One technique is abstracting the wide variety of issues related to architecture and design into smaller and more manageable bites. One way of accomplishing this is through the Enterprise Application Model, a new conceptual application framework introduced by Microsoft with Visual Studio 6.0. The Enterprise Application Model is part of the MSDN Library documentation that ships, with Visual Studio 6.0.

## Enterprise Application Model Overview

The Enterprise Application Model is a framework comprised of six submodels, each of which describes a specific area of the application's architecture and requirements. These submodels are:

- The Development Model, which describes the parts of the development process, including the development team, the testing process, source code control, and development milestones and deliverables.

- The Business Model, which describes issues such as expected return on investment, schedule constraints, available infrastructure, and business policies.

- The User Model, which describes requirements for the user interface, as well as user training and support requirements.

- The Logical Model, which describes the structure of the application, including component modeling, data modeling, and interface definitions.

- The Technology Model, which describes the technologies used to implement the application, from server platform to development tools.

- The Physical Model, which describes the physical distribution of the application, including servers used and component location. This model is the culmination of the decision-making process for all other submodels.

By breaking the application up into smaller chunks, it's easier for a development team to grasp the needs and available choices for each of the submodels individually, yet have a clear model for how those needs and choices affect the other related submodels. This allows various choices to be weighed based on what is best for the overall application, not on just what works for a particular tier or portion of the application. For example, it may be determined that a requirement of the development model is for the application to be delivered in six months. If the budget required by the business model only allows for hiring two developers, then it's a pretty good bet that the technology model will have to address the need for ultra-rapid development. The Enterprise Application Model is discussed in greater depth in Chapter 7, "Addressing Performance and Scalability."

Which tool or technique you use to make the architecture and design process more manageable is less important than that you *do* something to make it so. Enterprise applications, as we have already observed, are big, usually so big that it is next to impossible for one person to visualize the whole application without some method of abstraction. For very large, multi-developer projects, the Enterprise Application Model may be just the ticket.

## N-Tier Architecture Model

Another method for developing your application's architecture, which I will use in the remainder of this section, is to look at architectural choices as they relate to the tiers (as in n-tier development) of the application. In this method, you break the application up into N (where N represents the number of tiers) tiers, which abstract the application's services logically. Most often a Web application breaks nicely into three tiers, the *browser* or *client tier*, the *business tier*, and the *data tier*. For smaller or less complex applications (such as the Rent-A-Prize demo application that will be introduced in the next chapter), this method works well, particularly when used in conjunction with an application modeling tool such as Visual Modeler. Visual Modeler allows you to visually represent the tiers of your application, the services they provide, and the properties and methods that enable those services.

### Browser and Client Tier Choices

Just as in traditional client-server development, where often one of the first things developed is a user interface prototype, Web application development can be well served by looking first at the requirements and choices of the client, or user services tier. The choices that can and must be made here are many and varied, but almost inevitably, the first question to be addressed is, "Which browser(s) do we support?"

The answer to this question usually fits into one of two scenarios. If your organization already has an installed base that includes multiple versions of Internet Explorer, Netscape Navigator, and perhaps a few others such as NCSA Mosaic, your only choice may be to support all of these browsers, eschewing browser-specific functions or even functionality that requires a certain version of the leading browsers. On the other hand, your organization may allow you to require a specific browser or perhaps minimum versions of the leading browsers in order to access your application. Or you might end up somewhere in the middle, where your application tests for the type and version of browser the user has installed and tailors the application's functionality to that browser. Each of these are valid choices and involve tradeoffs. Choices should be made by balancing the business requirements (installed user base, cost of upgrades, functionality required) against the technological requirements entailed to deliver those business requirements within the allotted time and the project's budget.

In the first scenario, in which a varied installed user base and prohibitive upgrade costs demand a browser-neutral approach, you should determine the base level of functionality available from the installed browsers. Can you use frames? Can all the target browsers support JavaScript? Do all the target browsers support cookies? This one is especially important, since the tracking of session information in Active Server Pages is accomplished through the use of cookies. You may find that even in a browser-neutral environment, you still need to demand a minimum browser feature set, for example, any browser that supports both cookies and JavaScript. In doing so, you may be able to significantly increase functionality at minimal expense in terms of users who must change browsers in order to use your application. The consequence of not doing so is that all of your programming logic, including validation code, is relegated to the server. This results in more round-trips to and greater processing demands on the server, and ultimately in reduced scalability. If the target browsers do not support cookies, you also give up the ability to maintain session state using ASP's Session object. This means implementing a custom solution for session management, which can add substantially to the development effort and reduce the application's maintainability. Clearly, there are substantial benefits to establishing a minimum browser compatibility level.

**Figure 2-2.**
*Client-Side Validation Example.*

In the second scenario, in which you are able to require a specific browser or version of the leading browsers, there are more opportunities to be flexible in partitioning your application. For example, by simply requiring a JavaScript-compatible browser, you gain the ability to move to the browser code that validates form field entries before the HTTP POST request is sent to the Web server (see Figure 2-2). This can save a substantial amount of wasted processing on the server by preventing the server from having to process forms in which there are invalid values. This saves time by not having to send an error message to the client requesting that they re-input the data, then having to reprocess the form over and over, until all fields are correctly filled out. If you can also require Internet Explorer 3.0 or above, you can implement some of the functionality required by your application as ActiveX controls or client-side VBScript, increasing the amount of functionality you can enable at the client and again reducing the processing load on the server. In addition, the ability to use VBScript on the client gives you the opportunity to tap into the large pool of skilled Visual Basic developers. If you can go the next step and require Internet Explorer 4, you then have access to a full range of client options, including client-side script (JScript or VBScript), ActiveX controls and Java applets, and DHTML. Using DHTML, you can provide a very rich, interactive user interface while reducing the amount of code that has to travel over the wire, which can reduce the amount of time users have to wait while using your application, particularly those with slow modem connections.

In addition to providing substantial support for DHTML and client scripting, Visual InterDev 6.0 also offers the ability to switch between a mainly client-side solution using DHTML and client script, to a server-based solution using ASP, by changing a single option, either at the page level, or for your entire application. This feature allows for a great deal of development flexibility, and can save a great deal of development time when circumstances change. It should be noted, however, that this feature is only available with use of the Visual InterDev Design-Time Controls, which gain most of their functionality from either client- or server-side script. As you'll see in later chapters, this may have performance implications where scalability is concerned. You can read more about the Visual InterDev Design-Time Controls in Chapter 4, "Enter Visual InterDev 6.0."

## Server and Business Tier Choices

Decisions to be made on the server or business tier include which Web server to use (we've already established that if you're reading this book, you've likely decided on IIS), whether to use components instead of script to supply business services, where to host components (on the Web server?, on a separate component server?, on multiple component servers?), whether to use support services such as Microsoft Transaction Server and Microsoft Message Queue Server, and whether to host database(s) and data services on the same machine as the Web server or on a separate machine, in addition to many others. In this section we'll address some of these choices and look at the costs and tradeoffs associated with them.

## Scripts or Components?

Having chosen IIS as your Web server, one of the next issues to consider is that of scripts and components. Every Web application, large or small, will inevitably implement some of its functionality as either client- or server-side script. Some smaller applications may even implement all of their functionality in script, though this is not a recommended practice. The reason is simple: speed. There is a substantial performance advantage to using compiled components instead of scripts. In addition to speed, Web applications built entirely with script can be substantially more difficult to maintain and upgrade, compared to components. This being the case, it's safe to say that if you are designing an enterprise-level Web application and you're not planning to use components, you need to go back to the drawing board. Components are an essential part of building a Web application that will scale and perform well. Since IIS and ASP support the use of COM (more on COM later in this chapter), your components can be written in any language that supports COM, allowing you to leverage existing programming skills possessed by your developers.

**Component Location**   Once you've made the decision to use components, you must then decide where to install those components. That decision should be made based on the level of scalability required by your application. For smaller applications with minimal traffic, it might be acceptable to run your components on the Web server. This has the advantage of allowing IIS to run your components in its own process space, which can improve the performance of your components. The disadvantage of using Web server resources is that they could otherwise be used to service more user requests.

For larger applications, you could set up a components server, with IIS calling your components via DCOM (Distributed Component Object Model). This method of calling components is inherently slower, due to the fact that IIS and your component are running in separate processes (and all communication between them must be "marshalled" across the process boundary). However, this method does provide for greater scalability, since both the Web and components servers each have their own resources, rather than contending for shared resources. For applications requiring the utmost in scalability, you should enlist the services of Microsoft Transaction Server.

As discussed earlier, Visual InterDev 6.0 offers a number of features that make component management easier, including the ability to automatically register and add components to MTS packages (see Figure 2-3), as well as the ability to add components to Visual InterDev projects via drag-and-drop.

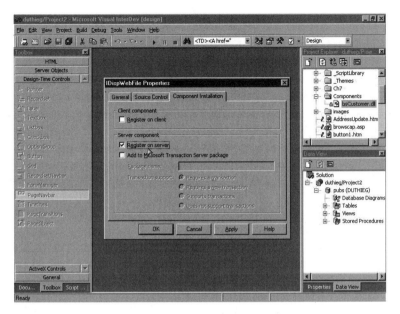

**Figure 2-3.**
*Setting up Component Registration in Visual InterDev 6.0.*

**Component Communication**   In addition to using Microsoft Transaction Server to improve performance for your application through connection pooling and component management, you can also choose to use the Microsoft Message Queue Server (MSMQ) to improve the reliability and responsiveness of your application.

MSMQ enhances application reliability by providing guaranteed delivery of messages between parts of your application. For example, if the network that connects your Web server and your component server is down, MSMQ can queue requests for your components, so that when the network connection is restored, the requests can be delivered and processed in the order in which they were sent.

MSMQ also improves the responsiveness of an application by providing for asynchronous communication and processing. For example, when a Web customer submits a registration request (which only requires an acknowledgment that the registration was received), the information submitted is packaged up into an MSMQ message and placed in a queue that has been set up for that purpose. The registration component can then check that queue periodically to see if there are any new registrations that require processing. By allowing the client process to continue without waiting for the registration to be processed, the response time of the application is reduced. This method also prevents slowdowns in response time during peak usage periods, when component backlog might otherwise equate to longer waits for your customers.

The advantages of using Microsoft Transaction Server and Microsoft Message Queue Server in your Web application are many, and the costs relatively small. Using these services dramatically improve the performance, scalability, reliability, and security of your application. All it costs for MTS is a few extra lines of code, shown below, and a reference to the MTS type library in your components.

```
'Create variable for MTS Object Context
Dim objContext As ObjectContext

'Get MTS object context for component
Set objContext = GetObjectContext

'Tell MTS the component has finished its work successfully
objContext.SetComplete

'Tell MTS the component did not finish successfully
objContext.SetAbort
```

For MSMQ, implementation is a little more complicated, but even at its most complicated, it is much simpler than trying to implement similar functionality on your own. In addition, Visual InterDev 6.0 provides easy access to features that can simplify the use of both MTS and MSMQ. MTS will be discussed in detail in Chapter 7, "Addressing Performance and Scalability," and Chapter 8, "Ensuring Transactional Integrity." MSMQ will be discussed in detail in Chapter 9, "Ensuring Reliable Communication."

**Database Location**   One architectural choice that should be a no-brainer, but often isn't, is where to locate the database for your application. That is, should the DBMS in which your data resides be installed on the Web server or on a separate machine? The answer to this question, for performance reasons, should almost always be that the DBMS should be installed on a separate server. Asking your Web server to perform both its job and the job of database server is asking for trouble, particularly if you want your application to scale. Unfortunately, this issue sometimes is decided solely on the basis of cost. This, however, is an area where the cost of a separate database server needs to be weighed against the cost of a failed development effort and against less room for application growth. Once you've made the decision to use a separate machine for your database, make sure that the network connections between the Web server, component server(s), and the database server are sufficient for the task. If possible, 100Mbps LAN connections are the ideal. We'll discuss the decisions that need to be made on the data tier next.

## Data Tier Choices

The first choice to be made on the data tier is which Database Management System (DBMS) to use. For enterprise purposes, Microsoft Access and other desktop databases should not be considered. Desktop databases generally cannot support the number of user connections required for a highly scalable application. Like the choice of which browser to support, the choice of DBMS is often affected by existing assets within the organization. If there is already data stored in an Oracle database that the application must access, and the organization's Database Administrators (DBAs) are all familiar with Oracle, then it probably makes sense to build the application around Oracle.

**Why Use SQL Server?**    For new development, or for situations in which migrating data is an option, there can be significant advantages to using Microsoft SQL Server. With the imminent release of version 7.0, SQL Server is truly poised to give its competitors a run for their money, both in terms of the size of databases it supports, as well as in transactions per second benchmarks. SQL Server 7.0 also offers substantially easier administration, with databases that automatically grow (and shrink!) as necessary, auto-configuration of memory, and a host of other configuration improvements. Much of SQL Server 7.0 will also be able to run on Windows 95 and 98, making it the only major DBMS to run the same code base on both Windows NT Server and Workstation and on Windows 95. This means that in situations where some of your application's data need to be replicated to a laptop of a busy executive, it can be accomplished without losing any of SQL Server's features.

**Data Access Choices**    Another choice that needs to be made for your application's architecture is the method of accessing data. This choice includes decisions of how to retrieve data, how to store data, and how (and where) to process data. There are many, many ways to access and process data, so I will not attempt to enumerate them all here. One method common in Visual Basic applications is to dynamically build a Structured Query Language (SQL) query string based on user input, and pass that string to the database to retrieve a recordset of matching rows. This method is also often used to do database inserts and updates. Although this method allows a fair amount of flexibility, and is relatively easy to code, it has a few disadvantages. One is performance. When you pass a SQL query string to your database, the database driver has to parse that string and convert it to a format the database can understand. In an app with a large number of users, that time can add up rapidly. Additionally, using this method for inserts and updates can be inefficient, particularly if the same (or close to the same) SQL string is being passed over and over. Each call to the server requires a certain amount of communications overhead, so wherever possible, inserts and updates should be sent as batches. Another potential problem is that all of the logic for your data access and manipulation resides on the business tier, not only reducing the degree of abstraction between the business and data tiers (potentially limiting reuse), but also locking up your data code inside a compiled component. This means that any changes you need to make to your data access code will require recompiling your component.

**Using Stored Procedures**   Another more efficient as well as more flexible method is using stored procedures. Stored procedures are precompiled chunks of SQL code that can be as simple as a SELECT statement and can contain conditional and looping structures. Using stored procedures allows you to simply pass in appropriate parameters, and allows the stored procedure to access and modify the data at the database. This minimizes the amount of data that has to travel over the network, and keeps the data access code with the data. Stored procedures also allow you to edit them at any time, without having to worry about bringing the application down to recompile and reinstall a DLL. Stored procedures are available with a number of DBMSs, including Microsoft SQL Server, Sybase, and Oracle. Visual InterDev 6.0 makes it very easy to create, use, and edit stored procedures for Microsoft SQL Server and ORACLE through the Data View and Query Designer.

## Architecture Summary

In this section, we've discussed a couple of different ways of abstracting the complexity of an enterprise Web application into models or tiers as a way of simplifying the process of making architectural choices. We've also looked at a number of architectural choices, including browser choice, use of scripts and components for business logic, use of MTS and MSMQ for application support, choices of physical locations for your components and DBMS, and use of stored procedures. I hope we've successfully demonstrated that each of these choices must be carefully considered based on a number of factors, including cost, performance, and maintainability. Architectural design is an iterative process. Each choice made in the course of designing an application's architecture invariably affects other decisions you have made as well as those you have yet to make. This means that you'll need to go through the process repeatedly until you're sure that you've addressed all of the requirements of your application, as well as all of the issues raised by decisions made in the course of designing the application. Documentation is the key to making sure this happens. All documents pertaining to the design and architecture of an application should be placed under source code control (Microsoft Visual SourceSafe, or other source code control system) as soon as they are created, so that the progress of the design, and all changes to it, can be tracked. Following the steps and suggestions outlined in this section may not guarantee that your application will be successful, but it will almost certainly improve its chances of success.

# A Brief History of COM

Another way to improve your chance of success with any development project is to increase your understanding of the Component Object Model (COM). COM is central to what can be done today on the Windows platform, and a basic understanding of COM is essential to any Windows developer, Web or otherwise. Without at least a basic understanding of COM, it will be much more difficult for you to figure out what to do when the COM operations happening "under the hood" in languages such as Visual Basic don't do what's expected. In particular, an understanding of COM can be very helpful when working with binary compatibility in Visual Basic. In this section, we'll take a look at where COM came from and what it offers us as developers, as well as what the future holds for COM.

## Once, All Inter-application Communication Was Custom

In the beginning, there was chaos. Each application had its own unique way of storing document information, and anyone needing to share information between applications or documents had to do so manually. This sharing could be accomplished by writing a custom program—assuming the person wanting to share the document was a programmer—or, more often, by saving to some intermediate format, such as flat text. For example, if a user wanted to include spreadsheet data in a word processor document, he or she would need to either save a snapshot of that data as flat text, or copy a range of cells to the clipboard (in a Windows application), again as flat text. The flat text could then be imported to the word processor document, and formatting added as necessary. There are some fairly obvious disadvantages to this kind of static integration of documents, the most important of which is that static integration assumes that the documents being integrated won't change, or at least that each time there is a change in the spreadsheet whose data is integrated into the word processor document, someone will manually go through the process of updating the integrated spreadsheet data to reflect its current state. From today's perspective, it hardly seems likely that it would be worth the trouble. If you were very lucky, you'd have access to spreadsheet and word processing programs made by the same company, meaning these applications might have a common format that made sharing data between the programs easier. But even among such programs this is not always the case. This conundrum is what sparked the desire to create OLE, or Object Linking and Embedding, a technology that, in the name of sharing data between applications, would revolutionize Windows programming. So, what does this have to do with COM? It was from the technical needs addressed by OLE, that COM would be born, as we'll see in the next sections.

## OLE — Object Linking and Embedding

Object Linking and Embedding (OLE) was not the first attempt to solve the problem of sharing data between applications. Other attempts to address this problem resulted in the Windows clipboard, which is still in use today (though enhanced from its original form), and Dynamic Data Exchange (DDE), a rather complicated method for sharing data between running applications.

## OLE 1 Enabled Compound Documents

The first version of OLE, OLE 1.0, was built on the concept of "document-centric" computing. That is, the desire was to allow users to think about documents instead of thinking about the applications used to create those documents. OLE, for the first time, enabled users to not only embed a spreadsheet into a word processing document, but also to edit that document in-place, rather than having to manually open a different application, make the desired changes, then re-embed the spreadsheet into the document. This paradigm was referred to as *compound documents*.

### OLE Servers Provide Document Editing Services

OLE applications are divided into two categories, *OLE servers* and *OLE containers*. It should be noted that an application does not have to be one or the other, many applications perform both roles. An OLE server provides document editing services. In our example of a spreadsheet embedded in a word processor document, the spreadsheet program would act as an OLE server, providing the services necessary to edit the spreadsheet in-place.

### OLE Containers Provide Site for Displaying Data

An OLE container program, in our example the word processor, provides a place to display the spreadsheet data, and in the case of an embedded document, also provides a storage area for the spreadsheet data. In OLE, compound documents can either be linked or embedded. In a linked document, the linked document is stored separately from the host document. This means that any changes to the linked document will automatically be reflected in the host document, since it's merely displaying the linked document, which is stored externally. In an embedded document, the embedded data is stored with the host document, but retains information about the format of the data and the application used to edit that data. This means that once a document has been embedded into another document, it is divorced from its original source file.

Although OLE was a giant step forward in sharing data between applications, it had its limitations. In addition, its designers realized that the problems of creating and managing compound documents was part of a larger issue of how applications in general should provide services to one another. This led to the creation of OLE 2, and tangentially, to the creation of COM.

## OLE 2 and COM

In order to address the larger issue of sharing data and services between software components, the OLE team created a set of technologies that provided an infrastructure for creating and communicating with reusable and extensible software component objects. It is this set of technologies that comprises the Component Object Model (COM). Since the release of OLE 2, all OLE-enabled technologies have been built using the infrastructure provided by COM. Now the term "OLE" was used not only to describe technologies that provided for compound documents, but to any COM-based technology.

A few years after the release of OLE 2, another technology came along, called *ActiveX*. The term ActiveX, which was initially used by marketing to describe those COM-based technologies that related to the Internet, gained enough popularity in the technical and marketing groups at Microsoft that it began to be used to describe technologies that had little or nothing to do with the Internet. Needless to say, this has caused quite a bit of confusion over the years. Recently, however, COM has begun to be described and recognized as its own, separate technology, and the terms *OLE* and *ActiveX* have been gradually reduced to their original areas of compound documents and Internet technologies, respectively.

## What COM Does for Us

Now that you have an idea of where COM came from, you'd probably like to know what COM can do for you. The most important service that COM provides—and that makes everything else possible—is a consistent method of component communication. With COM, any component built to the COM specification, regardless of the language used to create the component, can reliably communicate with, and use the services of, any other COM-compliant component. This magic happens through the use of interfaces.

### COM Interfaces

The central concept behind a COM component, or object, is that it is a "black box," in which the implementation of any services it provides are hidden from the client of the object. The only way the client of the object can access the services of the object is through interfaces defined by the component. An *interface* is a contract between the component and the outside world that guarantees that the object always provides that interface, and further that it will not change the external implementation of that interface. One of the most important rules of COM components is that once a component has defined an interface, that interface *cannot* change, not ever. This rule ensures that clients of your COM components will always be able to use your components, even if you upgrade them.

So what is an interface? An interface represents a method or methods exposed by a COM component (see Figure 2-4). The interface provides a way for external clients to call that method, to pass any required arguments, and to retrieve any return values. The interface defines the name(s) of the method(s), and any arguments or return values of the method(s), as well as the data types of arguments and return values. In this way, a client application can know exactly how to call a given method of a COM component. But how does a client application find out about these interfaces in the first place? Well, in order for a component to be considered a COM component, it must implement at least one interface, IUnknown (by convention all interface names begin with the letter I, as in IMyInterface).

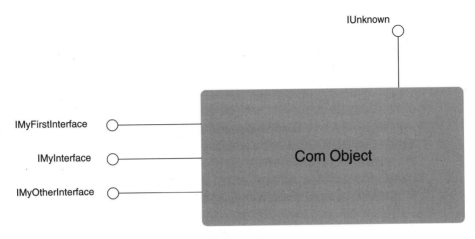

**Figure 2-4.**
*A COM Object with Four Interfaces.*

## IUnknown, the Mother of All Interfaces

IUnknown is the single interface every COM object is required to provide. The IUnknown interface is required to support three methods, QueryInterface, AddRef, and Release. When a client application creates an instance of a COM component, it receives a pointer to the component's IUnknown interface. Both COM components and the interfaces they support are identified on the computers on which they are installed by 128-bit integer values called GUIDs, or Globally Unique Identifiers that are stored in the system registry. Components are identified by Class IDs (CLSIDs), while interfaces are identified by Interface IDs (IIDs). Using the QueryInterface method of IUnknown, the client application can interrogate the component to find out whether the component supports a particular interface by calling QueryInterface and passing the IID of the interface it is looking for. This ability of a client to interrogate a component at runtime, combined with the rule of immutable interfaces, makes it possible to support upgrades of your components without breaking existing client applications. With COM, a component can be extended to offer new functionality by adding new interfaces. Since existing interfaces cannot change, existing clients of your component will be able to use the new component, while upgraded clients of your component can use QueryInterface to verify that the component supports the updated functionality.

## Using Type Libraries

None of the COM functionality described above would be much use without a way for developers to program their client applications to use the various interfaces of COM components. Type libraries provide this ability. A *type library* is a file, either separate or embedded in a DLL, that provides a description of publicly exposed classes, methods, and properties of a COM DLL, in other words, its interfaces. Applications such as Visual Basic use type libraries to provide a higher-level view of interfaces, and to allow developers to view the available methods and properties of the COM components they wish to use. If you've ever used Visual Basic's Object Browser (see Figure 2-5), then you have seen the power of COM and type libraries.

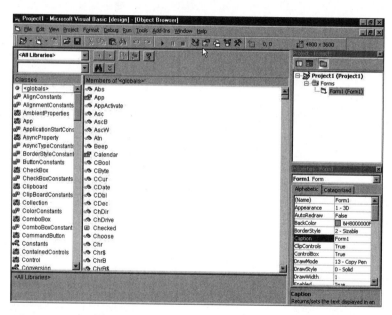

**Figure 2-5.**
*Visual Basic 5.0 Object Browser.*

In addition to using type libraries to enable browsing of COM components properties and methods, you can also use a type library to enable use of constant definitions in your ASP applications. By using the Project References... command of Visual InterDev 6.0 (see Figure 2-6), you can insert into your application's Global.asa file a reference to a component's type library. With this reference any page in your application can use named constants defined for that component.

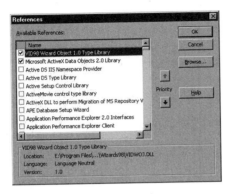

**Figure 2-6.**
*Visual InterDev's Project References Dialog Box.*

## Other Services Provided by COM

In addition to providing for communication between software components and their clients, COM also provides some other fundamental infrastructure services. COM provides the ability to create instances of components, assists in tracking the number of clients using a given component, and takes care of destroying the component when the last client using it has finished with it. These and other services provided by COM enable many of the technologies we take for granted today, including OLE and compound documents, as well as ActiveX controls. Much of the simplicity of using the Visual Basic programming language is enabled by COM. One of the advantages to using a higher-level language such as Visual Basic is that it hides much of the complexity of COM from the developer, allowing him or her to take advantage of COM's services without worrying about the messy details. Nonetheless, it is wise for every developer to gain at least a basic understanding of COM in order to better understand what is going on "under the hood." Such an understanding can be invaluable in figuring out what's wrong when things don't work the way you expected them to. For developers new to COM, I heartily recommend *Understanding ActiveX and OLE*, by David Chappell (Microsoft Press, 1996); it provides an excellent look at COM, at a level that is easy to understand.

## The Evolution of COM — COM, DCOM, and COM+

As time has gone by, COM has evolved, first from merely supporting compound documents, to providing a comprehensive infrastructure for enabling component software, later extending component support services from a single machine to multiple machines through DCOM. The next step in COM's evolution is approaching. COM+, the next generation of COM, will extend COM's already impressive services by, among other things, integrating the services of MTS and MMQS, as well as other OS services, with the goal of making much of this functionality transparent to the developer. The goal is for developers to be able to develop COM components as single-user objects written in the language of their choice. COM+ then takes care of the plumbing needed to make that component scalable, or make it communicate with other components reliably, regardless of their location. Within the next generation of Windows, COM+ will likely do as much for simplifying multi-user application development as COM did for enabling component development.

# Summary

In this chapter, we've discussed the Web application environment, including the server software, operating system services, and development tools available to support your Web applications. We've described some of the choices available in terms of designing an application's architecture and ways to reduce the complexity of those choices through abstraction, by using the Enterprise Application Model or an N-tier architecture model. We also took a brief look at the history of COM, the technology that supports many of the choices available to developers today. In the next chapter, we'll look at some of the challenges faced in developing an enterprise Web application and take a closer look at Visual InterDev 6.0, which promises to solve many of these challenges.

CHAPTER THREE

# Challenges Faced in Enterprise Web Development

Web development in general is a challenging field, and nowhere is this more evident than in developing for the enterprise. From architectural design to final implementation, enterprise Web development poses many challenges that will sorely test even the most skilled development team. These challenges, some of which we've touched on in earlier chapters, range from issues of browser compatibility to bandwidth, from implementing business logic to improving performance, and from accessing data to how and where to manipulate that data.

This book divides these challenges into three tiers, which correspond to the three tiers of our sample application, introduced later in this chapter. These tiers are also represented in the three "Solutions" sections of the book. Section 2 focuses on challenges encountered in the client tier. Section 3 looks at challenges of the business tier; and Section 4 discusses the challenges of the data tier. In each of these sections, we'll discuss the challenges faced, and the ways in which Visual InterDev 6.0, in combination with other Visual Studio tools, as well as the components of the Windows DNA architecture, can be used to address these challenges. Before we proceed, however, we'll stop to first identify these challenges in the following sections.

## Feature Richness vs. Application Reach

In building any Web application, one of the first challenges you'll run into is that stakeholders in the project may have the expectation that your Web application can do all the things a Visual Basic client application can do, and still have the reach granted by the Web. One of the few downsides to writing enterprise applications for the Web is that browser-based interfaces have not caught up to native Windows programs in terms of sophistication and control. While it is certainly possible with ActiveX controls or Active Document technology to provide some of the same UI features of a Visual Basic application, doing so will naturally limit the users of your application to those using Internet Explorer 3 or above, as well as those whose connection speed does not make downloading ActiveX controls or Active Documents prohibitively slow.

Likewise, Dynamic HTML (DHTML) can provide some of the functionality typically found only in a Windows application.

```html
<HTML>
<HEAD>
<TITLE>Menu Demo</TITLE>
<META HTTP-EQUIV="Content-Type" CONTENT="text/html; CHARSET=iso8859-1">
<META NAME="MS.LOCALE" CONTENT="EN-US">
<META NAME="ROBOTS" CONTENT="all">
<!-- Copyright 1997. Microsoft Corporation. All rights reserved. -->
<link rel="STYLESHEET" href="msmenu.css" type="text/css">
<script language="JavaScript" src="msmenu.js"></script>
<style>
.MenuBarItem {
  font-family: MS Sans Serif;
  font-size: 9pt;
  color: black;
  background-color:transparent;
  cursor:default;
  margin: 1;
  }
.MenuBar {
  position:absolute;
  left:0; top:0; width:100%;
```

*(continued)*

```
   background-color:#C6C3C6;

   margin:0 5 0 5;

   }

</style>

<script>

<!--

var MenuBarMenus = new Array()

var current = null

var popup

function DocOnLoad() {

   MenuInit();

   var MicrosoftMenu = new Menu(0,0)

   var ToolsMenu = new Menu(0,0)

   var ieSubMenu = new Menu(0,0)

   var HelpMenu = new Menu(0,0)

   var SearchMenu = new Menu(0,0)

   MicrosoftMenu.addItem(new MenuItem('Home Page', 'http://
www.microsoft.com'))

   MicrosoftMenu.addItem(new MenuItem('Internet Explorer 4.0', 'http://
www.microsoft.com/ie'))

   MicrosoftMenu.addItem(new MenuItem('MSNBC', 'http://www.msnbc.com'))

   ieSubMenu.addItem(new MenuItem('Windows 95/NT', 'http://
www.microsoft.com/ie/ie40/'))

   ieSubMenu.addItem(new MenuItem('Windows 95/NT', 'http://
www.microsoft.com/ie/win31/'))

   ieSubMenu.addItem(new MenuItem('Macintosh', 'http://
www.microsoft.com/ie/mac/ie40/'))

   ieSubMenu.addItem(new MenuItem('Unix', 'http://www.microsoft.com/ie/
?/ie/platform/unix.htm'))

   ToolsMenu.addItem(new MenuItem('NetShow', 'http://www.microsoft.com/
netshow'))
```

*(continued)*

57

```
    ToolsMenu.addItem(new MenuItem('NetMeeting', 'http://
www.microsoft.com/netmeeting'))

    ToolsMenu.addItem(new MenuItem('MS Chat', 'http://www.microsoft.com/
ie/chat'))

    ToolsMenu.addItem(new MenuItem('Internet Explorer', null, null,
ieSubMenu))

    HelpMenu.addItem(new MenuItem('IE Support', 'http://
www.microsoft.com/iesupport/'))

    HelpMenu.addItem(new MenuItem('Internet SDK', 'http://
www.microsoft.com/msdn/sdk/inetsdk', 'inetsdk.gif'))

    HelpMenu.addItem(new MenuItem('Search Microsoft', 'http://
www.microsoft.com/search', 'find.gif'))

    HelpMenu.addItem(new MenuItem(null, null, null, null, true))

    HelpMenu.addItem(new MenuItem('About', new Function("alert('The
DHTML Menu'); MenuBarClose();")))

    SearchMenu.addItem(new MenuItem('Infoseek', 'http://
www.infoseek.com'))

    SearchMenu.addItem(new MenuItem('Yahoo', 'http://www.yahoo.com'))

    SearchMenu.addItem(new MenuItem('WebCrawler', 'http://
www.Webcrawler.com/'))

    SearchMenu.addItem(new MenuItem(null, null, null, null, true))

    SearchMenu.addItem(new MenuItem('Cancel', new
Function('PupUpCmd()'), 'x.gif'))

    MicrosoftMenu.show(true)

    ToolsMenu.show(true)

    ieSubMenu.show(true)

    HelpMenu.show(true)

    SearchMenu.show(true)

    popup = SearchMenu

    MenuBarMenus[0] = MicrosoftMenu;

    MenuBarMenus[1] = ToolsMenu;

    MenuBarMenus[2] = HelpMenu
}
```

*(continued)*

```
function MenuBarClose() {
  if (current != null) {
    var menu = MenuBarMenus[current.menu]
    menu.hide()
    menu = null
    current.style.backgroundColor = 'transparent'
    current.style.color = 'black'
  }
}
function DocOnClick() {
  MenuBarClose()
}
function MenuBarOnClick() {
  var obj = window.event.srcElement
  var menu;
  window.event.cancelBubble = true;
  if (obj.className == 'MenuBarItem') {
    if (current != null) MenuBarClose()
    obj.style.color = 'white'
    obj.style.backgroundColor = '#000084'
    menu = MenuBarMenus[obj.menu]
    menu.left = obj.offsetLeft
    menu.top = obj.offsetTop + obj.offsetHeight
    menu.show()
    current = obj;
  }
}
function PupUpCmd() {
  if (helpbutton.value == 'Show Search') {
```

*(continued)*

```
    popup.left = helpbutton.offsetLeft + helpbutton.offsetWidth
    popup.top = helpbutton.offsetTop
    popup.show()
    helpbutton.value = 'Hide Search'
  } else {
    popup.hide()
    helpbutton.value = 'Show Search'
  }
}
-->
</script>
</HEAD>
<BODY onLoad="DocOnLoad()" onClick="DocOnClick()" TOPMARGIN=0
BGPROPERTIES="FIXED" BGCOLOR="#FFFFFF" LINK="#000000" VLINK="#808080"
ALINK="#000000">
<div onClick="MenuBarOnClick()" class="MenuBar">
  <span menu=0 class="MenuBarItem">  Microsoft  </
span>
  <span menu=1 class="MenuBarItem">  Internet
Tools  </span>
  <span menu=2 class="MenuBarItem">  Help  </span>
</div>
<input id=helpbutton
       type=button value="Show Search" onClick="PupUpCmd()"
       style="position:absolute; left:100; top:100">

</BODY>
</HTML>
```

Visual InterDev 6.0 provides great support for DHTML, including an excellent Cascading Style Sheet (CSS) editor, a Script Outline for access to scriptable events of DHTML elements, and drag-and-drop access to DirectAnimation controls, making implementation of such features a lot easier. Unfortunately, like ActiveX controls and Active Documents, a decision to use DHTML inherently limits your audience.

In fact, this highlights a general rule of Web programming. It can generally be said that as you increase the richness of a Web application's features, you decrease the reach of your application, that is, the number of people who will be able to use it. This is not unlike a similar trend in computer games, in which the newer and hotter the game, the fewer people can play it because of the increasing hardware demands made by it. The chart in Figure 3-1, albeit simplified, illustrates the relationship between features and application reach.

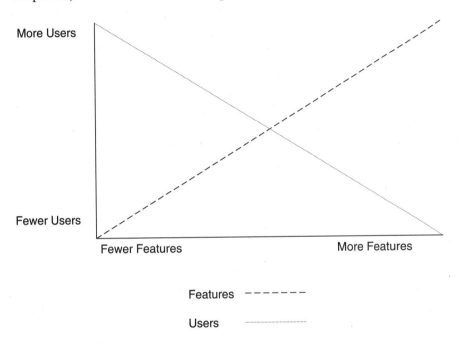

**Figure 3-1.**
*Relationship between Features and Users.*

Of course, there are technologies that allow you to get around the browser limitation somewhat on the client side. For one, ActiveX can be extended to work with Netscape Navigator through the use of plug-ins. Unfortunately, plug-ins tend to be a headache for users, and may not support all the functionality you need, so are not necessarily an ideal solution. After all, part of the point of implementing a Web application is to avoid having to install software on the client.

Java can supply a certain level of functionality that can be made available to a very wide audience, because most browsers provide at least some level of Java support. Unfortunately, Java, too, has its share of downsides, including uneven performance from one Virtual Machine (VM) to another, and multiple Java Development Kits (JDKs), meaning either limiting features used to the lowest-common-denominator JDK or limiting users to those with later JDKs installed. The Web is certainly the place where Java's "write-once, run everywhere" (WORE) mantra is closest to reality, but even on the Web it's not quite real just yet. Hopefully, as Java moves through the process of becoming a standard, WORE will get closer to reality. In the meantime, Java can still be a powerful weapon in your Web application arsenal, provided you use it for its strengths and understand its limitations.

Unfortunately, the reality is that if you need to reach the broadest audience, the Internet, you are essentially limited to plain vanilla HTML. Anyone who's tried developing a Web application with just HTML will tell you the results are often not pretty.

Fortunately, this is where Active Server Pages (ASP) steps in, giving you a relatively easy way to provide a substantial feature set enabled by server-side objects and ASP scripts, as well as the ability to easily check for browser capabilities at runtime and provide the richest features possible for each client. With ASP, you can provide a cross-platform-compatible HTML interface for clients with non-ActiveX and/or non-DHTML browsers, and provide a richer interface with ActiveX and/or DHTML for clients whose browsers can support these features. Sure, this approach may require a little extra coding and a few extra pages, but if your application requires a high level of functionality to be made available to a large user base, coding for multiple browsers may allow you to reach a close approximation of the project stakeholders' expectations.

The important thing to remember about features and reach is that it is not a simple either/or decision. What's required for success is a clear understanding of the available technologies for providing the desired functionality as well as the tradeoffs involved in using those technologies. Remember the Enterprise Application Model. When a decision is made in one submodel, related submodels will inevitably be affected by that decision. This is just as true when using a tiered approach to breaking up an application. When you make a decision in the client tier, that decision will have ramifications for your business tier, and possibly for your data tier as well. However you decide to implement the required functionality, you need to make sure that decision is made with a clear understanding of the ramifications of that decision on the other tiers. In Chapter 5, "Features vs. Reach—Cross-Platform Support," we'll take a look at how Visual InterDev 6.0 helps you provide some of the features most desired in Web applications, and does so in a way that gives us the greatest functionality along with the kind of application reach we need.

# Bandwidth Limitations

Hand-in-hand with the issue of features versus reach is the issue of bandwidth limitations. *Bandwidth*, for those of you who may not be up on Internet lingo, is a measurement of the amount of data that a particular communications medium can carry. Bandwidth is typically measured in multiples of bps, or bits-per-second, either Kbps (thousands of bits per second) or Mbps (millions of bits per second). Most modems in use today range in speed from 28.8Kbps to 56Kbps. Newer, faster (and more expensive) connections such as Integrated Services Digital Network (ISDN) or cable modems can move data at 128Kbps (ISDN) or even 500Kbps (cable). Unfortunately, these technologies are largely one-way for now. To get 128Kbps out of ISDN, you must use two 64Kbps channels. With Cable modems, you must still use an ordinary modem for the upstream connection, limiting you to 56Kbps at most. Most office LAN connections carry data at about 1.5Mbps, although some newer networks zip data through at 100Mbps. For a comparison of available technologies and their speeds, see Table 3-1. It's important to understand the communications technologies used by your application, since you may be limited by them.

If you are targeting the Internet with your Web application, you can expect a fair number of your users to have a 28.8Kbps modem. You should generally limit yourself to the weakest link of the communications chain, in this case the user's modem. For many applications, it may be reasonable to assume or demand at least a 28.8 or 33.6KBps connection as a minimum, but even that can dramatically limit the content of your application. When dealing with a 28.8Kbps modem connection, every graphic used in a page equates to more time the user must wait for that page to load. Any sounds you use can take a substantial bite out of available bandwidth, and don't even think about video. Streaming media technologies have improved the audio/video end of things somewhat, though they may still be unsatisfactory at 28.8kbps.

| Home/Home Office Use | |
| --- | --- |
| Standard Analog Modem | 14.4Kbps – 56Kbps |
| ISDN | 64Kbps – 128Kbps |
| Cable Modem | +/- 500Kbps |
| Asynchronous Digital Subscriber Line (ADSL) | 640Kbps – 7.1Mbps |
| **Office LAN Use** | |
| Standard Ethernet | 10Mbps |
| Fast Ethernet | 100Mbps |
| Token Ring | 4/16Mbps |
| **Internet Backbone Use** | |
| T1 | 1.5Mbps |
| T3 | 44.7Mbps |

**Table 3-1.**
*Comparison of communications technologies.*

Reducing the number and size of graphics can help mitigate bandwidth problems, but at the potential cost of a less visually interesting site/application. Other solutions include using specialized multimedia authoring tools, such as Macromedia's Flash to provide lightweight animations for your application, or using DHTML. DHTML, in particular, can be a great solution for providing a rich user experience at a low cost in bandwidth, but it requires either using Internet Explorer 4, or doing a fair amount of dual-coding to provide functionality for both Internet Explorer 4 and Netscape 4. Both Internet Explorer 4 and Netscape 4 implement DHTML quite differently (note that Internet Explorer's DHTML implementation is significantly closer to the HTML 4.0 standard from the W3C).

Why is bandwidth so important? What's a few extra seconds for a page to load? Well, those few extra seconds can be a major factor in how users perceive the performance of your application. If a page in your application takes over 10 seconds to load, the user won't care whether it's taking 10 seconds because the Web server is overloaded, or the component is slow, or whether it's because there are too many graphics to download. The user simply won't wait 10 seconds for the page to load. You may ask, "But doesn't the Web browser cache the page? Then the user should only have to wait the first time they visit the page." Well, that may be true for Web sites, but in some cases it is a business requirement that prevents the browser from caching pages, and all it takes is the following line of code:

```
<META HTTP-EQUIV="Pragma" CONTENT="NO-CACHE">
```

Imagine, for example, an online order form on which the user's credit card number is displayed as part of a purchase confirmation. It would be a really bad idea if the browser cached this page, since that would allow anyone to see the information simply by clicking the back button (if the user left the browser open and their computer unattended). The point is, you can't always count on caching to solve your bandwidth problems, particularly if your application deals with sensitive data. For solutions to the challenges posed by bandwidth and application reach, check out Chapter 5, "Features vs. Reach — Cross-Platform Support."

## Content Management

Another crossover issue between Web sites and Web applications is that of content management. Content management includes maintaining site structure, managing links between different parts of your application, maintaining consistency in your user interface and navigation, and simplifying application maintenance. Content management issues relate mainly to the client tier, but they may also affect the business tier if site navigation is managed by server-side components.

Creating and maintaining a consistent user interface is one of the first steps to making your application easy to use. An application in which each page uses a similar way to accomplish a given task is going to be much easier for users to learn than one in which each page has its own distinct approach. For example, in an application in which many pages use HTML forms to allow users to submit information, each page should format the form in a similar way. In addition, the manner of submitting the form, and the response the user gets, should be as consistent as possible. In this way, the user will have an idea what to expect, no matter which page or feature they are using.

In many ways, Visual Basic developers (and many others, for that matter) are spoiled because our tools do much of the work of maintaining UI consistency for us. In Visual Basic, most intrinsic controls are inherently visually consistent, which is not to say that it is impossible to design an inconsistent or unattractive Visual Basic user interface. Visual Basic and similar tools make creating a clean, consistent user interface much easier by providing grid-based, pixel-perfect, drag-and-drop control over the placement of user interface elements. In addition, properties of user interface elements can easily be modified to further control both placement and behavior.

Until recently, that kind of control in HTML was virtually impossible. The closest one could come was lining up UI elements by placing them within HTML tables, or by resorting to the use of the infamous single-pixel GIF file, techniques that are still widely used today. Unfortunately, that lack of control, and the lack of good editors for HTML, has resulted in much greater difficulty in achieving UI consistency in Web applications.

Visual InterDev 6.0 offers support for many tools that increase the level of control developers have over the user interface, including DHTML and Cascading Style Sheets and Positioning (CSS-P), as well as an excellent WYSIWYG HTML editor. Visual InterDev 6.0 also offers VB-style control over properties of DHTML elements and Design-Time Controls (DTCs), as well as of standard HTML elements. Figure 3-2 shows that Visual InterDev's Properties window displays the properties of an HTML tag when it is highlighted, or when the cursor is within the tag. With Visual InterDev 6.0, developers are finally gaining the level of control necessary to easily create a consistent user interface.

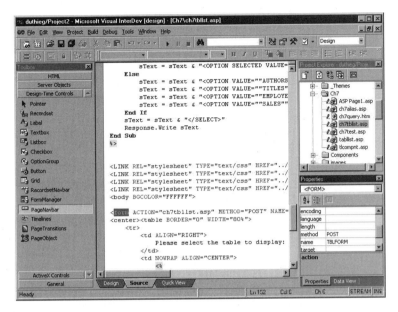

**Figure 3-2.**
*Visual InterDev's Properties box displaying properties of a <FORM> tag.*

An important part of a consistent user interface is navigation, or how the user gets from one page to another in your application. In a typical Visual Basic application, this is fairly straightforward; you create a main form and subordinate forms, then use buttons and/or menu items to connect the subordinate forms to the main form. The use of forms, buttons, and menus in Visual Basic is, as compared to HTML, rigidly structured. In a VB application, there is no way to get to a different part of the application without taking the intermediate steps required by the application. While this may potentially limit one's ability to be creative in navigating through a VB app, it also serves to make the app easier to use because users know that when they select File | Save As..., they can expect to see a dialog box that allows them to select a name and location to which to save a file.

This kind of consistency is precisely what makes graphical user interfaces such as those used by both IBM-compatible and Macintosh computers so popular, and is also what is generally lacking in Web applications. With Windows or Mac applications, once you've learned the general functional paradigm used on that platform, you've mastered a large part of using any application for that platform. With Web applications, each new application potentially means learning a new way of navigating and interacting with the application. Some apps use hyperlinks, some use buttons, and many use a combination of these and other methods.

Some Web sites and applications attempt to bring some order to the navigational chaos through the use of frames, but this technique, while useful, automatically excludes users whose browsers do not support frames. Frames also increase the complexity of your app, making application maintenance more difficult and correspondingly more costly. The bottom line is that navigation is an important element to consider in your Web application. Fortunately, navigation is also an area in which Visual InterDev 6.0 offers useful tools, including the Site Designer and navigation DTCs, which simplify the task of creating and maintaining your application's site structure. Figure 3-3 shows a very simple site structure consisting of a home page and a search page. The Site Diagram toolbar shown in the figure allows you to add new or existing pages to your site, and to change the order of pages on the global navigation bar provided by some of the navigation DTCs. The challenges encountered in the area of content management and their solutions are explored in Chapter 6, "Navigation and Content Management."

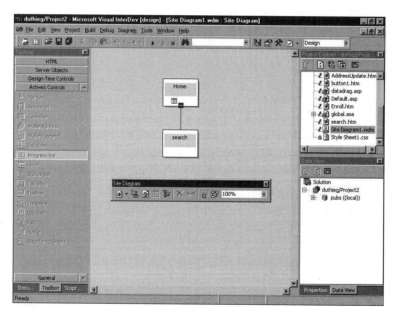

**Figure 3-3.**
*The Visual InterDev Site Designer.*

# User Authentication

Once you've taken care of the issues of supplying a feature set appropriate to your target audience, making sure those features use only the bandwidth available, and giving your app a user interface that's easy for your audience to learn and easy for you to maintain, you'll probably need to take steps to make sure that only your target audience uses your application.

Securing your application against unauthorized users by implementing user authentication can be relatively simple, or frustratingly complex. User authentication is simply a system by which you make sure that each user who accesses your application proves that they are who they say they are, and may go as far as making sure that user belongs to a group authorized to use the application. If your application is running on a corporate intranet that is standardized on the Windows platform, this may be as simple as checking the user's Windows NT login by enabling Windows NT Challenge/Response authentication (see Figure 3-4).

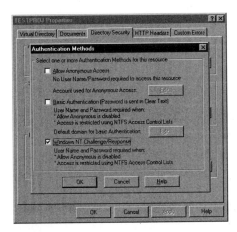

**Figure 3-4.**
*Setting NT Challenge/Response authentication.*

On the other hand, if your audience includes users accessing your application from the Internet, this can be a bit trickier. One common technique is to ask users both to register before using the application for the first time, then to log in before each subsequent use. Logins are then checked against a table of logins and passwords for registered users (the table might also include additional identifying information for greater security). This method also requires you to enable Anonymous authentication for your application in IIS.

Once a user has been authenticated and has successfully logged in, you can classify the user and grant more or less access to parts of your application based on the user's login. For example, in addition to a login and password, each user could have an assigned user level, which determines what parts of the application they can access. Or you could maintain a separate table with a subset of logins for users with greater access levels than the full user population. However you choose to get authentication information, and whatever you choose to do with it, what counts in a secure application is that you get it, and that you get it in such a way that a malicious person can't snoop and get it too. With IIS on a Windows-based network with Internet Explorer, the whole exchange can be made securely through Windows NT Challenge/Response. With authentication over the Internet, however, it is usually necessary to use clear text for logins and passwords, which means you must implement some form of encryption to avoid snooping of passwords. Clearly authenticating your users and securing your application can be a daunting task. We'll try to make the job seem a little more manageable when we look at security challenges and solutions in Chapter 10, "User Authentication and Security."

# Performance

Performance, or more to the point, getting good performance from your application, is a particularly difficult challenge because it is often hard to define just what "performance" means. Does performance refer to how fast the application is? Is performance measured by how accurately the application performs calculations? Or, is performance related to the failure rate of the application or percentage of downtime? The answer is often all of the above and more, depending on who you ask.

## What Defines Performance?

One of the first challenges in getting acceptable performance from your Web application is to define in a very specific and measurable way what is meant by performance as it applies to required application performance, such as the time it takes for your application to return results after the submission of an HTML form. It may be more important, in many cases, to concentrate on improving the responsiveness of the application rather than its overall speed, since it is often the responsiveness (or lack thereof) that users will perceive as performance.

In fact, what often matters most is how the users perceive application performance, not necessarily how many transactions per minute your database server can handle. If your user interface is slow, it won't matter to the user whether the cause is a slow SQL query or limited bandwidth, it only matters that it's slow. Ideally, performance expectations should be defined in cooperation with the project's stakeholders and users, and they should include such measures as numbers of concurrent users the application should be able to support, the acceptable load time for pages, and the acceptable response time for queries and updates performed by the application.

Having established quantifiable performance requirements, the next step is to design an application architecture that will allow your application to achieve those performance requirements. This involves many decisions, including choosing where to implement parts of your application, as well as choosing appropriate hardware on which to run your application. Many of these decisions were discussed in Chapter 2, "Defining the Web Application Environment," and will be revisited periodically throughout the book.

Having decided on an architecture, you can now begin developing your application.

Once you're certain that your application actually works and fulfills all its requirements, improving performance begins with establishing a baseline from which to judge the application's performance. Once an application is in the process of being built, or has been built, you should begin the process of profiling your application and measuring its baseline performance. *Profiling* or *baselining*, and measuring future performance against that baseline, are two of the most important things you can do to get a handle on performance, and to track performance as the application grows and changes. Without some sort of baseline measurements, it is virtually impossible to accurately assess whether steps taken to improve application performance were effective.

You can use Performance Monitor, a utility that comes with Windows NT, to generate charts, logs, and reports on specific aspects of your server, such as processor and memory usage, as well as statistics for services such as IIS and Active Server Pages. The logs and reports can be used to determine what the normal, or baseline, performance of your application looks like. Figure 3-5 shows a Performance monitor report that includes counters representing processor use, memory use, and several counters each for Active Server Pages and IIS.

Once you have a baseline against which to measure, it is much easier to determine the effect on performance of changes made to the application by measuring performance against the baseline before and after the changes are made. If you see a dramatic increase in the Active Server Pages Request Wait Time or Requests Queued counters, this may be an indication that something in your application is causing a bottleneck. If you find that there is a corresponding increase in processor or memory use, it may be that the number of users you are serving during peak periods is more than your processor or memory can adequately handle, in which case the solution may be to add processors or memory. Not every performance problem is as easy to diagnose, but if you have a baseline, at least you'll be able to see when things change, which should help you figure out why.

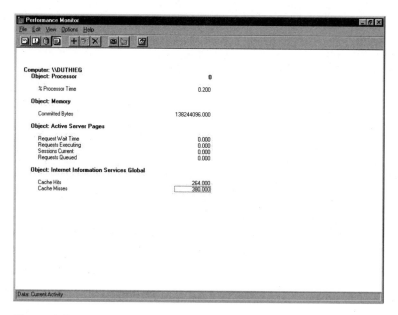

**Figure 3-5.**
*Performance Monitor report example.*

## What Factors Affect Performance?

Once you've established a baseline for your application through profiling, you can start taking a look at which parts of your application could be improved. As mentioned above, both server architecture and application architecture can have a major impact on performance. While it may not be feasible to redesign the application architecture once the application has reached a certain point in the development process, it may be possible to make changes in the hardware architecture that will improve application performance. Such changes might be suggested by discovering system bottlenecks through tools such as Windows NT's Performance Monitor. Such observations may suggest areas, including server resources such as RAM or processor speed, that are preventing your application from reaching its peak performance. Depending on your application's architecture, you may also want to look at whether resources on the client (or lack thereof) may be causing slow performance. If, for example, your application makes heavy use of DHTML and DirectAnimation, both of which are designed to take advantage of more powerful desktop machines, it's likely that users with older machines will experience less than optimal performance.

Another problem area for performance occurs when the application is being accessed by more users than it was designed to support. The number of users using a Web application can have a huge effect on the application's overall performance. Therefore it is especially important during the design and architecture phase of a project to get an accurate estimate of the number of users your application needs to support. It's also probably a good idea to build in a certain amount (perhaps 10-25 percent) of extra capacity above and beyond that estimate, both to account for peaks in application use, as well as for growth in the user base.

Another problem area that may affect your application's performance is database access. How you go about getting to and manipulating data can potentially make your application scream with speed, or make your users scream with frustration? In addition to the coverage of these and other performance-related challenges that can be found in Chapter 7, "Addressing Performance and Scalability," you can find information on improving the efficiency of your data access in Chapter 14, "Optimizing Data Access."

# Scalability

Scalability is closely related to performance. Unlike performance, however, scalability is a challenge that is somewhat unique to enterprise applications. Non-enterprise applications typically do not have a large enough number of users to make scalability a major issue. Of course, as with any challenge one faces, the first step is to define the challenge.

## Simple Concept

*Scalability* is the ability of an application to support large numbers of users as well as it supports small numbers. The larger the number of users an application can support without performance degradation (or outright collapse, for that matter), the better its scalability. This concept is especially important for Web applications that are accessible via the Internet, as the scalability required by such applications can be substantial, to say the least. A word to the wise: before you open the door, make sure it's big enough to accommodate the crowds you anticipate, and then some. As many Web site operators have found out the hard way, there are few things more embarrassing (not to mention damaging to a company's reputation) than having to shut down your Web application the day it's rolled out to the public because the application cannot withstand the load. The cost of building more capacity into your application than it needs may be one of the best investments your company makes.

Visual InterDev 6.0's strong support for components, its integration with MTS, and its ability to make use of MSMQ objects make it a particularly good choice for building scalable Web applications. Visual InterDev makes it easy to build a whole range of Web applications, from small applications with few users, to multi-developer enterprise applications with large numbers of users, using the same familiar tools.

## Factors in Scalability

Scalability is affected by many of the same factors as performance. Among these, of course, are application architecture and server architecture. Improving application scalability comes down to understanding where the work is being done. If all of the processing being done by your application occurs on the Web server (and the server hardware has not been designed to accommodate such demands), then it's less likely that your application will scale well. One of the advantages of building Web applications in the first place is that they are distributed applications, that is, the work they do is distributed between multiple machines. Even as simple a step as validating data entry at the client can relieve your servers of a substantial burden, as well as reduce network traffic by eliminating round-trips to the server for validation and for re-entering invalid data.

In addition to looking at where the work in your application is being done (or will be done), you need to understand the implications of decisions of which technologies to use for your application's infrastructure. For example, although Active Server Pages on IIS can provide a high-performance application platform, the performance advantage of business logic in compiled components over the same logic written in script code means that applications that make use of components to provide business logic will scale better than applications that use only ASP script. Applications that use components also gain the advantage of being able to take advantage of the component management services of Microsoft Transaction Server, as well as being able to offload the work those components perform onto a machine other than the Web server. Both of these abilities can translate to substantial improvements in an application's scalability. We'll discuss these and other factors in application scalability in Chapter 7, "Addressing Performance and Scalability."

## Ensuring Reliable Communications

Although there are many advantages to a distributed application architecture, there is one major disadvantage: reliance on networks. Any application that runs on more than one machine requires some method of communicating with the other machines involved. This communications method is most often a corporate Local Area Network (LAN) or Wide Area Network (WAN).

Networks, as anyone who has ever used one can attest, are not perfect. They have a nasty tendency to go down exactly when you need them most. Granted, this is a disadvantage shared by traditional client/server applications as well. Enterprise Web applications, however, are often considerably more vulnerable to network problems because they typically use a greater number of machines to provide the data and services of the application. Consequently, there are a greater number of potential failure points for the application, any of which could bring the entire application to a halt. In addition to network failures, the failure of individual machines may also prevent an application from functioning. In applications requiring 24 x 7 operation, this is clearly unacceptable.

So what are we to do about this? How do we insure that the failure of the network, or of servers used by our application, will not prevent our application from functioning? We could go through the time and effort of building our own custom inter-application communication solution to address these issues, but fortunately a solution has been provided for us in the form of Microsoft Message Queue Server (MSMQ).

MSMQ is comprised of an NT service (which in fact will be built-in to Windows NT 5.0) and client components that take advantage of the functionality provided by the Windows NT service. MSMQ provides a method for applications to communicate electronically in the same way people do via e-mail. It is, in a sense, e-mail for applications. MSMQ is not, however, meant to serve as a way of e-mail-enabling your applications. MSMQ enables the creation and management of public and private message queues. A *message queue* is an area in which an application (or part of an application) can place a message intended for another application (or another part of the same application). Using queues for enabling communication between the various parts of an application can effectively de-couple those parts, allowing (in many cases) one part of the application to continue working, even if the other part of the application is not. The challenges of inter-application communication will be explored further in Chapter 9, "Improving the Performance and Reliability of Enterprise Applications with Microsoft Message Queue Server (MSMQ)."

## Ensuring Transactional Integrity

*Transactional integrity.* It's yet another one of those terms whose meaning may not immediately jump out at you. By its simplest definition, a transaction is a unit of work. In the same simple terms, transactional integrity is about ensuring that for each unit of work, or transaction, all changes made or work performed are committed together, or if for some reason there is a failure during the transaction, any changes made are restored to their original state.

In a traditional client/server application using only one data source, we could rely on the DBMS to provide us with the ability to make changes within the context of a transaction. For example, an application using SQL Server could use the following code to ensure that an insert to two different tables both succeed:

```
Sub InsertRows(Data1 As String, Data2 As String)
    Dim Conn As New ADO Connection
    Dim Cmd As New ADO Command
    On Error GoTo InsertRows_EH
    'Open Connection with predefined connection string
    Conn.Open sConnectString
```

*(continued)*

```
'Set active connection for ADO command object
Set Cmd.ActiveConnection = Conn
'Set command properties
Cmd.CommandType = adCmdText 'SQL String
Cmd.CommandText = "INSERT INTO TABLE1 VALUES (" & Data1 _
    & ", " & Data2 & ")"
'Begin transaction
Conn.BeginTrans
'Insert row into first table
Cmd.Execute
'Set command property for second insert
Cmd.CommandText = "INSERT INTO TABLE2 VALUES (" & Data1 _
    & ", " & Data2 & ")"
'Insert row into second table
Cmd.Execute
'If no errors, commit transaction
Conn.CommitTrans
'Clean up
Conn.Close
Set Conn = Nothing
Set Cmd = Nothing
Exit Sub

'Error handling code
InsertRows_EH:

    'Rollback transaction
    Conn.RollbackTrans
    'Clean up
    Conn.Close
    Set Conn = Nothing
    Set Cmd = Nothing
End Sub
```

This method works fine if you are only dealing with a single data source. But what about enterprise applications that manipulate multiple data sources within the context of a transaction? We could write our own code to coordinate the updating of data from multiple sources, but we don't have to, thanks to Microsoft Transaction Server (MTS).

Microsoft Transaction Server is a transaction and component-management tool. Like MSMQ, MTS provides much of its functionality through a Windows NT service that is an extension of the Microsoft Distributed Transaction Co-ordinator (MSDTC). Clients access MTS services through the MTS COM component. By simply adding a reference to this component in a Visual Basic project, your application's components gain the ability to define a transaction that can include multiple data sources, as well as encompassing multiple components. MTS can also supply transactional control functionality to ASP pages. The best part is that all of this functionality is as simple to use (if not simpler) as the above code example.

MTS provides applications with the ability to implement "two-phase commit" transactions. In *two-phase commit*, the committing of a transaction begins when the process or component that began the transaction attempts to commit the transaction. At this point, MTS checks with all the other participants in the transaction to make sure that each participant signals that it's OK to commit. Once MTS receives this acknowledgment from every participant, the transaction is committed. If even one participant in the transaction signals a problem, the transaction is rolled back.

Once your components have been coded to take advantage of MTS functionality, Visual InterDev 6.0 provides the ability to manage your components, including where your components are registered, and how your component is packaged by MTS. The challenges of transactional integrity, and solutions based on MTS, are discussed in Chapter 8, "Enterprise Development Using Microsoft Transaction Server (MTS)."

# Accessing Heterogeneous Data Sources

Enterprise data is everywhere. From Microsoft Access and other desktop databases to Oracle and SQL Server DBMSs, you name it, your application may need to access it. Remember that your application is about data, and is nothing without it. Your users, however, don't want to and shouldn't have to think about where that data comes from. It can be a challenge to present data from numerous dissimilar sources as if it were all coming from the same place. Not too long ago, the effort involved was considerable.

Before Open Database Connectivity (ODBC), it might have been better in some cases to migrate data to a common platform than to try to write and maintain an application that communicated directly with several different data sources, each with their own method of accessing data. For Visual Basic developers, such a task might have been next to impossible. Today, tools such as ODBC, OLE DB, and ActiveX Data Objects (ADO) make this task much easier.

ODBC, which was introduced in 1992, provides developers with access to relational data sources such as Microsoft SQL Server, Oracle, and DB2. The ODBC architecture, as shown in Figure 3-6, consists of an ODBC driver for the data source to be accessed, and the ODBC driver manager, which communicates with the application, and takes care of loading the appropriate database driver and translating data access calls into a syntax appropriate for the data source. ODBC made data access a great deal easier by providing developers with a single method of accessing data in different databases, but since ODBC uses C syntax, its benefits were difficult to use from Visual Basic. Remote Data Objects (RDO), built on top of ODBC, was introduced to allow object-based access to ODBC data sources from Visual Basic. Unfortunately, neither ODBC nor RDO are usable from within an ASP page. Another area in which ODBC is lacking is the fact that ODBC does not enable access to nonrelational data stores, such as Microsoft Exchange message stores.

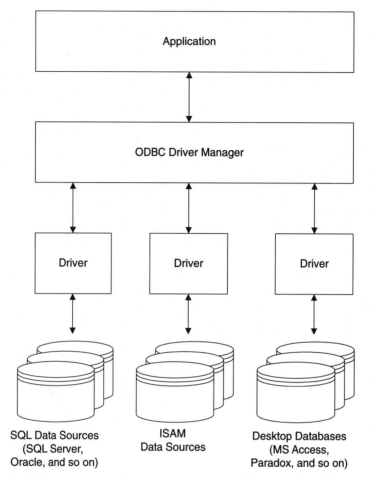

**Figure 3-6.**
*ODBC architecture.*

OLE DB, which was introduced in 1997, is designed to build on the success of ODBC, and to address some of its shortcomings, including access to nonrelational data stores. OLE DB provides a high-performance, COM-based interface to both relational and nonrelational data. In the world of OLE DB, data access is broken up into two parts, data consumers and data providers. OLE DB consumers consist mostly of applications, while OLE DB providers play a role similar to that of ODBC drivers. Each data source to be accessed through OLE DB requires an OLE DB provider, though there is an OLE DB provider for ODBC that allows access to data sources that do not yet have an OLE DB provider, but do have an ODBC driver available. ActiveX Data Objects (ADO) was designed as an object-based interface to any and all OLE DB providers.

Because ADO can be used with any OLE DB provider, developers now need learn only one method of data access to be able to access any data, anywhere (assuming of course that the data source has an OLE DB provider). An additional advantage of ADO is that it can be used directly from ASP pages, although for performance reasons (discussed further in Chapter 7), it is best to avoid doing so in applications requiring high scalability. The OLE DB/ADO architecture can be seen in Figure 3-7.

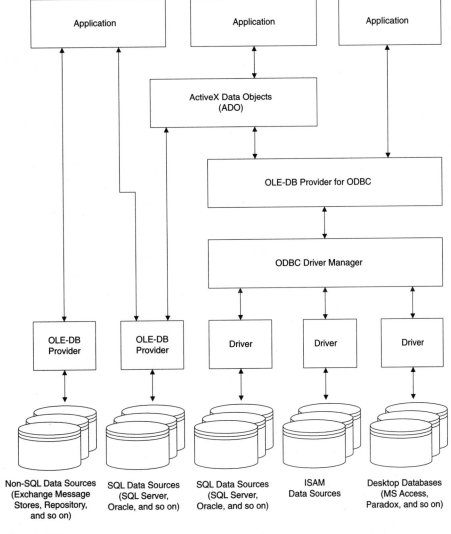

**Figure 3-7.**
*OLE DB/ADO architecture.*

Once you've managed to access the data your application needs, your next challenge is to present that data to users in a useful format. Visual InterDev 6.0 provides a number of useful tools for dealing with data. Among these are the Visual InterDev Design-Time Controls (DTCs).

NOTE:    To avoid confusion between the Design-Time Controls and the Microsoft Distributed Transaction Coordinator (which makes MTS possible), we'll refer to the Design-Time Controls as DTCs, and the Distributed Transaction Coordinator as the MSDTC. Perhaps if Microsoft had a Distributed Technology Naming Coordinator (MSDTNC), this confusion could be avoided.

The Visual InterDev DTCs are a group of controls that can be dragged-and-dropped onto an ASP page to enable data-bound HTML forms. The DTCs include Button, Textbox, Listbox, Label, Grid, Checkbox, OptionGroup, Recordset, and RecordsetNavBar. By simply dragging a Recordset DTC onto an ASP page, setting its properties to connect to a data connection defined for the project, and dragging the appropriate Textbox and other DTCs onto the page and setting their properties (see Figure 3-8, which shows a RecordsetNavBar DTC being dropped onto a page), you can enable access to data without writing a single line of code. In addition, when using the DTCs, it's possible to provide either server-based ASP functionality (including navigating from record to record) or client-based DHTML functionality at the project level or the page level. Moreover, you can change from one model to the other at the flip of a switch. Figure 3-9 shows the Properties dialog box for a Recordset DTC, which provides options to change the scripting platform.

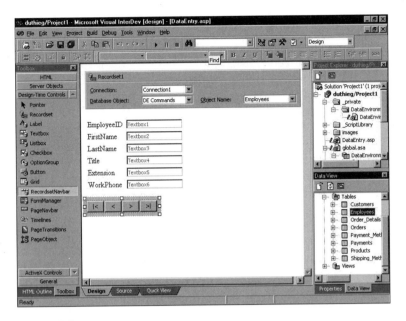

**Figure 3-8.**
*Using the Visual InterDev 6.0 Design-Time controls.*

Clearly, this is quite an exciting innovation, but hold on there. Before you build your entire enterprise application using DTCs, you need to be aware that the functionality of the DTCs is based on script code, and lots of it. As we've mentioned before, script code doesn't run as fast as compiled code, so the more you use, the more difficult it is for your application to scale well. Remember too that script code cannot be removed to a different server, which also limits scalability. That doesn't mean that you should never use DTCs, for they are an incredibly convenient way to enable data access. But if and when you do use them, you must understand the potential drawbacks, as well as the benefits. We can only hope that eventually the functionality of the Scripting Library (which provides the functionality of the DTCs as client- and server-side scripts) will eventually be implemented as a COM component, giving us the benefits of the DTCs, with the speed of compiled code (although client-side scenarios would require the downloading and installation of the component to work). Until then, the DTCs are still very useful for prototyping.

And, in situations where scalability is less of a concern, they are remarkably easy to use. We will revisit the topic of the Visual InterDev DTCs in Chapter 11, "RAD Database Development and Data Access."

**Figure 3-9.**
*Changing the scripting platform of a recordset DTC.*

# Accessing Legacy Data

Integrating legacy data. It can be one of the most painful experiences in developing an enterprise Web application. At best, it usually means searching for the few tools and protocols available that allow your disparate systems to talk to one another, and using brute force to coerce them into some form of cooperation. At worst, it means writing intricate custom code to provide an interface between the two systems, or worse yet, setting up potentially unreliable batch processes.

Legacy data exists. The unfortunate truth is that it will continue to exist for quite some time, as much as some developers might love to see it go away. Companies have far too much money invested in their legacy systems to simply throw them away. One might think with the approach of the Year 2000 problem, companies would want to migrate to platforms known to be Y2K compliant, rather than fix older systems, potentially at greater cost. But it seems that in reality, many companies are leery of taking on such a migration until after they've gotten beyond Y2K. It's probably safe to say that we won't see mainframe systems going away in large numbers for the next several years at least. Which means that, like it or not, developers will have to get at the data stored in these systems.

There is, however, a tool that can make the job easier when dealing with such standard systems as AS/400 and MVS: Microsoft's SNA Server, available as a part of Visual Studio 6.0 Enterprise Edition. SNA Server is a product that can simplify the process of connecting to and accessing data from legacy systems. With the addition of COM Transaction Integrator (COMTI), the technology formerly known as Cedar (TTFKAC), SNA Server can also provide the ability to integrate CICS applications running on MVS with Windows NT-based applications. The challenges involved in accessing and using legacy data and applications is discussed in depth in Chapter 12, "Accessing Legacy Data Sources."

# Application Maintenance

So once you've developed your application, deployed it, and your users are using it, your job is done, right? Wrong! A developer's job is never done. Now comes the task of application maintenance. Application maintenance can be roughly broken down into two areas, *bug fixes* and *upgrades*. A related area is *staged delivery*, in which parts of an application are rolled out as they are developed to reduce the amount of time users have to wait for a particular feature set.

## Bug Fixes, Or "One More Crash and You're Fired!"

So about now you're saying, "But our application won't have any bugs to fix." Yeah. Right. All applications have bugs. Enterprise applications are particularly vulnerable to bugs because of their size and scope. Hopefully, by implementing a good architecture, following sensible development guidelines, and implementing a thorough testing strategy, your development team can manage to keep bugs to a minimum. But let's face it, there will still be bugs to fix. What's especially challenging in enterprise development is fixing bugs without interrupting access to the application. You can't afford to have your application's site down for most of a day or even for a few hours while you make changes to pages and DLLs and test all of your changes.

Fortunately, Web applications developed with ASP are mostly pretty easy to upgrade. With changes that need to be made in ASP pages, the server doesn't even need to be stopped in order to make them. Once an ASP page has been modified, the next time a user requests the ASP page, they'll get the new copy (assuming of course that you've taken steps to prevent the page from being cached).

The problem arises when your bug fix involves a component used by your application. By default, components (in-process components, or DLLs) accessed by your application are run in the same process as IIS, which means that in order to replace the component, you must shut down IIS in order to get IIS to release the component. While this limitation is not true of out-of-process components (EXEs), they have a substantial performance deficit compared to in-process DLLs.

## Upgrades, Or "It's Just Not Good Enough Yet"

In addition to bug fixes, most Web applications will at some point need to be upgraded for one reason or another, whether to add additional functionality, or to integrate newly available technologies. Upgrades of a Web application bring up some of the same issues as bug fixes. While individual ASP and HTML pages may be easy to replace with the upgraded pages, components being run in-process require the IIS to be shut down in order to upgrade the component. In addition, upgrades may require a good deal more testing with the existing system than bug fixes.

## Staged Release, Or "Today the UI...Tomorrow the World"

Staged release is related to upgrades in the sense that staged release can be thought of as planned upgrades, in which each release stage is an upgrade that provides an additional set of the full application's functionality. Delivering an application via staged release has one primary advantage in that it gets functionality into the hands of your users weeks or months sooner than if you had developed the entire application before deploying it.

All three of the topics discussed, bug fixes, upgrades, and staged release, hinge on the same issue: how to reduce the amount of time the application is out of commission during the bug fix, upgrade, or installation of the staged release. The first step in solving this problem is planning. For each bug fix or upgrade, there should be a migration plan that details the files that need to be replaced and any new files that need to be installed, and changes to the system registry of affected systems, and so forth, as well as the planned time for the migration, or at least an agreed upon window during which upgrades and migrations may take place. In addition to having a migration plan, it is essential that any new code, bug fix or upgrade, be thoroughly tested on a test bed that is identical to the production environment (or as close to identical as is possible). The more accurate your test systems are, the less likely it is that you'll have problems once your code is in production. In addition, files being replaced should be renamed or archived so that they can be easily recovered in the event that the bug fix, upgrade, or new functionality doesn't perform as expected. All of these steps help reduce the amount of application downtime experienced during bug fixes and upgrades. For more information on application maintenance, see Chapter 6, "Navigation and Content Management," and Chapter 7, "Addressing Performance and Scalability."

# Introducing the Sample Application

In order to provide the best sample solutions possible, this book uses a single sample application as the basis for most of its code examples. This provides a single context in which to discuss the challenges and solutions of enterprise Web development. This is not to say that there will not be examples and code that do not relate directly to the demo application. It would simply not be practical in the context of a book such as this to develop an application that addressed each and every problem and challenge faced by enterprise developers. Even if it were possible, it would probably not be a particularly good example of how to develop an application.

The truth is, a developer probably will not face every challenge described in this book on a single development project. The point is to provide as many solutions and code examples in the context of the sample application as possible within the limits of sensible design. That said, let's introduce the sample application.

# The Rent-A-Prize Auto Rental Information Management System

• • • **GOAL: To Provide Universal, Web-Based Interface to Rental Reservations and Customer Information, and to Reduce Administrative Costs and Paperwork**

The demo application is designed for a fictional auto rental company called Rent-A-Prize, and was developed with the help of developers at Spectrum Technology Group. The fictional folks at Rent-A-Prize want a system designed that allows clerks in the individual Rent-A-Prize rental locations to enter customer information, access and enter rental reservation information, and check vehicles in and out for individual rentals via an Internet Explorer 4 DHTML-based interface. They also want their customers to be able to use their Web browsers (any browser) to register and enter reservations via the Internet.

## Requirements

The first step in producing an application such as the Rent-A-Prize sample application is to gather the requirements. Since Rent-A-Prize is a fictional company, we made up the requirements by having one member of the development team play the role of a stakeholder for the project. Remember that although the Rent-A-Prize application is intended to implement the best practices for enterprise development as we see them, its requirements are in part driven by the need to demonstrate solutions, which is not an entirely natural development paradigm.

## Interface Requirements

The user interface for Rent-A-Prize is Web-based, and is divided up into two interface areas, the clerk interface, and the customer interface.

### Clerk Interface Requirements

The clerk interface's requirements are as follows:

- Clerk interface will use Internet Explorer 4 as the browser.
- Clerk interface will enable clerks to retrieve information on customers, reservations, vehicle types, and vehicles at their location.
- Clerk interface will enable clerks to sort reservation and vehicle information locally, without querying the Web server.

## Customer Interface Requirements

The customer interface requirements are as follows:

- Customer interface will allow first-time users to register and select a password for future access to the application.

- Customer interface will allow users to update their registration information.

- Customer interface will allow users to view existing auto rental reservations placed via the system, and to update or cancel those reservations, or enter new reservations.

# Business Requirements

The business requirements for the Rent-A-Prize application include:

- The application should use compiled components for most business logic.

- The application should use a common set of components to provide functionality for both the clerk and the customer interfaces. Reusability should be maximized wherever possible.

- The application must provide access to potentially thousands of Internet users, without affecting the responsiveness of the clerk interface.

- When a customer enters a reservation via the Internet, that reservation will not affect the inventory of the location specified by the customer. If at the time of the reservation a vehicle of the type requested by the customer is unavailable, the customer will be upgraded to the next higher vehicle type for which a vehicle is available. If no vehicles are available, arrangements will be made through a competitor to provide a vehicle for the customer at the agreed rate. The latter will not be implemented as a part of the Rent-A-Prize application, but rather as a company policy.

## Security Requirements

Security requirements for the Rent-A-Prize application include:

- The clerk interface will be implemented on machines running Windows NT Workstation.

- Clerks must log in to their clerk interface machine at the beginning of their shift and log out at the end. Clerk logins will be validated against NT user accounts at the corporate headquarters.

- Clerk activity, such as entering new reservations and processing rentals will be tracked by including a Clerk ID with each reservation or rental processed by a clerk.

- All clerk activity should be protected by SSL.

- Customers must log in to the Rent-A-Prize application before they are able to view or enter reservations.

- Customer logins will be validated against a table of logins and passwords.

- Customer login page should use SSL or another encryption technology to prevent snooping of customer passwords.

- All records (registration, reservations, and so on) entered by a customer through the application will include a Customer ID field to enable tracking.

## Architecture

The architecture for the Rent-A-Prize sample application can be divided up into three areas: the logical architecture, the physical architecture, and the component architecture. The logical architecture is simply an n-tier architecture, in which the client, or user services tier consists of a browser and the Web server (running IIS 4.0), the business services tier consists of the Web server, and any component servers (running Microsoft Transaction Server) made necessary by scalability concerns, and the data tier consists of a database server (running MS SQL Server 6.5). The early drafts of the physical and component architectures are illustrated in Figures 3-10 and 3-11, respectively.

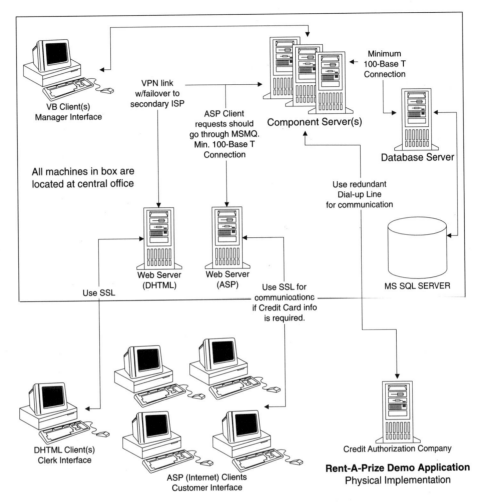

VPN link
w/failover to
secondary ISP

VB Client(s)
Manager Interface

ASP Client
requests should
go through MSMQ.
Min. 100-Base T
Connection

Component Server(s)

Minimum
100-Base T
Connection

Database Server

All machines in box are
located at central office

Use redundant
Dial-up Line
for communication

Web Server
(DHTML)

Web Server
(ASP)

Use SSL

Use SSL for
communications
if Credit Card info
is required.

MS SQL SERVER

DHTML Client(s)
Clerk Interface

ASP (Internet) Clients
Customer Interface

Credit Authorization Company

**Rent-A-Prize Demo Application**
Physical Implementation

**Figure 3-10.**
*Rent-A-Prize physical architecture.*

One thing to keep in mind about the physical architecture of Rent-A-Prize is that while this is a good solution for the particular situation of the application, it is not by any means the only solution available for such an application. In addition, the fact that this is a demo application means that this physical implementation will likely never actually be realized. All of the code described in the context of the sample application can potentially be run on one machine, although clearly at the expense of performance and scalability.

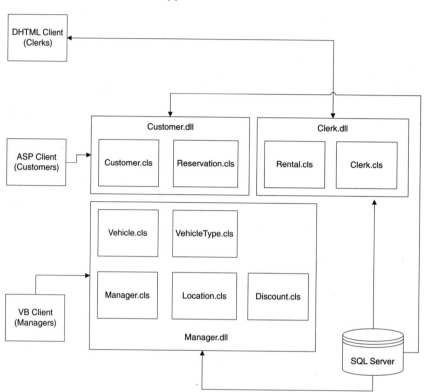

**Rent-A-Prize Application Architecture**

**Figure 3-11.**
*Rent-A-Prize component architecture.*

## The Rent-A-Prize Demo Application Is a Learning Tool

The important thing to remember as you read the book and play with the solutions provided by the sample application is that the Rent-A-Prize application is designed to be a tool for learning, not as an accurate picture of how one would develop an auto rental application. Each application you develop will have its own special needs that will have to be evaluated on their own merits. While you should use the solutions provided wherever they are useful to you, you should not try to shoehorn every application into the framework provided by the demo application.

NOTE:   The Rent-A-Prize application was developed internally at Spectrum Technology Group as a demonstration of the technologies discussed in this book, as well as for public presentations given by Spectrum consultants. The harsh reality of the consulting business, however, means that there was a limit to the resources that could be allocated for the development of an application that is, after all, just a demo. What this means is that there may be areas where corners were cut to save time in development. This is to our advantage, however, in that it gives us an opportunity to look at both the quick way to solve a problem *and* the right way.

# Summary

In this chapter, we've discussed the wide variety of challenges faced in Web development. We also introduced the Rent-A-Prize sample application. From client challenges such as features vs. reach and user authentication, to business challenges such as performance and scalability issues, to data challenges, including ensuring transactional integrity and accessing legacy data, enterprise Web development serves up a plateful of challenges sufficient to sate any developer's appetite. Starting in Chapter 5, "Features vs. Reach—Cross-Platform Support," we'll begin our in-depth look at the solutions provided by Visual InterDev 6.0 and related tools for these many challenges. Continuing on, in Chapter 4, "Enter Visual InterDev 6.0," we'll talk about the new features of the latest edition of Microsoft's premier Web-development tool, and provide a walkthrough of some Visual InterDev 6.0 basics.

# Enter Visual InterDev 6.0

Having discussed enterprise Web development, talked about the Web development environment as it currently exists, and enumerated some of the challenges faced in enterprise Web applications, it's time to take a closer look at what should become the central tool in your Web development Toolbox: Visual InterDev 6.0. First off, a note for those confused by the version number. After all, the last version of InterDev was 1.0. How did we end up at 6.0? Well, it all has to do with Visual InterDev as a part of the Visual Studio family of development tools. It was decided that for Visual Studio 6.0, all the Visual Studio products should carry the same version number. Thus, both Visual InterDev 1.0 and Visual J++ 1.1 become Visual InterDev 6.0 and Visual J++ 6.0, respectively.

## Visual InterDev 6.0

Visual InterDev 6.0 is a development environment for building Web applications. It's aimed at a wide variety of developers, from the new developer with a strong Web background, to Visual Basic programmers getting started with Web development. Visual InterDev provides both experienced and less experienced developers with wizards to get you up and running quickly. Of course, it also provides advanced Web developers with the kind of control they need to really make their applications sing.

Visual InterDev is primarily a Rapid Application Development (RAD) environment for HTML and Active Server Pages (ASP) pages. While ASP scripting and HTML can be combined to create powerful and flexible Web applications, until now, there have been no tools available that supplied the kind of powerful and easy-to-use development environment for Web applications to which users of languages such as Visual Basic and Visual C++ have become accustomed. Visual InterDev 1.0 was a good start, but it did not supply nearly the functionality Web developers were looking for. Features like drag-and-drop functionality, debugging, and WYSIWYG editing were conspicuous by their absence.

With Visual InterDev 6.0, that's all changed. Now, developing a Web application is much more like developing a Visual Basic application. In fact, the new Visual InterDev Integrated Development Environment (IDE) is suspiciously similar to that of Visual Basic. This is because the Visual Studio development team is finally beginning to realize the dream of a single IDE for all the Visual Studio tools, and Visual Basic is the model for that IDE. Visual InterDev 6.0 provides many improvements over the first version of Visual InterDev, including drag-and-drop of data-bound Design-Time Controls (DTCs) and even standard HTML elements, as well as end-to-end debugging of applications, and a WYSIWYG editor descended from the editor found in Microsoft FrontPage. With these and other new additions, Visual InterDev 6.0 is poised to solve many of the problems that have been plaguing Web developers for years. So without further ado, let's take a look at some of the features of Visual InterDev 6.0.

# Features of Visual InterDev 6.0

Like a kid in a candy shop, Visual InterDev has so many new and improved features, it's hard for a developer to know where to begin. While we won't be able to cover every feature of Visual InterDev in this section, we'll at least try to give you a look at the notable new ones as well as those that have been substantially improved.

## Site Designer

To begin our exploration of the features of Visual InterDev 6.0, let's start where you might logically start with the development of your application, *prototyping*. The Site Designer is a new tool in Visual InterDev that enables rapid prototyping of your Web application's structure and navigation. With Site Designer, you create a Site Diagram, which is a visual representation of the relationship between pages in your application. Figure 4-1 shows the Site Designer. It consists of the window that contains your pages, the individual pages that make up your site, and the lines representing the relationships between your pages.

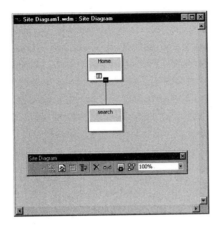

**Figure 4-1.**
*Visual InterDev Site Designer.*

You can use the Site Designer to manage the hierarchy of your site by simply dragging-and-dropping pages. You can add new content to your site through drag-and-drop as well, or by using context menu commands. If you're using the Visual InterDev PageNavBar DTC (more on this control later in the section entitled "Adding Content"), changes made to the Site Diagram will automatically update the navigational links provided by this DTC when the changes are saved. Site Designer and Site Diagrams provide an excellent way to rapidly develop the structure of your Web application to define site navigation and to maintain site structure.

## WYSIWYG Page Editor

Once you've created pages for your application using the Site Designer, naturally you'll want to edit those pages to add the features and functionality they require. Visual InterDev 6.0 now has an integrated WYSIWYG editor (see Figure 4-2), allowing you to design your HTML and ASP pages visually, without having to constantly preview the pages in a browser as you are designing them.

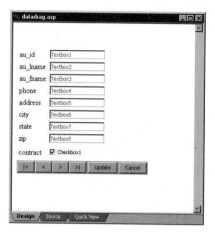

**Figure 4-2.**
*Visual InterDev's WYSIWYG editor.*

The WYSIWYG editor allows you to add content to your pages by dragging HTML elements from the Visual InterDev Toolbox onto the page. You can then set properties for these elements in much the same fashion as you would set properties of controls in Visual Basic. In addition to HTML elements, Visual InterDev DTCs may be dragged from the Toolbox and dropped onto the page. Items such as graphics and record sets can also be dragged from the Visual InterDev Project Explorer window and dropped onto the page.

If you are developing for IE 4 (or other browsers supporting CSS 3.0 and CSS-P), you can use the WYSIWYG editor to position elements on the page exactly where you want them, down to the pixel. The WYSIWYG editor also enables word processor-like editing of text, tables, and so on.

## Cascading Style Sheets (CSS) Editor

Cascading Style Sheets (CSS) offer developers the ability to exercise a great deal of control over the appearance of their Web application's pages, without a great deal of effort. The CSS editor included with Visual InterDev 6.0 makes creating and editing style sheets a breeze. The CSS editor allows you to specify tags and classes for your style sheets, then set properties for those tags and classes, including font properties, background properties, and positioning properties, all visually, without writing a single line of CSS code. The positioning properties are particularly powerful, allowing you to set the absolute position of elements of an HMTL page, including the z-order. Positioning requires a browser that supports the Cascading Style Sheets with Positioning (CSS-P) specification. The editor's Preview pane (see Figure 4-3) lets you to take a look at how the style will look when applied, and even lets you preview the style sheet on a page of your choice.

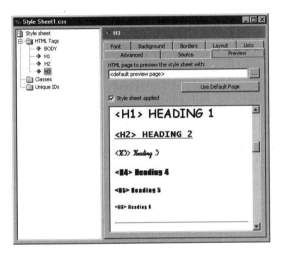

**Figure 4-3.**
*Cascading Style Sheet editor Preview pane.*

## IntelliSense Statement Completion

IntelliSense statement completion, one of the most useful features to be added to Visual Basic in recent years, has finally made it to Visual InterDev 6.0. With IntelliSense, there's no more struggling to remember the names of properties and methods, and consequently, a lot less time spent cleaning up after errors in your code. When writing script code in Visual InterDev's Source window, IntelliSense prompts you each time you enter the dot object separator with the methods and properties available for the object you are scripting (see Figure 4-4). IntelliSense works with server objects, such as the Session and Application objects, client objects, such as the Document, Window, and Form objects, as well as with components, including Microsoft components such as ADO, third-party components, and your own custom COM components. IntelliSense also helps out when using methods that call for arguments by prompting you with a ToolTip showing the required arguments of the method you are calling, just as in Visual Basic.

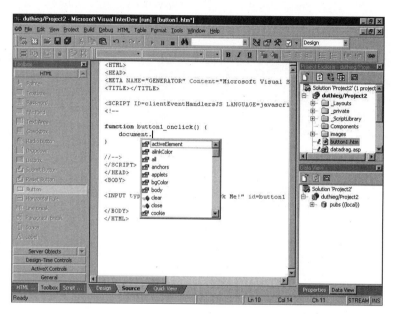

**Figure 4-4.**
*IntelliSense in action.*

## Scripting Object Model and the Scripting Library

The Scripting Object Model introduces a new paradigm to Web development: programming with objects. The Scripting Object Model, which is implemented by a series of HTML and ASP files containing JavaScript collectively known as the Script Library, provides all the functionality necessary for creating forms, binding data to input fields, such as textboxes or radio buttons, and providing access to the functionality of your Web pages to other pages in your application as page objects. With the Scripting Object Model, HTML and ASP pages are created using Design-Time Controls (see next section) and script objects instead of solely by writing code. Using DTCs and script objects abstracts the tasks of building application functionality with the "properties and methods" paradigm so familiar to Visual Basic developers. One important note about the Script Library: all of the functionality of the Design-Time Controls and script objects is provided by the files in the Script Library, so Microsoft recommends that you do not alter any of those files, or you may find that the controls do not function properly.

## New and Enhanced Design-Time Controls (DTCs)

We talked briefly about the Design-Time Controls (DTCs) earlier in the book, but only just scratched the surface. The DTCs shipping with Visual InterDev 6 include: the Button control, Check box control, FormManager control, Grid control, Label control, Listbox control, OptionGroup control, PageObject control, PageNavBar control, PageTransitions control, Recordset control, RecordsetNavBar control, Textbox control, and Timelines control. Figure 4-5 shows the location of the DTCs in the Visual InterDev Toolbox.

**Figure 4-5.**
*DTCs are located in the Visual InterDev Toolbox.*

DTCs provide a very simple object-based interface for creating and dealing with script objects. By dragging a DTC onto the page and setting a few properties, you can quickly and easily create an input form for your application.

101

All it takes is the following steps (you should already have an open project with a database connection defined to try this example).

1. Create a new ASP page.

2. Drag a DTC Recordset onto the page and set its Connection property to the name of the database connection you've defined in your GLOBAL.ASA file. Set its Database Object property to *Table*, and its *Object Name* property to the name of a table in the database to which your connection refers.

3. Drag and drop a Textbox DTC onto the page for each field in the table named in step 2. Right-click each Textbox DTC in turn and select Properties. Set the Recordset property to the name of the Recordset DTC in step 2, and the Field property to the field you want the Textbox to display.

4. Save the page, then right-click the file in the Project Explorer and select View in Browser. Voila! You've got data.

Although it takes a few more steps to add sufficient functionality to be able to scroll through and update records, data access truly doesn't get much easier than this. But as we alluded to earlier in the book, there is a price. Because the functionality of the DTCs is provided by script, Web applications built with extensive use of DTCs are not likely to scale as well as sites in which similar functionality is provided by components. That said, if there are plenty of areas in your application that don't require the ultimate in scalability, you can use the DTCs to save yourself a great deal of time and aggravation.

Another improvement of the DTCs in Visual InterDev 6.0 is the ability to target either client-based DHTML implementations or server-based ASP implementations, at the flip of a switch. We'll discuss this in the next section.

## One-Click Management of
## Reach vs. Features with DHTML and ASP

DHTML is going to do wonderful things for Web developers. DHTML makes *data-binding* (in which DHTML elements are bound to recordset fields, allowing display of an entire recordset with a minimum of code) considerably easier, regardless of whether or not you're using DTCs. The difficulty arises from the fact that DHTML is not yet consistent from browser to browser. Suppose you write an application using the DTCs, which are targeted at Internet Explorer 4, to allow client-side recordset navigation and updates without server round-trips. The application works great, but one day your boss walks in and tells you the application now has to support users of Internet Explorer 3 and Netscape. Normally, this would be the kind of thing guaranteed to make a developer pull his or her hair out, but in this case, since you used the DTCs, you can simply change the target platform of your pages by changing one property.

1. For each page to be converted, open the page in the Visual InterDev IDE. In Source view, right-click an empty area of the page and select Properties.

2. In the resulting dialog box (see Figure 4-6), change the DTC Scripting Platform property from Client (IE 4.0 DHTML) to Server (ASP). Save the page, and you're ready to roll on virtually any browser.

Sounds pretty simple and it is. In reality there will probably be at least a little bit of manual coding to be done, since an application will probably not implement all of its functionality with DTCs, but this feature alone will save developers a great deal of time re-coding. One thing to note: In order to change all the DTCs by changing the scripting platform of the page, you need to make sure all DTCs on the page are set to inherit their scripting platform from the page (data-bound DTCs that are bound to a DTC recordset will automatically inherit the scripting platform of the recordset).

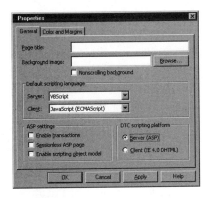

**Figure 4-6.**
*Document Properties dialog box.*

## Support for Internet Explorer 4 DHTML

Visual InterDev's support for DHTML goes well beyond support for data-binding with DTCs. The Visual InterDev editor provides IntelliSense statement completion for the DHTML object model, and the Script Outline window allows you to view (and add script to) the entire DHTML object model, as well as the server object model, and access any scripts on the client or the server. Double-clicking a script entry in the outline takes you to that script in the text editor, while double-clicking an event entry in the outline inserts an event handling function for that event into the page. As if this weren't enough, Visual InterDev also ships with the PageTransitions DTC, which allows developers to specify transition effects for when a page is loaded or unloaded. All of this adds up to unprecedented control over your Web application's user interface via DHTML. Although these features are only supported in Internet Explorer 4 at the moment, look for better cross-platform compatibility in the next generation of browsers supporting HTML 4.0.

## Drag-and-Drop Access to Database
## Objects through the Data Environment and Data View

While all of these fun toys for the user interface are great, in an enterprise application they won't amount to a hill of beans without access to data. The DTCs, as powerful as they are, only provide the ability to simplify access to a data source that's already been set up. So how do you set up your data sources? Well, those of you who've used Visual InterDev 1.0 will be happy to know that you add a connection to a database in much the same way as you did previously. In Visual InterDev 6.0, you can add a data connection to your project by right-clicking either the project folder or the GLOBAL.ASA file, and selecting Add Data Connection…, which brings up a series of dialog boxes in which you select (or set up) a data source, and set the desired properties for the connection. Once the connection has been established, you'll notice a window new to Visual InterDev 6.0, the Data View (see Figure 4-7). Here's where the fun with data begins.

**Figure 4-7.**
*The Visual InterDev Data View.*

Once the Data View is open, you can perform some pretty neat drag-and-drop magic. You want an ADO Command object representing a table from the database? No problem, simply drag a table from the Data View onto the Data Environment, and the Command object is automatically generated for you. You can then drag the Command object from the Data Environment onto your page to generate a DTC recordset, and drag individual columns from the Data Environment to generate data-bound controls for each column. Even Visual Basic can't claim to make data access that simple (at least in VB 5). Even bigger news is that the Data Environment supports Oracle as well as SQL Server, so those wanting to use drag-and-drop simplicity are not limited to only one DBMS. Clearly, data access has been simplified, but what about creating and maintaining database objects?

## Improved Visual Database Tools

The answer is that Visual InterDev 6.0 has made some stellar improvements here, as well. The version of the Visual Database Tools that shipped with Visual InterDev 1.0, while providing a fair amount of functionality for building queries visually, were somewhat limited. The Visual Database Tools that ship with the Professional Edition of Visual InterDev 6.0 provide developers with the ability to visually generate and edit queries against a database in real time, as well as to execute stored procedures. With the version that ships with Visual Studio Enterprise Edition, developers gain a host of features that support the creation and editing of tables, views, and stored procedures, as well as the ability to modify the structure of a table (including changing datatypes) *without* affecting existing data. The best part is that like the new Data Environment, the new Visual Database Tools support Oracle databases as well as SQL Server databases.

## Support for Many Data Sources through ODBC and OLE DB

In addition to extending the power of the Visual Database Tools to Oracle, Visual InterDev 6.0 extends your reach in terms of data sources you can use as well. Open Database Connectivity (ODBC), the grizzled veteran of data access, has advanced another generation in its drivers. In addition, Microsoft is continuing to expand its strategy for Universal Data Access with OLE DB. OLE DB is the logical extension of ODBC, which uses a consumer/provider model to deliver access to both relational and nonrelational data. OLE DB consumers (applications) can use the same data access techniques to access any data source for which there is an OLE DB provider. With ActiveX Data Objects (ADO), an object-based interface to OLE DB, data access is simplified even more than it was using ODBC and DAO or RDO. Until now, however, developers wanting to access SQL and Oracle data sources were limited to using the appropriate ODBC driver in conjunction with the OLE DB provider for ODBC. While this was not a huge problem, you can expect to see a performance improvement when using a native OLE DB provider. Fortunately, Visual InterDev 6.0 ships with OLE DB providers for both Oracle and SQL Server. In addition to accessing relational data in SQL Server and Oracle, third-party OLE DB providers are available for accessing nonrelational data, such as Microsoft Exchange message stores.

## Access Legacy Data with SNA Server, Developer Edition

For those folks who purchase Visual InterDev 6.0 as part of the Visual Studio Enterprise Edition tool suite, developing applications that access legacy data becomes substantially easier thanks to the inclusion of a developer edition of SNA Server. SNA Server allows developers to access data stored in mainframe and midrange systems that are accessible via the Systems Network Architecture (SNA) protocol. Systems accessible via SNA Server include AS/400 and VSAM, as well as mainframe relational databases. Data can be easily accessed directly, or for reduced network traffic (and in some cases, better performance), replicated to a local SQL Server database. In addition, a new part of SNA Server called Com Transaction Integrator (COMTI), formerly code named Cedar, provides applications running on Windows NT with the ability to use the functionality of Customer Information Control System (CICS) and Information Management System (IMS) applications, just as if they were ordinary COM components.

## Improved Scalability and Transaction
## Support with Microsoft Transaction Server (MTS)

Once you've got access to such a wide variety of data sources, one challenge you may well face is making sure that changes made in multiple data sources are committed or rolled back together. In an application using SQL Server 6.5, this was not a big problem, even with multiple servers, since SQL Server could use the Microsoft Distributed Transaction Coordinator (MSDTC) to ensure that transactional integrity was maintained between the servers involved. Applications using data sources other than SQL Server can now use this ability as well, thanks to Microsoft Transaction Server (MTS) 2.0, which ships with Visual Studio 6.0, and is also available as a part of the Windows NT 4.0 Option Pack. Currently, distributed transactions are supported with SQL Server 6.5 and 7, and Oracle 7.3.3 and 8. Future support is expected for distributed transactions on IBM DB2, Informix, Sybase, and Tandem databases.

Transactions aren't the only story of MTS, however—not by a long shot. As, or even more, important are Transaction Server's connection and component management features. COM components written for MTS automatically gain performance from Transaction Server's use of connection pooling for ODBC connections. When a COM component being managed by MTS requires a database connection, MTS supplies one from the connection pool it maintains. When the component is finished with the connection, MTS returns it to the pool. Connection pooling can substantially reduce the expense of making database connections, thereby reducing the need to maintain an open connection throughout the life of the application, a practice which is impractical for scalable applications.

Speaking of scaling, MTS helps out there as well with its component management functionality. When an application requests that the OS create an instance of an MTS-managed component for the application's use, MTS intercepts the call and creates a proxy object for the application instead. When the application calls one of the methods of the proxy object, MTS checks to see if an instance of the component is already running, and if so, whether the component is currently in use. If there is a component that is currently idle, MTS maps the method call to the appropriate method of the component. If there is no available instance of the component, MTS creates a new instance of the component, and maps the method call. When the application signals that it is finished with the component, MTS can then allow other client applications to use it. In future releases, MTS will likely go the next logical step of providing component object pooling.

## More Reliable Communications with Microsoft Message Queue Server

Distributed systems increase the potential for network problems. As we discussed in the last chapter, in an enterprise Web application, you can't afford to let network problems cripple your application. Visual InterDev 6.0 provides one of the easiest ways around this problem, as well as the ability to provide your applications with asynchronous communications for improved performance. All this functionality is provided through drag-and-drop by MSMQ objects in the Visual InterDev Toolbox (see Figure 4-8). Dragging an MSMQ object onto the page inserts the HTML tags necessary to create the desired MSMQ object, as shown below, which may then be manipulated with script.

```
<OBJECT RUNAT=server PROGID=MSMQ.Query id=objQuery> </OBJECT>
```

**Figure 4-8.**
*MSMQ Objects in the Visual InterDev Toolbox.*

## Team Development Support
## through Integration with Visual SourceSafe

One area of applications development that can be particularly difficult in enterprise applications is maintaining source code. When multiple developers are accessing the same source code, the development team must have a way to make sure that one developer cannot accidentally overwrite the work of another. One of the best ways to accomplish this is through the use of a source code control tool. Visual InterDev 6.0 provides integrated access to Microsoft's Visual SourceSafe source code control tool. By using Visual SourceSafe in your Web development efforts, you can substantially reduce the amount of time your development team spends rewriting code that has been accidentally overwritten by another developer. In addition to Visual SourceSafe integration, Visual InterDev 6.0 also supports developer isolation through Local Mode development. This allows a developer to get a local copy of the Web application files from the Web server. This in turn allows the developer to make changes and test them locally without affecting the files on the Web server. The developer then explicitly commits the changes to the Web server when they are finished by releasing their local copies or synchronizing the project.

## End-to-End Debugging

We've saved the best for last. One of the most anticipated and welcome features of Visual InterDev 6.0 is its support for end-to-end debugging. With Visual InterDev 6.0, you can debug scripts from client to server, and even debug custom-built Java components. Users of Visual Studio EE can also take advantage of the ability to debug SQL Server stored procedures from within Visual InterDev 6.0.

# Visual InterDev's Place in the Visual Tools Family

Visual InterDev 6.0 is first and foremost a Rapid Application Development (RAD) tool for Web development. It is also a member of the Visual Studio 6.0 development tools suite, and given the rapid pace of growth in Web application development, a very important part. It is Microsoft's intent with this release of Visual InterDev to advance the state of Web development tools to match that of the other tools in Visual Studio, including Visual Basic and Visual C++, in terms of power, flexibility, and ease of use. In this effort they have been largely successful. While there is room for more improvement, and areas in which Visual InterDev falls short of the features available in Visual Basic or Visual C++, there is little doubt that Visual InterDev 6.0 provides one of the most powerful and flexible development environments for Web applications available today. For enterprise developers, however, Visual InterDev 6.0 is only part of the solution. Other tools, including Visual Basic, SQL Server, Visual J++, Microsoft Transaction Server, Microsoft Message Queue Server, and SNA Server are designed to work with and extend Visual InterDev 6.0 to truly provide enterprise-level Web application solutions. There's a reason that Visual Studio is one of the most-used development tool suites ever. Part of that reason is that with the Enterprise Edition of Visual Studio, all of the tools mentioned above are included (developer editions of SNA Server and SQL Server are provided).

For developers needing to provide enterprise solutions quickly and efficiently, Visual Studio Enterprise Edition provides all of the "out of the box" functionality necessary. Visual Basic 6.0 provides an excellent environment for rapidly developing custom COM business components to support Web applications. Microsoft SQL Server 6.5 provides an excellent database solution for Visual InterDev 6.0 Web applications, and SQL Server version 7.0 promises substantially greater scalability and performance, combined with improved ease-of-use. Visual J++ 6.0 can be used either for developing server-side business components or client applets. Finally, Visual InterDev 6.0 can be used to bring all these pieces together into a coherent and highly functional application. Just remember that in an enterprise world, Visual InterDev 6.0 is only *part* of the Web application solution.

# Visual InterDev 6.0 Basics

Now that we've discussed some of the new and neat features of Visual InterDev 6.0, let's look at how to put some of them into action. If you've used Visual InterDev (1.0 or 6.0), you may wish to skim through the rest of this chapter, or skip on to Chapter 5, "Features vs. Reach—Cross-Platform Support."

## Creating a New Web Project

One of the first things you'll need to do on most projects is to create a new Web project. Creating a new Web project in Visual InterDev 6.0 takes care of all of the details required for the application to function properly, including setting up a new Web site on the server, copying the necessary FrontPage extensions to the new Web site, and creating skeleton GLOBAL.ASA and, if you choose, SEARCH.HTM files. The best part is, it's as easy as 1-2-3. Try it for yourself.

1. Open Visual InterDev. The New Project dialog box will appear. Make sure that the New Web project icon is highlighted, and choose a name and location for your new Web project. Click the Open button when you're finished.

2. Follow the instructions in the Web Project Wizard (see Figure 4-9) by choosing a Web server, selecting your development mode, deciding whether to create a new Web application or add to an existing application, choosing a layout for navigation components, and applying a theme. (Note that you do not have to use either layouts or themes in your Web application.)

NOTE: Visual InterDev 6.0 themes, which are based on Cascading Style Sheets, provide a simple way to add a consistent look to your application. Themes specify fonts, colors, background graphics, and other visual elements of your pages.

3. When you've made all your choices, click Finish. That's all you need to do. Visual InterDev now does all the work for you.

Once Visual InterDev 6.0 has finished copying files, you'll be returned to the Visual InterDev Integrated Development Environment (IDE), where you can begin work on your new project. While it's great to be able to get up and running with a project this quickly, it's probably a good idea to take a look at how the Web Project Wizard got us here.

**Figure 4-9.**
*The Visual InterDev Web Project Wizard.*

## Using Wizards to Speed Project Setup

Visual InterDev 6.0 provides two wizards for your use: the Web Project Wizard (which we've already seen in action), and the Sample App Wizard (which helps you install sample applications such as the Gallery sample application that comes with Visual InterDev 6.0). You also have the ability in the New Project dialog box to create a new Database Project, new Distribution Units (a *distribution unit* is a file that contains application components and related files, allowing an application to be deployed from one computer to another), including CAB and ZIP files, as well as self-extracting setup files, and new utility projects (a *utility project* simply sets up a Solution in Visual InterDev 6.0, to which you can add any files you choose). Right now, let's take a closer look at the Web Project Wizard, and what it's doing, step-by-step.

1. Choose the Web server you want to use, as well as the working mode you'll start in. The Web server entry is the machine name of the server you want to use for the master Web server, on which the master copies of all the Web application files reside (note that the master Web server must have FrontPage 98 server extensions installed). The working mode specifies whether you'll be making changes to the files on the master Web server, or working with local copies, then updating the master Web server once you've tested and debugged your changes. You can change the working mode for your project at any time.

2. Choose whether to create a new Web application or add your new project to an existing Web application. The first option will result in a new Web being created in the wwwroot folder of the InetPub folder on the server you specified in Step 1, while the second option will add the files for the new Web project to an existing Web of your choosing. When you create a new Web, you are also given the choice of enabling full text searching of your site.

3. Choose a layout for your Web project. *Layouts* are essentially templates that use the Visual InterDev PageNavBar DTCs to provide navigation controls for your pages. If you choose not to add a Layout at this point, you can still add a Layout later, either to the entire project, or to individual files. You can also later remove Layouts on a per-project or per-file basis if you choose to enable them in this step. Note that the PageNavBar DTC is especially dependent on the FrontPage extensions and will not function if they are not installed

properly. If you choose to apply a Layout to your Web application, the wizard will create a _Layouts folder in the project.

4. Apply a Visual InterDev Theme to your project. Visual InterDev Themes are a tool for providing a consistent look to the files in your Web project, based on Cascading Style Sheets. Like Layouts, you can add Themes later on a project or file basis. You can also change or remove Themes on a project or file basis if you enable them at this point. Once you've made all your choices and clicked Finish, Visual InterDev will chug away for a bit, and you'll be presented with your new Web project in the Visual InterDev IDE. At this point, you should see several folders and files in the Project Explorer (see Figure 4-10).

**Figure 4-10.**
*The Visual InterDev Project Explorer.*

NOTE: It's also a good idea if you are going to be using components in your Web application to create a folder in your project for them. Simply right-click the project name in the Project Explorer, select New Folder..., and give the folder a name (*Components* usually works pretty well).

So, what's going on "under the hood?" The wizard does a number of things. It creates a new Web site on the Web server (assuming you chose this option), complete with all the folders and files necessary to work with the FrontPage 98 Server extensions. To this folder, the wizard then adds all the folders and files required by the functionality you've chosen. By default, this includes a _private folder, a _ScriptLibrary folder (which contains a copy of the Script Library files that enable DTC functionality), and an images folder. If you choose to apply a Layout or a Theme to your project, the wizard will create a folder

(_Layouts or _Themes) for each of these as well, each containing the appropriate files. The Script Library, Layout, and Theme files are copied from Visual InterDev's master copy of these files. It is very important that you do not change these master copies, as you may inadvertently prevent these features from functioning. Once these folders and files have been copied to the master Web server, the wizard creates a local copy of the project's structure in the location you specified for the project.

## Adding Content

So now that we have a project, it's time to add some content to it. Adding content can be as simple as selecting File | New File..., or you can go a step further and plan your site's structure as you add content. We'll start by adding a home page to our new project using the Visual InterDev Site Designer.

### Using the Site Designer to Plan Your Site

Visual InterDev's Site Designer is a powerful tool that allows you to visualize the structure of your Web application's pages, add and remove pages, and modify the relationship between those pages. This section assumes that you've created a new Web project without using Layouts or Themes, and that you chose to enable the creation of a search page for your site. To add a home page to your new project and establish a relationship between the home page and your search page, use the following steps:

1. Create a new Site Diagram by right-clicking the project name in the Project Explorer, then selecting Add | Site Diagram.... Choose a name for your new Site Diagram or accept the default and click Open. The Site Diagram file will be added to the project and opened in the Site Designer. Note that if you do not already have a home page (DEFAULT.HTM, DEFAULT.ASP, or INDEX.HTM), the Site Designer will automatically display a home page the first time it is opened.

2. Click the delete button on the Site Diagram toolbar to remove the existing home page from the Site Diagram.

3. To add a new home page, click the Add Home Page button on the Site Designer toolbar (it's the one that looks like a little house).

4. By default the home page file will be named DEFAULT.HTM. You can change this by right-clicking the home page and selecting Property

Pages, then changing the URL property to the desired filename. For this example, change the URL property to DEFAULT.ASP.

5. Save the Site Diagram by selecting File | Save Site Diagram1.wdm... (note that Site Diagram1.wdm can be replaced by whatever you choose to name your site diagram). You'll notice when you save the Site Diagram that the file, DEFAULT.ASP, is created in your Web project.

6. To establish a relationship between your new home page and the search page created when you first created the project, you must add the search page to the Site Diagram.

7. From the Site Diagram toolbar, select the Add Existing File button. Alternately, you can select Add Existing File... from the Diagram menu. In the Choose URL dialog box that appears, select the search page, SEARCH.HTM. Accept the defaults for the other choices by clicking OK. The search page is added to the Site Diagram and is set by default to have a child relationship with your home page (see Figure 4-11).

8. Save your Site Diagram again.

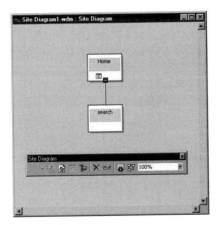

**Figure 4-11.**
*Site Designer example.*

## Adding Pages

Adding new pages to the Site Diagram is as easy as clicking the New HTML Page or New ASP Page button from the Site Designer toolbar, or selecting the matching commands from the Diagram menu. Of course, one of the advantages of using the Site Designer to create and manage your application's site structure is that the relationships defined in the Site Diagram are used to control how Visual InterDev's PageNavBar DTCs and Layouts provide navigation for your site. When you use PageNavBar DTCs or Layouts, any change made in the Site Diagram will automatically update the navigation controls on each page, saving you a great deal of work when you need to rearrange the pages in your site.

## Adding Navigation

Adding navigation ability to your pages is also relatively simple, and can be done in several different ways:

■ Navigation bars may be inserted into pages by applying a Layout to the project. This can provide a consistent navigational format.

■ Navigation bars may also be inserted into pages by applying Layouts to individual pages. This can provide greater page-by-page control over navigation.

■ Navigation bars may be added by inserting PageNavBar DTCs into each page. This affords the greatest control when using Visual InterDev's built-in navigation tools.

Let's walk through the process of applying a Layout to pages in a Web project. Using the same project as in the previous example, open the Site Diagram (if it is not still open).

1. Right-click the home page in the Site Diagram, and select Apply Theme and Layout.... In the Apply Theme and Layout dialog box, select the Layout tab if it is not already selected, and select the Apply layout and theme: radio button.

2. Highlight several of the available Layouts and observe how they appear in the preview window. When you've finished, select the Top and Left 1 Layout, and click OK.

3. Next, right-click the search page, and select Apply Theme and Layout....

4. In the Apply Theme and Layout dialog box, again select the Top and Left 1 Layout and click OK.

5. Save your changes, and open the home page in your browser by right-clicking it and selecting View in Browser.

You'll notice when you have the page loaded in the browser that even though we've added no content to the home page, the navigation controls allow us to navigate to the search page, and from the search page back to the home page. If we add more pages in the Site Designer, those pages too, would appear on the navigation bars, without any further assistance from the developer.

## Using the Visual InterDev Editor

The Visual InterDev editor has grown up in a number of ways. It now sports two new windows, a WYSIWYG editor, as well as a Quick View, which allows you to view your page as it will appear in the browser. It also has better syntax color-coding, including color-coding of script code. And of course, as we discussed earlier, the Source view now has IntelliSense statement completion, which helps eliminate typos in your code, as well as informing you of arguments required by various methods of the objects you script. Let's start by talking about how to use the WYSIWYG editor.

### Using the WYSIWYG Page Editor

So, now you've got a project with a couple of pages. Unfortunately, your home page is blank except for the navigation controls. It's time now to add some HTML content to the page. So open up the home page, DEFAULT.ASP, from the previous two examples (you can open the file by double-clicking it), and follow these steps:

1. Select the Design tab view for the editor if it is not already selected.

2. In the Visual InterDev Toolbox, select the Toolbox tab. Click the HTML bar, and take a look at all of the HTML elements that can be inserted into your page.

3. You should see several bars in the Design window that say "Add Your Content Below" or "Add Your Content Above" (see Figure 4-12). These are part of the PageNavBar DTCs designed to help you locate your content in a way that works well with the controls.

**Figure 4-12.**
*Design View window.*

3. Locate the cursor at the end of the first "Add Your Content Below" bar and double-click the Horizontal Rule element in the Toolbox. An HTML horizontal rule is created.

4. Now drag and drop a Horizontal Rule element onto the page, positioning the cursor at the beginning of the second "Add Your C ontent Above" bar before releasing the mouse button to complete the action. A second horizontal rule is created.

5. Position the cursor directly below the first horizontal line and type *Rent-A-Prize Login Page*. You can modify the size, font, color, alignment, etc., of the text by highlighting the text and using the buttons on the HTML toolbar. Try changing the font to Arial, making the text Bold, and changing the alignment to Center.

6. In addition to modifying text elements with the HTML toolbar, you can also modify properties of many HTML elements within the Properties window (see Figure 4-13).

**Figure 4-13.**
*Visual InterDev Properties window.*

6. Select the topmost horizontal rule. Make sure the box in the top of the Properties window is displaying the <HR> tag.

7. Scroll down in the Properties window to find the width property of the horizontal rule element. Enter 80% for the new width. Repeat for the lower horizontal rule.

8. Save your work and open DEFAULT.ASP in your browser (right-click the file in the Project Explorer and select View in Browser). The result should look similar to Figure 4-14.

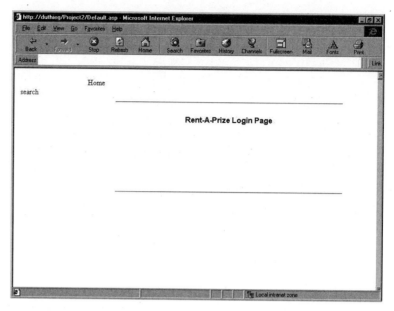

**Figure 4-14.**
*Viewing DEFAULT.ASP in browser.*

## Using the Source View

Of course, for you HTML junkies who can't get enough of code, there is the Source view of the editor. The Source view allows you to add or change tags directly. You can also perform some of the same drag-and-drop operations in the Source view as you can in Design view. The Source view is also where you'll do your coding when you finally roll up your sleeves and start writing scripts, with the assistance of IntelliSense statement completion.

If you view the home page we've been using in Source view, one of the first things you'll notice that's very different from Visual InterDev 1.0 is that the Design-Time Controls we've used are represented graphically, just as they are in Design view. This is in part to encourage developers to use the Properties window and Property pages to manage the options available with the DTCs, rather than attempting to edit the scripts themselves. If you want to see the code behind the DTCs, however, simply do the following:

1. Open DEFAULT.ASP and select the Source view editor window.

2. Right-click one of the PageNavBar DTCs, and select Show Run-Time Text. The text for the DTC will be displayed beneath the graphical representation of the DTC.

You can also select the Convert to Run-Time Text command, which does pretty much what the name implies, converting the selected graphical representation of the DTC to the HTML and script that it represents. Use this feature with caution, as some controls may lose functionality when converted to run-time text, and this operation cannot be undone. It might be better to use the command Always View As Text, which allows you to see the text behind the DTC. Unlike the Convert to Run-Time Text command, this command can be toggled on and off. Both of these commands are available from the context (right-click) menu for each control. You can also choose whether to view controls graphically or as text by selecting the appropriate command from the View menu.

One thing you may notice about the Source view, particularly if you're running at a desktop resolution of 800x600 or less, is that the Source view doesn't give you a lot of room for code, what with the Toolbox window, the Project Explorer window, and the Properties window. What's more, when you start InterDev for the very first time, you'll also see the task list window, leaving even less real estate for code. What's a developer to do?

Well first off, close that task list. Don't forget that it's available, since it can be a useful tool for helping you manage your projects, but for now it's just in the way. Next, take a look in the upper right-hand corner of the screen. There you'll see a combo box with the word "Design" in it. Open up the combo box, and select the Full Screen option. Isn't that *much* better? Play around a bit with the options available and see which ones you like. Visual InterDev 1.0 users will probably take to the DevStudio option, since it mimics the environment of Visual InterDev 1.0.

If you're concerned about giving up your other windows, don't be. You can add any window you like as a tab in the Toolbox simply by dragging the window to the title bar of the Toolbox. Before you go rearranging your entire environment, it's a good idea to create your own window layout in the combo box for your experiments. To do so, simply select View | Define Window Layout..., enter a name for your layout in the dialog box, then click Add. Now select the new layout in the combo box, and customize to your heart's content. Once you've got the IDE just the way you want it, call up the dialog box again, select your layout's name from the list, and click Update. From now on, whenever you want to edit in your custom layout, simply select it from the combo box.

### Viewing Your Progress with Quick View

As you proceed through designing the pages in your site, you may want to check periodically that your pages will appear in the browser as you expect them to. While the Design view gives you a pretty good idea of what the page will look like, it shows graphical representations of the DTCs on the page, which can alter the layout of elements on the page. To see what the page will look like in a browser, select the Quick View editor window. Two things to note about the Quick View window:

1. Since the file being viewed is not run through a Web server, it will not show the result of any server-side code. To see the result of ASP code, use the View in Browser command.

2. You may not edit the file while in the Quick View window.

## Controlling Interactivity

Interactivity and programmatic power are what separate a Web site from a Web application, and Visual InterDev 6.0 is no slacker when it comes to supporting developers writing lots of script. There are a number of features that support the insertion and editing of, as well as navigating to script blocks. If you're the type who doesn't want a lot of help with your script, but want a quick way to insert a script block for client or server script, follow these steps:

1. Select the Source view tab in the Visual InterDev editor and position the cursor where you want the script block to appear.

   NOTE: It is common practice to put script blocks containing functions to be used on a page between the <HEAD> and </HEAD> HTML tags.

2. Select HTML | Script Block | Client (or Server, depending on your needs). Visual InterDev inserts a pair of <SCRIPT> tags with the *Language* parameter set to the default language for the platform, plus the HTML comment brackets necessary for browsers that do not recognize script. If you insert a server script block, Visual InterDev will also insert the *Runat* parameter set to *Server*.

3. Write your script. As installed, the default language for the client is JavaScript (ECMAScript) and for the server it's VBScript. You can change these defaults on a per-file or per-project basis by accessing the Properties page for the file or the project, respectively (see Figure 4-15).

**Figure 4-15.**
*Using Property Pages to set the default Script language.*

A second and faster way to write script is to use the Script Outline. The Script Outline is one of the many available panes for the Visual InterDev Toolbox window. It is designed to make adding scripts, viewing scriptable events, and navigating to the various scripts in your page faster and easier. The Script Outline displays the object model and available events for the objects on your page, as well as available server objects. It also shows the existing scripts on the page. The Script Outline is available when you are in Source view. If the Script Outline is not visible in the Toolbox, simply select View | Other Windows | Script Outline.

So let's take a look at how we can insert a script handler for a client event with the Script Outline:

1. Add a new HTML page to your project. Name the file BUTTON.HTM, in case you wish to refer to the file later on.

2. Add a button to the page by dragging it from the HTML Toolbox to the Source view of the editor.

3. Using the Properties window, change the value property of the button to *"Click Me!"*.

4. Select the Script Outline tab from the Visual InterDev Toolbox, and expand the node marked button1 (the name of the node in the Script Outline corresponds to the ID property of the <INPUT> tag.

5. In the list of events for the button that appears in the Script Outline, double-click the onclick event (see Figure 4-16). An event-handling code block is inserted into the page, as well as an inline onclick handler in the <INPUT> tag.

6. In the event handler function, add the line, *alert("You Clicked Me!")*. Yes, it's silly, but it's better than using *"Hello World!"* yet again.

7. Switch to the Quick View window, and click the button. A message box should pop up saying, *"You Clicked Me!"* That's it! You've successfully handled a client event and only had to write one (very short) line of code. You may now remove this file from your project, or save it for later reference. We will not be using it again.

**Figure 4-16:**
*The onclick event of button1 in the Script Outline window.*

One of the things you may have noticed while entering the code in the above example is that as soon as you typed the opening parentheses a ToolTip appeared, informing you about the expected argument (in this case, [Message], with the square brackets indicating that the argument is optional). This is Visual InterDev's IntelliSense working to reduce the number of errors in your code. Between the Script Outline, IntelliSense, and the Visual InterDev DTCs, there are going to be a lot of opportunities for you to save time on your scripting tasks.

## Accessing and Manipulating Data

All that help with scripting, however, won't amount to a whole lot without data. Certainly it's true that not every application needs to be able to access and manipulate data, but most of them do. Until recently, this has been one of the most difficult aspects of Web development. With new data access technologies like OLE DB and ActiveX Data Objects (ADO), things have gotten easier. Visual InterDev 6.0 takes things a step further by adding the Data View and Data Environment.

The Data Environment, which is created below your GLOBAL.ASA file in the Project Explorer when you add a Data Connection to your project, is a graphical environment for data access. In combination with the Data View, which is simply a window that provides a hierarchical view of the objects in the database to which you are connected, the Data Environment provides drag-and-drop access to the functionality provided by ADO. In fact, the Data Environment is an abstraction of ADO that is designed to make it easier to use (which is interesting, given that ADO itself is an object layer that abstracts OLE DB in order to make it easier to use).

So, how do you enable the Data Environment? It's pretty simple. Just follow these steps (this example requires access to a SQL Server with the Pubs sample database installed):

1. If it's not already open, open the project used in the earlier examples, and open the DEFAULT.ASP file.

2. Right-click either the project name, or on the GLOBAL.ASA file. Select Add Data Connection... from the context menu.

3. In the Select Data Source dialog box, select the Machine Data Source tab. If there is no entry for the Pubs sample database, click New.... If there is an entry for Pubs, go to step 6.

4. In the Create New Data Source wizard, select System Data Source, then click Next. On the next page, select SQL Server as the driver and again, click Next. Now click Finish, and the Create New Data Source to SQL Server Wizard will launch.

5. On the first page of the Create New Data Source to SQL Server Wizard, supply a name (*Pubs*), a description (Pubs sample database), and a server name (the server where SQL is installed), and click Next. On the next page, select SQL Server Authentication (you can only use Windows NT Authentication with SQL Server if your Windows NT login has been associated with a SQL Server login) and enter a valid SQL Server login and password, then click Next. On the following page, check the Change the default database to: check

box and select Pubs from the combo box, then click Next. Click Next again as the default setting works fine, then (finally) click Finish. Then, click the Test Data Source button, and if all goes well you're in business. Move on to step 6. If the test fails, check your ODBC installation, and make sure you have connectivity to the SQL Server you are trying to access.

6. Now that we have a Data Source Name (DSN) defined for the Pubs database, select it from the list in the Select Data Source dialog box and click OK. The SQL Server login box will appear, type in the password for the login you specified and click OK.

7. Next you'll see the Properties dialog box for the connection. Here you can give the connection a descriptive name, and change other properties of the connection. For example if you'd prefer not to have to enter your password every time you open the project, select the Authentication tab and click the Save Design-time Authentication check box. When you are done with the properties dialog box, click OK. That's it! The Data Environment is created for you. You'll see that the Data View window has been added (sharing the space occupied by the Properties window).

With the Data Environment and Data View windows available you can now create database objects such as commands and recordsets simply by dragging and dropping objects from the Data View to the Data Environment or from the Data Environment to the page. For example, to create a command object in the Data Environment, follow these simple steps:

1. If it is not already open, reopen the example project we've been working on in this chapter. In the Data View of the project, expand the Pubs database, and the tables node under it.

2. Drag the authors table from the Data View and drop it onto the Data Environment in the Project Explorer (if the Data Environment is not visible, expand the GLOBAL.ASA node). A new command object called *authors* is created under the Data Environment node. The authors command represents the authors table in the Pubs database. We could also have dragged a View or a Stored Procedure from the Data View onto the Data Environment to create the command.

3. Add a new ASP file to the project and call it *DATADRAG.ASP*. Make sure the editor is in Source view.

4. Drag the authors command object from the Data Environment to the page. Position the cursor between the <HEAD> and </HEAD> elements before releasing the mouse button. When you release the command object, you're prompted to enable the Scripting Object Model for the page. Click OK. A Recordset DTC is inserted on the page with properties set to retrieve the authors table of the Pubs database.

5. To actually make use of the data retrieved by the Recordset, highlight one or more fields from the author command in the Data Environment, and drag them onto the page, between the <BODY> and </BODY> tags. For each field dropped, a data-bound DTC is added to the page of an appropriate type for the field, along with a label DTC (by default, the column name).

6. Save the file, then right-click in an empty area of the page and select View in Browser. Houston, we have data! Repeat, we have data! But right now, we're just seeing a single row. Wouldn't it be more useful if we could see all the rows and move back and forth between them?

7. So let's go to the old Toolbox, open the Design-Time Controls section, and drag a RecordsetNavBar DTC onto the page, just below the closing </TABLE> tag, and above the closing </BODY> tag. Right-click on the control, and select Properties, then set the Recordset property to Recordset1 (the recordset created by the authors command).

8. Resave the page again, and again right-click in an empty area and select View in Browser. Voila! Without writing a single line of code, we've created a page by which we can view the data for the entire table. But wait! There's more! In order to truly make this page useful, shouldn't we also be able to update the data?

9. So it's back to the Toolbox one more time. Drag two Button DTCs onto the page, right after the RecordsetNavBar DTC. Set the Caption property of the first button to Update, and the Caption property of the second to Cancel.

10. Now switch to the Script Outline (if it's not already open, hit Ctrl - Alt - S), and locate the entries for button1 and button2 in the Server Objects and Events. Expand each of these nodes. For each button, double-click the onclick event. An event handler (in VBScript, the default server language) is created for each button's onclick event.

11. Now comes the tricky part. You actually have to write some code. In the *button1_onclick* event handler (the Update button), add the following code:

    Recordset1.updateRecord

    In the *button2_onclick* event handler (the Cancel button), add this code:

    Recordset1.cancelUpdate

    OK, you can open your eyes again. That's it for the code. Save the page, then view it in the browser again. Having written a grand total of two lines of code, we now have a page that can view and update a database table (see Figure 4-17).

By using variations on this technique, you can build similar pages based on views, stored procedures, or SQL queries. With the Data View, the Data Environment, and the DTCs, you can quickly prototype your site's data access. For the most highly scalable sites, you may want to move your data access to components, as we'll discuss in Chapter 7, "Addressing Performance and Scalability."

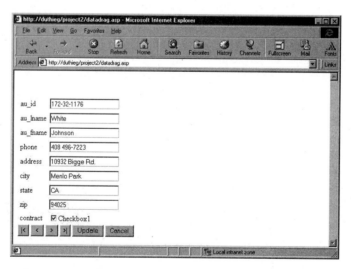

**Figure 4-17.**
*Data access with the Data Environment and Design-Time Controls.*

Building a SQL query has also gotten a bit easier in this edition of Visual InterDev with the new and improved Query Designer. Let's suppose we wanted to limit the records we returned to the page we just created to authors living in California. Here's how we'd do it:

1. In the DATADRAG.ASP page, right-click Recordset1 (the Recordset DTC), and select Properties.

2. Under Source of Data, change the selection from Database object to SQL statement, then click the SQL builder button (if you know the SQL statement you wish to use, you can enter it in the text area below the button and bypass the SQL builder).

3. Once the Query Builder has opened, if the Query toolbar (see Figure 4-18) is not visible, select View | Toolbars | Query. With the Query toolbar available, we're ready to begin by dragging the authors table into the upper or Diagram pane of the Query Builder. Notice that in the SQL pane, the SQL query is already being built.

4. Select the * (all columns) check box in the authors table, then drag the state column entry down to the second, or Grid, pane, and drop it on the grid field labeled Column, just below the *. In the same row of the grid, deselect the Output check box and enter = 'CA' into the field labeled Criteria.

5. Check the SQL query by first clicking the Verify SQL Syntax button on the Query toolbar. If the Query checks out, click the Run Query (!) button, then check the Results pane to make sure the results are what we expected.

6. Click the Save button on the toolbar, then close the Query Builder. View the page in a browser again, and you will see that our page is now limited to authors living in California. Pretty simple, eh?

**Figure 4-18.**
*The Query toolbar.*

The Data View, Data Environment, and DTCs provide a powerful set of tools for rapidly developing data access and update functionality. This can be great for providing simple functionality for smaller sites or for prototyping data access for larger sites. Whichever way you use it, just remember, like any other technology that abstracts programming complexity, there will be tradeoffs in performance and flexibility for using these data tools. Whether those tradeoffs are worth the ease of use and speed of development is something you'll have to decide on an application-by-application basis, based on experience.

# Summary

In this chapter, we've discussed a number of the new features in the 6.0 release of Visual InterDev, as well as some extras available when you get Visual InterDev as a part of the Visual Studio 6.0 Enterprise Edition development tool suite. We've also tried to give you a good grounding in the basics of Visual InterDev 6.0. What we've shown you so far, though powerful, has been pretty simple. Eventually, you'll get into situations when you need to adapt the code written by the DTCs, or write your own code. Inevitably, you'll run into situations where you'll need more functionality than just the DTCs can provide. In the next three sections of the book, we'll get deeper into the functionality in Visual InterDev, as well as show how complementary technologies such as MTS, MSMQ, and SNA Server can help you craft a Web application you (and your project manager) will be proud to call your own.

# PART II

# SOLVING CLIENT TIER CHALLENGES

CHAPTER FIVE

# Features vs. Reach—Cross-Platform Support

• • • **GOAL: To Provide the Richest User Interface, Given the Limitations of Client Platforms**

*Features vs. Reach.* It sounds very "either-or" doesn't it? Sometimes that is truly the case with Web applications. There are some features that you may want to implement in your application (for example, ActiveX controls) that will, of necessity, limit your audience. But that doesn't always have to be the case. This chapter will focus on some of the functionality available when you choose a specific target browser (in this case, Internet Explorer 4), as well as ways to get the most out of the browser-agnostic world of Active Server Pages (ASP). We'll also look at customizing the application experience for different browsers using the ASP browser capabilities component.

## DHTML—Providing a Rich User Experience

While the Web's *lingua franca*, HTML, has provided an adequate basis for developing Web applications, it is limited in many ways. For example, standard HTML doesn't allow you to specify precisely where to place an element on a page. Virtually every interaction your application has with a user requires a round-trip to the server. Standard HTML also provides no direct support for animation.

Dynamic HTML, or DHTML for short, is the next step in the evolution of HTML. DHTML is designed to address many of the shortcomings of HTML, including the ones mentioned above. DHTML uses standard HTML elements, Cascading Style Sheets, and script to provide interactivity, precise positioning, data-binding, and animation and special effects, all without burdensome round-trips to the server.

NOTE: A note on compatibility: While the Internet Explorer and Netscape Navigator implementations of Dynamic HTML differ in significant ways, the Internet Explorer implementation of DHTML is based on specifications that have either been accepted by or submitted to the W3C, the standards body for the Web. This means that Internet Explorer 4 DHTML, while not completely compatible with the standard for DHTML, is much closer, and should be completely in line with the standard in the next version of Internet Explorer. More information about HTML and CSS standards is available at: http://www.w3.org/TR/.

## Greater Interactivity

One of the difficulties with developing applications using HTML is that using standard HTML, interactivity and feedback to user actions (such as highlighting text links when the mouse moves over them) is next to nonexistent. While both Netscape Navigator 3.x and Internet Explorer 3.x do support scripting to provide a limited amount of interactivity, their implementations are not completely compatible, and both are limited in scope. DHTML promises (and delivers with Internet Explorer 4) much greater interactivity, with the power to script events of every HTML tag, thanks to the Document Object Model (DOM), which we'll discuss in the next section. DHTML allows a page to be modified in response to user actions or time elapsing, without a return to the server. This allows developers to take advantage of the power of today's desktop computers, and to make their Web applications more scalable by removing some of the burden from their Web servers. And since Internet Explorer 4 DHTML is standards-based, the chances are good that it will be compatible with the next generation of both major browsers.

### Event-Driven Document Object Mode (DOM)

The Document Object Model is the very heart and soul of DHTML. Without the Document Object Model, there would be no way to script events for HTML tags. The DOM defines a set of objects, properties, and methods for you to use in your HTML programming.

■ **Objects** The objects defined by the DOM include an object for each HTML element, and various collection objects, including the All collection, which is a collection of all of the elements beneath a given object. Objects and collections use a *parent/child* structure, where tags that contain other tags or elements are considered the parents of those tags or elements. In the following code, the <BODY> tag is a parent element to the <H1>, <DIV>, and <P> tags, while the <DIV> tag in turn, is a parent to the <IMG> tag. The All collection of the BODY element would allow you to access its child tags (<H1>, <DIV>, and <P>), which would then allow you to access the child of the DIV element (<IMG>).

```
<BODY id=myBody>

    <H1 id=myH1>Header Text</H1>

    <DIV id=myDiv>

       <IMG SOURCE="myImg.gif" id=myImg>

    </DIV>

    <P id=myPara>

</BODY>
```

■ **Properties**  In the DOM, each element has one or more properties. Some of these properties are read-only, such as the *appName* property of the navigator element. Others, such as color and font, can be changed as well as read in script. You can use the properties of various elements to make changes to your text, move elements on the page, hide or display elements, as well as many other uses. The code below uses the *fontFamily* property of the <P> element to change the font of the text within the <P> tags to Arial.

```
<BODY id=myBody>

    <H1 id=myH1>Header Text</H1>

    <P id=myPara onclick="myPara.fontFamily = 'Arial'">

    This is some text

    </P>

</BODY>
```

■ **Methods**  Methods are provided that allow actions to be taken, including navigating to a new page (without having to use a hyperlink), resizing the browser window, or changing an attribute of an element. For example, the code below will resize the browser window when the user clicks on the text between the <P> tags.

```
<HTML>

<HEAD>

<META NAME="GENERATOR" Content="Microsoft Visual Studio 6.0">

<SCRIPT ID=clientEventHandlersJS LANGUAGE=javascript>

<!--

function myPara_onclick() {

   window.resizeTo(400, 300)

}

//-->

</SCRIPT>

</HEAD>

<BODY>

<P id=myPara LANGUAGE=javascript onclick="return
myPara_onclick()">Hello World!</P>

</BODY>

</HTML>
```

The Document Object Model is built around events. By adding an event handler to a given tag, you can trap events for that tag and execute inline code, or pass execution to an event-handling subroutine. With the large number of objects, properties, methods, and events that make up the DOM, keeping track of all the elements and event-handlers could be challenging to say the least. This is where Visual InterDev comes in with its Script Outline, which we'll discuss in the next section.

The DOM is said to be event-driven because events are what cause the scripts you write for the various elements to be executed. These events can include the document object's *onLoad* and *onUnload* events, individual HTML elements' *onClick* or *onmouseover* events, and many more. This is quite similar to how events are handled in Netscape Navigator 3.x or Internet Explorer 3.x, with a couple of notable exceptions:

■ In Internet Explorer 4 DHTML, every HTML element can fire events that can be scripted. This provides Web developers with a much greater degree of control over a user's interaction with the application.

■ Internet Explorer 4 uses *event bubbling,* in which any event fired by a particular element that is not handled by that element will be passed *(bubbled)* up to its parent element. If the parent element does not handle the event, it is passed up to *that* element's parent, and so on. This continues until either the event is handled or the event reaches the Document object.

Event bubbling can be very useful, since it allows you to provide centralized handling for commonly used events, such as mouseovers or clicks, without giving up the ability to control individual elements differently. The biggest advantage of being able to handle events centrally is that it reduces the amount of code you need to write to handle a given event, which, in turn, makes your application easier to maintain and update. The following code uses event bubbling to display the name of the background color of the element that fires the event:

```
<HTML>

<BODY>

<DIV id=myDiv style="background-color: red"
onmouseover="alert(window.event.srcElement.style.backgroundColor)">

   This is some text

<P id=myPara style="background-color: blue">

   Some more text

</P>

</DIV>

</BODY>

</HTML>
```

Despite the fact that there is no code defined for handling the *onmouseover* event for the <P> tag, the name of its background color will still be displayed when you mouse over that element on the page. This is because the event is bubbled up to the parent element, <DIV>, which does have an *onmouseover* event handler.

There are four different ways to connect events to event handlers in Internet Explorer 4 DHTML (four when using VBScript):

■ **Inline**   In this method, which is used in the previous example, all the code needed to handle an event is placed inline with the HTML tag for which the event handler is responsible.

■ **<SCRIPT> blocks**  All the code needed to handle events for a particular element is placed inside a set of script blocks, with a FOR attribute specifying the ID of the element whose event is being handled, and an EVENT attribute specifying the event to handle. This allows us to create event handlers for specific elements while separating the event-handling code completely from the HTML element itself (with the exception of the ID attribute required for this method). An example of this method would look like the following:

```
<SCRIPT LANGUAGE=VBSCRIPT FOR=myPara EVENT=ONCLICK>

    MsgBox "Click!"

</SCRIPT>

<P ID=myPara>

    Some text

</P>
```

■ **Function-based**  We can also create functions (or subs in VBScript) that contain the event-handling code for an element (or set of elements). This function is then called by a snippet of code inline with the HTML element. This method allows us to write complex, multi-line event handlers, while keeping our code cleaner and easier to read. This is the method used by Visual InterDev's Script Outline when the default client scripting language is JavaScript. Using this method, the code above would look like this:

```
<SCRIPT ID=clientEventHandlersJS LANGUAGE=javascript>

<!--

function myPara_onclick() {
    alert('Click!');

}

//-->

</SCRIPT>

<P ID=myPara LANGUAGE=javascript onclick="return
myPara_onclick()">

    Some text

</P>
```

■ **Visual Basic style**    As mentioned above, when using VBScript, there is a fourth method that allows you to build event handlers that separate event-handling code from the HTML element code. In this method, as with the script block method, an ID attribute is required. This method is used by the Script Outline when VBScript is specified as the default client scripting language. Using this method, our example would look like the following:

```
<SCRIPT ID=clientEventHandlersVBS LANGUAGE=vbscript>

<!--

Sub myPara_onclick

   MsgBox "Click!"

End Sub

-->

</SCRIPT>

<P ID=myPara>

   Some text

</P>
```

Any of these methods can be used effectively within your application, so which method you choose will depend on the needs of the application, as well as the level of control you wish to have over event handling for each element.

## Scripting Events Using the Visual InterDev Script Outline

So how can you actually use DHTML event handlers in your application? Well, let's take a step-by-step look at implementing one of the most commonly scripted effects, the mouseover. First off, we're going to take advantage of Visual InterDev's Script Outline to help us generate our event handler, so you'll want to open up a new solution in InterDev and add a new HTML file (name the file *mouseover.htm*). Once you've got that all ready, follow these steps:

1. In the Visual InterDev Design window, add the following lines of text to the page:

```
This is the first line.

This is the second line.
```

2. Now switch to the Source window. You'll see that where you typed those lines, InterDev automatically inserted opening and closing <P> tags for you. In order to access these tags from the Script Outline, we need to give them an ID attribute. Give the first line an ID of "Line1" and the second "Line2." The code should look like the following:

```
<P ID=Line1>This is the first line.</P>

<P ID=Line2>This is the second line.</P>
```

3. Next, switch to the Script Outline tab of the Toolbox window (see Figure 5-1). If you cannot see the Script Outline tab, you can view it by selecting View | Other Windows | Script Outline.

**Figure 5-1.**
*Script Outline window.*

4. Expand the node labeled Client Objects & Events. Note that there are entries for both Line1 and Line2. We'll start by writing an event handler for Line1, so expand the node labeled Line1.

5. Now look in the event list for the *onmouseover* event entry and double-click it. Note that Visual InterDev writes virtually all the event-handling code for you. All you need to do is fill in the action you want to happen in response to the event.

6. Add the following code to the *Line1_onmouseover* event handler (note that each time you type the dot separator, IntelliSense™ offers you a list of available properties and methods for that object):

```
window.event.srcElement.style.fontSize = 20;
```

7. Now switch to the Quick View window, and mouse over the first line of text. You should see the font size increase as in Figure 5-2.

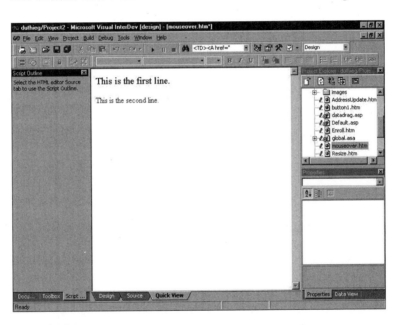

**Figure 5-2.**
*Using a mouseover event to increase font size.*

You may notice right away that there is at least one problem with this event handler: it only goes one way. When you mouse over the text, the font size increases, but the font doesn't return to normal when you move the mouse off the text. What we need is a way to do both, and with a little modification, this event handler will do just fine:

1. Change the name of the event handler function to *increaseFontSize*. Now copy the entire function and paste a copy below the existing function. Rename this function *decreaseFontSize*, and change the size of the font to 16. The code should now look like the following:

```
<SCRIPT ID=clientEventHandlersJS LANGUAGE=javascript>

<!--

function increaseFontSize() {

    window.event.srcElement.style.fontSize = 20;

}

function decreaseFontSize() {

    window.event.srcElement.style.fontSize = 16;

}

//-->

</SCRIPT>
```

2. Change the *onmouseover* calling code in the Line1 element to call the new function, and add an *onmouseout* call (using the same syntax) to call the *decreaseFontSize* function. The finished code will look like this:

```
<P ID=Line1 LANGUAGE=javascript

    onmouseover="return increaseFontSize()"

    onmouseout="return decreaseFontSize()">

    This is the first line.

</P>
```

3. Now switch to the Quick View window and test the code. Because the function we've written uses the *window.srcElement* object to determine which element to change, we can call this function from any element that contains text and get the same effect. To demonstrate this, change the <P> tags of the Line2 element to <A> tags (to

see the text as a hyperlink, add an HREF= attribute with an empty string as the target), then copy the code that calls the *increaseFontSize* and *decreaseFontSize* functions from the Line1 element and paste it into the Line2 element. The final product will look like this:

```
<P ID=Line1 LANGUAGE=javascript

    onmouseover="return increaseFontSize()"

    onmouseout="return decreaseFontSize()">

    This is the first line.

</P>

<A HREF="" ID=Line2  LANGUAGE=javascript

    onmouseover="return increaseFontSize()"

    onmouseout="return decreaseFontSize()">

    This is the second line.

</A>
```

Now we have a quick-and-easy method of doing text mouseover effects for any HTML element with a minimum of code. With the Script Outline and a little bit of tweaking in the Source view, there are many other things you can do to make your Web application behave more like a Windows application. The best part is that by handling events through DHTML, you reduce the number of trips back and forth to the server. This can be an important step toward improving the scalability of your application.

## Cascading Style Sheets (CSS)

Cascading Style Sheets (CSS) is a standard for formatting HTML elements, allowing you to provide pages that are stylistically richer and more consistent than pages created solely with HTML. Internet Explorer 3 supported a subset of the CSS-1 specification, while Internet Explorer 4 supports the full CSS-1 specification (as does Netscape Navigator 4), the proposed CSS-2 properties, inline styles (a part of the HTML 4 specification), as well as CSS-Positioning (which is currently a W3C working draft). This means that although browser support for CSS is somewhat limited at the moment, you can expect CSS support to grow now that the CSS-2 standard has been adopted.

Cascading Style Sheets allow you to specify styles for given HTML elements in four ways:

- **Inline**  Inline styles are specified by adding a STYLE attribute to the HTML element, followed by the CSS properties and their values (with each property:value pair separated with a semicolon) as follows:

```
<B STYLE="color:blue; font-size:20">This text is blue.</B>
```

- **Embedded**  Embedded styles are specified by creating a style block for an HTML page using the <STYLE> and </STYLE> tags, which contain the style rules for that page. Note that like script blocks, you should place CSS style rules within HTML comments to hide them from non-CSS browsers. Style rule declarations are written with the syntax: *TagName { property: value }* as shown below.

```
<STYLE>

<!--

B { font-family:Arial; text-transform:uppercase; }

P { background-color:silver; text-align:center; }

-->

</STYLE>
```

- **Linked**  Linked styles are specified in almost exactly the same way as embedded styles, but are stored in a separate file with a .CSS extension. It is this file that you edit when using Visual InterDev's Cascading Style Sheet editor. The only difference in defining the style rules within the file is that since the rules are in a separate file that will only be loaded by CSS-aware browsers, the comment tags are unnecessary. To use the defined styles in an HTML page, you simply link the HTML page to the style sheet with the following syntax:

```
<LINK REL="stylesheet" TYPE="text/css" HREF="myStyle.CSS">
```

- **Imported**  No these aren't the latest designer style sheets from Paris or Milan. Imported styles simply refer to using the *@import* statement to include an external style sheet within a style block or style sheet. The *@import* statement should appear at the beginning of the block or style sheet as follows:

```
@import: url(mystyles.css) ;
```

Which type of style sheet you use depends on what your goals are in using CSS. If you are striving for consistency over an entire site, it's probably best to use linked style sheets. If, on the other hand, you want the ultimate control over individual elements, inline styles would probably work best. But the greatest advantage to using CSS is that it isn't an either/or choice. You can use all of the methods described above to get both across the board consistency *and* by-page or by-element control over styles.

Here's how it works: The methods defined above are reverse-ordered by their precedence, that is, the order in which they will be applied, from inline styles (which are applied last) to imported styles (which are applied first). Each subsequent style sheet applied overrides any style information defined by previous style sheets. This is like having four different size paint brushes with which to paint your pages. Imported and linked style sheets are like wide brushes, allowing you to create a visually consistent site, the way a painter lays down a base coat. Embedded and inline styles are like detail brushes, allowing you to add accents and details to draw attention or contrast certain areas.

## CSS Positioning (CSS-P)

CSS-P is an extension of the Cascading Style Sheets specification that deals with the placement of HTML elements on the page. As mentioned above, CSS-P is currently a W3C working draft, which means it still has at least a little way to go before becoming a standard, but if you are able to require Internet Explorer 4 for your Web application, CSS-P has some nice features to offer. Just as the CSS specification can help you maintain a consistent style across your application by specifying fonts, colors, and backgrounds, CSS-P allows you greater control over the visual layout of your application by specifying pixel-precise placement of HTML elements on the page (no more single-pixel GIFs!). Using positioning with CSS is essentially the same as what we've discussed already, the difference being that you must specify both the type of positioning method and the actual position through CSS property attributes, as seen in this code:

```
<IMG SRC="myGif.gif" STYLE="position:absolute; left:50; top:50">
```

There are two methods of positioning HTML elements using CSS-P: *absolute positioning* and *relative positioning*.

## Absolute Positioning

With absolute positioning, an HTML element is placed on the page either in relation to its first positioned parent element (if there is one), or in relation to the BODY element. You use the *top* and *left* CSS attributes to set an element's position relative to the top-left corner of its positioned parent element (or the document body), which represents 0, 0. The following code would create a <DIV> with a red background containing some text 50 pixels from the left border of the document body and 30 pixels from the top:

```
This is some text.<BR>

This is some more text.<BR>

This is some more text.<BR>

This is some more text.<BR>

This is some more text.<BR>

This is some more text.<BR>

<DIV STYLE="position:absolute;left:50;top:30;height:150;width:150;
background:red">

    This text will appear inside the &lt;DIV&gt;.

</DIV>
```

The result would look like Figure 5-3, shown below:

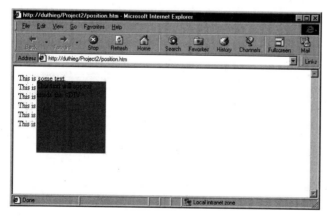

**Figure 5-3.**
*Absolute positioning of a <DIV> tag.*

Note that when positioned absolutely, the <DIV> element covers up some of the text. This is because an element that is positioned absolutely is removed from the normal flow of the document.

## Relative Positioning

By contrast, relatively positioned elements are placed on the page relative to their position in the normal flow of the HTML document. If we use the same code as above, but change the positioning to relative, the results would look like Figure 5-4 below. Note that now, the DIV is positioned 50 pixels to the left and 30 pixels from the top of where it would have been positioned without any positioning information.

```
This is some text.<BR>

This is some more text.<BR>

This is some more text.<BR>

This is some more text.<BR>

This is some more text.<BR>

This is some more text.<BR>

<DIV STYLE="position:relative;left:50;top:30;height:150;width:150;
background:red">

    This text will appear inside the &lt;DIV&gt;.

</DIV>
```

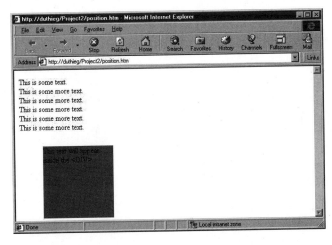

**Figure 5-4.**
*Relative positioning of a <DIV> tag.*

145

In both absolute and relative positioning, element overlap may occur depending on where various elements are placed on the page. The z-index CSS attribute can be used to control the z-order of elements. The *z-index* of an element is a number that describes how the element is placed on the page with respect to other elements occupying the same X-Y coordinates. By setting the z-index of an element higher than an element occupying part or all of the same space on a page, the element with the higher z-index will appear in front of the element with a lower z-index. For example, an element with a z-index of 100 will appear to be in front of an element with a z-index of 1 if both are positioned at 50, 50 on the page. This allows you to control the appearance of depth in your pages.

## CSS Wrap-Up

CSS offers a great deal of flexibility and power to application developers in making their applications look and feel more like the applications users are accustomed to. You can create a consistent look and feel for your entire application with a single style sheet; and with CSS-P, you can place elements on your pages with pixel-perfect precision. You should keep in mind when using CSS that although CSS-1 is supported in both Netscape and Microsoft's fourth-generation browsers, CSS-2 features, and such extensions as CSS-P, are only supported in Internet Explorer 4. In addition, the Internet Explorer 3 and Internet Explorer 4 implementations of CSS-1 are slightly different, due to the fact that Internet Explorer 3 supported CSS-1 before it was a fully formed standard. It is usually a good idea if you may have users with non-CSS browsers (or with Internet Explorer 3), to test your pages in such browsers to make sure that they degrade gracefully.

## • • • SOLUTION: Onscreen Help with DHTML and CSS

While developing the Clerk interface for the Rent-A-Prize sample application, we decided that one of the things we might want the interface to provide was simple onscreen help. The thought was that training new employees is an expense every company faces, and having onscreen help available might serve to reduce the amount of training necessary for new employees, and might also make the interface easier to use for existing employees as well.

One way to implement onscreen help, which we will demonstrate in this solution, is to use a mouseover effect to alert the user to the availability of help for an item on the screen, then use the *onclick* event to display help text for that item. To accomplish this, we'll use a variety of the techniques we've discussed, including inline and function-based event handlers and various CSS attributes.

To begin, open a Visual InterDev solution and add a new HTML page, then add the following code between the <BODY> and </BODY> tags:

```
<FORM METHOD="post">
<P ALIGN="center">
<TABLE ALIGN="center" BORDER="0" CELLPADDING="3">
  <TR>
    <TD>
      <DIV ID=PickUp>
        Pick-up:
      </DIV>
    </TD>
    <TD>
      <INPUT ID="txtPU" NAME="txtPU">
    </TD>
    <TD>
      <DIV ID=VehType>
        Vehicle Type:
      </DIV>
    </TD>
    <TD>
      <INPUT ID="txtVehTp" NAME="txtVehTp">
    </TD>
  </TR>
```

(*continued*)

147

```
<TR>
  <TD>
    <DIV ID=DropOff>
       Drop-off
    </DIV>
  </TD>
  <TD>
    <INPUT ID="txtDO" NAME="txtDO">
  </TD>
  <TD>
    <DIV ID=VIN>
       Vehicle VIN
    </DIV>
  </TD>
  <TD>
    <INPUT ID="txtVin" NAME="txtVin" >
  </TD>
</TR>
<TR>
  <TD>
    <DIV ID=StartDt>
       Start Date:
    </DIV>
  </TD>
  <TD>
    <INPUT ID="txtStartDate" NAME="txtStartDate">
  <TD>
    <DIV ID=Credit>
       Credit Card
    </DIV>
```

(*continued*)

```
    <TD>
      <INPUT ID="txtCreditCard" NAME="txtCreditCard">
    </TD>
  </TR>
  <TR>
    <TD>
      <DIV ID=EndDt>
        End Date:
      </DIV>
    </TD>
    <TD>
      <INPUT ID="txtEndDate" NAME="txtEndDate">
    </TD>
    <TD>
      <DIV ID=Mileage>
        Auto Milage:
      </DIV>
    <TD>
      <INPUT ID="txtMileage" NAME="txtMileage">
    </TD>
  </TR>
</TABLE>
</P>
<TABLE ALIGN="center" border="0" cellPadding="1" cellSpacing="1"
  width="75%">
  <TR>
    <TD>
      <DIV ID=Total>
        Total Amount:
      </DIV>
    </TD>
```

(*continued*)

```
        <TD>
            <INPUT ID="txtTotal" NAME="txtTotal">
        </TD>
    </TR>
    <TR>
        <TD ALIGN="right">
            <INPUT ID="btnSave" NAME="btnSave" type="submit" value="Save
                Rental">
        </TD>
        <TD ALIGN="left">
            <INPUT ID="btnPrint" NAME="btnPrint" type="button" value="Print
                Invoice">
        </TD>
    </TR>
</TABLE>
</FORM>
```

The results from this code is shown in Figure 5-5. To add onscreen help
to this page, we'll need to add code to change the text color and cursor when
the mouse is over a field name, event handlers for mouse and click events, and
code to display and hide the help text for each field.

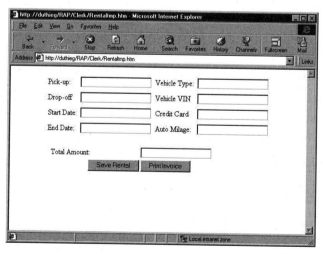

**Figure 5-5.**
*Rental page before onscreen help.*

First, we'll deal with the mouseover effect, for which we'll use a variation of the technique we used earlier. In this case we'll use VBScript for the event handlers, since we're developing for Internet Explorer 4 (and VBScript can simplify our procedures), but we'll still use JavaScript to actually call the functions:

1. In Source view, add a script block to the page by placing the cursor just before the </HEAD> tag and selecting HTML | Script Block | Client. Since we want to use VBScript for this script block, change the LANGUAGE attribute to VBScript.

2. Add two Sub procedures to the page, *ShowHelpCursor* and *HideHelp*. The code should look like the following:

```
Sub ShowHelpCursor()

End Sub

Sub HideHelp()

End Sub
```

3. To change the look of the field name and the cursor, we'll take advantage of the event object's *srcElement* property, which gives us access to the element that fired the event we are handling. We then use the style property to make the desired changes. Add the following code to the *ShowHelpCursor* procedure:

```
window.event.srcElement.style.cursor = "help"

window.event.srcElement.style.color = "red"
```

4. To change the cursor and text back to normal, we'll add the following code to the *HideHelp* procedure:

```
window.event.srcElement.style.cursor = "default"

window.event.srcElement.style.color = "black"
```

So far, our code can't do anything, since it's not connected to the elements firing events, so let's take care of that next. Since we've added an ID attribute to each of our field names (which we put in DIVs for easy scripting), we could use the Script Outline to set up the event handlers, but let's do it by hand just for the experience.

5. Find the <DIV> tag with the ID of PickUp, and add the following code to handle *mouseover* and *mouseout* events, then use the Quick View window to view the effect:

```
LANGUAGE=javascript

onmouseover="return ShowHelpCursor()"

onmouseout="return HideHelp()"
```

6. To add this effect to other field names (or any other element), you can simply add the code in step 5 to that element.

So now we've got our mouseover effect. Now comes the tough part, displaying help text. Well, really it's not so tough, just follow these steps:

1. Start by adding a <DIV> to the page just before the <TABLE> element. Set its attributes as ID=HelpDiv ALIGN=CENTER STYLE="border:1px solid white; font-family:arial; font-weight:bold".

2. Add two more Sub procedures to our script block, *ShowHelpText* (which we'll call from the *onclick* event) and *HideHelpText* (which we'll call from the *HideHelp* procedure).

3. Again, we'll use the *srcElement* property of the event object, but this time, we'll use a string variable to store the ID of *srcElement*:

```
Dim strElement

strElement = window.event.srcElement.id
```

4. Next we'll add some formatting to our <DIV>, using the style object (note that the property names for the style object are not always identical to the CSS Style attributes they represent):

```
HelpDiv.style.backgroundColor = "infobackground"

HelpDiv.style.border = "1px solid black"
```

5. We'll also need to decide which field the user clicked, which we'll do by using a Select Case statement on the ID property we stored in step 3. To display our help text, we use the Select Case to change the *innerText* property of our *HelpDiv* element to the desired message:

```
Select Case strElement

   Case "PickUp"

      HelpDiv.innerText = "Date of vehicle pick-up. Enter at
pick-up"

End Select
```

6. Next, we'll add code to the HideHelpText procedure to clean up (we set the *innerHTML* property to   to act as a placeholder for the help text to avoid having the document reflow repeatedly):

```
HelpDiv.innerHTML = " "

HelpDiv.innerText = ""

HelpDiv.style.backgroundColor = ""

HelpDiv.style.border = "1px solid white"
```

7. Almost there. Now we'll call the *HideHelpText* procedure from the *HideHelp* procedure by adding the following line:

```
HideHelpText
```

8. Finally, we need to connect our new event handlers to the field name element(s) by adding the following line:

```
onclick="return ShowHelpText()"
```

9. Now save the page and test it by right-clicking on the page and selecting View in Browser... (Internet Explorer 4 should be your default browser for this to work). Move the mouse pointer over the field name "Pick-up", then click. The result should look like Figure 5-6.

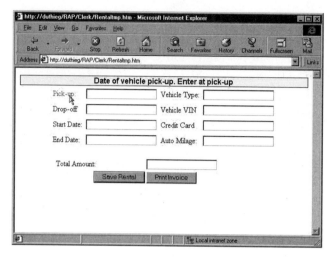

**Figure 5-6.**
*Onscreen help in action.*

The techniques used in this section are only the beginning of what is possible with CSS and DHTML, and the best part is that none of them add to the burdens of your overworked servers. For complete listings of DHTML and CSS objects, and their properties and methods, see the Internet Client SDK, downloadable from Microsoft's Web site (http://www.microsoft.com/IE). You can also view the Internet Client SDK online as part of the MSDN online library (http://www.microsoft.com/msdn). Other technologies offered with Internet Explorer 4, including Remote Data Services, offer additional functionality, as we'll see in the next sections.

## Remote Data Services and DHTML Data-Binding

Remote Data Services (RDS), formerly known as the Active Data Connector and now integrated with ActiveX Data Objects (ADO), is a technology designed to allow data to be transmitted to the client and manipulated locally without an active database connection, then allow the modified data to be returned to update the server. The advantage in using RDS is that in situations where data must be sorted, or where users need to be able to scroll through a group of records, these operations can be enabled without the expense of an open database connection, which greatly increases the scalability of the application, and also increases the responsiveness for your users.

With Visual InterDev 6.0 using RDS couldn't be much easier, or more transparent. By using VI's Design-Time Controls, all the hard work is done for you—from opening the database connection to binding data to individual form fields. All it takes is three easy steps (the DTC scripting platform for the page should be set to Client (Internet Eplorer 4 DHTML), the default for HTML pages):

1. Add a recordset to an HTML page by dragging a command object from the Project Explorer window onto the page.

2. Add DTCs for editing data (labels and textboxes) by either dragging them from the Toolbox, or by adding a data command to the Project Explorer and dragging the available fields from the command onto the page. In either case, you should make sure the *Recordset* property of the DTCs is set to the recordset created in step 1.

3. Add a RecordSetNavBar DTC to the page by dragging it from the Toolbox onto the page. Set its *Recordset* property to the recordset created in step 1, and make sure the Update on Move box is checked.

That's all there is to it. Of course, just using the DTCs will only get you so far. To move beyond simply scrolling through and updating records, perhaps adding such features as reordering a recordset by clicking on a column head in a table, we'll once again have to roll up our sleeves and write a little code of our own, using one of a number of other available alternatives, such as one of the variety of Data Source Objects (DSOs) included with Internet Explorer 4. Available DSOs include:

- **Tabular Data Control (TDC)**   A DSO designed to allow access to delimited text files. Useful for simple data access. Implemented as an ActiveX control.

- **Remote Data Service**   A more complex DSO that offers access to ODBC and OLE DB data sources. Allows insert, update, and delete functionality. Implemented as an ActiveX control.

- **XML DSO**   A read-only DSO. Well-equipped for displaying hierarchical data. Implemented as a Java applet.

- **MSHTML DSO**   Another read-only DSO. The MSHTML DSO allows developers to define data sets as HTML pages. The DSO uses ID attributes to parse out columns and rows. Implemented through the <OBJECT> tag.

- **JDBC DSO Applet**   A DSO similar to the RDS DSO. Offers access to ODBC data sources, including insert, update, and delete functionality. Implemented as a Java applet. This DSO may be downloaded from Microsoft Data Source Object Gallery at http://www.microsoft.com/gallery/files/datasrc/.

Whether you use the drag-and drop simplicity of the Visual InterDev DTCs, or the greater flexibility of one of the variety of DSOs available, bringing data to the client offers the same advantages: speedier response for your users, and fewer round-trips to burden your server and database resources. If you have the ability to use these technologies, your application will reap substantial benefits in scalability.

## DHTML *Can* Be Cross-Platform

Although certain parts of CSS and DHTML are currently supported only by Internet Explorer 4, this does not necessarily have to be considered a limitation. If you can require the use of Internet Explorer 4, your application can still reach a broad audience, due to the increasing number of platforms on which Internet Explorer 4 will run.

### Platforms Supported by Internet Explorer 4

Currently, Internet Explorer 4 has versions available for Windows 3.x, Windows 95/98/NT, Macintosh, and several flavors of UNIX. What this means to developers is that if you want to make use of the power and flexibility of DHTML, you can do so without eliminating large numbers of users from your potential audience. Although this may not be a realistic solution for applications available via the Internet, intranet and extranet applications may be able to take advantage of CSS, DHTML, and data binding to provide Windows-like application functionality without placing extra burdens on your servers.

### Limitations of Cross-Platform Authoring for Internet Explorer 4

Although the vast majority of DHTML and CSS features are available for cross-platform development, other new features may not be, depending on the platform. In general, any feature implemented as an ActiveX control (including non-Java DSOs) will only be available on Win32 platforms. With the delivery of COM support for UNIX, however, perhaps this limitation may soon be a thing of the past.

# ASP—Providing the Greatest Reach

At the opposite end of the features versus reach spectrum is Active Server Pages. Although ASP is the most common solution when you must support multiple browsers, it can be useful for delivering content for specific platforms as well. In this section we'll discuss both uses.

## Useful When You Cannot Control Client

So you wish you could use DHTML, but you just can't convince the project stakeholders of the wisdom of migrating an entire department to Internet Explorer 4. Or perhaps your application needs to be accessible to the Internet, and you're not prepared to ask customers to download a new browser just to use your application. Neither of these situations is particularly unusual, and if you're faced with them, your technology of choice is Active Server Pages. ASP allows you to perform many of the same tasks that a DHTML-enabled application performs, but for many it requires a server round-trip. For example, we could implement an onscreen help system similar to the one described earlier in this chapter by making our form field labels into hyperlinks to a page of definitions. The down side, of course, is that each time a user wants to see a definition, they have to go to another page, then click the back button (or a link) to get back to the original page.

This may sound like a criticism of ASP, however it is anything but. ASP is an excellent solution to one of the biggest problems plaguing Web developers: browser incompatibility. The simple fact is that at least for the time being, developing for multiple browsers involves making compromises. An old saying goes that there are three ways you can ask for any project: fast, good, and cheap, *pick two*. Turns out, developing for multiple browsers is not so different, you can make it easy (fast), powerful (good), and simple (cheap), but generally not all three at once.

## Making It Easy

Making it easy is the role of Visual InterDev 6.0. When you need to get an application prototyped and up and running in no time, Visual InterDev provides the Data Environment and data-bound DTCs to get your ASP application functional, as well as Visual InterDev themes to make it look good. Although the DTCs aren't as scalable or customizable as a custom component-based solution, they are excellent for prototyping and for smaller applications. Visual InterDev themes allow you to take advantage of CSS for those clients who support it, without excluding those who don't. The down side to making it easy is that you give up a certain amount of flexibility. Remember, the easier the tool, generally the less that can be done with it.

## Making It Powerful

You can also use InterDev to code your solutions by hand. If you want more data-access flexibility than the DTCs allow, you can code all your ADO logic by hand, or better yet, create your own server-side data-access components to use ADO from Visual Basic. If you want, you can even use the Browser Capabilities component (or JavaScript) to determine which features your application should implement. Any of these possibilities can make your application more powerful, but they too have a cost in complexity and development time.

Coding your own data-access components (and business logic components) takes more time and skill than using the DTCs, but can pay for itself many times over in performance (as we'll see in Chapter 7, "Performance and Scalability"). Providing different features for each browser requires an in-depth knowledge of the common and browser-specific features of a wide range of browsers, and typically means maintaining a much larger code base. But to provide the greatest level of functionality, no matter the platform, there may be no other way.

## Making It Simple

Making it simple refers to keeping both implementation and maintenance from becoming overly complex. In different situations, this may mean different solutions. For example, one way of simplifying maintenance is to remove complex business logic to components. Unfortunately, this has the consequence of increasing the complexity of the implementation (somewhat). Coding your entire application in ASP script code can simplify the implementation, but at the cost of much greater difficulty in maintaining that code.

The point of all this is that the old saw about a free lunch (or lack thereof) holds true for Web development. When deciding which browsers to support, or which features to implement, there is no one right answer. Each application must be designed based on its individual needs. Keep this in mind as we look at the next couple of solutions.

• • • **SOLUTION: Browsing Reservation Information on the Server**

In the Rent-A-Prize Customer interface, which is to be made available via the Internet, we need a solution for allowing customers to view their current reservations, and to select and edit them if they choose. For reasons of scalability, we chose to implement this functionality through a custom COM component. By creating a COM component to take care of looking up reservations and updating records, we reduce the amount of scripting code running on our Web server, and allow our business logic to be run within MTS for even greater scalability. We can also run our component on a different machine if we choose, to reduce the load on the Web server.

For this solution we take the following steps:

1. Create a new DLL project in Visual Basic (5.0 or later). Our component will be named *bsReservation.dll*, so change the name of the project to *bsReservation* using the properties window.

2. Select the predefined class and change its name to *CFetchReservation*. For this solution, we are going to concentrate on this class.

3. Set a reference to the ADO type library by selecting Project | References…, then browsing to the Microsoft ActiveX Data Objects 2.0 Library entry. Select the check box next to the entry and click OK.

4. Add the following code to the class:

```
Option Explicit

Function vGetReservations(CustomerID As Integer) As Variant

'-------------------------------------

' Purpose: Fetches all reservation

'     IDs for the given customer ID

'     Returns a Variant Array of

'     Reservation IDs. The first
```

*(continued)*

```
'     Array element (0) indicates
'     the length of the array
'------------------------------------

    'Declare required ADO objects
    Dim Conn As New ADODB.Connection
    Dim cmd As New ADODB.Command
    Dim rs As New ADODB.Recordset
    Dim vResIDArray() As Variant
    ReDim vResIDArray(25) 'Expand array if necessary to support
                          'more reservations
    Dim iRecordNum As Integer
    iRecordNum = 0

    'Set query parameters
    cmd.CommandType = adCmdText
    cmd.CommandText = "SELECT reservation_id " & _
        "FROM reservation " & _
        "WHERE customer_id = " & CustomerID
    'Open Connection
    'NOTE: Replace connection string as
    '   appropriate for your machine
    Conn.Open "DSN=RAP;UID=sa;PWD="

    'Set Conn as Active Connection for command object
    cmd.ActiveConnection = Conn
    'Execute command
    Set rs = cmd.Execute
    'Return value
```

*(continued)*

```
If rs.EOF Then

    vGetReservations = "0"

Else

    Do While Not rs.EOF

        iRecordNum = iRecordNum + 1

        vResIDArray(iRecordNum) = _
            rs("reservation_id").Value

        rs.MoveNext

    Loop

    vResIDArray(0) = iRecordNum

    ReDim Preserve vResIDArray(iRecordNum + 1)

    vGetReservations = vResIDArray

End If


'Close Connection

Conn.Close

Set Conn = Nothing

Set cmd = Nothing

Set rs = Nothing

End Function
```

5. Save the project and compile the DLL.

6. Open Visual InterDev and add a new ASP page named *CustomerHome.asp*.

7. Add the following code to the page:

```
<%@ Language=VBScript %>

<HTML>

<HEAD>

<META NAME="GENERATOR" Content="Microsoft Visual Studio 6.0">
```

*(continued)*

```
</HEAD>
<BODY>


<P align=center><STRONG>Rent-A-Prize</STRONG></P>
<P align=center><STRONG>Customer Home Page</STRONG></P>
<P><STRONG>Current Reservations:</STRONG></P>


<TABLE>
<%
Dim objReservation
Dim vResIDs 'Variant Array for function return
Dim iCounter 'Counter variable


Set rs = Server.CreateObject("ADODB.Recordset")
Set objReservation  v
  Server.CreateObject("bsReservation.CFetchReservation")
'Call method to get reservations
'Note that the Customer ID argument is hard-coded here
vResIDs = objReservation.vGetReservations(1)


Response.Write "<TR><TH>Reservation ID</TH></TR>"


For iCounter = 1 To vResIDs(0)
   Response.Write "<TR><TD>"
   Response.Write vResIDs(iCounter)
   Response.Write "</TD><TR>"
Next
```

*(continued)*

```
%>
</TABLE>


</BODY>

</HTML>
```

8. Save the page, then right-click and select View in Browser. This should display a list of the current reservations in the Rent-A-Prize database. Note that this solution assumes that you have used the scripts included on the CD-ROM to create and populate the Rent-A-Prize database, and that you have set up a DSN.

9. While this solution is relatively simple, it demonstrates how we can easily use custom components to implement data access and business logic. This simplifies the coding of our ASP pages, and also allows us much greater control over how we display our data than we might get from a DTC.

## ASP Browser Capabilities Component

With the Browser Capabilities component, you can create a server-based object that you can query at runtime to find out about the features of the browser being used by a given client. The component takes advantage of the USER_AGENT HTTP header that is sent with each HTTP request by comparing it to a list of USER_AGENT headers found in a file called *browscap.ini*. The Browser Capabilities component finds the header matching that passed by the client browser, then reads the properties listed, which allows you to query for them. Keeping up to date with the latest browsers is as simple as downloading a new BROWSCAP.INI file.

Although you can also interrogate the USER_AGENT header manually through script, the advantage of using the browser capabilities component is that you don't need to remember all of the capabilities of a given browser. You only need to query the component for the particular feature you desire and use it if it is available. Table 5-1, from the Visual Studio documentation, shows some of the properties you can query for.

| Property | Description |
|---|---|
| ActiveXControls | Specifies whether the browser supports ActiveX™ controls. |
| backgroundsounds | Specifies whether the browser supports background sounds. |
| beta | Specifies whether the browser is beta software. |
| browser | Specifies the name of the browser. |
| cookies | Specifies whether the browser supports cookies. |
| Frames | Specifies whether the browser supports frames. |
| Javaapplets | Specifies whether the browser supports Java applets. |
| Javascript | Specifies whether the browser supports JScript™. |
| Platform | Specifies the platform that the browser runs on. |
| Tables | Specifies whether the browser supports tables. |
| VBscript | Specifies whether the browser supports VBScript. |
| Version | Specifies the version number of the browser. |

**Table 5-1.**
*Browser properties found in BROWSCAP.INI.*

Now let's take a look at how we'd use this component:

## • • • SOLUTION: Dynamically Providing Features for Different Browsers

1. First open a Visual InterDev Solution and add a new ASP page. Call it BROWSCAP.ASP.

2. From the Server Objects pane of the VI Toolbox, drag the Browser Capabilities component onto the page (in the <HEAD> section of the page). Visual InterDev will add the component to the page using <OBJECT> tags. Note that you could also create the object by using the ASP *Server.CreateObject* syntax.

3. Change the object's ID attribute to *MyBrowsCap*.

4. Add the following code to the body of page:

```
<%

If MyBrowsCap.Browser = "IE" Then

    Response.Write "You're using Internet Explorer " & _
        MyBrowsCap.Version

    'Code to use an ActiveX Control
```

(*continued*)

```
ElseIf MyBrowsCap.Browser = "Netscape" Then

    Response.Write "You're using Netscape " & _
        MyBrowsCap.Version

    'Code to use a Java Applet

Else

    Response.Write "You're using " & MyBrowsCap.Browser & " " & _
        MyBrowsCap.Version

    If MyBrowsCap.ActiveXControls = True Then

        'Code to use ActiveX Control

    ElseIf MyBrowsCap.Javaapplets = True Then

        'Code to use a Java applet

    Else

        'Code for lowest-common denominator browser

    End If

End If

%>
```

5. Save the file and browse the new page in both Internet Explorer and Navigator (you *do* have both installed, right?) by right-clicking the file in the Project Explorer and selecting View in Browser and Browse with... (which allows you to browse the page in any installed browser). The results should appear similar to Figures 5-7 and 5-8.

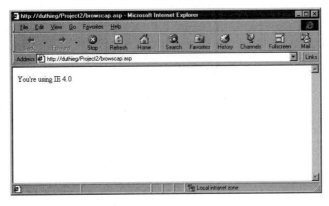

**Figure 5-7.**
*Browser Capabilities component with Internet Explorer.*

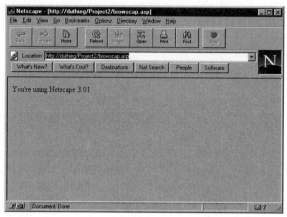

**Figure 5-8.**
*Browser Capabilities component with Netscape Navigator.*

## Summary

In this chapter we've looked at some of the issues facing developers who want greater functionality in their Web applications, including the conflict between feature richness and wide application reach. We've also looked at some of the difficulties with implementing those features in a world of incompatible browsers, which can include testing and writing code for multiple browsers. We looked at solutions based on DHTML and CSS, and how Internet Explorer 4 can help make those features available across a wide range of platforms. We've also looked at using ASP and the browser capabilities component to deal with situations in which we have little or no control over the client browser.

In the next chapter, we'll take a look at managing navigation and content in your Web application. We'll also look at planning for application maintenance and review the tools Visual InterDev 6.0 provides to assist you with these tasks.

## CHAPTER SIX

# Navigation and Content Design and Management

• • • **GOAL: To Make the Rent-A-Prize Application Easy to Use and Maintain**

One of the natural goals of any application is that it be easy to use. Another is that it be easy to manage and maintain. Visual InterDev 6.0 offers a number of tools to make these goals a reality, including the Site Designer, PageNavBar Design-Time Controls (DTCs), and automatic link repair functionality. In this chapter we'll discuss how to use these tools to make ease-of-use and maintainability a reality.

## Ease-of-Use Issues

Ease-of-use is a quality that most applications strive for, yet many applications lack. It is a combination of factors, including user interface and navigation, that make the task of finding and exploiting the features of your application simpler for even the unfamiliar user. Applications that have ease-of-use encourage repeat visits. Applications that lack it may force users to seek another method of fulfilling their needs (such as visiting a competitor's site).

Whether you are developing an in-house system for automating your internal business processes, or creating an online commerce solution for a retail or catalog business, ease-of-use is key to getting users to use your application—and to keep them using it. If you need any more motivation, just think what the chances are of winning another development contract with a client if the first application you build for them is rarely used.

In this section we'll discuss the two main issues relating to ease-of-use: *user interface consistency*, and *navigation consistency*. Both of these issues are especially important in Web applications because until the release of Visual InterDev 6.0 there were few tools to assist developers in addressing them, compared to development environments such as Visual Basic and Visual C++, which provide rich sets of tools that make it easy to create consistent user interfaces.

## Consistent User Interface

When developing an application with Visual Basic, the use of forms and controls makes creating a consistent user interface relatively easy (though these tools don't necessarily guarantee consistency). By comparison, it can be difficult to create a consistent user interface for a Web application, mainly because much of the interface traditionally has been built from scratch in HTML.

One of the many advantages offered by the Visual InterDev 6.0 development environment is a Toolbox that offers Web developers the drag-and-drop simplicity of controls for the first time. While this by itself does not guarantee consistent design, it does free the Web developer from having to look up and type in HTML tags and tags for DTCs, ActiveX controls, and commonly used server objects. This in turn gives the developer more time to spend planning the user interface.

### User Interface Planning

As the old saying goes, "People don't plan to fail, they fail to plan." Web developers would do well to heed this saying. Planning is one of the most important steps in creating a consistent user interface, and it's one you can ill afford to skip. At a minimum, the planning for your site's interface should consist of the following:

- **Use-case analysis**  Asks the questions: "Who are our users?" "What do they need to do at our site?" "How do they get to our site?" As well as other questions specific to your business needs. The answers to these questions will help determine the basic interface you use, as well as provide answers to some of the questions we'll discuss in the section on navigation.

- **Storyboarding**  Storyboarding is the process of sketching out the major elements of your user interface, including forms, buttons, graphics (or at least their placement), headers and footers, and navigational elements. Whether done on paper, on a whiteboard, or in a diagramming program such as Visio™, storyboarding can help you understand the flow of each page in your application, as well as the flow from a given page to others. Storyboarding can also help you catch inconsistencies before they make it into code. And fixing a storyboard is much cheaper than fixing the code.

■ **Flow charts**  You should create a flow chart addressing all the paths that a user can take in your application. This could get pretty elaborate for a large application, so it's probably a good idea to break the application down into sections (such as the clerk interface and the customer interface of the Rent-A-Prize application). Figure 6-1 shows an early flow chart of the process a customer would go through to log into the Rent-A-Prize application. It's also a good idea to do a separate flow chart for each page or section. These flow charts can give you a starting point for your site design, and like storyboards, they can help call your attention to trouble areas before you start writing code.

NOTE: If you are working on an enterprise application in which you intend to use components, you should probably also take time at this point to plan out the architecture of those components. This planning should include how the business processes you need to implement will be broken out (for example, which functions go into which components?), where components will be located, and how the components will communicate with the user interface (for example, how will arguments and results be passed back and forth?). This planning will save you the trouble of rewriting a lot of your user interface code. For more information on planning your architecture and implementing components, see Chapter 7, "Addressing Performance and Scalability."

# Rent-A-Prize Demo Application
## Customer Login/Registration Process

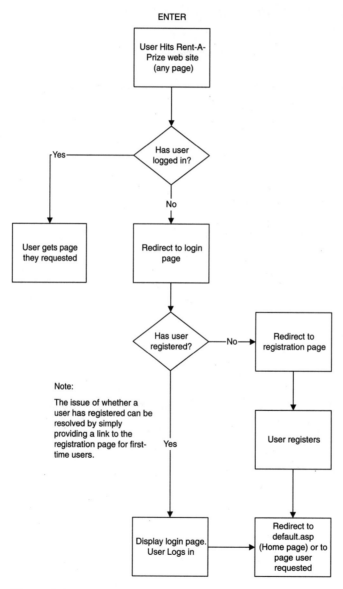

**Figure 6-1.**
*Customer login process.*

Whether you use the techniques listed here, or find or create others that better meet your particular needs, what *is* important is that you take the time to plan. Once you've taken this time, you should have a good enough idea of how you want your user interface put together to start working on implementation. We'll take a look at implementation in the section entitled, "Using Visual InterDev's Site Designer to Plan Your Site Structure."

## Using InterDev Themes to Provide a Consistent User Interface

Another important aspect of creating a consistent user interface is making sure that the visual elements used are consistent from page to page. This is another area where Visual Basic users have it pretty easy. In Visual Basic, you would have to try hard to make the visual elements used to build an application look inconsistent. Making a Web application look inconsistent is a piece of cake, but it's exactly what we want to avoid. Fortunately for us, there are the Visual InterDev Themes.

### How Visual InterDev Themes Work

Themes in Visual InterDev are made up of one or more Cascading Style Sheets (CSS), and a set of graphics, all of which are stored in your project in a folder labeled _Themes. The style sheets specify settings for the fonts, styles, and graphics that will be used in the pages to which the themes are applied. Themes can be applied at the project or page level, so you can specify a theme for your site as a whole, then override that by choosing a different theme for a specific file. Themes are defined for individual pages through a series of links to the CSS files as shown in the following code:

```
<LINK REL="stylesheet" TYPE="text/css" HREF="_Themes/raygun/THEME.CSS"
VI6.0THEME="Raygun">

<LINK REL="stylesheet" TYPE="text/css" HREF="_Themes/raygun/
GRAPH0.CSS" VI6.0THEME="Raygun">

<LINK REL="stylesheet" TYPE="text/css" HREF="_Themes/raygun/
COLOR0.CSS" VI6.0THEME="Raygun">

<LINK REL="stylesheet" TYPE="text/css" HREF="_Themes/raygun/
CUSTOM.CSS" VI6.0THEME="Raygun">
```

Keep in mind when using themes that pages may not display the way you expect them to in non-CSS browsers, although they should degrade gracefully. It is best to test your pages with both CSS and non-CSS browsers to be certain your application will work with any browser.

### Adding Themes

The process for adding themes to a project is roughly the same as adding a theme to a page, as is the process for adding a theme using the Site designer window. Just follow these simple steps:

1. In the Site Designer or Project Explorer window, right-click the file or project you wish to add a theme to.

2. Select Apply Theme and Layout... from the context menu.

3. In the Apply Theme and Layout dialog box, select the Apply Theme: radio button, then select the theme you wish to apply.

4. Click OK. Then theme will be applied to your project or page.

NOTE: If your HTML or Active Server Page (ASP) page is missing certain tags (in particular the <HEAD> and </HEAD> tags), Visual InterDev will report an error when you try to apply a theme to that page. This is because Visual InterDev needs these tags in order to determine where to insert the links to the theme's CSS files.

### Creating and Using Your Own Themes

With Visual InterDev 6.0, as with the earlier version, it is possible to create your own custom themes. The process (and the storage locations for themes), however, is a bit different for Visual InterDev 6.0. Despite the differences, creating a custom theme is very simple.

### • • • SOLUTION: Creating a Custom Theme for Rent-A-Prize

In this solution, we'll create a simple custom theme for the Rent-A-Prize application. This will involve creating a Cascading Style Sheet for the theme, adding the desired graphics, and saving the CSS file and the graphics to the Themes directory. The first thing we'll need is a place to store our theme.

1. Open the Rent-A-Prize project in Visual InterDev (see Appendix B, "Installing the Sample Application," for more information).

2. If one does not already exist, add a folder to the project called *Themes*, by right-clicking the project name in the Project Explorer and selecting New Folder....

3. In the Themes folder, create a folder named *RAPTheme* using the same technique. We now have a place to store our theme.

Next, we'll need to create a Cascading Style Sheet that will define the styles used in our theme. We'll build a style sheet that uses HTML tag name selectors. The technique for creating styles is similar for all three available CSS selectors: HTML tag name, Class, and ID.

> NOTE: A *selector* is the HTML tag name, class name, or unique ID that is associated with a particular style. Styles referenced by HTML tag name selectors are automatically applied when the given HTML tag is used. To apply styles associated with a class or ID selector, you reference the class or ID as a parameter of the HTML tag to which the style will be applied. For example, to apply the style associated with a class selector named *clsBlueItal*, you would use the following syntax:

```
<P CLASS="clsBlueItal">Some Text</P>
```

To discontinue the application of the style, you close with the closing tag for the element you are using.

To set up our style sheet:

1. Right-click the RAPTheme folder, and select Add | Style Sheet.... Name the file *RAPStyle*, and click OK. A new style sheet will appear in the Visual InterDev CSS editor (for the time being, close the Toolbox window to give yourself a little more screen real estate).

2. Set up a tag-based style for paragraph (<P>) tags by right-clicking on the HTML Tags folder in the left-hand pane of the CSS editor, and selecting Insert HTML Tag.... In the Insert New HTML Tag dialog box, use the drop-down box to select the <P> tag, as shown in Figure 6-2.

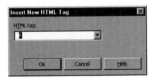

**Figure 6-2.**
*The Insert New HTML Tag dialog box.*

3. Now use the Font tab of the right-hand pane of the CSS editor to modify the font for the <P> tag style. Add Arial and Verdana to the Selected fonts list box (it's always a good idea to specify two or three fonts in case your first choice isn't installed on the user's system), change the color to Blue, and set the size to Absolute and Large, as shown in Figure 6-3.

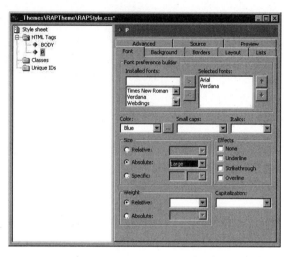

**Figure 6-3.**
*Changing font attributes in the CSS editor.*

4. Use the Preview tab of the CSS editor to view the effect of the changes on text within the <P> tags, then use the Source tab to view the style sheet code generated by the editor.

That's about all it takes to define our theme, though obviously a little more effort is involved if you want your theme to use custom images for bullets or other purposes, such as banners or navigation buttons. Using images for bullets is as easy as copying the images to your theme folder, then using the Lists tab of the CSS editor to specify the image(s) you want to use.

NOTE: For examples of using custom images for banners or navigation buttons, take a look at the GRAPH0.CSS and/or GRAPH1.CSS files included in each of the predefined Visual InterDev themes. These files demonstrate the various other ways you can use graphics in your themes.

Our last step is to apply the new theme to our project. In order to do that, we'll define an INF file for our theme by following these steps:

1.  Create a new text file in your project by selecting File | New File..., and selecting Text File, then clicking Open.

2.  The easiest way to define the INF file is to copy the information from an existing theme (browse to the Themes folder of your Visual InterDev installation, select a theme folder, open the INF file, and copy its contents to the Clipboard). The file only requires a few lines, as shown below (note that the only line that changes from theme to theme is the title line. If the INF file is stored in your local folder, the refcount should be 1):

```
[info]

title=RAPTheme

codepage=1252

version=01.02

readonly=true

refcount=1
```

3.  Save the file as *RAPTheme.inf*. Even if you save the file in the Themes folder of your project, you need to add the file to the project by right-clicking your _Themes folder, selecting Add | Add Item..., selecting the Existing tab and browsing to the file, then clicking Open.

4.  Once the INF file is in place, you can apply your theme to the project (or to individual pages) in the same way as the preinstalled themes.

NOTE: Developers who share projects between Visual InterDev and FrontPage 98 should use caution when customizing Visual InterDev themes. If you modify a Visual InterDev theme, then apply the theme using FrontPage, your modifications may be overwritten by FrontPage. This behavior can be avoided by always renaming themes you have customized, including changing the theme's INF file to reflect the new theme name.

## Consistent Navigation Paradigm

Navigation is actually a part of your user interface, but it's an important enough part to address on its own. The consistent use of navigational elements will have a greater impact than almost any other factor in determining the ease-of-use of your application. How you implement that navigation will also have a sizeable impact on the maintainability of your site (see the section, "Ease-of-Management Issues," for more details).

If each page in your application has an entirely different method for getting to other pages, users are going to have a hard time getting around, which in turn will reduce the likelihood of your getting that second development contract. If, however, each page has navigational elements that are consistent both in their location, and in the paradigm they use (buttons, link, image maps, and so on), it won't ultimately matter how many pages there are in your application, because each time a user visits a new page, they will already understand how to get around.

### Navigation Planning

Of course, having a consistent navigational paradigm also requires some planning, since how you implement navigation is intertwined with how you set up the structure of your site. As with the flow charts described above, mapping out the structure of a large Web application can be pretty complex. The best strategy in this case, as with flow charts, is to break the application up into manageable chunks, based on functionality or other factors (again, a good example of this would be the customer and clerk interfaces of the Rent-A-Prize application, which would be treated as separate "chunks").

One thing to keep in mind at this point in the process is using your pages efficiently. In most ASP-based Web applications, you will likely have a large number of pages with HTML forms. If you choose to implement each form as an HTML page with a matching ASP page to process the form input, you are effectively doubling the number of pages in your application to be planned, created, and maintained. Another option is to make the pages self-submitting. By using a simple If...Then statement to check the value of the REQUEST_METHOD HTTP header string using *Request.ServerVariables* (*"REQUEST_METHOD"*). When the request method is *GET* (for example, when a user is browsing the page), you display the form. When the request method is a *POST*, you process the form input and return any necessary response. While this method necessitates extra code in each page, it can be a much more efficient use of your application. The code for such an page would look like this:

```
<%
If Request.ServerVariables("REQUEST_METHOD") = "GET" Then
   'Code to display HTML Form
ElseIf Request.ServerVariables("REQUEST_METHOD") = "POST" Then
   'Code to process form input and display results
End If
%>
```

Once you have things broken down into reasonable pieces, it's time once again to use storyboarding, or your trusty whiteboard, to sketch out graphically the relationship between your pages. Are there a few parent pages with many subordinate pages? Or do you find that there are a large number of pages of equal importance? The answers to these questions, which you will gain as you go through the process of sketching out the relationships, will help determine the method of navigation that will work best for your application.

Some navigation methods to consider include:

■ **Visual InterDev's PageNavBar DTCs** Here again is an area where Visual InterDev's built-in tools can save you time and aggravation. By simply dragging and dropping a VI PageNavBar DTC onto a page (or using Layouts) and creating a site diagram, you can set up navigation from page to page based on the pages' relationships in your site diagram. The advantage to this method is that when you change the relationships of the pages by changing the site diagram, the navigation bars created by the DTCs are automatically updated. For details on this method, see the Solutions, "Planning and Implementing Pages for Rent-A-Prize" and "Making Changes to Site Navigation for Rent-A-Prize."

■ **Custom headers and/or footers** You can use custom headers and/or footers to provide global navigation bars on your pages. To reduce the amount of code you have to write, these headers and footers could be implemented as include files. The advantage of this method is that it may offer more flexibility than using the DTCs. Unfortunately, this method may not be practical for sites with a large number of pages, or with a complex hierarchical structure.

NOTE: Another method of reducing the amount of code you need to write for headers and footers is to take advantage of the ability in Visual InterDev 6.0 to customize the Toolbox by adding your own code snippets. Simply open the HTML pane of the Toolbox (or whichever you wish to add your code to), highlight the section of code representing your header or footer, then drag and drop the code snippet into the Toolbox. Right-click the resulting entry and select Rename Item to give the entry a meaningful name. Now whenever you want to use that header, you merely position the cursor in your HTML or ASP page where you want the code and double-click the Toolbox entry (you can also drag and drop the code onto the page).

- **Custom tree control**   For sites with complex hierarchical structures (or if you're feeling ambitious) a custom tree control might be an ideal solution. Such a control might allow you to maintain a database table of the pages in your site, along with their relationships and their URLs. The control could then display a context-based listing of links, depending on which page the user was viewing. Although this method has the expense of added development time, it also has the substantial advantage that if you are planning numerous Web applications with similar structures, the control could be made highly reusable. Such a control would also provide navigational consistency within an application, as well as across multiple applications.

- **Frames-based navigation**   Another method of providing navigational consistency is to break the page up into several areas using HTML frames. By adding a header or footer or sidebar frame (or a combination), you can set up navigational links that do not change as the user moves from page to page within the content frame. This method can be attractive because of its flexibility, but often ends up being fairly complicated in execution. A frames-based method suffers from the same problem of headers and footers in that it is not very useful for sites with many pages or a complicated site structure. It also excludes any users whose browsers do not support frames.

Whether you choose one of the methods listed here, or come up with one of your own, you should remember that while ease-of-implementation and ease-of-use are important factors in planning your navigation, you also need to be able to easily maintain navigation in your application. And don't forget that the maintenance phase of an application is apt to be much longer than the development phase.

## Few Things Are More Annoying Than Broken Links

It's probably fair to say that aside from applications that cause GPFs, there are few things likely to annoy your users more than links in your application that return "404 – Not Found." Broken links, particularly when they result in obscure or unhelpful error messages, can be very frustrating to your users. Fortunately, with Visual InterDev 6.0 and Internet Information Server 4.0, you can attack this problem two ways, through automatic link repair, and by creating meaningful error messages.

## Automatic Link Repair

*Automatic link repair* is a feature of Visual InterDev 6.0 provided by the FrontPage extensions. Automatic link repair is enabled by default in all new Web projects. When you move or rename files in your project, automatic link repair changes links that refer to these files to reflect the changes you made. To enable or disable automatic link repair for a project, follow these steps:

1. Right-click the project name in the Project Explorer window, then select Properties.

2. In the General tab of the Project Properties dialog box, select the On or Off Link Repair radio button and click OK or Apply.

To specify how Visual InterDev handles link repair:

1. Select Tools | Options.

2. In the Options dialog box, expand the Projects node. Select the Web Projects subnode, which displays the Web Projects options.

3. Select the Link Repair option you prefer.

Once link repair is enabled, whenever you rename or move a file or folder, Visual InterDev will ask you whether or not to repair links to the moved or renamed files. This feature can save you a great deal of headaches, particularly in sites whose structure is constantly in flux.

## Using Custom Error Messages

Although in an ideal world, you would never have broken links, most of us are aware that there's no such thing as an ideal world. Therefore, it makes sense to prepare for those occasions when a user will run up against a broken link by customizing the error message they receive. Internet Information Server 4.0 allows you to customize HTTP error messages by Web site, virtual directory, directory, or file, so each application can have messages suited precisely to its needs. To configure a custom error message for your application, simply follow these steps:

1. Open the Internet Information Server Microsoft Management Console snap-in.

2. Locate the Web site or virtual directory for which you want to configure custom error messages, right-click it, and select Properties.

3. In the Properties dialog box, select the Custom Errors tab.

4. Locate the HTTP error you want to supply a custom error message for and highlight it (see Figure 6-4). Click the Edit Properties... button.

**Figure 6-4.**
*Selecting an HTTP Error for a custom message.*

5. In the Error Mapping Properties dialog box, enter the message type (default HTTP error string, file, or URL) and the location of the file or URL containing the custom error message.

Custom error messages are not only useful for pacifying the angry mobs that can result from broken links. You can also conceivably use them to allow your users to help maintain your application. By setting up your custom error file with a mailto: link to the application administrators, problems can be caught and fixed quickly, before your boss comes beating on your door. Figure 6-5 shows an example of what such a page might look like.

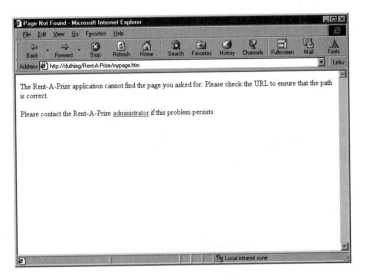

**Figure 6-5.**
*Providing a contact link for application errors.*

# Ease-of-Management Issues

Although ease-of-use is probably a more important concern for most applications, you should not overlook the issue of ease-of-management. *Ease-of-management* describes the effort required to keep your application running efficiently and to integrate new functionality into your application after it's been deployed.

## Designing Your Application with Maintainability in Mind

Like user interface and navigational consistency, ease-of-management and maintainability don't happen by accident, they happen through planning. One good place to start with this planning is Visual InterDev's Site Designer.

## Using Visual InterDev's Site Designer to Plan Your Site Structure

Site Designer, as discussed in Chapter 4, is a new tool for creating and maintaining the structure of your Web application's pages. Site Designer lets you define the structure of your application through the use of site diagrams. Site diagrams are graphical representations of the pages in your application and of the relationships between them. These relationships are then used by the Visual InterDev PageNavBar Design-Time Controls (DTCs) to define and update site navigation. Each site has a Global Navigation Bar that can be accessed through the PageNavBar DTCs. In a site diagram, you can:

- Create new ASP and HTML pages within your site

- Add existing pages to your site, either by menu or by drag-and-drop

- Create hierarchical relationships between pages in your application

- Expand or collapse branches of the trees that make up your site, allowing you to minimize onscreen clutter and focus in on the areas you're working on

- Add important pages to the Global Navigation Bar for your site

- Modify the order of the pages on the Global Navigation Bar

One great feature of site diagrams is that you can have more than one hierarchical tree per diagram, and you can have more than one diagram per application. One thing to remember, though, is that if you are using Site Designer to prototype a complex application, you should probably partition your content and store separate site diagrams for each partition.

**Figure 6-6.**
*Using folders to partition your application.*

## • • • SOLUTION: Planning and Implementing Pages for an Online Store

Let's say you want to build an online store called *MyOnlineStore* that you'll use to sell widgets and gizmos. You might choose to segment your application based on those categories, as shown in Figure 6-6. Having created separate folders in your project for widgets and gizmos, it's now relatively simple for you to manage the content for both sections of your application independently, by creating separate site diagrams for widgets and gizmos (see Figure 6-7) and keeping the diagrams and content for widgets and gizmos in the folders you created for them. This partitioning helps simplify the task of managing your application. It also allows for future expansion of your application to proceed more smoothly. Let's take a look at some of the steps involved.

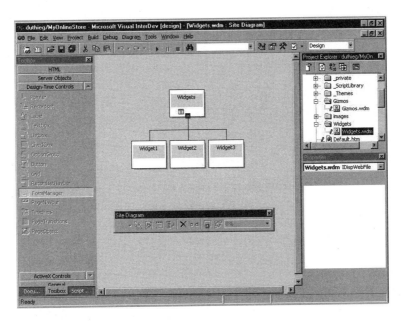

**Figure 6-7.**
*Using multiple site diagrams.*

## Adding Pages and Managing Links

Adding pages to the MyOnlineStore project is fairly simple. You've already created a site diagram for the project as a whole, called *MyOnlineStore.wdm*, to which you'll want to add your home page. You might decide later to add other pages, such as a full-site search page, to this diagram, but for now all you need is the home page, with links to the Widgets and Gizmos sections of your site. The links, as shown in Figure 6-8, are implemented by applying a layout to the home page in MyOnlineStore.wdm.

**Figure 6-8.**
*Links implemented with Visual InterDev Layouts.*

You add the links with the following steps:

1. With MYONLINESTORE.WDM open in Site Designer, right-click anywhere in the Site Designer window and select Add Home Page. You can also add a home page to a site diagram with the corresponding button on the Site Diagram toolbar.

2. Right-click the home page and select Apply Theme and Layout... from the pop-up menu (see Figure 6-9).

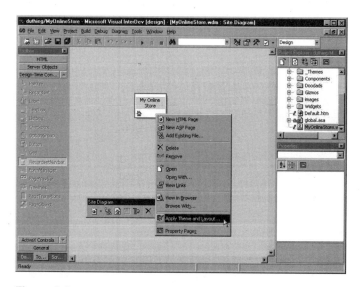

**Figure 6-9.**
*Applying a Layout using the Site Designer.*

3. In the Layout tab of the Apply Theme and Layout dialog box, select the Apply Layout and Theme radio button, choose a layout, then click OK.

For this example, we chose the Top and Bottom 4 layout, which provides a banner at the top of the page, and a global navigation bar at the bottom of the page. Note that the appearance of the global navigation bar links will depend on whether or not you've applied a theme to the page on which the global navigation bar is displayed. This is also true of other links provided by the PageNavBar DTCs. You can change the default appearance of these links by using the property page for the PageNavBar DTC you want to change.

Once you've got a home page for the MyOnlineStore application set up, you'll need to connect it to the widget and gizmo areas in order for the links to appear so that customers can browse and purchase widgets and gizmos. To make this possible, we'll add parent pages to the widgets and gizmos site diagrams, then add those pages to the global navigation bar using the following steps:

1. With the WIDGETS.WDM diagram open in Site Designer, use the Site Designer toolbar to add a new HTML page. Change the page's title in the site diagram to *Widgets*.

2. On the Site Designer toolbar, click the Add to Global Navigation Bar button (this button is also used to remove pages from the Global Navigation Bar). The page will now display the icon shown in Figure 6-10.

**Figure 6-10.**
*Site diagram page with global navigation bar icon.*

3. Save the site diagram. When a site diagram is saved, all of the pages created within that diagram are actually created in the project.

4. Repeat the process for the gizmos site diagram.

Note that even though your site diagram may be in a separate folder in your project, any pages created in that site diagram will be stored initially in the root of the project, which means that you'll need to move the widget and gizmo pages into the folders created for them. This also requires releasing the working copy of these files. While this process is somewhat less than intuitive, and a bit inconvenient, Visual InterDev's automatic link repair does make it incredibly simple to update all of the associated links. So simple, in fact, that all you have to do is confirm that you want the links modified to reflect the pages' new location (see Figure 6-11).

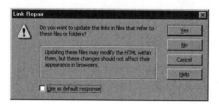

**Figure 6-11.**
*Link repair dialog box.*

Now we have a working structure for the MyOnlineStore application. We can navigate from the store's home page to the main page for both widgets and gizmos, even though those pages don't yet contain any content. Setting up navigation for the widget and gizmo sites is just as simple. Just keep in mind that the parent/child and sibling relationships displayed in the site diagrams are what determines the links presented by the PageNavBar DTCs and layouts (how the links are displayed will depend on the type of layout you choose). In the next solution, well see how the structure we set up with the help of the Visual InterDev Site Designer will make extending and maintaining MyOnlineStore much easier.

## Using Site Designer to Maintain Content and Navigation

### • • • SOLUTION: Extending and Making Changes to Site Navigation for MyOnlineStore

So your online store is up and running and the widgets and gizmos are selling like hotcakes. But you've decided that widgets and gizmos aren't enough to ensure the success of your store, you need to start selling some doodads. As many businesses have discovered, you've got to grow to survive, much less to succeed. The trick in this case is for the growth to be controlled and organized, so that your application doesn't get out of hand.

In addition to extending your application with a site for doodads, you've received feedback from your customers that they'd like to be able to browse all of the items in each category without having to go through the main page for the category each time they move from one item to another. This will require modifying the navigation for the page for each item so that each one contains a link to the next and/or previous item, as well as to the main page for that category.

## Extending a Site with the Site Designer

First, let's tackle adding an area to your site for selling doodads. This process will be relatively easy, since we designed the application with this type of expansion in mind by partitioning the application with a separate folder for each category of product we decide to sell. To add a new category, follow these simple steps:

1. Add a new folder in the project Explorer window named DOODADS by right-clicking the project, selecting New Folder..., and entering the appropriate information in the New Folder dialog box.

2. Add a new site diagram to the Doodads folder by right-clicking the folder and selecting Add | Site Diagram.... Name the file *Doodads.wdm.*

3. With the DOODADS.WDM site diagram open in Site Designer, add a new HTML page to the diagram. Change its title in the diagram to *Doodads,* and use the Add to Global Navigation Bar button to set the page up for navigation. The button works as a toggle. Click it once to add the page to the Global Navigation Bar, click it a second time to remove it.

4. Save the site diagram. This will create the file DOODADS.HTM in the project root. Release the working copy of the HTML file, rename it as *Doodadshome.htm,* and move it to the DOODADS folder. Now the page is accessible from the store's home page, as shown in Figure 6-12.

**Figure 6-12.**
*MyOnlineStore home page with link to doodads page.*

5. Add child pages to the site diagram for each doodad you want
   to sell.

Remember that you can add pages to your site diagram either by using
the Site Designer to create new pages, or by adding existing pages to the diagram.
Adding existing pages can be done with menu commands or by drag-and-drop.
Remember also that when you use the Site Designer to create new pages, you
must save the diagram before the pages are actually created.

## Modifying Site Navigation with Site Designer

Our other task, modifying the navigation for our item pages, turns out to be
just as easy thanks to Visual InterDev 6.0 Layouts, as well as a feature left over
from Visual InterDev 1.0, templates. We'll use a four-part process: creating a
template for each category, creating a file from that template, adding it to the
site diagram, and adding the appropriate layout.

## Creating a Template

Creating a template for the individual category items is a simple process. You can even use an existing item as the basis for creating the template. Just follow these steps:

1. Open an existing widget page in the Visual InterDev editor.

2. Replace all existing data specific to a particular widget with place-holder text, such as $XX.XX for dollar amounts (see Figure 6-13). You can also use special tags to add replaceable parameters as described in the section, "Replaceable Parameters."

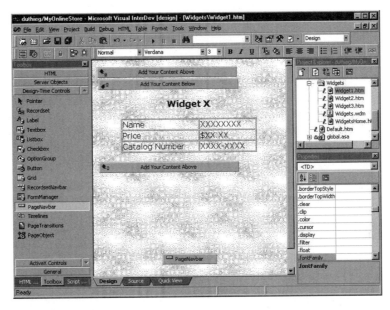

**Figure 6-13.**
*Replacement text for a widget template.*

3. Select Save...As... from the File menu. Browse to the Templates folder of the folder where you have Visual InterDev installed. Save the file as *Widget.htm* in the Web Project Items folder (which will cause the template to be displayed when you use the Add Item button). You can also add templates to the NewFileItems folder, which will cause the template to be displayed when you select File | New File....

4. In order for the new items to appear properly in the Add Item dialog box (or the New File dialog box), you also need to add entries for your templates to the VSDIR file for the corresponding template folder (NEWWEBITEMS.VSDIR or NEWFILEITEMS.VSDIR). The VSDIR file provides information about your template to the dialog boxes. Each line of the VSDIR file represents one template, and consists of a series of fields delimited by the pipe ( | ) character. These fields are described in Table 6-1, in the order in which they appear. Open the NEWWEBITEMS.VSDIR file by selecting File | Open File... and browsing to the appropriate folder.

5. Parameter fields for a VSDIR file. The easiest way to add an item is to copy one of the existing lines and modify it. Copy the last line (which begins with NEW SITE DIAGRAM.WDM) to the Clipboard, then paste it in the next available line.

6. Change the first field to *Widget.htm* (*Widget.vsz* if you're using the Template Wizard), leave the second field as is (change to {0} if you're using the Template Wizard), change the third field to a text label to be displayed with the icon for the template, change the fourth field to a number according to where in the sort order you want the template displayed, change the fifth field to a text description of the template action, leave the sixth field as is (if you wanted to use different icons, you could change this field to point to a different DLL, EXE, or ClassID), change the seventh field to the number of the icon for the file type of your template (HTML files are 296, ASP files are 294), leave the eighth field as is (enabled), and change the ninth field to a text string for the default file name of your template. Save the NEWWEBITEMS.VSDIR file.

7. Close and re-open Visual InterDev. This will allow you to access the new template.

8. Repeat the process for each category for which you want to create a template.

| Field Name | Purpose |
|---|---|
| RelPathName | Specifies the name of the template file or VSZ file (if any). A VSZ file is not needed unless you are using replaceable parameters (see "Replaceable Parameters" below). |
| {clsidPackage} | Specifies a Class ID of a DLL containing localized resources for your template. Optional. |
| LocalizedName | Specifies the name of the template displayed by the Add Item dialog—can be a string or a resource identifier of the form: "#ResID." Optional. |
| SortPriority | Specifies the sort order of the templates, lower numbered templates will be displayed first. Number by tens (for example, 10, 20, 30, and so on) to allow for new templates to be added without renumbering. |
| Description | Specifies the description of the template displayed by the Add Item dialog box—can be a string or a resource identifier of the form: "#ResID." |
| DLLPath or {clsidPackage} | Specifies a DLL or EXE containing icon resources for use with the template. Use either the full path, or a ClassID pointing to the desired DLL or EXE file. |
| IconResourceId | Specifies the number of the icon to display. If this entry is omitted, the default icon for a file with the same extension as the item will be used. Optional. |
| Flags | Specifies whether to disable or enable the Name and Location fields of the Add Item dialog box. The following values are valid:<br><br>Space (" "): enabled<br>8192: disabled |
| SuggestedBaseName | Specifies the default name for the template—either a string or a resource identifier of the form: "#ResID." This default name is displayed in the name field in the dialog box. |

**Table 6-1.**
*Parameter fields for VSDIR file.*

## Replaceable Parameters

As in Visual InterDev 1.0, it is possible in Visual InterDev 6.0 to put placeholders in your templates (delimited by <%# and #%> tags) that query the user for specific replacement values to be used in the file based on the template. In order to use this functionality you must, in addition to creating a template file, create a VSZ file (which invokes the Visual InterDev Template Wizard) with the same name as the template. This file should contain the following lines for use with the Template Wizard:

```
VSWizard 6.0

Wizard=VIWizard.CTemplatePageWizard

Param=<Path to the location of the template>
```

Replace <Path to the location of the template> with the full path where your template is stored. For this process to work most efficiently, store the VSZ file(s) in the template folder (for example, Web Project Items) and store your template(s) (for example, WIDGET.HTM) in a separate folder that is referenced by the VSZ file's path parameter. Remember that when you are using replaceable parameters with the Template Wizard, the VSDIR parameters need to be modified as described above.

## Using Templates and Adding Layouts

Using the templates you've created is even easier:

1. Highlight the WIDGETS folder, so that your new file will be created there.

2. Click the Add Item button or select File | New File to bring up the Add Item (see Figure 6-14) or New File dialog box, depending on where you chose to save your template.

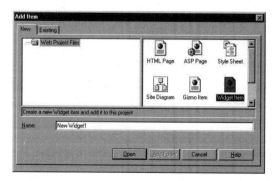

**Figure 6-14.**
*The Add Item dialog box.*

3. Select the WIDGET.HTM template from the Add Item dialog box. Note that the default filename is WIDGETX.HTM, where *X* is the first available unique number (for example, if your project already contained a file named WIDGET1.HTM, the default file name would be WIDGET2.HTM). Click the Open button.

4. Replace the placeholder text with the specific text for the new widget and save the new file. Note that if your template uses replaceable parameters, you will be prompted for the appropriate values when you create a new file based on the template (see Figure 6-15).

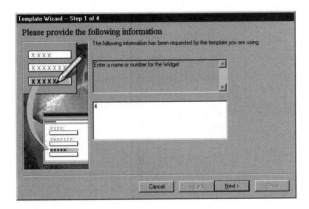

**Figure 6-15.**
*The Visual InterDev Template Wizard.*

## Adding the New Page to Navigation

The last thing we need to do with the new widget is to integrate it into our navigation. This requires the following steps:

1. Open the site diagram for the Widgets category in Site Designer.

2. Drag the new widget page we just created into the site diagram. Drop it so that it has a sibling relationship with the existing widget items (all the widget items should have the same parent) as shown in Figure 6-16.

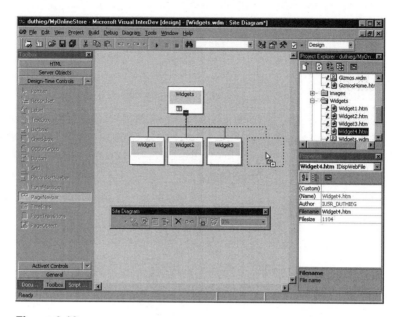

**Figure 6-16.**
*Dragging and dropping a new file into a site diagram.*

We've now added a new item to our widgets area. If you were to open this page in your browser, it would look something like Figure 6-17.

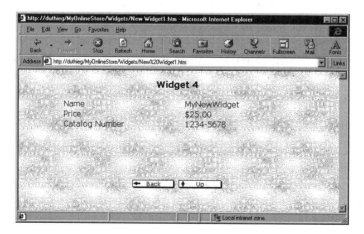

**Figure 6-17.**
*New widget page.*

This example is somewhat simple, but it demonstrates some of the techniques you can use to plan your site, as well as the powerful tools Visual InterDev 6.0 offers to help you manage and maintain your applications.

## Managing and Maintaining Larger Applications

The strategies described in previous sections also apply to larger applications that make use of databases and components. Partitioning of your application can include maintaining a special folder or folders for the components you use. Doing so ensures that when you need to find a specific component, you won't have to waste time searching for it. You can add components to your project by simply dragging and dropping them into the folder you've created for them. Another major advantage of storing and managing your components from your Visual InterDev project is that Visual InterDev can automatically register your components for you, using the property page for the component as shown in Figure 6-18.

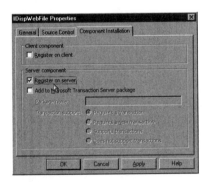

**Figure 6-18.**
*Setting up a component for automatic registration.*

Setting up a site like MyOnlineStore to get database access to widget, gizmo, and doodad data is beyond the scope of this chapter, but it would be relatively simple to use the data-bound DTCs to set up a page that gets most or all of its item-specific data, including field labels, from a database. Once having created such a page, you could then use it as a template for each new category of items added to the site. For more information, see Chapter 11, "RAD Database Development and Data Access."

The moral here is that whether the application you're developing is small or large, don't make the mistake of simply planning for today. Think about your application's future needs, and make development choices that will help support those needs.

# Summary

In this chapter, we've discussed the need for consistency in user interface and navigation for your applications. We've also described some of the planning techniques you can use to make this consistency possible, including:

- Use-case analysis
- Storyboarding
- Flow charts

We've also looked at some of the tools Visual InterDev provides to deal with the challenges of creating and maintaining consistent sites. These include:

- Site Designer
- Themes and Custom Themes
- Layouts
- Templates

These and other features of Visual InterDev 6.0 make it an ideal tool for the creation of consistent applications that are both easy to use and easy to maintain. For the first time, creating and maintaining a robust Web application does not have to be an arduous process.

In the next chapter, we'll begin our discussion of business tier challenges with a look at performance and scalability. Some of the issues we'll discuss include:

- Using the Enterprise Application Model to plan your architecture
- Using Active Server Pages (ASP) properly
- Making design choices that support scalability

The coverage of these and other issues will help prepare you for the choices you'll need to make to design and develop robust, scalable Web applications.

# PART III

# SOLVING BUSINESS TIER CHALLENGES

## CHAPTER SEVEN

# Addressing Performance and Scalability

• • •   **GOAL: To Improve the Performance and Scalability of the Rent-A-Prize Application, and Minimize Application Downtime Due to Component Upgrades**

*Performance* and *Scalability*. They're buzzwords that developers hear a lot these days. Everybody wants great performance, and everybody wants their applications to be scalable. So what does that mean? How many managers and developers can actually define performance and scalability objectively?

Performance may mean something very different to a developer of an application than what it means to the application's users, while the project's stakeholders may have a third perspective. A generic definition of *scalability* is that scalability is that property that allows your application to continue to provide acceptable performance as the number of users increases. This, of course, brings us back to how we define performance. This could become circular rather quickly. To be able to both provide performance and scalability, it's important to explicitly define benchmarks that the application is expected to meet. For a Web application, this can be expressed as an expected response time less than or equal to $X$, given $Y$ concurrent users. When the benchmark is met, we can confidently say that the application is performing acceptably and is scalable to the expected number of users.

In this chapter, we'll take a detailed look at the issue of performance and scalability in Web applications, and the ways to go about improving both. These include application architecture, using Active Server Pages (ASP) properly, using components for business logic, and using Microsoft Transaction Server (MTS). We'll also briefly discuss the issues of component maintenance and running applications in isolated process mode.

# Architecture, Architecture, Architecture

For those few of you who haven't heard it, the saying in real estate goes, "The three secrets of real estate are location, location, location." In a similar fashion, architecture is one of the most important factors in application performance and scalability. In most commercial and client-server applications, designing the application's architecture is one of the first steps in the development process. Often in Web application development, this step is skipped entirely, or is not given the same focus it receives in traditional life-cycle development. This probably stems from the fact that many Web applications are extensions of existing Web sites. While extending an intranet or Internet Web site with additional functionality may seem logical and may work fine for sites with few visitors or simple functionality, such a path can be disastrous for high-volume sites. When the architecture is lacking, any substantial growth in number of users or additional functionality can strain Web servers and databases to the breaking point.

Let's take as an example a company that sells amusements such as video games, pinball machines, and jukeboxes. Some time ago, this company had a Web site put together to allow customers and potential customers to view their available products and to find out a little more about the company. This initial Web site was all static content, and when new products were added, the Web site was manually updated to reflect the new offerings. Later, someone at the company decided that it would be a great idea for customers to be able to find the nearest distributor or salesman for their products right from the Web site. The number of distributors was too large to list statically without making the user scroll through a very long page, so the decision was made to give users the option of picking a distributor or salesman from list boxes or using a simple search engine to find the nearest distributor or salesman. Because of the limited scope of the data, the current number of hits the site was receiving, and financial considerations, the development team decided to implement this functionality with a Microsoft Access database. While this may have seemed like a logical decision at the time, it failed to take into account the fact that adding this functionality could potentially increase site traffic substantially. Then when site traffic increases, it may be decided that more functionality, such as online ordering, needs to be added. At this point, the company may discover that their initial architecture cannot support the functionality that they want, and that the site needs to be redesigned from the ground up. In many cases, this means greater expense and the potential for downtime at a critical point in the site's (and the company's) growth.

So the obvious answer is to put sufficient time and resources into designing the application's architecture. As we've discussed in earlier chapters, *architecture* can refer to the design of the hardware used to support the application, the software tools used to create the application, the structure of the application, and the components that comprise it. The decisions that make up the overall framework of the application can be incredibly complex, especially in enterprise applications. Fortunately, in addition to providing robust tools in Visual InterDev 6.0 for creating enterprise applications, Microsoft has also come up with a model for simplifying enterprise application design called, appropriately enough, the Enterprise Application Model, which we introduced in Chapter 2, "Defining the Web Application Environment."

## The Enterprise Application Model

The Enterprise Application Model is a conceptual design tool that abstracts the complexity of the decision-making process into six submodels. By separating the myriad number of requirements and decisions into distinct areas and using a graphical representation of the relationships between submodels, the potentially overwhelming array of choices can be reduced to manageable proportions.

The Enterprise Application Model is made up of the following submodels:

- **Business Model** The business model describes the budgetary requirements of the application, the security and robustness required of the application, as well as the application's delivery requirements. The business model is not limited to the business rules that will be implemented in the application, although it includes them to a degree.

- **User Model** The user model describes the qualities of the application's end users. These include the expected skill level of users, the amount of documentation the application will require, the ease of use necessary to satisfy the targeted users, and the hardware the users can or will be expected to have in order to run the application.

- **Logical Model** The logical model describes the entities, such as orders and customers, with which the application deals, and the rules and policies that are applied to them. The logical model is made up of two submodels, the logical data submodel and the logical object submodel. The logical data submodel describes the data entities used by the application, while the logical object submodel describes the implementation of the business rules and algorithms that act on those entities (i.e., how they are grouped together as properties and methods of specific class objects).

- **Technology Model**  The technology model describes the technologies that will support the application. This includes operating systems, browser types supported, network protocols used, and the tools used to create the application, to name a few. The technology model deals with deciding how to implement certain features given the technological limitations under which most applications must operate.

- **Physical Model**  The physical model describes the resources such as servers, networks, databases, operating system services, and third-party resources, and how these resources will be used to fulfill the requirements of the application. In conjunction with the other models the physical model can be used to help decide where certain parts of the application, such as *components* or *databases*, should be implemented.

- **Development Model**  The development model describes such details as the order in which tasks of the various submodels should be done, the size and makeup of the development team, how the application should be deployed, and how the application should be maintained and managed. The development model is made up of two submodels, the process submodel and the role submodel. The process submodel deals with issues related to planning and scheduling, while the role submodel deals with issues of organizing and managing development teams.

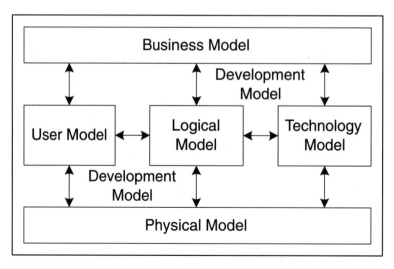

**Figure 7-1.**
*The Enterprise Application Model.*

The overall purpose of the Enterprise Application Model and its graphical representation of the six submodels is to act as a template both for new projects and for redesign of existing applications. In the case of new applications a developer is best served by using the model from the top down, since business requirements tend to be the most important driving force in the development of the application. On a project in which a Web application is being redesigned, it might make more sense to start with one of the other submodels, for example if requirements were driven by a certain set of existing hardware that cannot currently (for whatever reason) be replaced.

For the purposes of this chapter, the most important thing to remember about the Enterprise Application Model is its ability to assist developers in understanding and modeling how the effects of decisions and requirements for one submodel can affect each of the other submodels. This level of understanding can also make it easier for developers to predict potential bottlenecks and failure points in the overall architecture before they become problems. Whether or not you choose to use the Enterprise Application Model, it's very important to the performance, scalability, and robustness of your application that you take the time to create a viable architecture, and that you consider carefully the effects, both immediate and long-term, of changes to the application on that architecture. For an in-depth treatment of the use of the Enterprise Application Model see the Enterprise Application Model topic in the Visual Studio 6.0 documentation.

## Visual Modeler

Another tool available to assist in planning your application is Visual Modeler, which ships with Visual Studio 6.0 and Visual Basic 6.0. Visual Modeler is based on Rational Rose, a popular application modeling tool, and allows you to graphically plan out your application. You place objects representing business objects, such as *user classes*, *business classes*, and *data classes*, on a whiteboard representing the three-tier architecture, as shown in Figure 7-2. You can then add properties and methods to these objects and map relationships between them. This allows you to visualize the interaction between your user interface and business logic components. In addition, Visual Modeler can also generate framework Visual Basic code for you, which can simplify the implementation of your components. Visual Modeler can be a powerful tool for abstracting the required functionality of your application in a way that makes it easier to make decisions about how that functionality will be implemented.

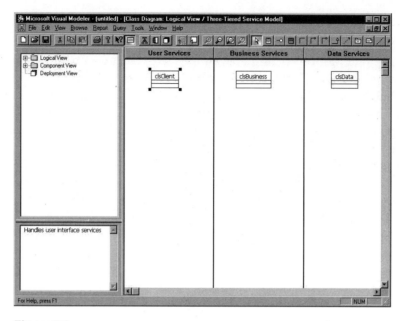

**Figure 7-2.**
*Adding classes in Visual Modeler.*

For smaller projects, using Visual Modeler alone may be sufficient to plan and implement an efficient and effective architecture. On larger projects, however, it is advisable to combine the visualization available with Visual Modeler with the abstraction of the Enterprise Application Model. This will increase the likelihood of your team developing an architecture that will stand up to the necessary strain, as well as reducing the amount of effort it takes to develop it.

## Architectural Choices That Support Scalability

Every architectural choice made during the design process affects performance and scalability to one degree or another. Some of these decisions choices will have a greater impact than others. We'll focus on these in order to get the most out of an application. Following are some of the architectural choices that have a relatively large impact on how our application scales.

### Choose the Appropriate Hardware to Support Your Application

There are a lot of Web applications being written on hardware that the application is destined to outgrow. It may seem like a bit of a no-brainer to have adequate hardware support for an application, but there are a lot of misunderstandings and misconceptions about this issue. For example, some Web applications may be running or being designed to run on a server that is used to run the Web Server software, the components used by the application, and the DBMS that the application uses to store and manage its data. In addition, in many cases these servers may have multiple Web applications running on them. In a situation where a single server is running the entire application (except for the UI), as well as housing the database, it would be surprising for one application on the server to scale well, not to mention multiple applications. While the three-tier architecture does not *require* a different machine for each tier, you can bet that implementing the architecture that way will lead to better scalability. It is especially important to separate the database from the Web server, as both can be quite demanding of resources and both are likely to experience peaks at the same times in a data-driven Web application.

Though it may seem obvious, it's also important to be sure that your application does not become processor or I/O bound by periodically monitoring your servers with Windows NT's Performance Monitor, or having Performance Monitor generate logs for you. If you notice that the CPU utilization is consistently high, it may indicate that you could benefit from extra processors. If the Disk I/O counters are reading high, you should check the IIS counters for cache hits or cache hits percent. If these counters are low, your server could probably benefit from more RAM, which would increase the size of the cache IIS can use. In general, cache hits or misses affect static content the most, while dynamic content, such as ISAPI and ASP, will take a greater toll on the processor, and are most likely to benefit from multiple processors.

## Choose to Move Work to the Client Where Feasible

It's important to always keep in mind that the main limitation to scaling in a Web application is always going to be the resources of the server. Since those resources are hardly infinite, we must use them as wisely as possible. Given that client machines are continually getting more powerful and are certainly more plentiful, it makes sense to make the client share some of the load. "But wait," you say, "if my users are coming in from the Internet, how do I know whether their machines can handle the work I am asking them to do?" Well, the answer is that sometimes you don't. One of the less fortunate aspects of developing Web applications that are accessible from the Internet is that you may have to design for the ultimate in thin clients, a generic browser (or browsers). That said, there are certainly plenty of options that can allow you to make the most of what you can find out about your clients.

First, you can use a process called *sniffing* to determine the browser that your client is running, which will tell you something about its capabilities. Sniffing is the process of interrogating the *USER_AGENT* string from the HTTP request headers sent by the browser, which includes the product name and version of the browser, and may also contain other information about that browser. You can also use sniffing to determine (to some extent) the processor architecture of the client, which, for example, can help you determine whether the client can use ActiveX controls. The Browser Capabilities component supplied with ASP can make sniffing even easier, as mentioned in Chapter 5, "Features vs. Reach-Cross-Platform Support."

Once you've determined the browser that the client is running, and perhaps even the type of machine (x86, Mac, or UNIX) they are running on, you can choose to push as much work to the client as the client will support. This can range from relatively simple client-side JavaScript/JScript validation code for data entry to ActiveX controls or Java applets that can provide a richer UI or even supply some of the application's business logic. The downside to this approach of course is that it means writing and maintaining multiple versions of pages and/or scripts for different browsers and processors, but the ability to move work to capable clients can help make up for a substantial number of less-capable clients.

In situations where your Web application will only be accessible to an Intranet community, or to a members-only subset of the Internet, you may be able to make some demands about the client software and hardware required to work with your application. For example, if you require your clients to run Internet Explorer 4 as their browser, you opens up many opportunities for both enriching the UI and moving work to the client, including the use of ActiveX controls (assuming an x86 processor), DHTML, and data binding. You can also make some reasonable assumptions about the processing power of machines that are running Internet Explorer 4. Whether you have control over the desktop, or must use sniffing or the Browser Capabilities component to determine client capabilities at runtime, the important thing to remember is that every job your server doesn't have to do leaves it available for one more job that it does.

### Choose to Implement Coding Standards

Though the connection to architecture may not seem obvious at first, the importance of committing to a set of coding standards cannot be overstated. In addition to making code easier to maintain, which is especially important in sites that use a substantial amount of scripting code or a large number of components, coding standards make it easier to develop your applications quickly and consistently. Most important from the standpoint of performance and scalability, the more consistent your code is, the easier it will likely be to track down performance bottlenecks. Coding standards allow you to see more easily the big picture, since you won't be spending all of your time trying to figure out what each section of code is doing, and how it relates to other parts of the application.

Implementing coding standards for your project can be as simple as making available to all developers on the project a document that describes standards for variable naming, code formatting (including the use of indents, and their required width, as well as the use of white space), and standards for commenting code. The use of consistent, clear commenting is among the most important practices for ensuring code maintainability. The code sample below illustrates some of these practices.

Another important step in the same vein as using coding standards is including the *Option Explicit* statement in any page using VBScript. The *Option Explicit* statement should immediately follow the @LANGUAGE directive, as follows:

```
<@ LANGUAGE=VBScript %>
<%
' Require all variables to be declared explicitly using Dim
Option Explicit
%>
<HTML>
<HEAD>
<TITLE>Coding Standards Example</TITLE>
</HEAD>
<BODY>
<H1>Coding Standards</H1>
<%
' Variable declaration is required by Option Explicit
' Prefacing variable names with type information (as in Hungarian
' notation) can make the purpose of variables much clearer
Dim strMyText
'Without sufficient white space, code can be difficult to read
strMyText = "Hello World!"
Response.Write strMyText
%>
</BODY>
</HTML>
```

*Option Explicit* operates the same way in VBScript as it does in Visual Basic, in that it requires that any variables used in your code be declared explicitly using the *Dim* statement. Even though VBScript uses only *Variant* variables, *Option Explicit* can still save you a great deal of debugging time by alerting you to misspellings and other problems that might not be obvious without explicit variable declaration. While this may not translate directly to an improvement in performance, it will certainly save you time, time that can then be devoted to improving the performance of your application.

## Choose to Limit the Use of ASP Include Files

One of the bad habits encouraged in the first version of ASP was the inefficient use of Include files. *Include* files can be very powerful because they allow the reuse of code in ASP by loading the code of the Include inline with your ASP page before it is executed. If you need to create the same header on each page, easy, just slap the code in an Include, and include it on every page. One important advantage of this is that it allows you to update that header simply by changing the code in one place, rather than on every page where the header is used. Unfortunately, in the rush to use Includes, many developers may put more code than is necessary in their Includes, such as creating an Include file full of utility functions, many of which are used infrequently at best. Such an Include provides a convenient way of accessing a library of functions. The problem with this, however, is that each line of code in an Include that is not called on a given page is a waste of resources, a waste that is multiplied by the number of pages in which the code is never used. For this reason, it is wise to limit the use of Includes to situations in which they will substantially improve efficiency, and to keep Includes as lean and mean as possible. Only put code in an Include that will (or may) be used every time you use the Include.

Another use of Includes that was more problematic was the use of Include files to provide named constants for components and their methods. A prime example of this is the files ADOVBS.INC, and its JScript companion ADOJAVAS.INC, supplied with ADO. By including one of these files (which file depends on which scripting language you choose to use), you are able to use ADO objects and their methods using named arguments, which makes for more readable and easily maintainable code. Unfortunately, this convenience comes at a cost. Even if you only use one named constant on your ASP page, the inclusion of ADOVBS.INC means that ASP must interpret and load into memory the entire file, which may be many times longer than your entire ASP page. When dealing with large numbers of users, this can cause a dramatic slowdown. Fortunately, in IIS 4.0, there is a better way.

IIS 4.0 allows the use of *type libraries* from ASP. To use the type library for ADO 1.5, you use the <METADATA> tag in your application's GLOBAL.ASA file as follows:

```
<!--METADATA TYPE="typelib" FILE="c:\program files\common
files\system\ado\msado15.dll -->
```

You are then able to use the constants in the type library as named arguments for method calls to ADO from any page in the application associated with the GLOBAL.ASA file. This use of type libraries has the advantage of reducing the performance overhead required to use named constants with components like ADO. It also has the advantage of making the components easier to upgrade. Since you are accessing the type library from one place for your entire application, if you upgrade the component of that type library, you only have one place where you need to change the code that references the type library. Using Includes, you would need to update every single page that used the Include file, assuming that the component continued to support the use of Includes at all. The best part about using type libraries in your Web applications is that with Visual InterDev 6.0, all it takes is two simple steps:

1. In an open Visual InterDev solution, select Project | Project References...

2. In the References dialog box, select the type library you wish to have access to from the list, or use the Browse... button to find the type library (or DLL containing a type library), then click OK. It's really that simple. VI then takes care of adding the reference to your GLOBAL.ASA file, and you're ready to go.

## Choose to Move ASP Code Into COM Components

One of the easiest ways to substantially improve the performance and scalability of your Web application is to move as much code as possible into components. While it may be tempting to write applications solely using ASP code, for reasons ranging from your available developer resources to desiring to avoid having to frequently recompile components as they are developed, this is generally not a wise practice. While ASP does a pretty good job of handling multiple users, the mere fact that ASP code has to be loaded and interpreted at runtime can substantially reduce your application's ability to scale. Because components are precompiled, their performance is many times faster than equivalent scripting code. In addition, by using components, we are also able to take advantage of the services of Microsoft Transaction Server, which include object, thread, and database connection management. We will discuss these concepts in-depth in the sections "Moving Business Logic and Data Access into Components," "Using Microsoft Transaction Server for Object and Resource Pooling," and "Component Maintenance."

# Proper Use of ASP

One of the problems that can plague a Web application as it grows is that of improper use of Active Server Pages. Often, a Web application is designed and developed to support a nominal set of users, then must be expanded to support more users at a later time. The difficulty here is that coding practices in Active Server Pages scripts that have negligible effect on an application with few users can rapidly destroy the performance of an application as it scales up to more users. Even in new ASP development there are a number of common misconceptions that can lead to poor application performance. This section addresses some common problems with the use of ASP in applications.

## Using ASP Objects

For both those who have never used ASP, and occasionally for those who use it regularly, the use of ASP's intrinsic objects can be cause for confusion. Certain uses that seem natural from a common-sense approach can have negative effects on performance and scalability. In other cases, there are more efficient ways of using ASP objects that are neither obvious, nor particularly well-documented. In this section, we'll try to cover a number of both of these cases.

### Application Object

The ASP Application object provides relatively few methods compared to other ASP objects but is very powerful in that it allows you to share information between users of your application. One of the first things many developers may try to do with the ASP application object is to implement a *page hit counter*. A simple way to do this is to create an application variable that stores the number of hits to that site. The variable could be updated by placing code to increment the application variable in the *Session_OnStart* event of GLOBAL.ASA. But what happens when two users hit your site at the same time? Can you be sure that the counter will be updated as expected? One way to be absolutely certain is to use the *Lock* method of the application object to prevent others from changing any application variables until you're finished updating the counter variable. Since only one session can lock the application at any given time, this solves the problem of simultaneous attempts to update application variables. Unfortunately, this method may create an additional problem. When your site is experiencing a high volume of traffic, you may find that requests are beginning to be queued. Why? Because by locking the application to reliably update your page counter variable, we have effectively prevented any other users from changing the variable until the application object has been unlocked (see Figure 7-3). In addition, if you've implemented any other application variables, users attempting to change those variables will be denied as well. The greater the number of application variables used, and the longer it takes to update them, and the more vulnerable our application is to queueing problems under heavy loads. To avoid these problems, it's a good idea to minimize the use of application variables, and to ensure that where they are used the amount of time that the application is locked is kept to an absolute minimum.

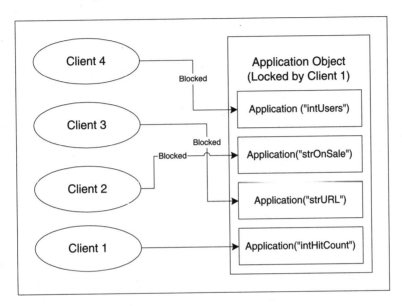

**Figure 7-3.**
*Processes blocked by application locking.*

## Session Object

The ASP Session object is similar to the application object in that one of the things that you can do with it is share information, in this case between multiple pages accessed by the same user. This is accomplished by storing information as variables within the Session object as follows:

```
<%Session("UserName") = "John Smith"%>
```

You may also create instances of components and store them in the Session object. This practice, however, can be problematic depending on the threading model of the component, as discussed below in "Using Application and Session Variables for Storing and Sharing Objects."

The Session object is also important in managing user's sessions in your application. When a user browses to a page within your application for the first time, and your application uses the *Session_OnStart* event in its GLOBAL.ASA file, ASP creates a session for that user, which is identified by a unique SessionID. The *SessionID* is a property of the session object. By using the SessionID you can keep track of users in your application, including which pages they access and other information. If your users are required to log in, you can also apply any information you track to the specific user, rather than to the more generic SessionID. More important for purposes of improving the scalability of your application is the ability to terminate a user's session, provided by the *Session.Abandon* method and the *Session.Timeout* property.

> NOTE: A session can also be started in two other ways: 1) If a user requests a page in which the GLOBAL.ASA file uses the <OBJECT> tag to create an instance of a component with session scope, or 2) If a user stores a value in the session object. Neither of these methods require the GLOBAL.ASA file to use the *Session_OnStart* event.

The *Session.Abandon* method immediately terminates the session of the user calling it, freeing up resources being used by that session, including variables and components with session scope. The ability to terminate sessions is important because it allows you to build into your application the ability for a user to log out of the application when they are finished, conserving resources on the server that otherwise would remain in use until the session timed out. A logout feature can also help in securing your application against unauthorized use, assuming of course that users are required to log in the first place. Implementing a logout feature can be as simple as providing a hyperlink to a page with the following code:

```
<%@LANGUAGE="VBSCRIPT">

<HTML>

<HEAD>

<TITLE>Logout Page</TITLE>

<%
' Destroy user's session and release resources
Session.Abandon


'You can also send the user to another page, such as the start page.
Response.Redirect "default.asp"

%>

</HEAD>
```

*(continued)*

```
<BODY>
<H1>Logging Out... Please Wait</H1>
</BODY>
</HTML>
```

The *Session.Timeout* property, which is set by default to 20 minutes, determines the amount of time ASP will wait for a request from the user before terminating his or her session. This can help alleviate one of the biggest potential problems in browser-based applications, which is users walking away from their computer while in the middle of your application or leaving your site without logging out. Because users are accustomed to being able to stop and start browsing whenever and wherever they please, it may be difficult to get them in the habit of treating a Web application the same way they would a standard Windows application. The problem with this is that every time a user leaves your application without logging out, their session continues to consume resources in storing its variables and objects. To reduce the impact of this problem it's important to set the *Session.Timeout* value to something more restrictive than the default 20 minutes, if possible. If your application does not require users to do a lot of reading on a page between actions, you may be able to set this value as low as 5 minutes before users are impacted by timeouts. The actual setting appropriate for your application is best determined through discussions with users and a healthy dose of experimentation. To set the *Session.Timeout* value for an individual session, you can use the following code:

```
<%
'Set the Timeout to 5 minutes
Session.Timeout = 5
%>
```

To set the timeout value at the application level, follow these steps:

1. Open the Internet Service Manager in the Microsoft Management Console.

2. Expand the structure of the appropriate server and Web site until you get to the folder containing your Web application.

3. Right-click the folder containing your application, and select Properties.

4. On the Virtual Directory tab of the Properties dialog box, click the Configuration button.

5. In the Application Configuration dialog box, select the App Options tab (see Figure 7-4).

6. From the App Options tab, you can set the desired timeout value, as well as several other defaults.

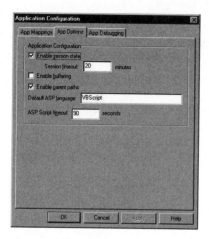

**Figure 7-4.**
*Application Configuration dialog box.*

You can also disable session state for certain pages in your application with the following code as the first line in your ASP file:

```
<%@ EnableSessionState=False %>
```

Depending on the pages on which you use it, this code can have the effect of delaying the point at which your application begins tracking a user's session, conserving resources on the server. You can also disable session state at the application level by clearing the Enable session state check box on the App Options tab of the Application Configuration dialog box.

NOTE: In IIS 3.0, session state can be disabled by setting the EnableSessionState parameter of ASP to 0. This parameter can be found in HKEY_LOCAL_MACHINE\SYSTEM\CurrentControlSet\ Services\W3SVC\ASP\Parameters.

WARNING: Editing the Registry improperly can result in serious problems that may prevent your computer from booting. Always use caution when making changes in the Registry, and be sure to back up any Registry entries you plan to change.

## Server Object

The ASP Server object is used primarily to create instances of component objects for use in ASP pages. This is accomplished through the use of the *Server.CreateObject* method, which takes as an argument the ProgID of the component. The ProgID is the component's human-readable name, which takes the format *ComponentName.ClassName*. For example, the ProgID of the ADO Connection object is ADODB.Connection. Strategies for using components more efficiently are discussed below in "Using Application and Session Variables for Storing and Sharing Objects." The Server object offers a single property, the *ScriptTimeout* property, which determines how long a script can run before it times out. In some cases it might be desirable to reduce the timeout value in order to prevent long-running scripts from having a negative effect on your application as a whole. You can set the timeout value with the following code:

```
<%Server.ScriptTimeout = 10 'Sets the timeout to 10 seconds %>
```

Keep in mind, however, that the value set by *Server.ScriptTimeout* cannot be less than the *AspScriptTimeout* property in the IIS Metabase. Both the *Server.ScriptTimeout* property and the Metabase *AspScriptTimeout* property are set by default to 90 seconds.

## Request Object

The ASP *Request* object is used to retrieve responses from a user's HTTP request via a variety of collections associated with the *Request* object. The *Request* object has five collections associated with it, the *QueryString* collection, the *Form* collection, the *Cookies* collection, the *ClientCertificate* collection, and the *ServerVariables* collection. Although the *Request* object allows values to be retrieved by the following syntax,

```
<%MyVariable = Request("VariableName") %>
```

it is recommended to explicitly name the collection in which the value is stored as follows:

```
<%MyVariable = Request.Form("VariableName") %>
```

The reason is that when you access collection values by the first syntax, ASP searches all of the collections of the *Request* object for the named value (the search order is the same as the order of the collections above). If you do a lot of work with the *Request* object, it will be well worth the extra code to avoid the overhead of repeatedly searching the collections.

## Response Object

The ASP *Response* object allows your application to communicate information to the client browser in a variety of ways, from writing strings to passing cookies. The *Response* object offers a property that can be of particular use in avoiding costly operations on the server for a client that is no longer connected. The *IsClientConnected* property reports whether the client has disconnected from the server since the last call to *Response.Write*. This property would return *False*, for example, if a user clicked the stop button while waiting for your page to load. By checking the value of this property before performing particularly expensive tasks, you can reduce the amount of wasted processing that your application performs, an important step toward better scalability.

NOTE: The *IsClientConnected* property is only available with IIS 4.0.

Another performance improvement that can easily be made in the use of the *Response* object has to do with its *Write* method. Often when an ASP page needs to write a number of lines of text to the client, the code is written like this:

```
<%
Response.Write "<H1>When writing text to the browser,</H1>"

Response.Write "<BR>it is less efficient to call the Response.Write"

Response.Write "method multiple times."

Response.Write "<B>It is <EM>better</EM> where possible to
concatenate"

Response.Write "strings together and call Response.Write once.</B>"
%>
```

The problem with this code is that each time *Response.Write* is called, ASP must stop and write the specified string to the HTML stream. This is somewhat akin to trying to eat soup with a baby spoon. As long as you're not very hungry, it'll work fine, but it's really not very efficient. Instead, it's a good idea wherever possible to concatenate strings together and call *Response.Write* once as follows:

```
<%
Dim sText
sText = "<H1>When writing text to the browser,</H1>"
sText = sText &"<BR>it is less efficient to call the Response.Write"
sText = sText & "method multiple times."
sText = sText & "<B>It is <EM>better</EM> where possible to
concatenate"
sText = sText & "strings together and call Response.Write once.</B>"
Response.Write sText
%>
```

## ObjectContext Object

The *ObjectContext* object is new with IIS 4.0. It allows your transactional ASP pages to access the Microsoft Transaction Server ObjectContext in order to commit or abort any transaction initiated by your application in that ASP page. In order to use the *ObjectContext* object, an ASP page must be made transactional by inserting the following code:

```
<%@Transaction = Required %>
```

This ensures that both the ASP page and any components created by the page (assuming they support transactions) will not commit any of the work they are doing until all of them have agreed to do so by calling the *SetComplete* method of the *ObjectContext* object (the *ObjectContext* is also available to components written to be compatible with MTS). If an error occurs, the ASP page can call the *SetAbort* method of the *ObjectContext* object in order to signal all parties to the transaction to rollback their work.

The danger in transactional ASP is that for the entire time that the transaction is uncommitted, any resources that are updated by the transaction are locked. This has the potential to reduce scalability if used carelessly. In general, it is best to only use transactions where necessary. When you must use a transaction, make sure that the transaction is either committed or aborted as soon as possible. Try to avoid performing time-consuming procedures as a part of a transaction or, if possible, break the work up into multiple transactions.

## Using Application and Session Variables for Storing and Sharing Objects

One of the most common misconceptions in ASP development relates to the use of application and session variables. application and session variables are storage areas within the ASP intrinsic application and session objects that allow developers to store values or objects globally to the application or to the user's session. It is in the storage of objects (components) in application or session variables that performance problems can be encountered.

The first problem is simply one of scope. When designing an application that stores component instances in application or session variables, it is important to realize that those component instances will be consuming resources for the entire life of the application or session, respectively. In other words, using application or session variables to avoid the inconvenience of creating instances of components on multiple pages is generally a bad idea. The only time when you should consider storing a component instance in an application or session variable is if that component must share information between users or pages. Even then it is important to remember that in most cases this functionality can be provided by storing properties, rather than components, in application and session variables.

In a way, the root of these problems lies in the fact that it is so easy to create objects with application or session scope. All it takes is the following code:

```
Set Session("MyObject") = Server.CreateObject("MyComponent.MyClass")
```

Of course, you can also use the <OBJECT> tag with the RUNAT and SCOPE parameters from within your GLOBAL.ASA file, but this has its own pitfalls, depending on the scope of the object you are creating.

Because of the ease of creating objects with application or session scope, many developers see them as an easy solution to providing components to multiple users or pages, without considering the possible consequences. One common instance of this is storing an ADO Connection object in an application or session variable, on the theory that it will allow the application to provide faster data access. In fact, the opposite is often the result of such a strategy, as doing this defeats IIS's built-in ODBC *connection pooling* (assuming it is enabled) and prevents any user other than the one currently using the Connection object from getting data access.

## Threading Issues

In addition to issues of connection pooling, another problem in storing components in application and session variables relates to *threading*. Threading is the process by which an application or component can provide more than one path of execution (thread) at any given time. applications and components that are multi-threaded are able to process requests from more than one client simultaneously. Multi-threading provides greater efficiency, but typically increases programming complexity. Fortunately, the Active Server Pages engine itself is actually fairly efficient at managing threading issues for your application. It is possible, however, through the injudicious use of components with application or session scope to prevent ASP from efficiently managing threading.

The problem arises when one uses application or session scope objects without regard to the threading model of those objects. For example, creating an object with session scope from a single-threaded component results in ASP locking that session down to a single thread. The same is true for apartment-threaded components. This results in all activity for that user's session being serialized, which can seriously impact performance. Although the use of application and session scope objects should be avoided if possible, you will get the best possible performance by using only components marked as Both (Free- and Apartment-threaded). The following table shows the relationship between scope and threading model.

| | Single--Threaded | Apartment-Threaded | Free-Threaded | Both Apartment- and Free-Threaded |
|---|---|---|---|---|
| Page Scope | Poorer Performance | Best Performance | Poorer Performance | Best Performance |
| Session Scope | Locks Session to Single Thread | Locks Session to Single Thread | Poorer Performance | Best Performance |
| Application Scope | Poorer Performance | Poorer Performance. | Poorer Performance Must be created with <OBJECT> Syntax | Best Performance |

**Table 7-1.**
*Effect of threading model and object scope on performance.*

As one can see from the table, unless you are using components marked as *Both*, you are likely to suffer performance degradation from giving those components application or session scope. Since in many cases a developer will be using either custom components built in Visual Basic (which only creates single- or apartment-threaded components) or third-party components for which the threading model may not be known, it is advisable to only give components page-level scope.

## Using ActiveX Data Objects (ADO) Efficiently

Although ActiveX Data Objects (ADO) is not strictly speaking a part of ASP, it is both the recommended and most commonly used method to access data from ASP pages. As such, it deserves a place in the discussion of the proper use of ASP.

ADO is another technology that can create difficulties because it is so simple to use. Because of its simple object model, and the novel ability to use some of its objects without explicitly creating an entire object hierarchy (as is common with other data-access methods, such as DAO), developers may fall victim to common misunderstandings about how ADO operates, and how to use it most efficiently.

### Marking ADO as Both-Threaded

The ADO component as installed by default is marked in the System Registry as being apartment-threaded. This is in order to support the Jet database engine, which is limited to apartment threading. If your application will only be accessing SQL Server data sources or other sources that use drivers or OLE DB providers known to be thread-safe, you should use the batch file provided with ADO called MAKEFRE15.BAT to mark ADO as Both-threaded in the System Registry. If you must use ADO objects with application or session scope, it is highly recommended that you use this procedure to set the threading model of ADO.

### Using ADO Connections

Visual Basic programmers may fall victim to another pitfall of ADO use. In VB programs, particularly programs in which opening a database connection was expensive, it was not uncommon for programmers to hold database connections open for long periods to avoid the expense of repeatedly opening and closing connections. Because IIS uses *connection pooling* for ODBC drivers that support it, this practice is unnecessary, and will likely result in slower data access for the application overall, as certain clients will likely have to wait for connections until other users are finished with them.

In general, using ADO connections efficiently merely requires following a few simple rules:

- Enable ODBC Connection Pooling: This simple procedure can make a substantial difference in data-access performance. To turn Connection Pooling on in IIS 3.0, set the *StartConnectionPool* parameter of the Registry key, HKEY_LOCAL_MACHINE\System\CurrentControlSet\Services\W3SVC\ASP\Parameters, to 1.

WARNING: Editing the Registry improperly can result in serious problems that may prevent your computer from booting. Always use caution when making changes in the Registry. In IIS 4.0, Connection Pooling is enabled by default for the SQL Server ODBC driver.

NOTE: Connection Pooling cannot be enabled for ODBC data sources that use the Jet database engine, due to threading limitations of Jet.

- Open ADO Connections as late as possible and close them as early as possible. Set all required properties (*CommandType*, *CommandText*, *ConnectionTimeout*, and so on) and stored procedure parameters before opening the ADO Connection.

```
'BAD!
'Create ADO Objects
Set Conn = Server.CreateObject("ADODB.Connection")
Set Cmd = Server.CreateObject("ADODB.Command")
Set RS = Server.CreatObject("ADODB.Recordset")


'Set Connection String to our Secure DSN
sConnectString = "DSN=MyConnection;UID=SA;PWD="


'Open Connection
Conn.Open sConnectString


'Set ADO Command Properties
Cmd.CommandType = 4 'Stored Procedure
```

*(continued)*

```
Cmd.CommandText = "MyProcedure"
Set Cmd.ActiveConnection = Conn


'Execute Stored Procedure
Set RS = Cmd.Execute


'Code to process recordset


'Close Connection
Conn.Close


Set Conn = Nothing
Set Cmd = Nothing
Set RS = Nothing


'GOOD!
'Create ADO Objects
Set Conn = Server.CreateObject("ADODB.Connection")
Set Cmd = Server.CreateObject("ADODB.Command")
Set RS = Server.CreateObject("ADODB.Recordset")


'Set Connection String to our Secure DSN
sConnectString = "DSN=MyConnection;UID=SA;PWD="


'Set ADO Command Properties
Cmd.CommandType = 4 'Stored Procedure
Cmd.CommandText = "MyProcedure"


'Open Connection
```

*(continued)*

```
Conn.Open sConnectString

Set Cmd.ActiveConnection = Conn        'Active Connection must
                                       'be set after Open.


'Execute Stored Procedure

Set RS = Cmd.Execute


'Code to process recordset


'Close Connection

Conn.Close


Set Conn = Nothing

Set Cmd = Nothing

Set RS = Nothing
```

■ Where possible, use the ADO Command object and its *Execute* method. This allows you to retrieve a recordset, update a row, or call a stored procedure in one step (not including setting properties, and so on).

■ Use connection strings that are as generic as possible. Since ODBC Connection Pooling looks for a connection in the pool that will satisfy the user's data-access needs, making the connections as generic as possible (i.e., all connections in the application use the same login and password) allows your application to make the most of connection pooling. Since clients in three-tier applications should not access data sources directly, only one connection string per application should be necessary, since the application is the only client from the perspective of the data source.

■ Store connection strings in application or session variables. Storing connection strings in application or session variables allows multiple components to use the same connection information, which can both improve the performance of connection pooling and can simplify the maintenance or updating of connection strings.

## Aliasing Recordset Fields

Another relatively simple procedure can improve the speed of accessing recordset fields in a loop. The following code retrieves a recordset and creates an HTML table by looping through the recordset. The code assumes that you have a DSN set up with the name *MYSERVER_PUBS* pointing to the PUBS SQL Server sample database. You should change your settings for the DSN, User ID, and Password as appropriate.

```
<%@LANGUAGE="VBSCRIPT"%>
<HTML>
<HEAD>
<TITLE>Creating a table from a recordset</TITLE>
</HEAD>
<BODY>
<H1>The following table is generated from an ADO recordset.</H1>
<TABLE BORDER=2>
<TR>
<TH>Author ID</TH>
<TH>Last Name</TH>
<TH>First Name</TH>
</TR>

<%

tBeginTime = Time

sConnectString = "DSN=MYSERVER_PUBS;UID=sa;PWD="
Set Conn = Server.CreateObject("ADODB.Connection")
Set Cmd = Server.CreateObject("ADODB.Command")
Set RS = Server.CreateObject("ADODB.Recordset")

Cmd.CommandType = 1 'Text
Cmd.CommandText = "SELECT au_id, au_lname, au_fname FROM authors"
```

*(continued)*

```
Conn.Open sConnectString
Set Cmd.ActiveConnection = Conn


Set RS = Cmd.Execute


Do While Not RS.EOF
sText = sText & "<TR>"
   sText = sText & "<TD>" & RS("au_id") & "</TD>"
   sText = sText & "<TD>" & RS("au_lname") & "</TD>"
   sText = sText & "<TD>" & RS("au_fname") & "</TD>"
   sText = sText & "</TR>"
   RS.MoveNext
Loop


Conn.Close


Set Conn = Nothing
Set Cmd = Nothing
Set RS = Nothing


sText = sText & "</TABLE>"


Response.Write sText


tEndTime = Time


Response.Write "<BR>Begin Time = " & tBeginTime & _
   "<BR>End Time = " & tEndTime
%>
</BODY>
</HTML>
```

Now, if we've done everything correctly, the results should look like the following:

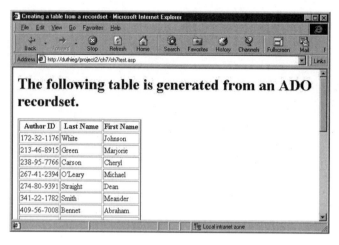

**Figure 7-5.**
*HTML table generated from an ADO recordset.*

You may have noticed in the code above that we have implemented a simple but effective script timer by checking the system time at the start of the script and at the end. If you run the code above, you will likely notice that the page takes a while to load the first time. This is because of the expense of making the initial database connection. If you refresh the page, you'll see that the script execution time is significantly reduced. This is because the database connection is taken from the connection pool, assuming that you have Connection Pooling enabled. The implementation of the timer allows us to measure the performance gain of modifications to ASP scripts. Also note that we explicitly destroy the ADO objects using *Set Object = Nothing*. This is not strictly necessary in ASP, as the objects will be destroyed automatically when the pages goes out of scope, but the object destruction code does no harm and we have included it to encourage consistent coding habits between Visual Basic and VBScript in ASP. It can be easy to forget to add such code when migrating code from ASP pages to Visual Basic components.

That said, the above code does an effective job of displaying data from a table based on a SQL query. Like many of the examples in this book, this ASP page will perform adequately in most situations. But as requests for this page increase, the cost of accessing the data will accumulate. In order to compensate for this accumulation, we need a way to make even a simple query such as this more efficient. Fortunately, one answer is provided by the ASP Field object.

Using the ASP Field object, we can alias the recordset fields we are retrieving in order to speed access while looping through the recordset. By aliasing the recordset field as an ASP Field object, we can avoid the time it takes to look into the data structure and resolve the RS ("fieldname") syntax during each trip through the loop. For ASP pages that bring back lengthy recordsets, or that are frequently accessed, this can result in substantial data-access savings. Here's what the modified code would look like:

```
<%@LANGUAGE="VBSCRIPT"%>
<HTML>
<HEAD>
<TITLE>Creating a table from a recordset</TITLE>
</HEAD>
<BODY>
<H1>The following table is generated from an ADO recordset.</H1>
<TABLE BORDER=2>
<TR>
<TH>Author ID</TH>
<TH>Last Name</TH>
<TH>First Name</TH>
</TR>

<%

tBeginTime = Time

sConnectString = "DSN=SERVER2_PUBS;UID=sa;PWD="
Set Conn = Server.CreateObject("ADODB.Connection")
Set Cmd = Server.CreateObject("ADODB.Command")
Set RS = Server.CreateObject("ADODB.Recordset")

Cmd.CommandType = 1 'Text
Cmd.CommandText = "SELECT au_id, au_lname, au_fname FROM authors"
```

*(continued)*

```
Conn.Open sConnectString
Set Cmd.ActiveConnection = Conn

Set RS = Cmd.Execute

'Alias recordset fields
Set fldAuthID = RS.Fields("au_id")
Set fldLName = RS.Fields("au_lname")
Set fldFName = RS.Fields("au_fname")

Do While Not RS.EOF
sText = sText & "<TR>"
    sText = sText & "<TD>" & fldAuthID & "</TD>"
    sText = sText & "<TD>" & fldLName & "</TD>"
    sText = sText & "<TD>" & fldFName & "</TD>"
    sText = sText & "</TR>"
    RS.MoveNext
Loop

Conn.Close

sText = sText & "</TABLE>"

Response.Write sText

tEndTime = Time

Response.Write "<BR>Begin Time = " & tBeginTime & _
    "<BR>End Time = " & tEndTime
%>
</BODY>
</HTML>
```

NOTE: With a small recordset such as the one in this example, there will be little noticeable difference in execution time between non-aliased and aliased versions. The performance benefit increases with the length of the recordset.

Now, having put you through both code and explanation, it's time to do a reversal and say that you should almost *never* write an ASP page such as the above. The why goes back to the issue of architecture, and of using resources efficiently. Although we may be able to improve the overall efficiency of the query and the process of looping through and displaying the records, our efforts in this case are misplaced, since in this case ASP is the wrong tool for the job. If all you want to do is display the results of a query, there are easier ways to do it than through ASP, ways that also have the advantage of better client response. One such way is to use the Microsoft SQL Server Web Assistant.

One should *always* look carefully at sample code, both in the Microsoft documentation, and in Microsoft Press and third-party books, with an eye toward performance issues. Many code samples, unless specifically targeted at demonstrating performance issues, are not necessarily fully optimized. As such, when using sample code as the basis for your own work, be sure you're aware of performance issues related to the work you are performing or the objects you are using, and make appropriate modifications.

## The Microsoft SQL Server Web Assistant

The Microsoft SQL Server Web Assistant is an easy-to-use wizard that allows you to create a static Web page based on a table or view, on a SQL Query, or on a stored procedure. You can choose to have the Web Assistant create a Web page immediately, or set up a scheduled task to update the Web page periodically, even when the data is updated. You can also specify a template for the Web Assistant to use, so that you can format the page to fit in with your site design. If your application needs to give users access to static pictures of Microsoft SQL Server data, for statistical or other purposes, the SQL Web Assistant can provide that functionality without the processing overhead of ASP or the expense of opening a data connection every time a user wants to look at the data. The results of a page created by the Web Assistant based on the same query used in the ASP example above would look something like the following:

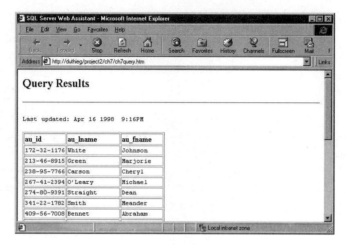

**Figure 7-6.**
*HTML table generated by the Microsoft SQL Server Web Assistant.*

## • • • SOLUTION: Dynamically Building a Table of Information

Now let's take a look at how we can implement some of the performance tips discussed above as we retrieve data from a table selected at runtime. In this sample solution, our requirement is to set up a page that allows a user to select a table to view from a set of predefined choices. In this example the table choices will be hard coded, but it would not be much more difficult to drive the combo box from a table as well. Instead of displaying data from a set of tables, we could built SQL statements. We will be using the Pubs sample database that comes with Microsoft SQL Server for our data source.

In order to provide the solution, follow these steps:

1. Open Visual InterDev. You do not need to open a new or existing Solution unless you wish to use a data source from the Data Environment.

2. Add a new ASP page, either by clicking the New Item button on the toolbar and selecting the ASP page icon, or by selecting New File... from the File menu and selecting the ASP page icon (see Figure 7-7; note that in Figure 7-7 we have added the *Option Explicit* statement, as well as a set of TITLE tags for the page).

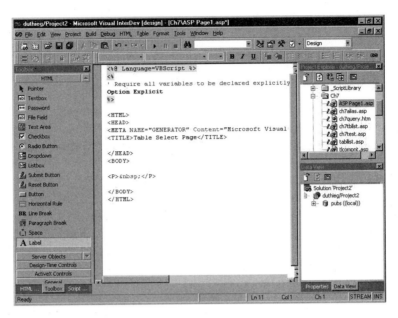

**Figure 7-7.**
*New ASP page in Visual InterDev Source View.*

3. Add the code from the listing below to the page. Note that the VBScript procedure code is kept between the <HEAD> tags.

4. Change the following line to refer to an ODBC DSN on your Web server that points to the Microsoft SQL Server Pubs database. If no DSN exists for the Pubs database, one should be created using the ODBC control panel applet.

```
sConn = "DSN=MYSERVER_PUBS;UID=sa;PWD="
```

5. Save the ASP page as *TABLLIST.ASP* to a folder set up for use with IIS. This will likely be under the \INETPUB\WWWROOT\ folder.

6. Browse the page by entering *http://myserver/MYWEBFOLDER/New ASP Page1.asp*, where *MYSERVER* is the name of your Web server and *MYWEBFOLDER* is the name of the folder in which you saved the ASP file.

7. Select a table from the drop-down list and then click the Show Table button. The results should look like Figure 7-8 below.

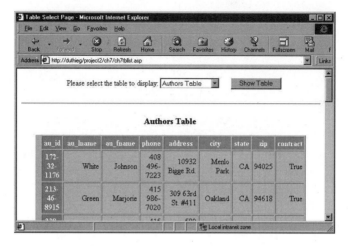

**Figure 7-8.**
*Dynamically generated table using ASP and ADO.*

8. Take a close look at the ASP code for this page. Identify the places where techniques described in this chapter have been used to improve its performance.

```
<%@ LANGUAGE="VBSCRIPT" %>

<%

' Require all variables to be declared explicitly

Option Explicit

%>


<html>

<head>

<meta NAME="GENERATOR" Content="Microsoft Visual Studio 6.0">

<title>Table Select Page</title>


<%

Private Sub WriteTable(SelectedTable)
```

*(continued)*

```
'---------------------------

' Purpose: Generates an HTML

' table based on the user

' selected database table

'---------------------------


' Declare ADO Object Variables

Dim Cmd

Dim Conn

Dim rs

' Declare string variables

Dim sConn        'Connection String

Dim sText        'String variable for Response.Write

' Declare counter variables

Dim H

Dim I


sConn = "DSN=PUBS;UID=sa;PWD="


Set Cmd = Server.CreateObject("ADODB.Command")


Cmd.CommandTimeout = 0

Cmd.CommandType = 2              ' adCmdTable


If SelectedTable = "AUTHORS" Then

   Cmd.CommandText = "Authors"

   sText = "<P ALIGN=""CENTER""><FONT SIZE=""4""><B>Authors
Table</B></FONT></P>"
```

*(continued)*

```
ElseIf SelectedTable = "TITLES" Then

    cmd.CommandText = "Titles"

    sText = "<P ALIGN=""CENTER""><FONT SIZE=""4"">" & _
        "<B>Titles Table</B></FONT></P>"

ElseIf SelectedTable = "EMPLOYEE" Then

    cmd.CommandText = "Employee"

    sText =   "<P ALIGN=""CENTER""><FONT SIZE=""4"">" & _
        "<B>Employee Table</B></FONT></P>"

ElseIf SelectedTable = "SALES" Then

    cmd.CommandText = "Sales"

    sText =   "<P ALIGN=""CENTER""><FONT SIZE=""4"">" &_
        "<B>Sales Table</B></FONT></P>"

ElseIf SelectedTable = "" Then

    Exit Sub

End If


Set Conn = Server.CreateObject("ADODB.Connection")

Set rs = Server.CreateObject("ADODB.Recordset")


Conn.Open sConn


Set cmd.ActiveConnection = Conn


Set rs = cmd.Execute


sText =   sText & "<CENTER><TABLE WIDTH=""90%"" " & _
    "CELLPADDING=""3"" BORDER=""1"" BGCOLOR=""D3D3D3"">"

sText = sText & "     <TH>"

For H = 0 To rs.Fields.Count - 1

    sText = sText & "<TD WIDTH=""" & 100 /(rs.Fields.Count) & _
```

*(continued)*

```
        "%"" ALIGN="""CENTER""" BGCOLOR=""A9A9A9"">"

    sText = sText & "<FONT COLOR=""FFFFFF""><B>" & _
        rs(H).Name & "</B></FONT>"

    sText = sText & "</TD>"

Next

sText = sText & "</TH>"


Do While Not rs.EOF

    sText = sText & "<TR>"

    sText = sText & "<TD>"

    sText = sText & "</TD>"

    For I = 0 To rs.Fields.Count - 1

        If I = 0 Then

            sText = sText & "<TD ALIGN=""CENTER"" & _
                "BGCOLOR=""A9A9A9"">"

            sText = sText & "<FONT COLOR=""FFFFFF""><B>" & _
                rs(I).Value & "</B></FONT>"

            sText = sText & "</TD>"

        Else

            sText = sText & "<TD ALIGN=""RIGHT"">"

            sText = sText & rs(I).Value

            sText = sText & "</TD>"

        End If

    Next

    sText = sText & "</TR>"

    rs.MoveNext

Loop


sText = sText & "</TABLE></CENTER>"

Response.Write sText
```

*(continued)*

```
        Conn.Close


        Set Conn = Nothing

        Set cmd = Nothing

        Set rs = Nothing


        SelectedTable = ""


        End Sub


        Private Sub BuildSelectList

        '---------------------------

        ' Purpose: Generates a dropdown

        '   listbox from which the user

        '   can choose a table to view

        '---------------------------

            Dim sText


        sText =  "<SELECT ALIGN=""LEFT"" NAME=""LISTTABLE"">"
        If Request("LISTTABLE") = "AUTHORS" Then

            sText = sText & "<OPTION SELECTED " & _
                "VALUE=""AUTHORS"">Authors Table"

            sText = sText & "<OPTION VALUE=""TITLES"">Titles Table"

            sText = sText & "<OPTION VALUE=""EMPLOYEE"">" & _
                "Employee Table"

            sText = sText & "<OPTION VALUE=""SALES"">Sales Table"
        ElseIf Request("LISTTABLE") = "TITLES" Then

            sText = sText & "<OPTION VALUE=""AUTHORS"">" & _
                "Authors Table"
```

*(continued)*

```
        sText = sText & "<OPTION SELECTED VALUE=""TITLES"">" & _
            "Titles Table"

        sText = sText & "<OPTION VALUE=""EMPLOYEE"">" & _
            "Employee Table"

        sText = sText & "<OPTION VALUE=""SALES"">Sales Table"

    ElseIf Request("LISTTABLE") = "EMPLOYEE" Then

        sText = sText & "<OPTION VALUE=""AUTHORS"">Authors Table"

        sText = sText & "<OPTION VALUE=""TITLES"">Titles Table"

        sText = sText & "<OPTION SELECTED VALUE=""EMPLOYEE"">" & _
            "Employee Table"

        sText = sText & "<OPTION VALUE=""SALES"">Sales Table"

    ElseIf Request("LISTTABLE") = "SALES" Then

        sText = sText & "<OPTION VALUE=""AUTHORS"">Authors Table"

        sText = sText & "<OPTION VALUE=""TITLES"">Titles Table"

        sText = sText & "<OPTION VALUE=""EMPLOYEE"">" & _
            "Employee Table"

        sText = sText & "<OPTION SELECTED VALUE=""SALES"">" & _
            "Sales Table"

    Else

        sText = sText & "<OPTION VALUE=""AUTHORS"">Authors Table"

        sText = sText & "<OPTION VALUE=""TITLES"">Titles Table"

        sText = sText & "<OPTION VALUE=""EMPLOYEE"">" & _
            "Employee Table"

        sText = sText & "<OPTION VALUE=""SALES"">Sales Table"

    End If

    sText = sText & "</SELECT>"

    Response.Write sText

End Sub

%>
```

*(continued)*

```
</head>

<body BGCOLOR="FFFFFF">


<form ACTION="ch7tbllst.asp" METHOD="POST" NAME="TBLFORM">

<center><table BORDER="0" WIDTH="80%">

   <tr>

     <td ALIGN="RIGHT">

        Please select the table to display:

     </td>

     <td NOWRAP ALIGN="CENTER">

        <%

        'Call method to build the dropdown listbox

        BuildSelectList

        %>

     </td>

     <td NOWRAP ALIGN="LEFT">

        <input TYPE="SUBMIT" NAME="CTRLSUBM" VALUE="Show
Table">

     </td>

   </tr>

</table>

</center>

</form>


<hr>


<%

Dim SelectedTable
```

*(continued)*

```
If Len(Request("LISTTABLE")) > 0 Then

    SelectedTable = Request("LISTTABLE")

Else

    SelectedTable = ""

End If


WriteTable(SelectedTable)

%>


</body>

</html>
```

In this example,

■ We have avoided the use of Include files by using the integer value for the ADO *Command CommandType* property in the following line (we use a comment to clarify the meaning of the integer value):

```
Cmd.CommandType = 2     'adCmdTable
```

■ Since the above is the only value we refer to that is contained in the ADO 1.5 type library, we have not included a reference to the type library in this page. This means that the type library does not need to be loaded into memory along with the ADO DLL.

■ We have used *Option Explicit*, comments, and other coding standards, such as variable naming and use of whitespace to make our code more efficient and more easily maintained. We have also put almost all of our ASP code into two procedures, *BuildSelectList* and *WriteTable*. Doing so has allowed us to largely separate ASP code from HTML, which allows ASP to parse the page more efficiently. It also has the added advantage of making it much easier to move our ASP code into a component, as we will demonstrate in the next section.

■ We have explicitly named collections of the Request object and Recordset object when we refer to them, to reduce the amount of time ASP must spend searching through collections for the named or indexed value we are using, as shown in the following lines:

```
SelectedTable = Request.Form("LISTTABLE")

sText = sText & rs.Fields(I).Value
```

- We have used a variable, *sText* to concatenate the HTML to be sent to the browser, avoiding repeated calls to *Response.Write.*

- We have opened our ADO Connection as late as possible, and closed it as early as possible, for more efficient use of connection pooling.

In short, we have used a variety of techniques to improve the performance of this ASP page. We have not yet, however, implemented the technique most likely to improve the performance of this page, that is, moving the code from this page into a component. We will demonstrate this at the end of the next section.

# Moving Business Logic and Data Access Into Components

One of the advantages provided by Visual InterDev is the ability to develop Web applications in a way that has never before been possible. One can access, retrieve, and update data, all available through simple drag-and-drop, thanks to the Visual InterDev Design-Time Controls (DTCs). This is an ability that rivals even the Visual Basic environment for ease of use. This advantage, however, comes at a price (as do most advantages). The price of admission for using the DTCs is that their functionality is provided by a set of files known collectively as the *script library*. The script library contains one set of files each for client and for server purposes, both written in JavaScript. Given that script languages must be interpreted at runtime, and the script library files can run into hundreds of lines (two of the files weigh in at over 750 lines), this can present a potential problem for sites that need the utmost in scalability. By the same token, ASP pages that you write that contain hundreds of lines of code can potentially lead to performance falloff. When you're looking for the best possible performance, the solution is to move as much code as possible into components.

## Advantages Provided by COM Components

Components provide many advantages, but the most important of them in terms of performance and scalability is that because they are compiled, they run substantially faster than equivalent script code. This translates to less work for your processors, which translates to better scalability. Other benefits provided by components include enhanced security, protection for proprietary business logic, and the ability to abstract data access and business logic from the user interface. This abstraction can provide further benefits, including the ability to selectively upgrade and/or replace individual components or tiers of the application, without throwing away the rest of the application. Perhaps more important, by abstracting business logic into components, you make it much easier to reuse that logic (i.e., the component) from other applications.

## Creating VB COM Components from Existing ASP Script

A good rule of thumb when writing scripted business logic is to base the script language you use on the tier on which that logic will be running. If you are writing client-side validation logic, it is a good idea to use JScript/JavaScript. This will give you the greatest reach since JavaScript is supported on both Internet Explorer 3.0 and up, as well as on Netscape Navigator 2.0 and up (be sure if you want cross-platform functionality that you use only those features of the language that are supported on all target platforms). On the other hand, if you are writing ASP code, there are at least a couple of compelling reasons to use VBScript. The first reason is that if you are a Visual Basic programmer VBScript provides a subset of a language with which you are already familiar, which of course translates to more efficient development. The more important reason to use VBScript when writing ASP pages is that when it's time to move your ASP code into components, those ASP pages that are written in VBScript are much more easily migrated into components using Visual Basic 5.0.

For the benefit of the reader who is not already familiar with Visual Basic (and for those who have not had reason to use Visual Basic to create server-side components), Visual Basic 4.0 and later provide the ability to create what Visual Basic refers to as *ActiveX DLLs*. Active X DLLs are compiled components that run in the process of the client application (the application that instantiates the component). The term *ActiveX DLL* is a bit of a misnomer, since at this point Microsoft has reduced the scope of the ActiveX branding back down to its original meaning of technologies that are specific to the Internet and light-weight control objects. Since a VB DLL may have no user interface, and may have nothing to do with the Internet, the term is perhaps misleading. The reason it got this name, however, is that DLLs created with Visual Basic (assuming you follow a few simple rules) are actually full-fledged COM objects, with almost all of the advantages COM provides, but little of the headaches that were once required to build a COM object. In fact, it is possible to create and use COM objects with Visual Basic without knowing anything about what's going on under the covers, though it is inadvisable in situations where performance is critical. For the purposes of this discussion, the reader may consider the terms *ActiveX DLL* and *VB COM DLL* interchangeable.

> NOTE: Although it is possible to create COM objects with VB 4.0, for performance reasons, as well as for the advantages offered by VB 5.0 and 6.0 (which include the ability to create apartment-threaded components), we recommend using VB 5.0 or 6.0 for the creation of COM DLLs for use in ASP development.

What all this means for Web application developers is that it is possible to create simple COM components by dropping your existing VBScript code with only minor modification into a Visual Basic class module, and compiling the project into a DLL. This is exactly what we will demonstrate in the solution at the end of this section.

## Methods of Deploying COM Business Objects

By default, when you compile your Visual Basic project into a DLL, that DLL is registered on your development machine as a part of that process. If you want to use the DLL on another machine, however, there are a number of different ways in which you can deploy it. If you have the appropriate machine and file system permissions, you can simply copy the DLL to the remote machine and register it using RegSvr32.EXE. You could also use the Visual Basic Setup Wizard to create a setup package for the DLL that could then be installed on the target machine by someone with the appropriate permissions. If the DLL is to be accessed remotely, as would be the case if you've set up a server specifically for running components, then you must configure both the client and server machines using DCOMCNFG.EXE. Finally, you can also install your component into a Microsoft Transaction Server package, which can then be exported to a remote computer.

## • • • SOLUTION: Creating a Data Access Component

In this solution, we'll demonstrate how easy it can be to improve the performance of your Web application by moving your ASP code into custom Visual Basic COM components. We'll use the ASP page we created in the last solution as a starting point.

In order to provide the solution, follow these steps:

1. Start Visual Basic. From the New Project dialog box, select the ActiveX DLL icon, then click Open. A new Class Module called *Class1* will be created for you.

2. From the Project menu, select References.... Find the item labeled *"Microsoft Active Server Pages Object Library"* and select its check box. This will allow us to reference the calling ASP page and access the intrinsic ASP objects. Also find the item labeled *"Microsoft ActiveX Data Objects 2.0 Object Library"* and select its check box. This will allow us to create the necessary *Connection, Command,* and *Recordset* objects.

3. Create a new Sub procedure called *OnStartPage,* with the following argument:

```
iScriptingContext As ScriptingContext
```

The *ScriptingContext* object comes from the ASP Object Library and is passed by the calling ASP page whenever this component is called.

4. Dim a module-level variable called *sc As ScriptingContext.*

5. Start Visual InterDev and open the TABLLIST.ASP file that we created in the last solution. If you did not do the last solution, you can copy the code from the listing in the prior solution.

6. Copy the two sub procedures from the ASP file into the class module. Make sure that any procedures you want to call from your ASP page are preceded by the keyword *Public.* In order to use the ASP intrinsic objects from within the component, preface each use of an ASP intrinsic with the *ScriptingContext* object variable, *sc.* You should also remove the reference to the Server ASP intrinsic object before the *CreateObject* method call for each ADO object, since Visual Basic doesn't need it.

7. Rename the Project as *MyProject,* and the Class module as *TableList.* Save the Project and the Class module, then compile the Project. If the component is to be used on a computer other than the one on which it was compiled, it must be copied to and properly registered on that computer.

8. Using the Save File As... command from the File menu, save the TABLLIST.ASP file as *tlcompnt.asp.*

9. Delete the two sub procedures from TLCOMPNT.ASP.

10. Using the *Server.CreateObject* syntax, alter the code block in which the *BuildSelectList* method is called so it looks like the following:

```
<%

Dim TableList


Set TableList = Server.CreateObject("MyProject.TableList")


'Call method to build the dropdown listbox
TableList.BuildSelectList

%>
```

11. Alter the code block in which the *WriteTable* method is called so it looks like the following:

```
<%

Dim SelectedTable


If Len(Request.Form("LISTTABLE")) > 0 Then

    SelectedTable = Request.Form("LISTTABLE")

Else

    SelectedTable = ""

End If



TableList.WriteTable(SelectedTable)


Set TableList = Nothing


%>
```

12. Save the TLCOMPNT.ASP file.

13. Browse the file by entering *http://myserver/MYWEBFOLDER/ tlcompnt.asp*, where *MYSERVER* is the name of your Web server and *MYWEBFOLDER* is the name of the folder in which you saved the ASP file.

Assuming everything is configured correctly, the results should be identical to those obtained by running the previous solution.

As mentioned earlier, it's possible to use the code in this solution to present data from sources other than tables, including SQL statements and stored procedures. To implement this functionality, you would simply need to change the *CommandType* property of the ADO command object to the desired type, and the *CommandText* property to either the name of the desired stored procedure, or the SQL statement you wish to use.

# Using Microsoft Transaction Server for Object and Resource Pooling

If the performance advantages provided by moving your ASP code into COM components is not sufficient, then it may be time to take the next step in scalability, using Microsoft Transaction Server (MTS) to manage the objects your application uses. A full discussion of the advantages and implementation of MTS is beyond the scope of this chapter. MTS will be discussed in-depth in Chapter 8, "Ensuring Transactional Integrity." In this section, we'll provide an overview of the component management features of MTS related to scalability, as well as discussing some considerations you should use when developing components for MTS.

## Scalability Advantages of MTS

One of the main services that Microsoft Transaction Server provides is that of component management. MTS provides this service by intercepting the call when a client calls *CreateObject*. Rather than the expected component object reference, MTS passes the client a reference to a context object it creates. The context object acts as a proxy for the actual object, allowing the client to access the properties and methods of the object, yet still allowing MTS to maintain control of the actual object.

How does this translate to better scalability? By maintaining control of the object instance in question, MTS can keep track of when a client is using the object, and share that same object with other clients when it is not in use. This in turn means that fewer instances of the component object must be maintained, which means fewer resources will be consumed, which means greater scalability.

Although not currently implemented in MTS 2.0, future versions of MTS will support *object pooling*, in which a pool of identical object instances are maintained, saving clients the expense of creating a new object instance each time one is needed.

> NOTE: Until the release of COM+, it's necessary to code components in such a way as to notify MTS when they are finished with a given task, so that MTS can share the component.

## Considerations for MTS Components

In order to support the functionality described above, components written for use with MTS should make use of the *ObjectContext* object of MTS. In your component project, set a reference to the Microsoft Transaction Server type library. To get a reference to the MTS *ObjectContext* object, a component simply needs to call the *GetObjectContext* method. To make the most out of the services MTS provides, components should use the *SetComplete* and *SetAbort* methods of the *ObjectContext* to notify MTS that a given unit of work is complete, or that a failure has occurred. Once the *SetComplete* or *SetAbort* method has been called MTS can allow another client to make use of that component.

### Maintaining State with MTS Components

One of the consequences of writing a component for use with MTS is that in order to make a component available for use by another client, MTS must return that component to its initialized state, meaning any state information from the current client is lost. The effect of this is that any client of a component running under MTS must never require the component to maintain state information between method calls. Any properties necessary for the successful completion of a method call should be set prior to calling the method, or passed as arguments.

### Performance Issues

In order for MTS to do its job effectively, components must cooperate. Each discreet unit of work provided by a component should end with a call to *SetComplete*, and each error handler should end with a call to *SetAbort*. Additionally, it's important to remember that since MTS treats all data access in your component as existing within a transaction, components that take a long time to call *SetComplete* or *SetAbort* may cause data concurrency problems as the data source is locked during the transaction. This can result in less than optimal performance. For this reason, it's recommended that the unit of work a component does before calling *SetComplete* be as small as possible.

# Component Maintenance

*Component maintenance* is not necessarily an issue of performance, but it is important to the developer because poorly planned maintenance or upgrades can cause significant application downtime. For applications in production, upgrades must be well-planned in order to avoid disrupting the normal operation of the application, not to mention other applications running on the same Web server. For applications in development, IIS makes life a little easier by allowing applications to be run in a separate process, as described later in this section.

## Planning for Upgrades

One problem that can be especially troubling for Web applications is that of upgrading the components in use by the application. In IIS 3.0, it was necessary to stop the World Wide Web Service in order to be able to replace a component that is used by a Web application. Given that in IIS 3.0, all applications ran in the same process as the Web server, this meant that each time a component needed to be upgraded, every application on that Web server needed to be disrupted, if only briefly. Since components need to be upgraded frequently during development, this can be especially problematic during the early stages of a Web application's life. IIS 4.0 provides a solution to this problem, called *process isolation*.

## Running in an Isolated Process

*Process isolation* simply means that a given Web application is run in a process separate from that of IIS. The advantage of this is that a Web application being run in process isolation mode can be stopped independently from any other application on that server. This allows component upgrades to be substantially less disruptive. Process isolation also provides the substantial benefit of protecting the Web server from unstable applications, and protecting applications from one another. With process isolation, if an application crashes, it cannot affect other applications or the Web server. There is one catch to process isolation, a catch that should be fairly obvious given the name.

Applications can be run in one of two ways, *in-process* (typically DLLs) and *out-of-process* (typically EXEs). While it is possible to run out-of-process components with IIS, it is generally discouraged for performance reasons. When a component is run outside of the process from which it was called (in this case IIS) all property settings and method calls and arguments must go through a process called *marshalling*. Marshalling is a process by which the call is translated from the format of the client to an intermediate universal format, moved across the process boundary to the component, then translated back to a format understood by the component. The process of marshalling generally makes out-of-process components substantially slower than in-process components. This should be taken into account when deciding whether your application will run in process isolation mode.

### • • • SOLUTION: Developing the Rent-A-Prize Application in Process Isolation Mode.

In this solution, we'll demonstrate the steps necessary to run our sample application in process isolation mode.

1. Open Internet Service Manager in the Microsoft Management Console.

2. Expand the server on which your Web application resides by clicking the + symbol next to it.

3. Expand the Default Web Site, and look for the folder or icon corresponding to your application.

4. Right-click on the icon for your application and select Properties from the context menu.

5. On the Properties dialog box for your application, check the box marked, "Run in separate memory space (isolated process)."

6. That's it. Your application and all components used by your application will now run in a process separate from IIS, allowing you to stop and start your application separately from other applications, and protecting IIS and other applications from your application crashing.

## Summary

In this chapter, we talked about the many ways in which the performance and scalability of your application may be enhanced, from implementing coding standards, to the proper use of ASP, from reducing the use of Include files, to moving code into components. The important thing to remember is that although not all of these techniques will be useful in every situation, consistently using these techniques where appropriate for the solution you are implementing will definitely improve the overall performance of your Web application.

In the next chapter, we'll continue discussing the specifics of Microsoft Transaction Server, in particular its role in maintaining transactional integrity.

# Enterprise Development Using Microsoft Transaction Server

• • • **GOAL: Increasing the Scalability of the Rent-A-Prize Web Application Using Microsoft Transaction Server 2.0**

Microsoft developed the Windows Distributed interNet Architecture (DNA) as a scaleable, transaction-oriented framework on which to base the development and deployment of both Web and client/server solutions. The middle tier of a Windows DNA application typically consists of COM components, written in either Visual C++, Visual J++, or Visual Basic, running on one or more distributed Microsoft Transaction Server (MTS) machines. In an enterprise Web application, these components provide services to the Active Server Pages (ASP) created in Visual InterDev 6.0. MTS provides management services for the COM business components in a DNA Web application. Despite what the name suggests, the Microsoft "Transaction" Server acts not only as a Transaction Processing (TP) monitor but also facilitates the management of components and component resources that live and play in the middle tier of a distributed application. In theory MTS spends as much time managing transactions as it does managing component resources. In fact, some developers feel that a more suitable name for the product might be the "Microsoft Component Manager."

In this chapter we're going to discuss the underlying MTS architecture and how MTS performs its Transaction Processing (TP) and Object Request Brokering (ORB) magic. Then we're going to examine how you construct MTS Component Object Model (COM) components using Visual Basic 5.0 or later. Finally, we'll take a look at a practical example that demonstrates how to build, deploy, and call MTS components from the Rent-A-Prize Active Server application.

# Microsoft Transaction Server 2.0

MTS 1.0 provided a run-time environment that handled all the underlying system services, better known as the "plumbing," that needs to be addressed to scale single-user components called from a Visual InterDev application to the enterprise. MTS 2.0 now extends that environment by providing integration with Microsoft Internet Information Server 4.0, transactional connectivity to Oracle databases, integration with Microsoft Message Queue Server, and transactional mainframe connectivity via Microsoft SNA Server 4.0.

MTS lets developers build their applications as a collection of single-user COM components that can then be deployed with little or no additional coding in a multi-user middle-tier environment.

MTS 2.0 is an integral part of the Windows NT environment and can be installed by running the Windows NT 4.0 Option Pack installation program. In the next version of the Windows NT operating system, NT5, MTS will be installed, by default, as part of Windows NT Server 5.0.

Before you begin to write MTS components you should have an understanding of the types of scalability and resource issues MTS resolves and how it goes about resolving them. In the next several sections we are going to look at a few of the issues developers face as they begin to scale their applications to the enterprise. After examining the issues we will take an in-depth look at how MTS addresses each of them.

# Component Scalability and Transaction Management in Enterprise Web Development

Up until a year or so ago, COM objects and the word "scalability" were rarely found in the same chapter, much less the same sentence. Now, MTS has emerged as a premier player in the middle-tier component management arena allowing developers to write single-user COM components that can be scaled to the enterprise.

If you take a look at the Windows DNA architecture you'll find that the DNA framework is actually a combination of new and existing Microsoft technologies. Its primary purpose is to facilitate the integration of the client-server and Web application development models and to help alleviate some of the scalability issues associated with Internet application access. At the foundation of the DNA architecture is the Component Object Model (COM). Developers can build Windows-based and browser-based clients that call the same MTS COM components written to execute the same business logic from both applications.

COM components help resolve the traditional two-tier processing bottle-neck by distributing the application load across three distinct tiers. There is, how-ever, one catch; just because the business logic is moved to a different tier doesn't mean you don't need to worry about scalability. When applications call a com-ponent running on a middle-tier server, the server places the component in memory where it stays until the application releases it. In two-tier development, developers were often taught to grab onto resources early and hold them until they no longer needed them, thus avoiding the costs of re-creating components and database connections. This limits the number of expensive server processes but, in most cases, vastly increases the potential for a fatal database and/or resource contention error as application use increases. The server resources consumed by the dormant component remain unavailable to other objects until the application releases them, a situation that is inefficient at best, and fatal to the application at worst. The problems associated with distributed development are central to the scalability of the middle tier.

If you could somehow manage the resources of a middle-tier COM server, like some ORBs and TP monitors do in the UNIX and mainframe world, you could then squeeze more processing power out of the servers, thus accommo-dating the fluctuating demand for middle-tier resources. This is not an easy task. Although there are several advantages to a distributed component architecture, building robust, multi-user components is quite difficult and time consuming. In fact, some research shows that developers who attempt to build scalable components spend nearly 40 percent of their development time building plumbing leaving only 60 percent of their time for implementation of the core business, functionality. Several major issues tend to complicate the implementation of a scalable physical n-tier architecture:

- **Distributed Transaction Support**   The need for multiple data sources to be updated simultaneously, with assurance that all or none will be updated.

- **Security**   The need to ensure that only authorized users or processes can gain access to business login in components.

- **Multi-user Support and Scalability**   The need to make applications available to large numbers of users without performance degradation.

- **Performance**   The need to prevent long wait times (or any wait times) during application processing.

- **Administration**   The need to keep track of who is using components and how.

# The MTS Solution

Microsoft's solution to component management is Microsoft Transaction Server (MTS). MTS is designed to take the grunt work out of server-side component creation by combining a COM-based transaction processing monitor and an object request broker, allowing developers to create single-user, nontransactional components that run well in a multi-user, transactional environment with little or no additional coding.

MTS 2.0 currently provides the following services:

- **Thread/Process Management**  Tracks resource usage by running programs, making sure they are run efficiently.

- **Process Isolation**  Runs components in separate MTS packages. This allows each component to execute simultaneously with the other on the same server without either affecting the success or failure of the other.

- **Object Pooling and Recycling**  Stores released objects in a holding pool and then re-assigns them to the same or alternate calling components on an as-needed basis without having to re-instantiate them.

- **Automatic Security**  Automatically provides user- and role-based security to components installed in MTS packages by administratively assigning user roles and access rights to the components in a package. No additional coding is required on the developer's part.

- **Automatic Transactions**  Automatically provides transaction support to components installed in MTS packages by administratively assigning transaction properties to components in a package. No additional coding is required on the developer's part.

- **Point-and-Click Administration**  Manages components installed in the MTS environment using the Microsoft Management Console MTS snap-in.

- **Integration with Window NT Features and Microsoft Products**  MTS is fully integrates with the Windows NT 4.0 operating system and communicates with the Windows NT 4.0 suite of products, including IIS 4.0, MSMQ, Cluster Server, and Active Server Pages.

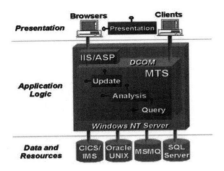

**Figure 8-1.**
*The MTS solution.*

So how does MTS do all this? To understand Microsoft's approach to component management we'll compare some of the more difficult component management issues to a more familiar scenario, consultant staffing. In this way, we'll use an everyday business scenario as an analogy for the techniques used by MTS.

# A Typical Consulting Firm—Consultant Pooling

A typical consulting firm's existence is based on its ability to acquire, maintain, and serve clients. The main commodity in this industry is the consultant. In a typical consulting firm the standard resource staffing scenario is usually described by these three actions:

1. A client calls with a project staffing requirement(s).

2. The consulting firm assigns a consultant(s) to the project.

3. The consultant completes the project and is placed onto another project.

For example, the XYZ firm has 70 consultants, each equally qualified, 20 of whom are currently available or "on-the-bench" (in the XYZ firm, consultants "on the bench" continue to draw a salary, which is how we keep them around). In this environment you could handle staffing in one of three ways:

## Dedicated Consultants

First, you could assign "dedicated" consultants to each client. When a developer works with a particular client they continue working with that client and only that client for their life at the firm, regardless of whether or not the client has work for them. This could become very expensive for the consulting firm. If the client doesn't have work for the consultant, the consultant isn't billable and isn't bringing any revenue into the firm to offset the expenses of retaining that consultant.

The parallel in the COM world is components that are created for an individual user and remain in memory for the life of that application. Server resources are allocated to this component until the component has been destroyed. Components are not destroyed until all client applications release the component. This results in resources (like our dedicated consultants) being consumed by components even though the component may be idle. Traditionally, developers were taught to acquire resources early and release them late to limit the number of network round-trips that were required. This can be expensive. When the application isn't using a component, the component is still in memory, consuming valuable server resources, possibly causing database contention problems and tying up resources that could otherwise be allocated to other applications.

### Minimalist Staffing

Second, you could decide that XYZ only hires consultants when a project staffing need arises and then terminates them when the project ends. This may solve the overhead problem associated with maintaining a dedicated consultant on the bench, however, over the long run it could turn out to be an even more expensive solution then the first. The costs associated with hiring a new employee can be staggering, that is if you can actually find one and then afford to pay him or her.

In the COM world, if an application requests a component, four things happen: the object is invoked on the server, the server allocates resources, the application invokes one or more of the objects methods, and the object is destroyed. If your application created an instance of a component each time it was requested and then released it each time it finished, the total number of network round-trips required to run the application would be staggering. Every time the application needed to invoke a method in a component the server would need to allocate the resources to support the Remote Procedure Call (RPC). This would require a substantial investment in server resources.

### Consultant Pooling

Finally, you could hire consultants based on projected, as opposed to immediate, needs and keep them in a consultant pool, traditionally called "the bench." When a consultant is not assigned to a client project he or she is "on-the-bench" awaiting re-assignment. Although the "benched" consultants are still drawing salary, having a bench minimizes the hiring and overhead costs associated with finding and keeping consultants. The bench can assure that no clients are turned away because you don't have enough consultants to staff a new project, but it does have a degree of risk. If the pool is too large, the company loses money because the overhead of the bench becomes larger than the costs associated with the hiring and firing of employees. So, the idea is to maintain a sufficient number of consultants in the consultant pool to service the firm's clients but not generate substantial overhead costs.

Pooling resources also has a few drawbacks. For example, what if the client is picky and wants the same consultant they used last year? This could be a problem if the company is not using the dedicated consultant model. In the pooled model, the chances of a client getting the same consultant are slim at best. This example of retaining previous knowledge is known in the component world as "state." The consultant that performed the work last year retains the previous engagement knowledge and the new consultant knows little or nothing about the project. The pooling example exemplifies a "stateless" environment. Now, this doesn't mean that the consultant does not remember anything during the engagement. What it does mean is that that knowledge is released, in this case because the consultant is not available, as soon as the consultant returns to the consultant pool.

COM components do not automatically provide the ability to share or pool resources. In fact, as we discussed several sections ago, it is fairly difficult to write components that can share resources reliably. You need to worry about things like resource and transaction management, multi-user access, connection pooling, and thread and process management.

MTS handles component management with an approach that is very similar to the pooling consultant staffing example. It provides component resource management that supports connection and resource pooling without the pain associated with creating the "plumbing."

## MTS Architecture

MTS components are actually in-process COM objects that are loaded into a process with the MTS Executive (MTXEX.DLL). The MTS Executive DLL provides the run-time services for MTS components, including thread and context management. The MTXEX.DLL is loaded into the same process as the MTS component DLLs and can be loaded in-process with the client or an alternate process named MTX.EXE. Most applications choose to load the components in the MTX process as opposed to the client process (see Figure 8-2).

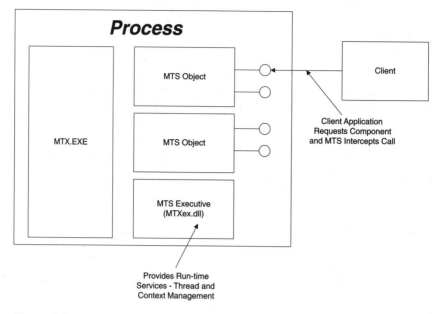

**Figure 8-2.**
*The MTS architecture.*

When a client application calls a component, MTS intercepts the call and creates a Context Object for the component. The Context Object is a COM object that implements the *IObjectContext* interface. This interface allows the components to tell MTS when the work they are doing is done and whether or not the work completed successfully (*Commit*) or unsuccessfully (*Abort*). There are several *IObjectContext* methods that are used, at runtime, to communicate with MTS. You use the *SetComplete* and *SetAbort* methods to tell MTS the status of a component's completed work, the *CreateInstance* method to enlist a component within the scope of an already existing transaction, and the *IsCallerInrole* to check a client's security settings.

## Component Resources

In most distributed object environments, instances of server-based objects remain active consuming server resources as long as one or more clients hold a reference to the object. In a multi-user environment, this would require significant server resources and could potentially even stall the server. To address this issue, MTS provides something called "just-in-time" (JIT) activation and "as-soon-as-possible" deactivation (ASAP).

MTS uses JIT and "deferred activation" to allow components to only consume server resources while they are executing. *Deferred activation* means that a component instance is not actually created until a client calls one of the object's methods. As soon as an MTS component indicates that it has finished, MTS deactivates the component and recycles its resources. As long as the component is deactivated, only limited server resources remain allocated to it. When the component is called again, MTS reactivates it by reacquiring the resources the component needs. From the client's perspective, only a single instance of the component exists from the time the client creates it to the time it's finally released.

MTS implements just-in-time activation using an *object context wrapper*. When a component is called by a client application, MTS wraps the component in the object context wrapper. The object context wrapper takes the place of the object the client application sees. The client application sees an object (the object context wrapper) that appears to be the component being called. The object context wrapper exposes the same methods as the actual component. The client just sees an ordinary COM object exposing a number of methods. When the MTS object calls *SetComplete*, MTS releases all its references to the object. Like any COM object when the references to the object are released, the object instance is destroyed. The client still holds what it thinks is a reference to the object, which is, in fact, a reference to the MTS object context wrapper (see Figure 8-3). This is called *deactivating the component*.

To take advantage of this feature client objects must reference an MTS object early and release it as late as possible. This lets MTS create an instance of the MTS object whenever an incoming method call comes in. When the component tells MTS that it's done processing, MTS destroys it but keeps the object context wrapper alive to service the next method call. This allows MTS to limit the number of times you actually create and destroy an object, thus reducing the number of network round-trips required. In many ways it is similar, in theory, to caching a component for future use.

In a perfect world, the components, along with the component instances, would be cached so that you would not need to re-instantiate the instance of the component each time you call it. Today, only the components themselves are cached, although Microsoft does have future plans to cache instances of components as well.

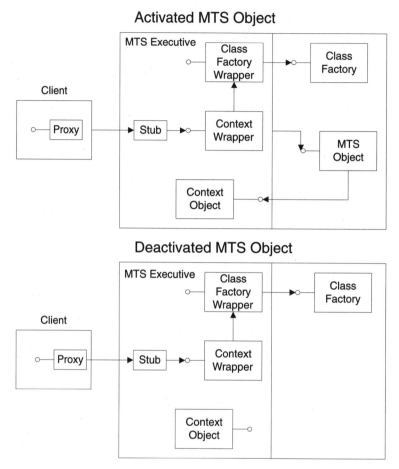

**Figure 8-3.**
*Just-in-time activation.*

## Managing Data Resources

Managing data resources is traditionally a complicated process. Developers have to plan how they are going to optimize the locking of a database and its tables to insure the integrity and scalability of the application. There are, however, some additional resource issues to think about. Obtaining and releasing ODBC connections is an expensive proposition. Just as component resources are finite so are the resources available to database connections. If the system does not manage the connections properly, the application could experience data concurrency problems. A few of the data resource challenges developers face are listed below.

- Configuring and maintaining a separate database connection for each client consumes significant database resources and limits scalability.

- The cost of establishing a connection to a database can far exceed the cost of the work the connection was acquired to accomplish.

- The process of establishing, managing, and closing multiple database connections usually requires complex transaction processing that spans several disparate data stores.

MTS allows you to manage database connections effortlessly with something known as *database connection pooling*. Connection pooling allows users to re-establish connections with the database without the cost of having to necessarily re-create a connection. As applications create and release connections they are placed in a pool. If an application requests a connection and a connection is available in the connection pool, the available connection is re-activated. This can yield significant performance gains because it eliminates some of the overhead associated with the opening and closing of an ODBC connection each time an application needs access to an ODBC data source.

Connection pooling is implemented in MTS with resource dispensers and resource managers. A *resource dispenser* provides an orderly way of acquiring and freeing shared nonpersistent resources (such as threads or database connections) on a system. When an object requests a resource the resource dispenser hands it one from a resource pool. If a connection does not exist in the pool, the resource dispenser requests a new connection from the appropriate resource manager. When the object releases the connection, the resource dispenser returns it to the pool. MTS ships with a component called the ODBC resource dispenser that automatically pools connections to ODBC databases.

## Resource Managers

*Resource managers* are services that manage durable data. MTS currently supports the Microsoft SQL Server 6.5 resource manager using the OLE transaction protocol as well as the X/Open or XA protocol. Microsoft SQL Server and durable message queues like those in Microsoft Message Queue 1.0 (MSMQ) are both examples of resource managers. The resource dispenser usually requests some data from the resource manager. The resource manager, in the case of SQL Server, simply executes requests as the resource dispenser makes them.

## Resource Dispensers

Resource dispensers manage nondurable shared state for application components within a process. The easiest way to think of a resource dispenser is to compare it to a type of driver. For example, the ODBC 3.0 Driver Manager is the ODBC resource dispenser that gives MTS components access to ODBC data sources. MTS currently provides two resource dispensers, the ODBC resource dispenser and the Shared Property Manager. The Distributed Transaction Coordinator (DTC) calls the appropriate resource dispenser based on a request from a component or process.

The Shared Property Manager provides synchronized access to application-defined, process-wide, properties. For example, you might use a shared property to maintain a Web page hit counter or cache system data in a component used in a Visual InterDev Web application.

## Thread and Process Management

System performance and scalability always seem to be an issue when the number of user requests increase. One way to increase the scalability of an application is to use Windows NT threads instead of a process for each user request, since threads are less expensive than processes where resources are concerned. MTS thread pooling creates and runs multiple component instances, one for each caller, within a single process. This enables single-user components to execute in a multi-user environment without requiring a process-per-user architecture. Now, instead of having to have a process per user, users can share processes, reducing the load on the middle-tier server (see Figure 8-4).

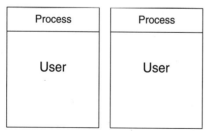
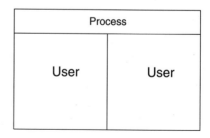

**Figure 8-4.**
*MTS thread pooling.*

This may sound like a good idea until you try to write the programming logic to implement it. So, to make it easier for developers to use threads, MTS provides an automatic thread pooling mechanism. When a request for component comes to MTS from a client, MTS automatically locates an available thread from a thread pool, executes the component on the thread, and returns the thread to the pool. This increases performance and simplifies programming by reducing the overhead of thread creation and destruction.

There are three threading models that currently exist for COM components, *single-threaded*, *apartment-threaded*, and *free-threaded*. Single-threaded components are the least scalable because component requests must execute in sequence within a single thread. The component access is serialized, meaning that the component can only process one user at a time. Clients that need to access the component must wait until the client in front of them has finished processing. This is generally unacceptable in situations where multi-user access is required.

Apartment-threaded components use more than one thread to process multiple client requests. Each thread, however, can only service one request at a time. This allows a single component instance to process multiple client requests simultaneously. However, it accomplishes this by creating a new instance of the component for each request. Visual Basic 5.0 (Service Pack 2 and later) and 6.0 support apartment and single-threaded components. The Rent-A-Prize components are compiled as apartment-threaded components. The threading model of a component may be changed using the General tab of the Visual Basic project properties dialog box (see Figure 8-10).

Free-threaded components, the most scalable of the three, can process many client requests at a time inside a single thread. MTS and Visual Basic do not yet support free-threaded servers.

In many environments, a failure within a thread or process can potentially cause the failure of an entire application. To prevent this problem, MTS provides the ability to package components so that they execute in their own Windows NT process. The most visible example of this is in the Visual InterDev development world. If you reference a COM component that fails from an ASP page and the component is executing in the same process as Internet Information Server (IIS) you have to kill the WWW IIS process to release the rogue component from the memory of the server. If you mark the application to run out-of-process, you only need to unload the application. You mark the application as out-of-process using the Internet Service Manager Microsoft Management Console snap-in (discussed in a later section). Process isolation ensures that a failure in one package or process doesn't affect another process.

## Distributed Transaction Management

Well-designed three-tier applications are not only scalable but they are *fault tolerant.* A fault tolerant application is an application that can automatically recover from a failure without the loss of data. Distributed Web applications built with Visual InterDev 6.0 can use transactions to guarantee the automatic recovery of an application failure. Transactions, by definition, allow a complex set of operations to appear as a single unit of work that either succeeds or fails. In the mainframe world, Transaction Processing monitors (TP monitors) have existed for years, allowing applications to recover without incident from potentially harmful failures. A *TP monitor* is a type of middleware that enables business applications to group two or more units of work into a single unit ensuring that all changes to the units involved either succeed or fail. Now, MTS affords Windows NT developers the same luxury.

MTS uses transactions to allow applications to achieve *atomic* (all or nothing) updates and consistency across components, database systems, and network boundaries. Each component designed and packaged for MTS has a transaction property that indicates the transactional attributes of the component, allowing the component to be automatically managed by MTS.

In order to understand why we need transactions in a Visual InterDev application, let's take a look at how a Web-based banking application might implement transactions. In this example, a bank application allows a user to transfer funds between two accounts existing in two different physical locations. If the customer transfers one hundred dollars from an account in Washington, D.C., to an account in Seattle, Washington, the system will need to credit the account in Seattle, Washington, and then debit the account in Washington, D.C. If both units of work succeed, the state of the transaction and the data integrity of the databases are maintained. Now, let's look at what happens if one of the units, the debit of the account in Washington, fails. If the debit fails and the credit in Seattle succeeds, the bank actually creates money. While account holders may love this arrangement, the bank president will no doubt feel differently.

In the Rent-A-Prize application, a transaction can be used to guarantee that a customer's credit card has been authorized before the clerk is permitted to rent the car to the customer. For example, the update rental component saves the rental information and then attempts to verify the customer's credit card. If the rental information is saved and the credit validation fails, the customer would still be able to rent the car unless both components were wrapped in a single transaction. With the use of a transaction, if one of the components fails, both fail.

Transaction-based systems must pass what's known as the "ACID" test. There are four primary attributes that govern transaction processing and define the ACID test. They are:

- **Atomicity**   Ensures that all work is either committed or rolled back as a single unit.

- **Consistency**   Ensures that work being performed is legal according to the business rules or database consistency rules we're using.

- **Isolation**   Ensures that concurrent transactions are independent from one another.

- **Durability**   Ensures that uncommitted transactions will survive system failures.

As long as business components follow these rules, the state and integrity of the business data will remain intact.

## Why Can't Database Transactions Do the Job?

It's very easy to create one or more SQL statements and then wrap them in a transaction within a stored procedure. The database will automatically roll back the data to its previous state if one of the SQL statements fail in a transaction. So, why can't database transactions handle the transaction processing? To better understand the issues associated with database transaction management, let's take another look at our bank transfer example. In that example, we wanted to transfer data between two accounts and wrap the debit and the credit of the accounts into one atomic unit or transaction. If the two accounts exist in the same physical database, the events can be grouped between begin transaction and end transaction statements in a database stored procedure. If one of the units fails, then the database server will automatically roll back the other. But what happens if the data is not in the same physical database? Until the introduction of MTS this type of transaction could only be accomplished with the creation of lengthy coding logic that would store the original information at the start of the transaction. If one of the units failed, the system could then re-create the initial state of the database from the stored data. MTS facilitates the coordination of transactions across disparate systems using the Distributed Transaction Coordinator (DTC)

## The Distributed Transaction Coordinator(DTC)

The Distributed Transaction Coordinator coordinates transactions that span multiple resource managers. The component calls the DTC, which then calls the appropriate resource dispenser for the resource manager. This allows work to be committed as an atomic transaction even if it spans multiple resource managers located on distributed servers. The Microsoft DTC was first released as part of the Microsoft SQL Server 6.5 product and is included in the MTS product. It implements a two-phase commit protocol that ensures that the transaction outcome is consistent across all resource managers involved in a transaction. In a two-phase commit, the committing of a transaction begins when the component that begins the transaction attempts to commit the transaction. At this time, MTS checks with all other transaction participants to ensure that each component acknowledges that it's OK to commit the transaction. Once MTS receives an acknowledgment from each participant, the transaction is committed. If even one of the transaction participants sends notification of a problem, the entire transaction is rolled back.

Microsoft has created what they call "OLE transactions" as the preferred Microsoft two-phase commit protocol. It is based on COM and is used by resource managers in order to participate in transactions that are coordinated by the Microsoft DTC. XA, defined by the X/Open DTP group, is another supported two-phase commit protocol. XA is natively supported by many UNIX databases, including Informix, Oracle, and DB2.

## MTS 2.0 and IIS 4.0

Microsoft Internet Information Server 4.0 is now fully integrated with MTS 2.0. The most noticeable IIS enhancement is its ability to provide run-time services such as transaction management. This means that Active Server Pages developed in Visual InterDev can now support and participate in MTS transactions. Like standard transactions, ASP transactions can involve database access logic, mainframe application integration, and message queues.

Another enhancement is that the IIS ISAPI DLL is now installed in a package in the MTS environment. This allows developers to specify whether or not components called from an ASP page will run in the same or a separate server process from the IIS process, regardless of whether they are in-process (DLL) or out-of-process (EXE) components. When the IIS server launches a component it can either place the component in the same physical package or create a new package for it. This solves an annoying problem encountered by Visual InterDev developers who modified COM components implemented in the IIS 3.0 environment. In IIS 3.0, the only way to unload a rogue or failing COM component from memory was to stop and start the IIS World Wide Web service, an unacceptable solution for a production Web server. IIS 4.0 allows you to create a Visual InterDev application and then set attributes for that application, one of which is whether the application runs in-process or out-of-process. An in-process Web application will be run in IIS's memory space, leaving it potentially vulnerable to crashes in other applications, while the out-of-process setting runs the application in its own isolated memory space.

NOTE: While the use of the out-of-process setting can help the stability of an application, there is a performance penalty for running an application out-of-process. This performance penalty should be weighed against the need for application stability when deciding which setting to use.

You set the attribute by right-clicking the application in the MMC Internet Service Manager snap-in and selecting Properties from the pop-up menu that appears. The dialog box in Figure 8-5 appears, allowing you to modify the properties of the Active Server application. To set the attribute, either select or deselect the Run in separate memory space check box.

**Figure 8-5.**
*The Microsoft Management Console IIS ASP application properties.*

## Transactional ASP

The integration of MTS and IIS 4.0 allows ASP pages to participate in transactions. An Active Server script can manipulate data and make calls to server components that participate in the transaction. As with any transaction, if any part of the transaction fails, the entire transaction will be rolled back. There is one problem with using transactional scripts, if the transaction aborts, the database changes will be rolled back but the script environment changes will not. For example, if you modified a row in a database table and then set a session variable to a new value, the changes in the database would be rolled back by the databases resource manager but the modification to the session variable would not. There are, however, transactional events that are triggered based on the outcome of the transaction that allow developers to manually reverse any script changes.

To define a page as transactional in a Visual InterDev project, you include the following directive at the top of your active server page:

```
<%@TRANSACTION = transParam %>
```

265

This directive must be on the first line in the ASP script. If it is not, then a script error will be generated when the page is run.

The *transParam* parameter can have the following values:

| transParam | Valid Values |
|---|---|
| Requires_New | Starts a new transaction regardless of the existence of an existing transaction. |
| Required | Starts a new transaction if one doesn't already exist. |
| Supported | Participates in a transaction if one exists. |
| Not_Supported | Does not participate in a transaction at any time. |

**Table 8-1.**
*Valid values for ASP transParam parameter.*

There is also a simple shortcut to add the @TRANSACTION = Required directive to your page. Simply follow these steps:

1. Open the page you wish to make transactional in the Visual InterDev 6.0 Source editor.

2. Right-click in an empty area of the page, and select Properties. The dialog box shown in Figure 8-6 appears.

3. Check the Enable Transactions check box, then click OK.

Visual InterDev then adds the directive to the top of your page.

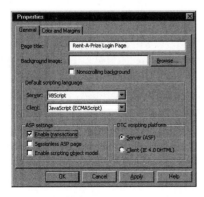

**Figure 8-6.**
*Visual InterDev's Page Properties dialog box.*

Although the script itself cannot determine the outcome of a transaction, you can write events that are called when the transaction commits or aborts. For example, suppose you have a Visual InterDev project that contains a page with a script that executes a component. Based on the outcome of that component, you want to display a different page. You can use the *OnTransactionCommit* and *OnTransactionAbort* events to have the application automatically display a different page, depending on whether the transaction succeeds or fails.

```
<%@TRANSACTION=Required%>

<%

'Buffer output so that different pages can be displayed.

Response.Buffer = True

%>

<HTML>

<BODY>

Welcome to my test.


<%

Set MyTest = Server.CreateObject("MyTest.TestIt")

MyTest.Test("1")

%>

<%

Sub OnTransactionCommit()

    Response.Write "<HTML>"

    Response.Write "<BODY>"

    Response.Write "Transaction Successful"

    Response.Write "</HTML>"

    Response.Write "</BODY>"

End Sub

%>

<%

Sub OnTransactionAbort()

    Response.Write "<HTML>"
```

*(continued)*

267

```
   Response.Write "<BODY>"

   Response.Write "Transaction Failed"

   Response.Write "</HTML>"

   Response.Write "</BODY>"

End Sub

%>
```

## The Microsoft Management Console (MMC)

Microsoft Management Console (MMC) provides a common interface and framework for system management applications. The MMC environment supports *snap-ins*. Snap-ins provide the management functionality inside MMC. Microsoft currently ships several prebuilt snap-ins, including the Microsoft Transaction Server (MTS) Explorer, Internet Service Manager (IIS 4.0), and the Microsoft Message Queue Server (MSMQ) Explorer. MMC was developed to provide an easy way for developers and ISVs (independent software vendors) to create and maintain system management functions for applications they write and or distribute. The console was designed to give system administrators the ability to create and save subsets of tools from various vendors.

MMC is currently installed with the NT 4.0 Option Pack and will be distributed as part of Windows NT 5.0. Throughout this chapter the MMC will be used to administer MTS as well as IIS (see Figure 8-7).

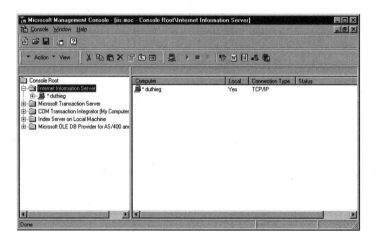

**Figure 8-7.**
*The Microsoft Management Console.*

# Building MTS Components

Building MTS components is as simple as building a standard COM component. They can be built using Visual C++, Visual J++, or Visual Basic. There are, however, some rules you should follow when designing and building COM components that can have an enormous effect on the scalability and performance of an application. We'll take a look at these rules and then discuss how they work together to make designing scalable components a reality.

## Rules for Scalable Component Design

Designing scalable components is easy if you follow a few simple rules:

- Make your components as granular as possible.

- Do not maintain state unless you have to.

- Make sure your components call *SetComplete* as often as possible. This notifies MTS that the component no longer needs to maintain state and releases the resources held by the component.

- Acquire resources early and let them go late. MTS only holds onto interface pointers and won't allocate the resources to the component until the first method is invoked. When you call *SetComplete* MTS releases the resources but not the pointer.

- Acquire database connections late and let go of them early, since they are pooled. The pooling of database connections makes acquiring these resources very cheap.

- Pass parameters by value whenever possible. Avoid passing parameters by reference.

- Use declarative security. An entry for each individual does not scale well.

- Use transactions whenever possible.

## Designing with Scalability in Mind

The above rules provide some much-needed guidance, but rules out of context are not sufficient. The discussion that follows explains how to combine these rules to create scalable components and will help focus the developer, allowing him or her to attack their development challenges clearly and confidently.

## Component Granularity

*Granularity* of a component is defined by the number of tasks it performs, and the scope of those tasks. Granularity can have an enormous effect on the performance of your application. Components can be divided into two types—fine-grained and coarse-grained.

*Fine-grained components* usually perform a single task that is limited in scope. Fine-grained components are easier to debug and are often called from many places throughout the application. They perform simple operations and are therefore usually more efficient consumers of system resources. For example, a customer component that contains a method to add customer information, a method to update customer information, and a method to delete customer information would be defined as a fine-grained component.

*Coarse-grained components* usually perform multiple tasks. For example, a component that creates a rental reservation, checks out the car, and then creates a receipt. This component performs several complex tasks and would most likely hold valuable system resources until the component finishes processing. This type of component is generally more difficult to maintain, harder to debug, less reusable, and should be avoided at all costs.

The components created for the Rent-A-Prize application are designed to be finely grained. Each method accomplishes a single task, allowing developers to mix and match them, as appropriate, to accomplish larger and more complex tasks. For example, the update method needs to update the rental table information and check the validity of the customer's credit card. The code to accomplish this could have been included in one component but to keep the components finely grained, the credit card validation functionality is located in a separate and distinct COM component.

## Stateless Versus Stateful

If you are accustomed to writing COM components, you are probably accustomed to using object properties to maintain state between client method calls. Maintaining state in this manner allows a component to pick up where it left off, a sometimes valuable asset in the COM programming world. MTS COM objects can also maintain internal state, but this can have a significant effect on the performance of an application. If you maintain state between client component calls, the component cannot be released from memory and must remain in memory until it is finished processing. This prohibits MTS from re-allocating the components resources for use by other components.

You release the state of a component by calling the *SetComplete* and *SetAbort* methods of the *ObjectContext* object. When you call one of these methods, you are notifying MTS that the component no longer needs to maintain state.

This frees server resources for use by other components and transactions. If the object needs to maintain state, it must remain activated, holding potentially valuable resources, such as server resources and database connections. Stateless objects are thus more efficient and are recommended by Microsoft to achieve maximum application scalability. The Rent-A-Prize components were designed as stateless components.

There are, however, circumstances that require that a component maintains state between client calls. In these instances it's recommended that you only maintain state within the scope of a transaction. The transaction boundary must not be crossed. If you cross it you will lose the state you have worked so hard to hold when one of the transactions completes (see Figure 8-8). Maintaining state between a client and a component located in different tiers is also not recommended. This type of call is slower than inter-tier calls and as a result, holding state in these instances can be expensive.

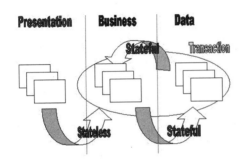

**Figure 8-8.**
*Holding state in objects.*

## Using the Object Context to Manage Component Transactions

Each MTS object has an associated context object. A *context object* is an MTS COM object that provides context for an instance of a component. When a client calls an MTS component, MTS automatically creates the context object. When the component is finished processing, it uses the MTS Object Context (to which it has obtained a reference) to communicate the status of the component to the MTS service. There are several *ObjectContext* methods, the four that help you manage transactions are: *SetComplete*, *SetAbort*, *EnableCommit*, and *DisableCommit*. When the component issues the *SetComplete* or *SetAbort* method of the *ObjectContext* object, MTS automatically deactivates the component and releases that component instance from memory. It retains the pointer to the component until the client application unloads or the client issues

271

the *SetObject = nothing* command. Once the component is destroyed, MTS will release the object from memory. A description of the four *ObjectContext* methods is listed below.

- **SetComplete**   Tells MTS that the object has completed its work successfully. MTS deactivates the component when it returns from the method that first entered the context.

- **SetAbort**   Tells MTS that the component's work can never be committed. MTS deactivates the component when it returns from the method that first entered the context.

- **EnableCommit**   Tells MTS that the component has not necessarily completed its work yet, but that its transactional updates can be committed in their current form.

- **DisableCommit**   Tells MTS that the component's transactional updates can not be committed in their current form.

The *UpdateRental* method of the *UpdateRental* class uses the object context to communicate the success or failure of the method. To use the *ObjectContext*, you must get a reference to the current *ObjectContext* by declaring an object of type *ObjectContext* and then calling the *GetObjectContext* function. At the completion of the method you then call either the *objContext.SetComplete* or *objContext.SetAbort* function.

```
Dim objContext As ObjectContext
Set objContext = GetObjectContext()
```

The code below checks to see if a return value is *True*. If it is, the code calls the *SetComplete* method. If the return value is *False*, it calls *SetAbort*. The *SetComplete* and *SetAbort* methods will produce a run-time error if the component is not installed in the MTS environment at the time it is executed. This can be a problem in the test and debug modes of development. To avoid this, the validity of the *ContextObject* is checked prior to calling the *SetComplete* and *Abort* methods by comparing it to "nothing." The *GetObjectContext* method will not produce a run-time error but will return a value equal to that of nothing when the component is not installed in the MTS environment.

```
If vRtnCode = True Then

    UpdateRental = 0


    If Not objContext Is Nothing Then
```

*(continued)*

```
        objContext.SetComplete
    End If
Else
    If Not objContext Is Nothing Then
        objContext.SetAbort
    End If
End If
```

The *EnableCommit* and *DisableCommit* methods are commonly used when an object's state must be maintained between client component calls. Although maintaining state is not recommended, it is sometimes a necessity. Objects that need to retain state across multiple calls from a client can protect themselves from having their work committed prematurely by calling the *DisableCommit* method before returning control to the client. When the component is finished processing it calls the *EnableCommit* method to allow the component transaction to successfully commit.

## Improving Performance with Just-In-Time Activation

Just-in-time activation allows MTS to release component resources without having to notify the client that the component is no longer available in memory. Components are in one of two states: *activated* or *deactivated*. Activated means that the MTS component is available in memory and deactivated means that only the context wrapper object that mimics the MTS object interface is available. It is this context wrapper object that provides transparent access to the component even when the component is deactivated. MTS components are initially created in the deactivated state. When a client invokes a method on a component that is in a deactivated state, MTS automatically activates the component. When the component is finished processing, it is placed back in the deactivated state. This ability to deactivate and reactivate while clients are still holding references to a component (actually the component's object context wrapper) is called "just-in-time" activation. From the client's perspective, only a single instance of the component exists from the time the client creates it to the time it is finally released, even though the client may make use of many different instances of the component during the time the client application is running. This makes the server applications more scalable by allowing server resources to be used more efficiently through recycling of components.

The context object wrapper exists for the lifetime of the MTS object across one or more deactivation and reactivation cycles. So how does an object get deactivated? Calling the *ObjectContext SetComplete* and *SetAbort* methods deactivates the object. Because deactivated components require the consumption of fewer resources, the performance and scalability of an application can be improved substantially by objects that remain stateless and deactivate immediately upon completion of their methods.

## Passing Parameters and ASP

Parameters are passed or marshaled between client applications and server components either by reference or by value. In the three-tier environment, an MTS object interface must be able to be marshaled across thread, process, and machine boundaries. Components that are invoked by Visual InterDev applications using VBScript are limited to specific parameter types. In VBScript 1.0, all parameters must be passed by value and the return value of a method must be of type variant. In VBScript 2.0 you can pass parameters by reference, but only if they are of type variant. ADO and ADOR Recordset objects can also be referenced and returned from method functions.

If you intend to pass variables by reference, you should consider carefully the performance implications that are associated with maintaining a reference to your variable across machine boundaries. Every time you refer to the variable, the component will communicate across machine boundaries. This can decrease the performance and scalability of an application substantially. Therefore, it is recommended that you only pass variables by reference when it is absolutely necessary.

There are two types of objects that can be passed by reference, *business* (COM) objects and *recordset* objects. Business objects are always passed by reference. Recordset objects can be passed by value or by reference. When returning a large amount of data you should consider using the ActiveX Data Object Recordset (ADOR). The Microsoft Remote Data Services (RDS), previously named the Active Data Connector (ADC), provides a mechanism that allows you to marshal ADOR recordsets back to a client by value. The recordset is essentially disconnected from the server and allows the server resources to be freed. You can also pass the recordset from the client back to a component, reconnect to the database, and then use the recordset's methods to save or discard changes. This, although appealing, should be considered very carefully before it is implemented in a Visual InterDev application as it can have a serious effect on the data integrity of a database.

The Rent-A-Prize application uses ADOR recordsets in its components to marshal data to and from the client applications. Before the existence of ADOR recordsets the "safe array" was the only efficient way to marshal large data sets between a component and a client. This usually resulted in lines and lines of grueling code to load and unload two-dimensional arrays. ADOR recordsets allow us to package the data and marshal it as an object. Although you could use the recordset's update method to save changes to the database, as mentioned before, the Rent-A-Prize components only use the ADOR recordset as a storage container to preserve the data integrity of the database.

## Declarative Security

You can control access to packages, components, and interfaces by defining user roles that are then assigned to MTS packages. User roles determine which users are allowed to invoke interfaces in a component that are installed in a package. This method of security is much more effective than its alternative—client impersonation. Client impersonation requires that you programmatically implement security in a component's procedural logic based on specific Windows NT user IDs. For more information regarding MTS component security, see the section entitled, "Setting Up User Roles," later in this chapter.

## Determining Transaction Outcome

A client application determines the success or failure of a transaction based on values returned by the method call that completed the transaction. The typical method of returning the outcome is to return it as the return value of the method or to pass in by reference a return parameter of type variant for the method. For example, the *RentalUpdate* method returns a variant as the return value. The calling client application checks this return value. If the return value is anything but -1, the method failed and the client can re-direct the user appropriately, as shown in the code below:

```
If Request("REQUEST_METHOD") = "POST" then

    If Request("btnSave") <> "" then

        rtnValue = UpdateRental()

        If rtnValue <> -1 then

            Response.Redirect("SelectRental.asp")

        Else

            Response.Redirect("ErrorPage.asp?Message=Save-Customer-Error")

        End If

    End If

Else

    ' GET from another form

    RentalId = Request("RentalId")

    ReservationId = Request("ReservationId")
```

*(continued)*

```
rtnValue = GetRental(RentalId, ReservationId)
```

```
End If
```

In this example the component sets the value of the method to *0* if the component succeeds and the error number if the component fails. The client checks the return value of the component and then re-directs the user to an error page if appropriate.

## Automatic Versus Client Controlled Transactions

MTS transactions can be controlled programmatically in the client application, or automatically by the MTS run-time environment. To control transactions automatically you need to set the component's transaction property as we just discussed to one of the following: *requires a transaction, supports transactions, requires a new transaction*, or *does not support transactions*. The component transaction properties tell MTS how to enlist the object in a transaction. Based on the value of the component's transaction property, MTS, on behalf of the component, automatically begins transactions and commits or aborts them.

When a client calls an MTS component, MTS intercepts the call and then creates and enlists the component in a transaction based on the component's transaction property. When a transaction is started the resource dispenser passes the transaction to the resource manager. For example, the ODBC driver manager is a resource dispenser for ODBC database connections. When a database connection is requested from a transactional component, the ODBC driver manager obtains the transaction from the object's context. The ODBC driver manager then associates or enlists the database connection with the transaction. When the transaction is completed, the ODBC driver manager communicates with the database to handle the commit or rollback of the command. When you call a component from client code MTS automatically follows the rules of the transaction attribute. The developer does not have to add any transaction-specific code to create and enlist components in a transaction.

You don't have to rely on MTS to create a transaction. The client application can control the component transaction by using the transaction context object. The client uses the *ITransactionContext* interface to create transaction server objects that execute within the client's already existing transaction and to commit or abort the transaction. For example, a Visual InterDev client can call a component that creates a transaction and then the component can enlist one or more components in that transaction by calling the *CreateInstance Object Context* method.

```
Dim objObjectContext As TransactionContext
Dim objCustomer As Customer.GetCustomer
Dim objReservation As Reservation.GetReservation


'Get Transaction Context
Set objObjectContext = _
CreateObject("objObjectContext.TransactionContext")


'Create instance of objects
Set objCustomer = CreateInstance("Customer.GetCustomer")
Set objReservation = CreateInstance("Reservation.GetReservation")


'Do work
objCustomer.GetCustomer(1)
objReservation.GetReservation(1)


'Commit the transaction
objObjectContext.Commit
```

Using the transaction context to create a transaction has its drawbacks. The main reason developers place code in components is to encapsulate and remove the business logic from the client. If you control the transaction from the client, thus calling multiple business components, you are in essence executing business logic. This business logic can only be executed in the specific base client implementation. This also means that any work you do in the client does not participate in the transaction because the client does not create a transaction context object.

Finally, if you use this method, you need to also be aware that MTS will need to exist on the base client. The *TransactionContext* object runs in process with the base client and is therefore required. This is actually how Transactional Active Server Pages work. The client in that case is really the IIS server machine.

There are, however, instances where you will want to use the *CreateInstance* method. If you are calling components from within another component and want the called component enlisted in the already existing transaction, you need to instantiate that component using the *CreateInstance* method. This sends a handle to the already existing transaction context to the called component and MTS so that the component can be enlisted properly. For example, if a client calls a component that requires a transaction, MTS creates transaction 1. If the first component that was called calls a second component that also requires a transaction and wants the second component to participate in transaction 1, then the first component would call the second component using the *CreateInstance* method of the *ObjectContext* object, as opposed to Visual Basic's *CreateObject* method. By using *CreateInstance*, both components participate in the same transaction, which means that only if both components complete their work successfully will the transaction be committed.

## How MTS Transaction Attributes Work

In the Rent-A-Prize example the RENTAL.ASP page calls the update rental business server to update the rental information. After the component updates the information it attempts to verify the credit card by calling the credit card authorization component. If one of these component methods fail then they will both fail. To facilitate this they are both installed in the MTS environment with "requires transaction" transaction attributes.

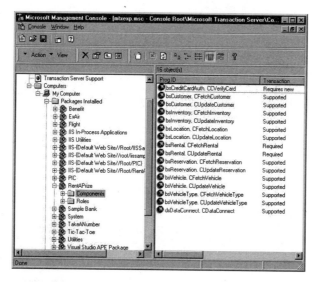

**Figure 8-9.**
*The components installed in MTS with transaction attributes set.*

## • • • SOLUTION: Creating the bsRental Business Server

In the Rent-A-Prize Clerk interface, which is to be made available via the Intranet, we need a solution for allowing clerks to view current rentals and to select and edit them if they choose. To implement this functionality we chose to build a custom COM component. The example below will read and return a reservation record from the reservation table in the Rent-A-Prize database. For this solution we take the following steps:

1. Create a new DLL project in Visual Basic (5.0 or later). Our component will be named *bsRental.dll*, so change the name of the project to *bsRental* using the properties window.

2. Select the predefined class and change its name to *CFetchRental*. For this solution, we are going to concentrate on this class.

3. Set the Project Properties for the component. You can set a component's properties by selecting the project properties dialog menu option for the component. There are several properties you need to set to have the component execute properly in the MTS environment (see Figure 8-10).

**Figure 8-10.**
*Setting a component's general properties.*

You'll need to make use of four settings in the Properties dialog box. Two are in the General tab, Unattended Execution and Threading Model (the other two can be found in the Component tab—see step 5). An MTS component, by design, is going to execute in an unattended environment and you specify this by selecting that option in the property dialog box. As discussed earlier, components execute best with a free-threaded model, but since Visual Basic does not yet support the free-threaded model we must settle for apartment-threaded instead.

4. The next property is the version number auto increment number (see Figure 8-11). This property is not required but is very helpful when you begin installing the components in production and test environments.

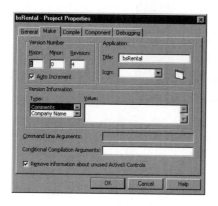

**Figure 8-11.**
*The Component Project Properties dialog box—Make tab.*

5. The next two properties are in the Component tab, the Remote Server and Version Compatibility options (see Figure 8-12). The Version Compatibility option is the more important of the two. Version Compatibility refers to the *GUID* (globally unique identifier) that is created and assigned to the component each time it is compiled. With no version compatibility, the GUIDs created for the component DLL, and each of its classes, are changed each time the component is recompiled. This can cause compatibility problems with existing clients of the DLL that are expecting to access the component with the old GUID. You can avoid this problem by setting the Version Compatibility property to Binary Compatibility. This will insure that the GUID for the component remains the same each time you compile the component. If you change the component interface (for example by changing the number or datatype of a public method's arguments), a new GUID must be created for the component DLL and the affected classes. You will be prompted to remove the Binary Compatibility option before you can recompile the component.

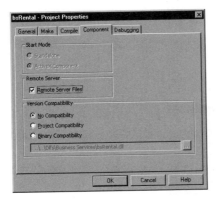

**Figure 8-12.**
*The Component Project Properties Component tab.*

6. Set a reference to the ADO type library by selecting Project |
   References..., then browsing to the Microsoft ActiveX Data Objects
   2.0 Library entry. Select the check box next to the entry and click OK.

7. Set a reference to the MTS type library by selecting Project |
   References..., then browsing to the Microsoft Transaction Server
   Type Library entry. Select the check box next to the entry and click
   OK. In the dialog box that appears, select the MTS Type Library
   item (Figure 8-13). You must do this before you can reference the
   *ObjectContext* interface.

8. Add the following code to the class:

```
Public Function GetByRentalID(ByVal vRentalId As Variant, _
    ByRef vRtnCode As Variant) As ADOR.Recordset


    Dim adoConnection As ADODB.Connection

    Dim adoRecordset As ADODB.Recordset

    Dim adoCommand As ADODB.Command

    Dim objContext As ObjectContext

    Dim strSQL As String

    Dim strSQLWhere As String

    Dim objConnect As CDataConnect
```

*(continued)*

```
On Error GoTo GetByRentalID_EH


Set objContext = GetObjectContext()

Set objConnect = MakeObject(objContext, _
    "dsDataConnect.CDataConnect")

Set adoConnection = New ADODB.Connection

Set adoCommand = New ADODB.Command


If Not objConnect.ConnectToDB(adoConnection) Then
 Err.Raise CONNECTION_ERROR, , "ConnectToDB failed."
End If


Set adoCommand.ActiveConnection = adoConnection


adoCommand.CommandType = adCmdText

adoCommand.CommandText = "{call sp_get_rental_id (" & _
    CStr(vRentalId) & ")}"


Set adoRecordset = New ADODB.Recordset

adoRecordset.CursorType = adOpenStatic

adoRecordset.LockType = adLockBatchOptimistic


adoRecordset.Open adoCommand


If vRtnCode = 0 Then
 If adoRecordset.EOF Then
  ' inform caller of no records
  ' no direct error, because it may be for a NewByRentalID()
  If vRentalId = -1 Then
   adoRecordset.AddNew
```

*(continued)*

```
        vRtnCode = INSERT
      Else
        vRtnCode = GET_NO_SUCH_ID_ERROR
      End If
    End If
    Set GetByRentalID = adoRecordset
  Else
    If Not objContext Is Nothing Then
      objContext.SetAbort
    End If
  End If


  Set adoRecordset.ActiveConnection = Nothing


  If Not objConnect.CloseConnection(adoConnection) Then
    'Close Connection error occurred.
    'Err.Raise CONNECTION_ERROR, , "CloseConnection failed."
  End If


  If Not objContext Is Nothing Then
    objContext.SetComplete
  End If


  Exit Function


GetByRentalID_EH:


  vRtnCode = Err.Number
  LogError Err.Source, Err.Description
```

*(continued)*

```
Set adoRecordset.ActiveConnection = Nothing


If Not objConnect.CloseConnection(adoConnection) Then
 Err.Raise CONNECTION_ERROR, , "CloseConnection failed."
End If


If Not objContext Is Nothing Then
 objContext.SetAbort
End If


End Function
```

9. Save the project and compile the DLL.

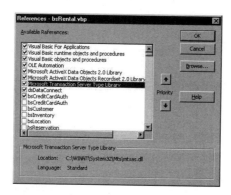

**Figure 8-13.**
*Setting the component project references.*

# Installing MTS Components from MMC

The Microsoft Management Console handles the management and administration of MTS components. To install components using the Microsoft Management Console, you create a package on the server within the console and then import components into the package. Once you've created the package and installed the components, you set the package and component attributes based on the required security and transaction requirements of the application.

Before you begin creating packages you should have an understanding of why it's important to group components in packages in the first place.

## Packaging MTS Components

MTS gives you the ability to configure DLL components into "packages" that serve as units of execution and deployment. Packages run in a single-system process and serve as security boundaries for component client access. Developers can choose to deploy their DLL's in one or more packages. The decision as to how many packages and which components to place in which should be a definitive result of three distinct issues: whether or not components share common resources, whether or not a failure in one component can shut down the processing in another component and whether or not components share security access rights.

### Sharing Resources

Components that share resources should be pooled together. MTS runs each package in a separate server process so the fewer pools you have running on your server, the more efficiently your server will pool resources.

### Fault Isolation

If two components are running in the same process and one of them fails, they may both fail. Components in the same package share the same process so to mitigate this problem, troubled components should be isolated in a separate package. With IIS 4.0, developers can now specify whether or not they want their components to run in-process with the Web server DLL or out-of-process in their own MTS package.

### Security Isolation

MTS security roles represent a logical group of user accounts that are mapped to Microsoft Windows NT domain users and groups during the deployment of the package. The security roles are assigned at the package level so users without access rights cannot access any component in that package. Because security authorization occurs between packages rather than between components within a package, it is best if you consider the security model of your application before packaging your components.

The package security authorization is checked when a method call crosses a package boundary (for example, when a component from one package calls a component in another package). It is not checked for calls between components in the same package. This is an important feature to note. When you package your components, make sure you group components that can safely call each other without requiring security checks within one package. If you need to package components in the same package that cannot safely call each other you'll need to add *IsCallerInRole* calls to manually block user access from within the component.

In the Rent-A-Prize application we've created one package to hold all of our components. In this example we're going to create a new package and add the component we just created, the BSRENTAL.DLL to it. To create the new package, follow these steps:

1. Expand the Microsoft Transaction Server, Computers, and My Computer nodes. Right-click the now-visible Packages Installed folder and select New | Package.

2. Click the Create an empty package button, then specify the name of the new package, in this case, *RAPBusiness*, and click Next. On the Set Package Identity page, either accept the default, or specify a user account to run the components under, then click Finish.

3. Next, set the package attributes for the new package, as follows.

To set the package attributes, right-click on the package in the Microsoft Transaction Server Explorer in the Microsoft Management Console and select the properties option in the pop-up menu that appears. There are five package property tabs, General, Security, Advanced, Identity, and Activation (see Figure 8-14).

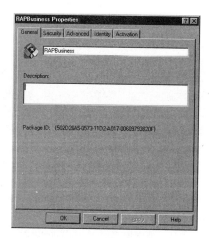

**Figure 8-14.**
*The Package Properties dialog box.*

The General tab allows you to enter a name and a brief description of the package. The Security tab enables authorization checking. If you do not enable security for the package, then roles for the component or interface will not be checked by MTS. The authentication level tells MTS how to check the security of a package. If you are not familiar with the specifics of authentication levels you should use the default setting, Packet.

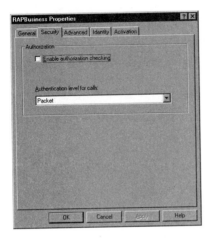

**Figure 8-15.**
*The Package Properties Security tab.*

The Advanced tab determines whether the server process associated with a package always runs, or whether it shuts down after a certain period of time (see Figure 8-16).

The Identity tab is used to set the user identity for the package. The default value is Interactive User, which is the user that is currently logged onto the Windows NT server account. If you want your components to execute under one designated user ID regardless of which user called the component, you can select a specific user by selecting a defined Windows NT account name from the user dialog box. The identity of a component defines the User ID of a component when it is executing. This user is also the user that is granted database access when a component requests it (see Figure 8-17).

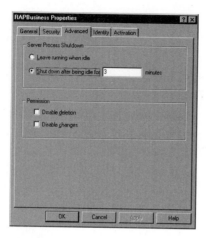

**Figure 8-16.**
*The Package Properties Advanced tab.*

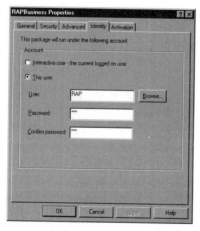

**Figure 8-17.**
*The Package Properties Identity tab.*

The Activation tab controls where the package is activated, in the creator's process or in a dedicated process on the server. You can either set the activation level to Library Package so components are activated in the creator's process or to Server Package so that the package runs in a dedicated server process. The Library option speeds up component processing by eliminating the need to marshal data across machine boundaries but is only available for clients that have MTS installed and configured. It also does not support component tracking, role checking, or process isolation. For these reasons it's recommended that most packages be designated as Server packages (see Figure 8-18).

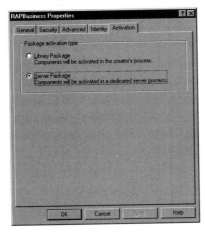

**Figure 8-18.**
*Package Properties Activation tab.*

## Setting Up User Roles

MTS implements component security using user roles. *User roles* are symbolic names that define a logical group of users similar to a User group in Windows NT. To implement role-based security you must first group your components into packages. Packages serve as units of execution and deployment for multiple COM DLLs. Components in a package run in single-system process and share security boundaries. You assign user roles to packages using the MTS Explorer. For example, in the Rent-A-Prize application there are three defined user roles,

Customer, Clerk, and Manager. At deployment time a Windows NT administrator assigns users to the roles you defined during development. Then, at runtime, users will only be permitted access to components in packages that allow access to that role.

Although this may seem fairly straightforward, there is one issue you should be aware of when using MTS package security. If a base client calls a component, MTS will check user roles for the component. If one component calls another component in the same package, MTS will not check user roles because components within the same package are assumed to "trust" one another. In instances where you need to restrict access to certain methods in a component you can use the *IsCallerInRole* method to programmatically restrict users access.

Two processes take place when a client calls an MTS object. First, MTS security checks to see if the client is actually who he or she says he or she is (*authentication*), then checks to see if the user's role has access to the component that was called (*access*). There are two ways to protect a component's interface access, *client impersonation* and *client authorization*. Of the two, client authorization is the preferred method.

## Client Impersonation

With client impersonation, access is explicitly provided to each client for methods the client is permitted to use. This means that to implement client impersonation you need to code your COM components to check each client's access privileges. This can be a nightmare for both application and database administrators. The system administrator would need to modify the component's interface and database table access rights each time a new user is added or a user's client access permissions change. It can also have a substantial effect on the performance of a system. This method of secure access does not effectively take advantage of database connection pooling. Database connections are dependent on the user ID of the user who requested the connection. If the user ID of the client is continually changing, the component will need to connect and disconnect to the database more often because two distinct users can not share a connection even if one is waiting and available in the connection pool.

## Client Authorization

Client authorization means that the component runs with its own user ID, not the ID temporarily borrowed from the client. During the development of your components, you define permissions for each component interface using user roles. When a component checks for access permission, all it does is check to see if the client is a member of the permitted role. This allows components to take advantage of database connection pooling and the sharing of database connections ,and substantially decreases the administrative tasks associated with the addition and deletion of users. Now, all you need to do to add the user to the Windows NT system is specify that that user is part of the Windows NT group or user role.

## Using IsCallerInRole

The *IsCallerInRole* method allows you to determine the direct caller of the method that is currently executing. You typically use this method to validate that a user is a member of a role that has access permissions to the components in a package. The *IsCallerInRole* method only applies to the direct caller of the currently executing method. The direct caller can be either a base client or another component server process.

The *IsCallerInRole* method returns *True* when the object that invokes it is executing in a client process so it's a good idea to call the *IsSecurityEnabled* method before calling *IsCallerInRole*. If security isn't enabled, *IsCallerInRole* will not return an accurate result. The code listed below demonstrates how to use the *IsCallerInRole* method to check a user's access permissions.

```
Dim objContext As ObjectContext

Set objContext = GetObjectContext()


If Not objContext Is Nothing Then
 If objContext.IsSecurityEnabled Then
  If Not objContext.IsCallerInRole("Clerk") Then
   ' If not, do something appropriate here.
  Else
   ' If so, execute the call normally.
  End If
 Else
 ' Error - Security not enabled.
 End If
End If
```

## Creating User Roles

Three user roles were defined for the Rent-A-Prize application, Customer, Clerk, and Manager (see Figure 8-19). In the following example we will add all three user roles to the application. To add the user roles, use the following steps:

1. Right-click the Roles folder in the Microsoft Transaction Server Explorer. In the pop-up menu that appears, select New Role and type in the name of the role.

2. Next, add one or more users to the role by right-clicking the role in the MTS Explorer. In the pop-up menu that appears, select the New User menu option. The selected user can be a defined Windows NT user or group on the server. Defining role users as a Windows NT group is sometimes an easier way to maintain access to an MTS component. In this scenario a system administrator would only need to assign the Windows NT user to the Windows NT group to grant the user access privileges to the system.

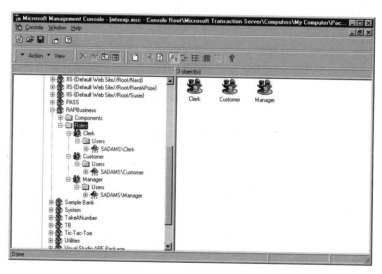

**Figure 8-19.**
*Rent-A-Prize user roles.*

292

## Setting Transaction Attributes

The transaction attributes of a component tell MTS how to enlist component instances within a transaction. You set the transaction attribute at the component level for each component. MTS uses this attribute during object creation to determine whether an object should be created within a transaction, and whether a transaction is required or optional. You set the transaction attribute of a component using the MTS Explorer, now part of the Microsoft Management. The four available transaction attributes are listed below.

- **Requires a Transaction**   The component's objects must execute within the scope of a transaction. When a new object is created, its object context inherits the transaction from the context of the client. If the client does not have a transaction, MTS automatically creates a new transaction for the object.

- **Requires a New Transaction**   The component's objects must execute within their own transactions. When a new object is created, MTS automatically creates a new transaction for the object, regardless of whether its client has a transaction.

- **Supports Transactions**   The component's objects can execute within the scope of their client's transactions. When a new object is created, its object context inherits the transaction from the context of the client. If the client does not have a transaction, the new context is created without one.

- **Does not support transactions**   The component's objects do not run within the scope of transactions. When a new object is created, its object context is created without a transaction, regardless of whether the client has a transaction.

In the following example we'll set the transaction attributes for the BSRENTAL.DLL component methods. To set the transaction attributes, do the following:

1. Select the component in the Microsoft Transaction Server Explorer and right-click.

2. In the pop-up-menu that appears, select the Properties menu option (see Figure 8-20).

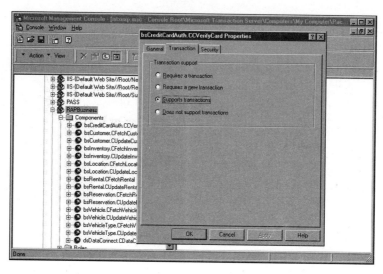

**Figure 8-20.**
*Setting the component transaction attributes.*

## Installing Components Inside Visual InterDev 6.0

In each of the previous examples we have had to navigate between Visual InterDev and the Microsoft Management Console to effectively install and run our middle-tier COM components. Visual InterDev 6.0 now gives the developer the ability to add COM components directly to the Visual InterDev project. These components live in the Project Explorer as any other Active Server Page or image would and are included in version control as part of the Web project.

Visual InterDev allows you to register a component on the client as well as the server machine. The server machine is the Web server you are publishing to. If you choose to publish your components directly to the MTS server on your server machine, you will be prompted to enter a package name for the components. You can choose an already existing package or have Visual InterDev 6.0 create a new package. When Visual InterDev creates a new package it sets the Activation level to Library and will not install security parameters on the package. If you want to change these default values. you'll need to open the Microsoft Management Console for MTS manually.

In this example we're going to use Visual InterDev 6.0 to add the BSRENTALL.DLL component to our Visual InterDev project. Then we are

Rent. To install the component, create the new package, and add the component to the package, follow these steps:

1. Create a new Visual InterDev project by opening the Visual InterDev 6.0 development environment. In the new project dialog box that appears, select the New tab and enter the name of the new project, *RentAPrize*.

2. Step through the wizard and enter the appropriate parameters to add the new project to your Web server.

3. Open the Windows Explorer and select the BSRENTAL.DLL file from the appropriate folder. Then drag and drop the component onto the Project Explorer as shown in Figure 8-21.

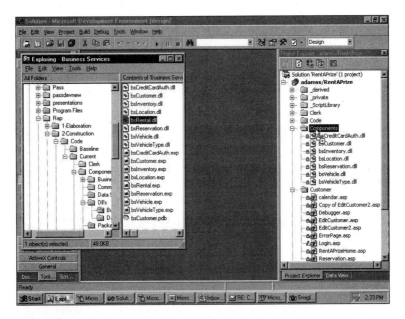

**Figure 8-21.**
*Adding a COM component to a Visual InterDev 6.0 project by drag-and-drop.*

4. Right-click the component in the Visual InterDev project folder and select the Properties menu option in the pop-up menu that appears. In the dialog box that appears select the component tab and set the appropriate MTS component attributes properties (see Figure 8-22).

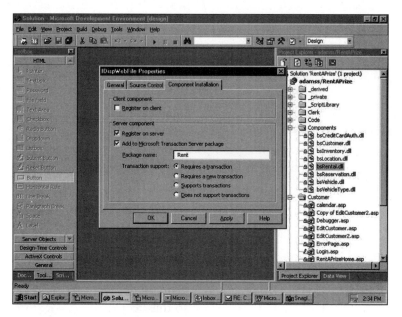

**Figure 8-22.**
*Setting the MTS component attributes in Visual InterDev 6.0.*

5. Open the Microsoft Management Console as you did in the previous example and reset the package attributes for the newly created package. Visual InterDev automatically sets the Activation for a package to Library. This sets components installed in this package to run in the same process space as the client. As we discussed earlier, this is usually avoided to improve the scalability of the application.

## Setting Up Remote Components

You can distribute a package between MTS servers by *pulling* and *pushing* components between one or more computers. You install the components on an MTS server and then either push them to a destination server or pull them from a source computer. The process of pushing or pulling components copies the component's type library and proxy/stub DLLs from one computer to another.

This does not, however, change the way components are run. A component always executes on the machine on which it was installed. Pushing and pulling simply copies the information needed to access the components remotely. This facilitates the static load balancing of COM components. In future versions of MTS and Windows NT, dynamic load balancing will be supported. *Dynamic load balancing* will allow client applications to point to a single server. When the component is run it will be instantiated on the least busy MTS server in the system.

In the following example we will install the BSRENTAL.DLL as a remote component on another server. To set up the remote component follow these steps:

1. Identify the remote computer in the Microsoft Management Console (see Figure 8-23).

2. Once you have added the remote computer to the management console you must make sure that the source and destination computers have the appropriate user identities assigned to the system package. You need to do this because the system packages on both machines need to call and send information between one another. If you are pulling components from a source server you need to assign the destination user as a member of the Reader or Administrator roles on the source server. If you are pushing you'll need to make sure that both machines can read and write from one another, that is, that both you are a member of the Administrator role on both machines.

3. To pull components from a source computer you'll need to add the source computer components to the MyComputer Remote Components folder. Right-click on the Remote Components folder in the pop-up menu that appears select New | Remote Component.

4. To push components from the WRAP computer to My Computer, simply add the components to the wrap Remote Components folder (see Figure 8-24).

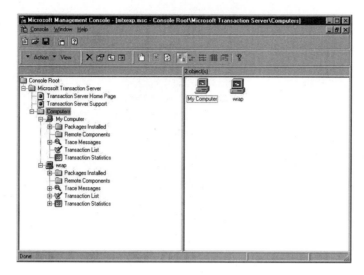

**Figure 8-23.**
*Adding new servers to MMC.*

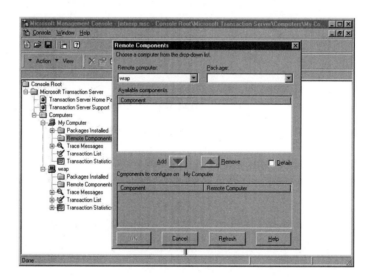

**Figure 8-24.**
*Adding remote components.*

# Calling MTS Components

MTS components are usually installed on a separate computer from the client that is accessing them. A client can call a remote MTS component using one of three transport methods, DCOM, HTTP, or Remote Automation (see Figure 8-25). In the Rent-A-Prize application we are using HTTP/DCOM for both the Visual InterDev Customer and Clerk Active Server Web applications.

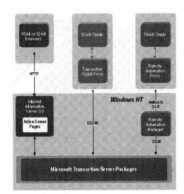

**Figure 8-25.**
*Calling MTS components.*

## Calling MTS Components through DCOM

DCOM is the standard transport for calling MTS components. To enable DCOM calls to MTS components, you must configure the client registry settings and the DCOM security settings for both the client and the server. The component must be registered on the client machine to call a remote MTS component. The easiest way to configure the Registry settings on the client is to create an application executable for the MTS component and then run that executable on the client. The application executable automatically registers the MTS component on the client machine. If you want to use Microsoft Windows 95 clients with MTS, you need to install DCOM for Windows 95 on the client machine.

The DCOM security settings are usually fine with the default values of Identify for the Impersonation Level and Connect for the Authentication Level. If you need to modify these settings, you should do so in the MTS Explorer package properties.

You can invoke an MTS object in Microsoft Visual Basic using one of three methods:

■ The *CreateObject* function

■ The *CreateInstance* function

■ The New keyword

The *CreateObject* function creates an instance of an object. The object context that is created will exist outside of any already existing context object. *CreateInstance*, on the other hand, will create an instance of the object inside an already existing context object. *CreateInstance* is only appropriate when an *ObjectContext* already exists. A run-time error will be generated if one does not exist when it is called. The Rent-A-Prize application uses a function called *MakeObject* to create an instance of the object dependent upon whether or not a *ContextObject* exists.

```
Function MakeObject(objContext As ObjectContext, & _
   strClass As String) As Object

 If objContext Is Nothing Then

  Set MakeObject = CreateObject(strClass)

 Else

  Set MakeObject = objContext.CreateInstance(strClass)

 End If

End Function
```

When you create an object using *CreateInstance*, the new object's context is derived from the current object's *ObjectContext* and the declarative properties of the new object's component. The new object always executes within the same activity as the object that created it. If the current object has a transaction, the transaction attribute of the new object's component determines whether or not the new object will execute within the scope of that transaction.

Do not use the *New* operator, or a variable declared *As New*, to create an instance of a class that is part of the active project. In this case, Visual Basic does not use COM to invoke the object.

## Calling MTS Components from an ASP Page

The Rent-A-Prize Clerk application has an ASP page named RENTAL.ASP that allows clerks to add and edit rental information for a customer. In the following example we are going to add a new Active Server Page to the "RentAPrize" Visual InterDev 6.0 project we created earlier. This page will allow users to view and modify rental data and will call the BSRENTAL.DLL *CfetchRental.GetRentalById*(ID) method to retrieve a rental record from the RentAPrize SQL Server 6.5 database. The page is called from the RENTFIND.ASP page and is looking for *btnFind* and *txtDrNo* request variables to retrieve the appropriate rental record.

NOTE: You can delete the request code and manually enter a *DrNo* to retrieve a rental record if you want to run the Active Server Page independently of the RENTALFIND.ASP page.

1. Open the Visual InterDev 6.0 RentAPrize project and add a new Active Server Page by selecting the project in the Project Explorer and right-clicking. In the pop-up menu that appears, select the add menu item's active server page submenu item. Name the page *Rental.asp*.

2. Add the following code to the page.

```
<%@ Language=VBScript %>

<% response.buffer = True %>

<html>

<head>

<meta name="VI60_defaultClientScript" content="VBScript">

<meta NAME="GENERATOR" Content="Microsoft Visual Studio 6.0">

</head>


<body>

<form method="POST">

<%

Dim rsRental
```

*(continued)*

```
isData = FALSE


If Request("REQUEST_METHOD") = "POST" then

    If Request("btnFind") <> "" then

        vRtnValue = FindRental(Request("txtDrNo"))

        If vRtnValue = -1 then

            Response.Write("Invalid ID Number!")

            isData = FALSE

        End If

    End If

End If

Function FindRental( vDrNo)

    Dim objFetchRental, vRtnCode, theCount

    Set objFetchRental = _
      Server.CreateObject("bsRental.CFetchRental")

    Response.Write("hi there "&vDrNo)

    Set rsRental = objFetchRental.GetRentalByDrNo(vDrNo, _
      vRtnCode)

    isData = TRUE

    FindRental = vRtnCode


End Function


%>

<p><font face="Garamond"></font>

<P align=center><STRONG><FONT color=blue face="" size=6>Select
Rental

<table border="1" cellPadding="1" cellSpacing="1" width="50%"
align="center" style="WIDTH: 50%">

    <tr>
```

*(continued)*

```
        <td>

            <BR></FONT></STRONG><STRONG>Driver's Licence No</
STRONG>:

            <INPUT id=txtDrNo name=txtDrNo><INPUT id=btnFind
name=btnFind type=submit value="Go!"  ></P></FONT></STRONG>

        </td>

    </tr>

</table> 

<table border="1" cellPadding="1" cellSpacing="1" width="65%"
align="center" style="WIDTH: 65%">

    <tr>

        <td>

            <div align="center">#</div></td>

        <td>

            <div align="center"><font
face="Garamond"><em><strong>Begin </em><font
face="Garamond"><em>Date</em></font></strong></font></div><font
face="Garamond"></font></td>

        <td>

            <div align="center"><font
face="Garamond"><em><strong>End Date</strong></em></font></
div><font><em></em></font></td></tr>

    <%

    theCount = 0


    If isData then

    Do While Not rsRental.EOF

        theCount = theCount + 1

%>

        <tr>
```

*(continued)*

```
            <td><a href="http://localhost/RentAPrize/Clerk/
    Rental.asp?RentalId=<%=rsRental("rental_id")%>">

            <%=rsRental("rental_id")%></td>

            <td>


            <%=rsRental("rental_start_date")%></td>

            <td>

            <%=rsRental("rental_end_date")%></td>

        </tr>
    <%

        rsRental.MoveNext

        Loop

        End If

    %>

    </table></p>

    </form>

    </body>

    </html>
```

3. Save the page and view the result by right-clicking and selecting View in Browser....

There are two ways a client can call an MTS component from an ASP page through HTTP:

- By Calling an Active Server Page, which then calls an MTS component using DCOM.

- By calling an MTS component from a Web browser Remote Data Service (RDS)

You can invoke an MTS object from an ASP by calling *Server.CreateObject*. Unlike Visual Basic, you can not invoke an object using the *CreateInstance* method. If the page you are calling is transactional and implements the

*OnStartPage* and *OnEndPage* methods, the *OnStartPage* method is called when the component is invoked. The Rent-A-Prize Rental.asp page creates the *CFetchRental* class using the *CreateObject* method.

```
Set objGetRental = Server.CreateObject("bsRental.CFetchRental")
    If ReservationId = "" Then
        Set rsRental = objGetRental.GetByRentalID(RentalId, rtnCode)
    End If
```

You can choose to run your MTS components in-process or out-of-process with the Internet Information Server (IIS) DLL. If you run your MTS components in-process with IIS and MTS encounters a problem, the IIS process will be terminated. IIS 4.0 allows you to specify whether or not you want COM components to run in- or out-of-process. By default, IIS 3.0 disables calling out-of-process components. You can enable calling out-of-process components by setting the following Registry entry:

```
HKEY_LOCAL_MACHINE\SYSTEM\CurrentControlSet\Services\W3SVC\ASP
\Parameters\AllowOutOfProcCmpnts key to 1
```

You can call MTS components from a client-side component by using the HTML <OBJECT> tag to call the component. If MTS is installed on the client machine you can also use the <OBJECT> tag to create an MTS object in-process with the browser client. Components called from a client should be made safe for scripting.

The Remote Data Service (RDS) also allows you to create client-side components using the <OBJECT> tag and supports the following transport methods:

- HTTP
- HTTPS (HTTP over Secure Socket Layer)
- DCOM
- In-process server

To call a RDS component you need to register it as an RDS component. You accomplish this by configuring the following Registry key to the ProgID of the object that you want to call:

```
HKEY_LOCAL_MACHINE\SYSTEM\CurrentControlSet\Services\W3SVC
\Parameters\ADCLaunch
```

## Summary

The Microsoft Transaction Server provides management services for the Component Object Model (COM) business components in a Windows DNA application. Developers can build enterprise applications that consist of Visual InterDev 6.0 client applications that call a collection of single-user COM components. These components can then be deployed with little or no additional coding in a multi-user middle-tier environment, thanks to MTS. MTS not only manages transactions but also manages how COM components allocate and share resources by providing both the transaction processing and object request brokering functionality to applications running in the Windows NT environment.

In this chapter we discussed:

- Why MTS is important
- How to build scalable MTS components
- How to install MTS components using the Microsoft Management Console
- How to install MTS components using Visual InterDev 6.0
- How to call MTS components

In the next chapter, we'll take a look at another new Microsoft technology, Microsoft Message Queue Server (MSMQ), that promises to improve the performance and scalability of your enterprise applications, as well as solve some of the other problems that plague enterprise applications.

## CHAPTER NINE

# Ensuring Reliable and High-Performance Communication

• • • **GOAL: To Reduce Customer Wait Time, Enable Offline Functionality, and Increase Application Reliability**

In this chapter, we'll take a look at one of the best friends a Web developer could ask for, Microsoft Message Queue Server (MSMQ). MSMQ can be used to solve a number of the cumbersome problems that you will face in enterprise development, including dealing with unreliable networks, using asynchronous processing to reduce bottlenecks, and enabling functionality, such as order entry, to be performed offline.

The goal of this chapter is to concentrate at a high level on what MSMQ is, what it brings to Visual InterDev developers, and the basic programming techniques used to develop MSMQ solutions. So, let this serve as a starting point for your learning about MSMQ. After reading this chapter you should be able to identify several areas within your current development projects where you can leverage MSMQ's abilities.

## The Need for MSMQ

So things are starting to come together with Rent-A-Prize. We've got a Web-based system up and running, and though it's not bug free or even pretty yet, it's got 90 percent of our required functionality. Everyone is happy, the end is in sight, and the development team is starting to think about a celebration at the end of the project. Oops, what's going on here? On the reservations page that in the real world is going to be hammered on by thousands of users a day, processing is taking four to five times longer than originally anticipated. Alarms go off, people get worried, you start to stress-test your application. Much to our horror, you discover that with numerous concurrent users during peak times of day (when the network is already being taxed by its normal duties) the response times become even slower.

How can this be? You broke out key business logic into individual COM components, placed them on high horsepower machines on the same LAN as the database servers (thereby reducing network traffic), ran these components under Microsoft Transaction Server (MTS) to take advantage of its object and database connection management and yet somehow, it's still running too slowly. After further investigation, you discover that the sticking point is the business logic contained inside the COM components.

This business logic started out innocently enough, in fact it screamed during the prototype stage. So what is the problem? Well, unfortunately, as real development began it turned out that the customer master database was on the mainframe, the inventory and reservations systems were on different UNIX platforms, and you had to access three other pre-existing Windows NT systems. This added complexity, when mixed with high user volumes, caused extremely slow performance which caused increased stress and anxiety to the development team.

Does this sound all too familiar? If it does, don't worry, you're not alone. This hypothetical situation based on the Rent-A-Prize application demonstrates a very real problem in enterprise Web applications. So how do we solve this problem? Fortunately, there is a new product called Microsoft Message Queue Server (MSMQ) that will help us solve this issue and several of Windows enterprise development's most nagging problems. To top it all off, MSMQ is an extremely easy technology to implement into your existing and/or new client/server and Web-based development projects.

## What Is Message Queuing?

So what is MSMQ? For that matter what is *message queuing* in general? Just another fancy name for MAPI and e-mail, right? Wrong. Don't be fooled into thinking that MSMQ constitutes an e-mail package such as Microsoft Exchange. What it provides is the infrastructure technology needed to write systems like Microsoft Exchange.

Message queuing, or Message Oriented Middleware (MOM), is software that allows both synchronous and asynchronous interactions between distributed computing processes. This interaction comes in the form of a message that can either be directly passed or placed in a queue for later retrieval. Messages are self-contained requests or responses that include source and destination information, as well as content. Both the sender and receiver of messages must agree on the meaning of the message's contents. Message queues are like mail boxes for messages that are waiting for delivery. These queues protect messages from being lost in transit and provide a place for receivers to look for messages.

Normally in the Microsoft world, we use Microsoft's Component Object Model (COM) and Distributed COM (DCOM) technology when we wish to have interprocess communications. Underlying these technologies is a much older technology, commonly referred to as *remote procedure calls* (RPCs). Simply put, you can write an application that calls a function or procedure that resides outside your application. This RPC can access logic on the same machine or on a remote machine. RPCs are an extremely powerful tool in that they allow for the creation of n-tier distributed systems, many of the benefits of which have been covered in previous chapters.

The problem with RPCs is that they are generally synchronous in nature and require tight coupling between the applications and the network. In many business situations, a developer might want to pass key information to another process, but not have to wait until the other process finishes processing. Another problem with RPCs is that they require both the client and server to be available to each other throughout their communication process. In today's distributed environment, this is not always a possibility and even in the situations where it is, 100 percent availability cannot generally be guaranteed.

Message queuing helps solve both of these dilemmas. Messages can be sent and received asynchronously therefore avoiding tying up applications. MOM technologies also do not require the receiver of the message to be directly accessible to the sender, or even be online when the sender sends the message.

One of the easiest analogies to illustrate the differences between RPCs and message queuing is to compare them to telephone conversations and e-mail messages (see Figure 9-1). Calling up a friend on the phone is a great example of an RPC call. A direct connection between both parties is required since information is constantly being passed back and forth throughout the conversation. If for some reason the caller cannot access the other party (the other party is on another call, the other party is not home, or the phone line has been severed) the information will fail to be passed.

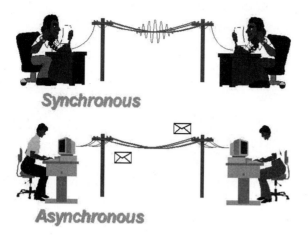

**Figure 9-1.**
*Illustration of e-mail and telephone communications.*

E-mail, on the other hand, would represent the message queuing solution. One party prepares the message and sends it to the other party. As soon as the sender has transmitted the message, he or she is free to continue with other tasks. The sender does not have to worry about the delivery of the message to the appropriate party, that responsibility falls upon the shoulders of the e-mail system or the message queuing system. The sender does not have to have direct access to the receiving party, the message queuing system takes care of the routing of the message. The receiving party does not have to be online at the time the sender sends the message, the message is simply placed in a mailbox (queue) where it can later be retrieved by the recipient.

"But what about the answering machine?", you say. The answering machine actually serves the purpose of a message queue in this scenario. The point is that when architecting a new system, it is not an RPC versus MOM decision that has to be made. Instead you can easily implement solutions that are a combination of RPC and MOM technologies.

## MSMQ Architecture

The intent of this chapter is to help you learn to develop MSMQ solutions with Visual InterDev, not to teach you how to set up and administer MSMQ systems. However, it is important to cover some basic terms and concepts that are involved with an MSMQ system. If you're familiar with MSMQ, skip to "Using MSMQ from Visual InterDev 6.0" later in this chapter, if not, continue reading below.

## MSMQ Topology

In MSMQ, all computers that run MSMQ belong to one enterprise and access information from the same Message Queue Information Store (MQIS). Within the enterprise, computers are broken up into *sites*, or a physical collection of computers where communication between any two computers is fast and inexpensive. Site boundaries in many cases correspond to the physical location of the computers (i.e., all computers within same building). All of the computers within a site need not be running the same protocols and need not even be able to directly communicate with each other.

Each site is connected to other sites through communication links called *site links*. *Inter-site routing* is the process of sending messages between sites on these links. MSMQ calculates inter-site routing based on site link costs. *Site link costs* are numbers assigned by administrators that represent the cost of communicating on a particular link.

All machines that participate in MSMQ can be classified into three categories: *dependent clients*, *independent clients*, and *servers*. All MSMQ servers can be broken out into four subcategories: Primary Enterprise Controller (PEC), Primary Site Controller (PSC), Backup Site Controller (BSC), and MSMQ Routing Server. All of these servers require Windows NT in order to run. Every MSMQ enterprise must contain one PEC. The PEC also functions as a PSC for one site. The PEC holds information about the enterprise configuration and the certification keys that are used in authenticating messages in a database. The PEC also functions as an MSMQ routing server. The PEC must be installed before any other PSCs can be installed.

A PSC must be installed for each additional site in an MSMQ network. The PSC holds information about the computers and queues in its site in a database and also functions as an MSMQ routing server.

A site does not require a BSC, however, one or more BSCs should be installed at each site to provide load balancing and failure recovery, should the PSC or PEC fail. The BSC holds a read-only replica of the PSC or PEC database and also functions as an MSMQ routing server.

MSMQ routing servers support dynamic routing and intermediate store-and-forward message queuing. They allow computers using different protocols to communicate.

MSMQ independent clients can be installed on computers running Windows 95, Windows NT Workstation, or Windows NT Server. MSMQ independent clients can create and modify queues locally and send and receive messages. Independent clients can also create queues and store messages on the local computer, without synchronous access to an MSMQ server. Independent clients can send messages to public queues while disconnected from the network, without any additional application design or configuration. The only caveat to this is that the independent client must be installed with a connection to PSC since it must have access to the MQIS on the PSC. The main difference between independent clients and servers is that the independent clients do not have the intermediate store-and-forward capability of MSMQ servers, nor do they store information from the distributed MSMQ database.

Dependent clients function very much like independent clients, except that they cannot function without synchronous access to a supporting server. Dependent clients rely on their supporting server to perform all standard MSMQ functions on their behalf (creating queues, sending and receiving messages). Dependent clients can be installed on computers running Windows 95, Windows NT Workstation, or Windows NT Server. MSMQ servers can support up to fifteen dependent clients each.

### MSMQ Queues

MSMQ queues can be broken into two main groups: *public* and *private*. *Public queues* are those published in the MSMQ Information Store (MQIS), which is a Microsoft SQL Server database containing information about your enterprise. All public queues are replicated throughout the enterprise by the MQIS, and can therefore be located by any computer within the enterprise. Private queues are not published in the MQIS, and therefore don't add to the MQIS replication load. *Private queues* can be accessed only by applications that have access to the full pathname or format name of the queue.

MSMQ routes and delivers messages based upon a combination of queue priority and message priority. Messages are routed and delivered first by queue priority, then by message priority.

### Message Delivery

MSMQ allows messages to be delivered one of two ways: *express* or *recoverable*. *Express messages* are stored in memory as opposed to the disk storage methods used by recoverable delivery. Express messages usually require fewer resources and are faster than recoverable messages. *Recoverable messages*, on the other hand, will not be lost in the event of computer failure while express messages will.

## When to Use MSMQ

Now that we've discussed what MSMQ is, let's talk about some scenarios where it would be useful. Bear in mind that MSMQ is an answer to some situations, but not all. Just as with any other tool, you should ensure that its use is justified for the situation. Using MSMQ for every situation will add to your programming complexity and could possibly hurt system performance.

So when should you use MSMQ? If your development effort requires one or more of the five basic communication situations outlined below, you should seriously consider using MSMQ.

- **Asynchronous**   When two or more systems need to communicate asynchronously with one another to avoid locking up the systems while waiting for communications to complete.

- **Connectionless**   When a direct connection between two applications is not available or is not guaranteed to be available.

- **Store and Forward**   When the sending application may be disconnected from the network yet still needs to send messages as if it were connected. These messages will automatically be communicated to their destinations when network connectivity is restored.

- **Journaled**   When journals are required to be kept for all communications activity between systems. Very useful for logging and audit purposes as well as for error recovery.

- **Defensive**   When all of the above scenarios occur. In many systems if one piece fails, the whole system fails. MSMQ will help ensure that the system stays up and running even in the event of certain components failing. In many cases this is a required feature of mission critical systems since the cost of message loss or interruption is very high.

Let's return to the example that began the chapter. The biggest obstacle that needs to be overcome is performance. The current solution has browser-based clients placing rental reservations over the Internet. After the user enters his or her reservation information and transmits it back to IIS, a call is made to a component called *bsReservation. bsReservation* in turn makes calls to other COM components, systems, and databases while processing a new reservation. The *bsReservation* component becomes a *hotspot*, or trouble area, because all Web-based orders must pass through it making processing time longer than deemed acceptable by the customer. This whole process is outlined in Figure 9-2.

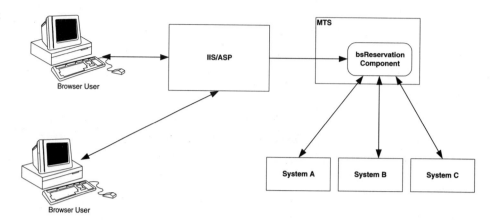

**Figure 9-2.**
*The existing architecture of IIS/ASP hitting against an MTS server.*

So, how do you use MSMQ to improve the performance in this situation? In order to solve this problem, an asynchronous solution is a good place to start. If the user could place his or her reservation without having to wait for the reservation to be processed, the problem would be solved. If that was possible, users would only transmit their information across the Web and receive a notification that their reservation had been received. All reservation processing would occur in the background while the user continued on with other unrelated tasks.

Granted, this whole solution is based upon the premise that the user only needs to know that the order request was successfully received, not that it was successfully processed. MSMQ does have the ability to send messages back to users as soon as a message is successfully processed, similar to a return receipt in an e-mail system. MSMQ could also send another message to a queue when the order is finished being processed. The customer could then return at a later date and time to see if the order was successfully processed or not. Just keep in mind that it does not make sense to use asynchronous processing in a scenario where the customer cannot do anything else until they know whether the order was processed correctly. In this situation, using MSMQ this way would just add additional overhead to the existing solution and could in fact cause the application to run more slowly.

If this was a traditional client/server application we would attack the problem in exactly the same manner, by way of an asynchronous solution. With some programming languages you can implement asynchronous functionality by methods such as *threads* and/or *callback servers*, although these are a rather advanced programming feature that should be used with caution. In the ASP/

VBScript development world, however, threads are not currently supported, so developers are limited in their ability to implement asynchronous solutions without the use of multi-threaded components, which can be difficult to develop and implement. However, with MSMQ, ASP developers can easily build asynchronous solutions within their Active Server Pages applications.

In our example, we need to modify the *bsReservation* component. Currently it receives reservation information from the calling, or client, application. By using MSMQ, *bsReservation* will never be called directly from the client application. Instead, it will now be responsible for reading the *NewReservations* queue to retrieve new order information. After retrieving the reservation information, it will continue in exactly the same fashion as it did before the introduction of MSMQ.

By changing the design, the customer who placed the reservation is now able to be off surfing the Web, while *bsReservation* is reading the new reservation information from the *NewReservations* queue and processing the reservation. The beauty of this solution is that all of this processing is taking place in the background and is not affecting the customer, regardless of how much processing time is required. In situations where the background components are lagging way behind, because of extremely large order loads, system administrators can simply instantiate more *bsReservation* components to handle the increased load. This redesigned process can be seen in Figure 9-3.

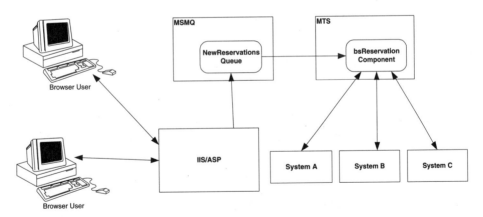

**Figure 9-3.**
*The proposed new architecture of utilizing MSMQ with MTS.*

With this new solution everyone is happy. The customer is happy because he or she can quickly place his or her reservation. The development team is happy because not only have they met their requirements for performance but have actually helped with the scalability of the system.

There are also several side benefits to solution. The front-end or data-capture portion of this system has only one responsibility—to capture new reservation information. In the old scenario, if for some reason one of the many pieces of the reservation process was to go offline, the whole system came to a halt. For example, let's say the link from the *bsReservation* component to the customer database that resides on the mainframe was severed. With the original solution, the *bsReservation* component would fail and reservations would not be processed. By using MSMQ, any of the back-end pieces can fail or be offline and the reservation will still be placed in a queue to be processed later when the system is restored. In fact, even in the event that the Web server is severed from the rest of the network, including the server where the *NewReservations* message queue is located, the system could work, thanks to MSMQ's store-and-forward mechanism. In this situation, the messages would be written to a local message queue and would then later be routed to the correct destination queue when system connectivity was restored. The greatest benefit of this is that you don't have to write any special code to enable the MSMQ store-and-forward logic.

Now it could be argued that the *bsReservation* component could be written in such a manner that it could handle partial system failures. In the event of a failure it could write the order to disk and later, when the system was completely functional, it could read this information from disk and finish processing the order. Basically what you would be doing is writing your own custom store-and-forward mechanism. By doing this you are falling victim to what is referred to as "reinventing the wheel" syndrome. MSMQ gives you an extremely powerful, yet easy-to-program store-and-forward mechanism. So why take days, if not weeks, to write your own, which probably will not be as versatile, efficient, or reliable?

## When Not to Use MSMQ

Message queuing is not a remedy for all inter-system communications problems. In fact there are some scenarios where message queuing introduces unnecessary overhead. Probably the most prevalent situation in inter-system communications where MSMQ should not be used is when a client application requires an answer back from the other system before it can continue processing. Sure, an MSMQ solution could be crafted where a client sends a message and then waits until another message is returned by the other system. Unfortunately, this solution would only cause increased programming effort and possibly decrease overall system performance.

# Using MSMQ from Visual InterDev 6.0

Let's assume that you've decided to use MSMQ within your Visual InterDev application. The biggest question now is "How do I start?" To stay true to one of the themes of the previous chapter, it is with "architecture, architecture, architecture." Let's step back a moment and figure out which method of implementing MSMQ makes the most sense for our needs.

## Ways to Access MSMQ Functionality

When it comes to implementing MSMQ within an application, developers have several basic options. One option is to do all the work within your ASP pages using VBScript code. One of the biggest benefits of MSMQ and its COM interface is that it does not require inordinate amounts of coding from the developer. With the introduction of Visual InterDev 6.0, creating MSMQ objects is as simple as dragging them from the VI Toolbox and dropping them onto your page. It doesn't seem as if implementing an MSMQ solution could get any easier, so do you really need to look any farther?

The answer is a definite yes. There are many situations where alternate architectures would provide benefits above and beyond those of easily coding MSMQ logic in VBScript. In these situations, developers can take the MSMQ logic and move it into an COM component. With Visual InterDev 1.0, this approach could be argued to make life easier for the developer, since COM components can be developed in a variety of languages, such as Visual Basic and Visual C++. These languages are far more feature-filled and easier to develop with than Visual InterDev 1.0. However, with InterDev 6.0 many of those arguments go away thanks to features such as drag-and-drop access to MSMQ objects, debugging, and so on.

So, why would a development team want to go the extra step of housing MSMQ logic in a COM component? One major reason is performance. In many situations, the driving factor to use MSMQ is to help increase performance. To keep true to this goal, developers should let IIS/ASP do what it is best at: handling requests for and producing Web pages. Complex business logic, including message queuing, will run much more efficiently if it is converted into compiled code and run outside the interpretive ASP environment. Once business logic has been broken out into a component, system administrators have the flexibility to use other Microsoft tools, such as MTS, to further boost performance.

Another great reason for breaking out the message queuing to a COM component is *code reuse*. In the enterprise arena, so much of the code developers write could be reused by multiple systems. Not always are these systems Web-based, many are traditional client/server applications written in a multitude of

317

languages. Placing key business logic in COM components cuts down on the "reinvention of the wheel" syndrome and allows tomorrow's development efforts to build on today's. In the end, if there is a chance the business logic can ever be reused by another system, it would probably be beneficial to package this logic into a component.

As the developer you have two basic options when it comes to adding MSMQ functionality to your Visual InterDev application: dragging and dropping an MSMQ object onto a page and then manually coding the MSMQ objects in VBScript within your ASP page, or developing a COM component providing the MSMQ functionality that can be used by your ASP pages. Both choices are similar in that you will have to use some variation of the standard MSMQ code.

Which method is the best to use? The simple answer is that there is no simple answer. There are definite benefits to implementing MSMQ functionality, or other types of functionality for that matter, with either method.

A new feature of Visual InterDev 6.0 that is very useful is the ability to drag and drop an object such as an MSMQQuery object on to your Web page as seen in Figure 9-4. This can save you from having to write the code to instantiate the object and set its initial properties. Once you've dropped an MSMQ object onto the page, you will have to roll up your sleeves, hit that "middle" Source tab, and get your hands dirty by writing some MSMQ code.

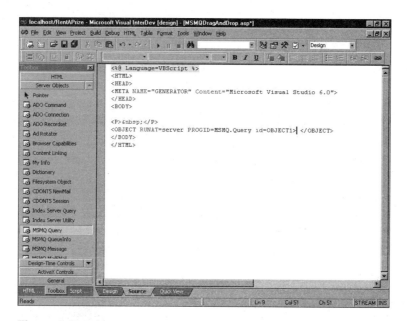

**Figure 9-4.**
*Dragging a MSMQ object onto an ASP.*

The other option is incorporating MSMQ logic in an COM component written in another language such as Visual Basic or Visual C++. Initially, this option will be more time consuming than coding all the logic within Visual InterDev, due to the fact that you have to use different tools to develop the components. However, in the long run, this type of approach will actually save you time since this code can be reused by other systems. This approach also allows for increased performance since components can be written in a compiled language and offloaded to machines dedicated to running COM components, thus freeing up IIS to do what it does best: manage Web pages. The biggest point to remember about these options is that there is no right answer, each choice has its own set of benefits and drawbacks. In order to give you a good feel on how to implement both of these solutions, both techniques will be demonstrated in this chapter.

## MSMQ Objects and Programming Basics

Programming MSMQ solutions in Visual InterDev is very easy thanks to the COM interface that Microsoft provides. There are only ten basic objects you'll have to deal with. The list is presented below. Of these ten, *MSMQQuery*, *MSMQQueueInfos*, *MSMQQueueInfo*, *MSMQQueue*, and *MSMQMessage* are the objects a Visual InterDev developer will use most often. Over the next few pages we'll show you some quick examples using each of these objects. More in-depth examples can be found later in this chapter in the "Solutions" section.

| MSMQ Objects | |
| --- | --- |
| MSMQQuery | MSMQMessage |
| MSMQQueueInfos | MSMQCoordinatedTransactionDispenser |
| MSMQQueueInfo | MSMQTransaction |
| MSMQQueue | MSMQTransactionDispenser |
| MSMQEvent | MSMQApplication |

**Table 9-1.**
*MSMQ Objects.*

### Searching for a Specific Queue

One of the most commonly used pieces of MSMQ functionality is to look up an existing queue. The *MSMQQuery* object allows you to query MQIS for existing public queues by way of its *LookupQueue* method. This method allows you to search for public queues based on the following queue properties: create time, label, modify time, queue identifier, and service type. If at all possible, try to search on *Label, QueueQuid,* or *ServiceTypeGuid.* The reason for this is that these searches will generally execute more quickly since these properties are indexed in MQIS. The results of the search are returned to MSMQQuery in a *MSMQQueueInfos* object. Let's quickly run through an example where we query MSMQ for a specific queue.

1. Create a Web page named GETQUEUENAME.HTM by selecting Project | Add Web Item | HTML Page. This page is responsible for querying the user for a queue name and then submitting this name to an ASP named SearchForQueue.asp.

2. From the HTML Toolbox, drag a Form object onto the newly created GETQUEUENAME.HTM.

3. If you are not already viewing the source code, click the Source tab.

4. Modify the Form tag that Visual InterDev created for you by entering *SearchForQueue.asp* as the action of the form. Also give more meaningful names for the ID and NAME properties. These changes can be seen below.

```
<FORM ACTION="SearchForQueue.asp" ID=frmNameSearch METHOD=POST
NAME=frmNameSearch>
```

5. Enter a text message asking the user to *"Please enter the name of the queue for which you wish to search"* within the form.

6. Drag a Textbox object from the HTML Toolbox onto the form. Make sure that you drag it to a point that is inside the form.

7. Give this textbox meaningful names for its ID and NAME properties.

```
<INPUT ID=txtName NAME=txtName>
```

8. Now drag a Submit button from the HTML toolbox onto the form. Once again make sure that this button is within the form.

9. Give this submit button meaningful names for its ID and NAME as shown directly below. All of the code for GETQUEUENAME.HTM can be seen below.

```
<INPUT ID=SUBMITNAME NAME=SUBMITNAME TYPE=SUBMIT VALUE=Submit>

<HTML>

<HEAD>
```

*(continued)*

```
<META NAME="GENERATOR" Content="Microsoft Visual Studio 6.0">

</HEAD>

<BODY>

<FORM ACTION="SearchForQueue.asp " ID=idQueueName METHOD=post

NAME=frmQueueName>

<P>Please enter the name of the queue for which you wish to

search</P>

<P>

<INPUT ID=idName NAME=txtName>

<INPUT ID=idSubmit NAME=submit1 TYPE=submit VALUE=Submit></P>

</FORM>

</BODY>

</HTML>
```

10. Let's now create an asp page called *SearchForQueue.asp*. You can easily do this by right-clicking the project within the Project Explorer window and selecting Add | Active Server Page.

11. From the server objects section on the toolbox, choose the *MSMQQuery* object and drag it onto the form.

12. Give the newly created object a better name than Object1, for example, *qryObj* by way of the properties window. If you now switch to the source tab, you should see that a *MSMQQuery* object has been created with the following code:

```
<OBJECT id=qryObj RUNAT=SERVER PROGID=MSMQ.MSMQQuery></OBJECT>
```

13. Dimension and initialize two new objects in code, one as a *MSMQQueueInfos* object and the other as a *MSMQQueueInfo* object.

```
Dim qInfo

Dim qInfos

Set qInfos = CreateObject("MSMQ.MSMQQueueInfos")

Set qInfo = CreateObject("MSMQ.MSMQQueueInfo")
```

14. Call the *LookupQueue* method of the *MSMQQuery* object. As stated previously, we can search for public queues by several properties:

create time, label, modify time, queue identifier, and service type. For our example, we are going to assume that all queues within our enterprise are guaranteed to have a unique label and therefore we will search for queues based upon their label. When calling the *LookupQueue* method, the value the user entered in the txtName textbox on the *SearchForQueue* html page will be passed as the third parameter, the label parameter. This method returns a collection of *MSMQQueueInfo* objects for all the queues that meet the criteria specified in *LookupQueue*.

```
Set qInfos = qry.LookupQueue(,,Request.Item("txtName"))
```

15. Call the *Reset* method of the *MSMQQueueInfos* object, qInfos. The *Reset* method returns the cursor to the start of the results of the LookupQueue query. Then call the *Next* method of qInfos. The Next method returns the next queue in the collection, which in this circumstance should be the first queue.

```
qInfos.Reset

Set qInfo = qInfos.Next
```

16. Finally, check to see if the query found any queues that match the name the user entered. If no matching queues were found, qInfo should be equal to nothing and the program will return a message stating that no matching queues were found. If qInfo has a value it will tell the user that the queue was found and display its format name on the page. Regardless of whether the queue was found or not, you should also set all created objects equal to nothing to help ensure proper clean up.

```
If qInfo Is Nothing Then%>

    <%="Sorry, the queue you requested was not found!"%>

<%Else%>

    <%="The queue was found. It has a format name of " & _
       qInfo.formatname%>

<%End If

'clean up of created objects

Set qInfo = Nothing

Set qInfos = Nothing
%>
```

One important point to note is that the information in the *MSMQQueueInfos* collection is *dynamic*, other clients can be changing the information at any time. For this reason there is not a queue count property available for the collection. Instead, *MSMQQueueInfos* provides an end-of-list (EOL) mechanism to indicate when you have completely moved through the collection.

## Creating, Updating, and Deleting Queues

In the previous example, we used the *MSMQQueue* object when we retrieved a particular queue from the *MSMQQueueInfos* collection. The *MSMQQueueInfo* object can be used for more than accessing existing queues. It can also be used to create new queues (transactional or nontransactional), change an existing queue's properties, and delete existing queues.

1.  Creating a new queue is quite easy. The only property that's required to be set by the developer is the *PathName*. The *PathName* property specifies the name of the computer where the queue's messages are stored, if the queue is public or private, and the name of the queue. All of the other properties of the *MSMQQueueInfo* object are optional. If the optional properties are not set, their default values are used. Below is an example for creating a new queue in an ASP.

2.  Create a Web page named PROMPTFORNEWQUEUENAME.HTM that queries the user for a queue name and submits this name to an ASP called *CreateNewQueue.asp*. The code for PROMPTFORNEWQUEUENAME.HTM is very simple code and can be seen below.

    ```
    <HTML>

    <HEAD>

    <META NAME="GENERATOR" Content="Microsoft Visual Studio 6.0">

    </HEAD>

    <BODY>

    <FORM ACTION="CreateNewQueue.asp" id=idQueueName METHOD=post
    NAME=frmQueueName>

    <P>Please enter the name of the new queue</P>

    <P>

    <INPUT ID=idName NAME=txtName>
    ```

*(continued)*

```
<INPUT ID=idSubmit NAME=submit TYPE=submit VALUE=Submit></P>

</FORM>

</BODY>

</HTML>
```

1. Create an asp called *CreateNewQueue.asp* by right-clicking the current project within the Project Explorer window and selecting Add | Active Server Page.

2. Drag an *MSMQQueueInfo* object from the Server Objects tab of the VI Toolbox to the ASP. From within the Source window, modify its tag to have an ID of *qInfo*. The following line of code should appear within the source:

```
<OBJECT ID=qInfo RUNAT=SERVER PROGID=MSMQ.MSMQQueueInfo></
OBJECT>
```

3. Add the following two lines of code. The first line sets the queue's pathname, the only property that is required to have a value. This name is submitted to the ASP from PROMPTFORNEWQUEUENAME.HTM. The pathname must specify both the machine on which it is to be created and the actual name of the queue, separated by a "/". After setting the pathname, the Create method of the qInfo object is called.

```
qInfo.PathName = Request.Item("txtName")

qInfo.Create
```

Most *MSMQQueueInfo* properties can be modified after the queue is created by using the *Update* method of the *MSMQQueueInfo* object. Update can only be used on *MSMQQueueInfo* objects that define public queues or local private queues. Properties for remote private queues are stored on the computer where the queue exists, and therefore cannot be updated. There are several queue properties that cannot be modified; these are: *BasePriority, CreateTime, QueueGuid, ModifyTime,* and *PathName*.

Both updating and deleting queues follow the same basic procedure of the *Create* method. In either scenario, a valid reference to queue information by way of the *MSMQQueueInfo* object must be obtained for a specific queue. A valid reference can only be obtained if the Windows NT user trying to access the queue has the appropriate rights. MSMQ's access control is based upon

Windows NT security and should be controled by system administrators. After obtaining this reference, the object's properties (other than those noted above) can be modified. After all the new property values have been set, the only remaining step is to call the *Update* method of the *MSMQQueueInfo* object.

Deleting a queue is even simpler. Once a valid reference to the queue information for a specific queue is obtained through a *MSMQQueueInfo* object, the developer only has to call the *Delete* method of the *MSMQQueueInfo* object.

## Sending Messages

Probably the most important and most frequently used MSMQ code that a Visual InterDev developer will work with is the code needed to send a new message. In order to send a new message two new objects must be used, *MSMQQueue* and *MSMQMessage*. The *MSMQQueue* object represents an MSMQ queue. It provides cursor-like behavior for traversing the messages of an open queue. At any given moment, it refers to a particular position in the queue. A valid *MSMQQueue* object can be obtained by calling the *Open* method of the *MSMQQueueInfo* object. After the queue is open, new messages can be sent to or read from the queue. When a queue is opened, the cursor points to the front of the queue, not the first message in the queue.

So what exactly is a message? In MSMQ a *message* is defined as an *MSMQMessage* object. Each message is defined by its properties, with the *Body* property containing the bulk of the information that is being passed in the message. The *Body* property of an MSMQMessage is extremely flexible in that it can contain strings, an array of bytes, numerics, dates, currency, or any persistent COM object that supports the *IDispatch* and *IPersist* interfaces. After a MSMQMessage object is created and its properties set, you can easily send the message to a queue by calling its *Send* method. A simple example of sending a message to a queue is outline below:

1. Once again, you need to create a Web page with an HTML page with a form that prompts the user for the required information. This page needs to have a text box for the queue label (txtQueue) and another text box for the message (txtMessage). The code for this page can be seen below.

   ```
   <HTML>

   <META NAME="GENERATOR" Content="Microsoft Visual Studio 6.0">

   </HEAD>
   ```

   *(continued)*

```
<BODY>

<P>

<FORM ACTION="sendmessage.asp" ID=idSendMessage METHOD=post
NAME=frmSendMessage>Queue

<INPUT ID=idQueue NAME=txtQueue></P>

<P>Message

<INPUT ID=idMessage NAME=txtMessage></P>


<P><INPUT ID=idSubmit Name=submit TYPE=submit VALUE=Submit></P>

</FORM>

</BODY>

</HTML>
```

1. Create a new ASP page called *SendMessage.asp* by clicking the Add Item button on the toolbar. You will then be presented with the Add Item dialog box from which you should choose to create a new Active Server Page named *SendMessage.asp*.

2. You now need to create the objects that are required for sending a message. These objects include *MSMQQuery*, *MSMQQueueInfos*, *MSMQQueueInfo*, *MSMQQueue*, and *MSMQMessage*. For this example we are going to do this through code, so if you are not already within the Source section, press the Source tab now and enter the following code:

```
<%

Dim qInfos

Dim qInfo

Dim qryObj

Dim msgObj

Dim queueObj


Set qInfos = CreateObject("MSMQ.MSMQQueueInfos")

Set qInfo = CreateObject("MSMQ.MSMQQueueInfo")
```

*(continued)*

```
Set qryObj = CreateObject("MSMQ.MSMQQuery")

Set queueObj = CreateObject("MSMQ.MSMQQueue")

Set msgObj = CreateObject("MSMQ.MSMQMessage")
```

3. Next, we'll perform a lookup by calling the *LookupQueue* method of MSMQQuery. As in the previous example, this search will look for the queue that has a label matching the one entered by the user on the HTML form. For the purposes of this example and to facilitate ease of searching, we are assuming that all queues will be given a unique label when created within the enterprise. This approach will help simplify MSMQ programming since developers are guaranteed that they have found the correct queue after issuing a search based upon queue label. After calling the *LookupQueue* method, the *MSMQQueueInfos* object needs to be reset and moved to the first *MSMQQueueInfo* object in the collection:

```
Set qInfos = qryObj.LookupQueue(,,Request.Item("txtQueue"))

qInfos.Reset

Set qInfo = qInfos.Next
```

4. Finally, check to see that the *MSMQQueueInfo* object, *qInfo*, is pointing to a valid queue. If it's not, return a message to the user saying that the system was unable to find the specified queue. If the queue is found, the *MSMQQueue* object, queue, needs to be initialized by calling the *Open* method of the *MSMQQueueInfo* object. After the queue is opened, the MSMQMessage object's *Label* and *Body* properties are given values. The *Body* property is filled with the text entered by the user on the HTML form. The next to last step is to call the *Send* method of the MSMQMessage object. This method requires only one parameter, a valid reference to a MSMQQueue object. The last step after sending the message is to call the *Close* method of the MSMQQueue object and to set all created objects equal to nothing, to help ensure proper cleanup. All of the code for SendMessage.asp can be seen below.

```
<%@ LANGUAGE=VBScript %>

<HTML>

<HEAD>

<META NAME="GENERATOR" Content="Microsoft Visual Studio 6.0">
```

*(continued)*

327

```
</HEAD>

<BODY>

<P>

<%

Dim qInfos

    Dim qInfo

    Dim qryObj

    Dim msgObj

    Dim queueObj


    Set qInfos = CreateObject("MSMQ.MSMQQueueInfos")

    Set qInfo = CreateObject("MSMQ.MSMQQueueInfo")

    Set qryObj = CreateObject("MSMQ.MSMQQuery")

    Set queueObj = CreateObject("MSMQ.MSMQQueue")

    Set msgObj = CreateObject("MSMQ.MSMQMessage")


    'for this example we are only searching on the queue label

    'this assumes that label names are unique within enterprise

    Set qInfos = qryObj.LookupQueue(,,Request.Item("txtQueue"))

    qInfos.Reset

    Set qInfo = qInfos.Next


    If Not qInfo Is Nothing Then

       Set queueObj = qInfo.Open(MQ_SEND_ACCESS, MQ_DENY_NONE)

       msgObj.Label = "Test Message"

       msgObj.Body = CStr(Request("txtMessage"))

       msgObj.Send queueObj

       queueObj.close

       %><%="Message sent successfully!"%><%
```

*(continued)*

```
Else

   %><%="Failed to find the queue specified!"%><%

End If


'clean up of created objects

Set qInfos = Nothing

Set qInfo = Nothing

Set qryObj = Nothing

Set queueObj = Nothing

Set msqObj = Nothing

%>

</BODY>

</HTML>
```

NOTE: Although it is not necessary in Active Server Pages to destroy objects created on a page (since they are automatically destroyed when the page is exited and the objects go out of scope), it is good programming practice to do so anyway. This has the advantage of encouraging consistency in coding between ASP and Visual Basic code and also makes it easier to move ASP code written in VBScript to components at a later date.

# Solutions

Let's now take a moment to look at some samples that show just how easy it is to implement an MSMQ solution in your enterprise Web application. These solutions illustrate three main points: guaranteed message delivery, store-and-forward functionality, and asynchronous communications.

### • • • SOLUTION: Inter-Component Messaging Over Unreliable Networks

In many enterprise systems, network reliability needs to be 100 percent guaranteed. Unfortunately, many times this is not a reality in the real world due to a variety of factors. In scenarios such as Web-based purchasing systems, a company's lifeblood, sales to new customers and repeat customers, depends completely upon the system being up and running twenty-four hours a day. If the system becomes unavailable to customers, business is lost, and worse yet, customers go looking elsewhere to do business. Because of this, companies need systems that are available to their customers twenty-four-hours-a-day, seven-days-a-week.

In some situations this may seem impossible, since many of a company's old legacy systems, such as inventory or accounts receivable processes, might be designed to run only once a day as a batch job. In other situations, a company's internal network might not be reliable enough to meet these exacting demands. In many cases, fixing either of these problems is not an option due to the amount of time and money that would be required and the risks involved with redesigning such important systems.

These situations are ideal for implementing a quick and inexpensive solution by way of MSMQ. MSMQ will allow you to write an online order entry system that can be available 100 percent of the time to customers, regardless of whether internal networks or systems are up and running. By using MSMQ, system administrators only need to worry about keeping IIS available to the outside world.

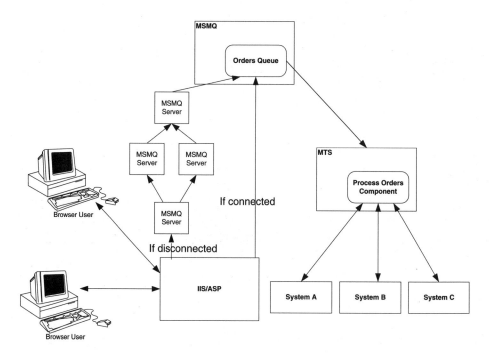

**Figure 9-5.**
*Architecture to ensure reliable communications over unreliable networks.*

Implementing the architecture shown in Figure 9-5, is rather simple.

1. You develop an ASP page that collects order information, which for the purposes of this example we'll keep simple; customer name, address, the product being bought, and the number of units purchased.

2. After the user enters this information and submits it to the Web server, an ASP script packages this data in a message and sends it to the Orders queue.

3. After the message has been successfully sent, the ASP page returns a message to the customer saying their order was processed. From the customer's viewpoint, they have ordered their product and are now free to place another order or leave the site.

Internally, the order process is just beginning. The message is automatically routed by MSMQ to the appropriate queue. In the event that the message is unable to reach its final destination because the route it is taking has been broken due to a network failure, MSMQ will try to send the message by a different route. MSMQ will keep trying different routes until the message has been successfully delivered to the final destination. Once the message reaches the destination queue another process will come along and read it from the queue and process the order. The specifics of this are not important for this example since we are only trying to show how MSMQ allows for messaging over unreliable networks.

Let's take a look at how easy it is to send this information to the Orders queue.

1. Start off by creating a simple order entry page (as shown below) for the Microsoft Fruit Stand (an attempt by Microsoft to branch out into new markets). This page collects basic user information such as user name, address, city, state, zip, as well as the type of fruit (notice Microsoft sells no lemons) and the quantity desired by the customer. After collecting this information from the user, the HTML form submits it to SENDORDER.ASP. The code for SENDORDER.HTM, the calling page, can be seen below.

```
<HTML>

<HEAD>

<META NAME="GENERATOR" Content="Microsoft Visual Studio 6.0">

</HEAD>

<BODY>
```

*(continued)*

```
<P><STRONG><EM><FONT color=#ff0000 face="" size=6>The Microsoft
Fruit Stand</FONT></EM></STRONG>
</P>


<P>
<FORM ACTION=SendOrder.asp ID=idOrder METHOD=post
NAME=frmOrder>
<TABLE BORDER=1 CELLPADDING=1 CELLSPACING=1 WIDTH=90%>


    <TR>
<TD>Name

        <TD>

    <INPUT ID=idName NAME=txtName STYLE="HEIGHT: 22px; WIDTH:
264px">

    <TR>

        <TD>Address

        <TD>

    <INPUT ID=idAddress NAME=txtAddress STYLE="HEIGHT: 22px;
WIDTH:264px">

    <TR>

        <TD>City

        <TD>

            <INPUT ID=idCity NAME=txtCity STYLE="HEIGHT: 22px;
WIDTH: 265px">

    <TR>

        <TD>State

        <TD>

    <INPUT ID=idState NAME=txtState STYLE="HEIGHT: 22px; WIDTH:
265px">

    <TR>

        <TD>Zip
```

*(continued)*

```
    <TD>

  <INPUT ID=idZip NAME=txtZip STYLE="HEIGHT: 22px; WIDTH:
265px">

    <TR>

      <TD>Fruit

      <TD>

      <!--METADATA TYPE="DesignerControl" startspan

<OBJECT classid="clsid:B5F0E450-DC5F-11D0-9846-0000F8027CA0"
height=21

id=cbFruits style="HEIGHT: 21px; WIDTH: 93px" width=93>

<PARAM NAME="_ExtentX" VALUE="2461">

<PARAM NAME="_ExtentY" VALUE="556">

<PARAM NAME="id" VALUE="cbFruits">

<PARAM NAME="DataSource" VALUE="">

<PARAM NAME="DataField" VALUE="">

<PARAM NAME="ControlStyle" VALUE="0">

<PARAM NAME="Enabled" VALUE="-1">

<PARAM NAME="Visible" VALUE="-1">

<PARAM NAME="Platform" VALUE="257">

<PARAM NAME="UsesStaticList" VALUE="-1">

<PARAM NAME="CLSize" VALUE="4">

<PARAM NAME="CLED0" VALUE="Apples">

<PARAM NAME="CLEV0" VALUE="1">

<PARAM NAME="CLED1" VALUE="Grapes">

<PARAM NAME="CLEV1" VALUE="2">

<PARAM NAME="CLED2" VALUE="Grapefruits">

<PARAM NAME="CLEV2" VALUE="3">

<PARAM NAME="CLED3" VALUE="Oranges">

<PARAM NAME="CLEV3" VALUE="4">
```

*(continued)*

```html
<PARAM NAME="LocalPath" VALUE="">

    </OBJECT>

-->

<script language="JavaScript" src="_ScriptLibrary/
EventMgr.HTM"></script>

<script language="JavaScript" src="_ScriptLibrary/
ListBox.HTM"></script>

<script language="JavaScript">

function _initcbFruits()

{

    cbFruits.addItem('Apples', '1');

    cbFruits.addItem('Grapes', '2');

    cbFruits.addItem('Grapefruits', '3');

    cbFruits.addItem('Oranges', '4');

}

CreateListbox('cbFruits', _initcbFruits);</script>


<!--METADATA TYPE="DesignerControl" endspan-->

    <TR>

        <TD># Fruit

        <TD>

            <INPUT ID=idAmount NAME=txtAmount></TD></TR></
TABLE>

            <INPUT ID=idSubmit NAME=submit TYPE=submit
VALUE=Submit>

</FORM>

</P>


</BODY>

</HTML>
```

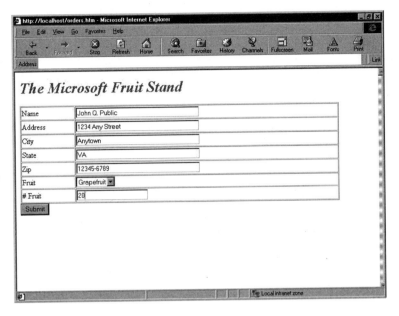

**Figure 9-6.**
*Web-based order form.*

2. SENDORDER.ASP is responsible for validating that the user enters all the required information and then sending the message to the "Fruit Order" queue. This code is based upon the assumption that the Fruit Order queue has already been created. The coding for this page is really quite simple: perform validation, search for the queue, and then send the message with the order information to the queue.

```
<%@ LANGUAGE=VBScript %>

<HTML>

<HEAD>

<META NAME="GENERATOR" Content="Microsoft Visual Studio 6.0">

</HEAD>

<BODY>


<%

Dim qInfos

Dim qInfo
```

*(continued)*

```
      Dim qryObj
      Dim msgObj
      Dim queueObj


      'validation checking, make sure user enters a value for every
         field
      If Trim(Request("txtName")) = "" Then
        %><%="You need to enter your name!"%><%
      ElseIf Trim(Request("txtAddress")) = "" Then
        %><%="You need to enter your address!"%><%
      ElseIf Trim(Request("txtCity")) = "" Then
        %><%="You need to enter the city in which you live!"%><%
      ElseIf Trim(Request("txtState")) = "" Then
        %><%="You need to enter the state in which you live!"%><%
      ElseIf Trim(Request("txtZip")) = "" Then
        %><%="You need to enter the zip in which you live!"%><%
      ElseIf Trim(Request("cbFruits")) = "" Then
        %><%="You need to enter the fruit that you wish to
           order!"%><%
      ElseIf Trim(Request("txtAmount")) = "" Then
      %><%=Request("txtAmount") & "You need to enter a correct amount
        for the fruit you wish to order!"%><%
      Else
        'process order
        Set qInfos = CreateObject("MSMQ.MSMQQueueInfos")
        Set qInfo = CreateObject("MSMQ.MSMQQueueInfo")
        Set qryObj = CreateObject("MSMQ.MSMQQuery")
        Set queueObj = CreateObject("MSMQ.MSMQQueue")
```

*(continued)*

336

```
Set msgObj = CreateObject("MSMQ.MSMQMessage")
'search for the queue with a label of 'Fruit Order'
'this code assumes that the 'Fruit Order' queue already
'exists and that only one queue exists with that label
Set qInfos = qryObj.LookupQueue(,,"Fruit Order")

qInfos.Reset
Set qInfo = qInfos.Next
If Not qInfo Is Nothing Then
    Set queueObj = qInfo.Open(MQ_SEND_ACCESS, MQ_DENY_NONE)
    ' the label consists of the fruit code for the fruit
    ' selected by the user on the submitting form
    msgObj.Label = CStr(Request("cbFruits"))

    'the body consists of the name, address, city, state, zip, and
    'amount of fruit all concatenated by the pipe symbol (|)
    msgObj.Body = Request("txtName") & "|" & _
        Request("txtAddress") & _
        "|" & Request("txtCity") & "|" & Request("txtState") & _
        "|" & Request("txtZip") & "|" & Request("txtAmount")

    msgObj.Send queueObj
    queueObj.Close
%><%="Order processed successfully.  Please expect your
    fruit to be delivered in two to three days"%><%
```

*(continued)*

```
Else

    %><%="Failed to process order.  Please try again"%><%

End If

'clean up of all created objects

Set qInfos = Nothing

Set qInfo = Nothing

Set qryObj = Nothing

Set queueObj = Nothing

Set msgObj = Nothing

End If%>


</BODY>

</HTML>
```

As you go through this and other examples you will notice that there really is not much difference in coding between the different scenarios, except for store and forward. This is because MSMQ has provided developers with an extremely simple and standardized way to send messages to queues. Once developers learn how to send messages for one situation, they basically have all the knowledge they need to send messages for all scenarios. This is a great feature because developers only have to worry about identifying situations where using MSMQ makes sense, not on how to specially code MSMQ for each situation.

When sending a message, developers only have a few choices on where to store the information in the MSMQMessage object. As you will notice, in this and several other examples within this chapter, we use the *Label* and *Body* properties for all of the information passing we do. In many cases we may need to send more than two values within a message. Instead of sending several messages for one order, we'll concatenate several pieces of data together delimited by the "|" symbol (also known as the pipe symbol) into a string and pass it as one of the properties. It is up to the recipient of the message to know the format of this message and to parse out this information once received.

• • • **SOLUTION: Implementing Store-and-Forward Functionality**

Another great feature of MSMQ is *store and forward*. This is an extremely powerful technology for systems in which the user might be disconnected from the corporate network while doing business. As long as the client is an MSMQ independent client, the messages will simply be placed in a local queue on the client machine and later be automatically routed to the correct destination, when network connectivity is restored. This is extremely useful for laptop systems where users spend the majority of their business day disconnected from the corporate network.

Sounds helpful doesn't it? You're probably wondering, though, how exactly this will help out a Visual InterDev developer who builds applications that require Internet connectivity in order for the user to access the system. Well the answer goes hand in hand with the previous example that dealt with building a solution over an unreliable network. In scenarios where it is imperative that data never be lost after the user enters it into the system, but the network is unreliable, store and forward can definitely help. It is possible that a user is able to access the Web server, by way of the Internet, while the IIS machine is completely disconnected from its internal network. This disconnection would probably be caused by a network failure. Thanks to MSMQ's store-and-forward capabilities, the user will be able to continue processing, never realizing a disruption has occurred. All of the user's information will be stored on the IIS machine in local queues until network connectivity is restored, at which time the information will be routed to the appropriate destination queues.

One important point to remember is that an MSMQ application is not automatically store-and-forward capable. Because of the very nature of store-and-forward scenarios, applications will be offline and unable to connect to the network and the Message Queue Information Store (MQIS). In an offline situation, public queues cannot be opened to retrieve or peek at messages, since they will be unavailable. Any code that normally accesses public queues must have adequate error handling, as an error will be raised or a timeout will occur. You must also ensure your application avoids any API or component calls that access the MQIS. These calls would force an attempt at network activity causing an error to be raised or a timeout to occur. A list of these calls is outlined below.

| API Functions | COM Methods |
|---|---|
| MQCreateQueue (for public queues) | Create (for public queues) |
| MQDeleteQueue (for public queues) | Delete (for public queues) |
| MQGetMachineProperties | MachineIdOfMachineName |
| MQGetQueueProperties | Refresh |
| MQGetQueueSecurity | IsWorldReadable |
| MQGetSecurityContext | AttachSecurityContext |
| MQLocateBegin | LookupQueue |
|  | Reset |
| MQLocateNext | Next |
| MQOpenQueue (public queues opened to receive messages) | Open (for public queues receive messages) |
| MQPathNameToFormatName |  |
| MQSetQueueProperties | Update |
| MQSetQueueSecurity |  |

**Table 9-2.**
*MSMQ methods that will raise errors when disconnected.*

One important point to remember, as mentioned earlier in our discussion of MSMQ messages, is that messages sent in express mode are only being held in RAM and will be lost when the computer is turned off. For this reason, you may want to send messages in recoverable mode, which guarantees that they are written to disk and successfully saved in case of a power failure. In order to send messages in recoverable mode, the delivery property of the message must be set to MQMSG_DELIVERY_RECOVERABLE.

When opening queues offline, you can use private, public, or direct format names. After opening the queue, all messages sent to the queue are stored locally by the client computer's Queue Manager. Upon reconnecting the client computer to the network, these messages will be passed on to the destination queue. In order to use a public format name, the identifier of the queue must be known by the caller, while accessing private queues requires the identifier of the client computer and the queue's name.

Direct format names require that you know the address of the queue where the computer is located and the local name of the queue. Direct format names will send the message directly to the queue, as soon as network connectivity is restored, bypassing the MQIS, since the exact network address is known. This is extremely helpful when you are trying to access a queue that is not in your enterprise, or when you want to ensure that MSMQ sends the message to the queue in one quick step. For all the examples in this chapter, direct format names are used simply for performance reasons. The downside to this strategy is that if for some reason a queue has to be moved to another machine, the new queue format name must be communicated to all the client applications that wish to send messages to the queue.

In order to illustrate the ease of implementing store-and-forward functionality into Visual InterDev application let's return to our Rent-A-Prize example. Suppose we want to require Rent-A-Prize employees to log the total amount of time and a description of the work they perform on a daily basis. To meet this requirement we'll build a sample timecard application with Visual InterDev and MSMQ. All employees will enter their daily time into an ASP application on the corporate intranet. Each of the time entries will be sent as messages to a queue named Time. In situations where network connectivity is available the messages will be quickly routed to the Time queue. However, in situations where network connectivity has been severed, the messages will be sent to a local queue and later be routed to the appropriate destination queue when network connectivity is restored.

The sample below consists of a main entry page (see Figure 9-7) and an ASP page that processes the information entered by the user on the main entry page.

1. We'll first build a standard HTML form called *Timecard.htm* that submits its information to an ASP called *SaveTime.asp*, by selecting Project | Add Item, and choosing HTML page. The code for TIMECARD.HTM can be seen below.

```
<META NAME="GENERATOR" Content="Microsoft Visual Studio 6.0">

</HEAD>

<BODY>


<P><FONT size=5><STRONG><EM>Timecard System</EM></STRONG></
FONT></P>

<FORM ACTION=SaveTime.asp ID=idTimecard METHOD=post
NAME=frmTimecard>

<P>

<TABLE BORDER=0 CELLPADDING=1 CELLSPACING=1 HEIGHT=127
```

*(continued)*

341

```
        STYLE="HEIGHT: 127px; WIDTH: 403px" width=90.56%>

    <TR>

        <TD><STRONG><FONT size=4>Date</FONT></STRONG>

        <TD>

            <INPUT ID=idDate NAME=txtDate>

    <TR>

        <TD><FONT size=4><STRONG>Employee #</STRONG></FONT>

        <TD>

            <INPUT ID=idEmpNum NAME=txtEmpNum STYLE="HEIGHT:
22px; WIDTH: 98px">

    <TR>

        <TD><STRONG><FONT size=4>Hours Worked</FONT></STRONG>

        <TD>

            <INPUT ID=idHours NAME=txtHours STYLE="HEIGHT:
22px; WIDTH: 99px">

    <TR>

        <TD><STRONG><FONT size=4>Work Description</FONT></
STRONG>

        <TD>

            <INPUT ID=idDesc NAME=txtDesc

    STYLE="HEIGHT: 88px; WIDTH: 212px"></TD></TR></TABLE></P>


<P>

<INPUT ID=idSubmit NAME=submit TYPE=submit VALUE=Submit></P>

</FORM>

</BODY>

</HTML>
```

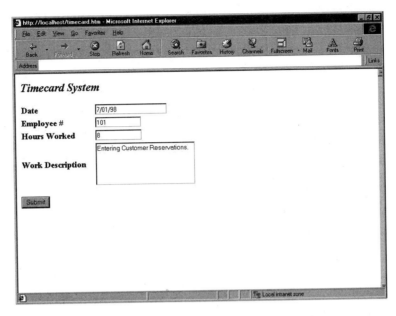

**Figure 9-7.**
*Time entry screen.*

2. Next, we'll create *SaveTime.asp* by selecting Project | Add Item, and choosing ASP page. SaveTime.asp first performs some error and validation checking to ensure that the user entered all the required information and that the information they entered is of the correct type. After performing the edit and validation checks, SAVETIME.ASP creates MSMQQueue, MSMQMessage, and a MSMQQueueInfo object. After initializing these objects, the MSMQQueueInfo objects FormatName property is set to a specific value (in this case a direct format name) and the Open method is called to return a reference for a valid queue to the MSMQQueue object. Finally, the MSMQMessage's Label and Body properties are assigned values that correspond to the information entered by the user and the message is sent.

As you can see in the code below, store-and-forward solutions require minimal coding. Developers, however, must adhere to the rules outlined above concerning which objects and method calls can be utilized. Notice that no calls that would directly access the MQIS (like LookupQueue) were used in the sample code below. The only other requirement that must be met in order to implement a store-and-forward application is that the IIS machine must be an MSMQ server or an independent client.

```
<%@ LANGUAGE=VBScript %>

<HTML>

<HEAD>

<META NAME="GENERATOR" Content="Microsoft Visual Studio 6.0">

</HEAD>

<BODY>


    <%

Dim qInfoObj

Dim queueObj

Dim msgObj


'perform validation


'check to see txtDate is a valid date

If Not IsDate(Request("txtDate")) Or _
    Trim(Request("txtDate")) = "" Then

    %><%="You need to enter a valid date!"%><%


'check to see that txtEmpNum is numeric and not blank

ElseIf Not IsNumeric(Request("txtEmpNum")) Or _
    Trim(Request("txtEmpNum")) = "" Then

    %><%="You need to enter a valid employee number!"%><%


'check to see that txtHours is numeric and not blank

ElseIf Not IsNumeric(Request("txtHours")) Or _
    Trim(Request("txtHours")) = "" Then

    %><%="You need to enter a valid number of hours!"%><%
```

*(continued)*

```
'check to see that a non zero length description is entered
ElseIf Trim(Request("txtDesc")) = "" Then
    %><%="You need to enter a description!"%><%
  Else
    'process entry
    Set qInfoObj = CreateObject("MSMQ.MSMQQueueInfo")
    Set queueObj = CreateObject("MSMQ.MSMQQueue")
    Set msgObj = CreateObject("MSMQ.MSMQMessage")

    'set the format name to the pre-existing Time queue
    'on a machine named rdu_nt4
    qInfoObj.FormatName = "DIRECT=OS:rdu_nt4\Time"
    Set queueObj = qInfoObj.Open(MQ_SEND_ACCESS, MQ_DENY_NONE)
    'label consist of employee number, entry date, and hours
    'concatenated by the pipe (|) symbol
    msgObj.Label = CStr(Request("txtEmpNum")) & "|" & _
       CStr(Request("txtDate")) & _
       "|" & CStr(Request("txtHours"))

    'the body of the message is simply the text description
    msgObj.Body = CStr(Request("txtDesc"))
    'send the message to the Time queue
    msgObj.Send queueObj
    queueObj.Close
    'clean up created objects
    Set qInfoObj = Nothing
    Set queueObj = Nothing
```

*(continued)*

```
        Set msgObj = Nothing
        %><%="Time entry was successfully sent!"%><%
    End If
%>
</BODY>
</HTML>
```

When developing enterprise level, Web-based solutions, you should definitely consider utilizing MSMQ's store-and-forward functionality. As you have just seen in the previous example, the coding is extremely easy as long as you follow several basic guidelines. This ease of development when mixed with the powerful functionality will make using MSMQ an easy decision for situations where message delivery must be guaranteed and network failure is a possibility.

## Asynchronous Communications

The last example deals with the Internet-based reservations portion of the Rent-A-Prize system. It is very similar to the situation discussed at the beginning of the chapter. The system is currently using a COM component running under MTS to process reservation orders. Unfortunately, the reservation business logic is running too slowly, thus causing the customer to have to wait too long after submitting a reservation.

MSMQ and its asynchronous capabilities are going to come to the rescue and allow us to reduce the amount of time a customer has to spend waiting for his or her reservation to process. We have several options when it comes to implementing MSMQ in the existing solution including changing the ASP page or changing the bsReservations component, which accepts the information required to make a reservation, processes the reservation, and finally records the reservation in the database. For example's sake, we will change the bsReservations component so that it only performs its existing validation and then sends the reservation information to a queue called Reservations. This change requires no modifications to the ASP page since the COM interface remains static. It does, however, require a new component to be created that periodically reads messages from the Reservations queue and then performs the logic that was originally contained within the bsReservations component, before it was modified.

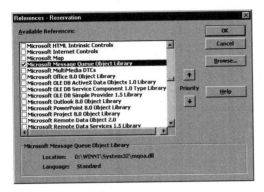

**Figure 9-9.**
*Visual Basic References dialog box.*

Modifying the bsReservations server is quite easy:

1. Add a reference to the Reservations project in Visual Basic (see Figure 9-9).

2. Strip out the logic for processing a reservation and replace it with code that sends all of the reservation information to the Reservations queue. These changes can be seen below. (Note that this code has been simplified for this example and may not reflect the code in the final version of the Rent-A-Prize application.)

```
Public Function MakeReservation(VehType As Long, StartDate As Date, _

    EndDate As Date, StartCity As Long, _

    EndCity As Long) As Boolean

    On Error GoTo EH:

    Dim qInfos As MSMQQueueInfos

    Dim qInfo As MSMQQueueInfo

    Dim qry As MSMQQuery

    Dim msg As MSMQMessage

    Dim que As MSMQQueue

    Dim sBody As String

        'error checking and validation
```

*(continued)*

```
Set qInfos = qry.LookupQueue(, , "Reservation")

qInfos.Reset

Set qInfo = qInfos.Next

If Not qInfo Is Nothing Then

    Set que = qInfo.Open(MQ_SEND_ACCESS, MQ_DENY_NONE)

    msg.Label = VehType

    sBody = StartDate & "|" & EndDate & "|" & StartCity & _
        "|" & EndCity

    msg.Body = sBody

    msg.Send que

    que.Close

Else

    MakeReservation = False

End If

MakeReservation = True

Exit Function

EH:

    MakeReservation = False

    Exit Function

End Function
```

By making these changes, the responsiveness of the reservations process can be greatly improved. Thanks to MSMQ's ability to provide asynchronous processing capabilities, the ASP page is only delayed for as long as it takes to pass the information to the COM component and send the message to the queue. As the message is being routed asynchronously to its appropriate destination, control is returned to the ASP page. The ASP page is then free to tell the customer that their reservation has been processed. By improving the responsiveness of the user interface, we have also improved the customer's opinion of the application's performance, meaning that customer is much more likely to come back again.

# Summary

In the past few chapters we have discussed several key ways to increase the performance, scalability, and reliability of Web-based enterprise applications. This chapter concentrated on utilizing message queuing to improve system performance and reliability, while providing functionality not directly available from Visual InterDev. One point to remember is that MSMQ, like any other tool, must be used wisely. In situations where system design is well thought out, using MSMQ will allow you to solve problems by leveraging its unique functionality and to increase system performance, reliability, and scalability.

In the next chapter, "User Authentication and Security," we will discuss security in Web applications, including methods of authentication, encryption, and security credential storage options.

**C H A P T E R   T E N**

# User Authentication and Security

• • •  **GOAL: Securing Rent-A-Prize from Non-Authorized Users, Providing Multi-Level Functionality Based on Employee Status, and Protecting Sensitive Data**

Teenage hackers. Financial fraud. Disgruntled employees. If you think your Web application is immune to these kinds of attacks, think again. If there is a security hole in your site, no matter how obscure, it can still be exploited. Students at high-tech colleges work night and day to find such holes, just so they can say they did; and criminal organizations have a lot to gain if they get hold of your customers' credit card numbers. Just as with any risk in life, you need to consider the expected impact—the chance that an event will happen, multiplied by the cost to your organization if it does—and balance the cost of the potential loss against the cost of prevention. In most cases, the cost of a potential loss far exceeds the cost of prevention. One large financial services firm applies the *Wall Street Journal* test—if a security breach occurred on our site, on what page of the *Journal* would it appear, and what would be the effect on our company's stock and customer confidence?

In this chapter, we'll discuss the features of Microsoft Windows NT, the Windows NT Option Pack, and Microsoft Site Server that apply to securing your site, and show you how to implement them. We'll discuss the basic concepts of Web application security—levels of content, authentication, and encryption—and show you how to implement the most common solutions. Finally, we'll show the design-time security features of Visual InterDev 6.0 that make remote design and management of your Web application even easier than before.

# Microsoft BackOffice Security Solutions

In this section, we'll discuss the security features you'll use most often, most of which are part of Windows NT. These features exist in Windows NT itself, as well as in Internet Information Server (IIS), Certificate Server, and the Personalization and Membership services (P&M) that are part of Microsoft Site Server.

## Windows NT Security

Windows NT provides a security solution that includes resource access control, user authentication, and confidential transmission. Windows NT keeps all system resources, including Web pages and application components, secure by requiring that they be accessed via an authenticated Windows NT user account. Users can be *authenticated* (positively identified) to Windows NT using many of the methods covered in this chapter, and their credentials and permissions are stored securely on the server.

Windows NT security integrates seamlessly with NTLM, basic, and client certificate authentication. With no code of your own, you can set rights to content administratively based on particular users or groups of users by assigning them to groups using Windows NT's User Manager, and assigning rights and permissions to resources such as files and folders through Windows NT Explorer. The Windows NT Security Provider also integrates with Microsoft Transaction Server (MTS) and Microsoft SQL Server, allowing you to protect application components and database objects on an individual or group basis. Even if you don't assign NT accounts to your individual Web users, IIS 4.0 gives you the power to assign different anonymous accounts to individual applications, letting you control and audit access to each application's resources separately.

There is another reason to allow the server operating system to manage security: Windows NT 5.0 will use a more secure, faster, and scalable security provider as part of the Active Directory Services Interface (ADSI). Under ADSI, all domain controllers in Windows NT 5.0 will be peers, allowing implementations to support larger account databases, up to 10 million server objects, than NT 4.0. NT 5.0 also makes use of *Kerberos*, an industry-standard authentication protocol developed by MIT that provides more secure authentication than the current NTLM protocol. Windows NT 5.0 will allow you to use its security provider for larger Internet applications where users are allowed to self-enroll. Until then, you should certainly use NT's security services for all of your intranet and smaller extranet applications. If you abstract security from your application now by taking advantage of the security built into Windows NT 4.0 (rather than coding your own custom security routines), you'll have less work to do when you move to Windows NT 5.0.

### Add User Accounts and Set Rights

The NT security provider is administered using the User Manager for Domains application located in the Administrative Tools folder. In general, the defaults that Windows NT assigns to a new user are too liberal for Web applications. Many of the settings, including group assignments and login hours, are loose enough to present security risks, so it's necessary to trim them down further. For any account that only accesses your network from over the Web, be sure to do the following:

- Remove the user from all NT-defined groups, such as Users, Administrators, and Domain Users. You should create application-specific groups that link accounts together by function.

- Under Policies, User Rights..., remove the user and any groups to which it belongs from all rights except Log On Locally. The account must have User Right to allow IIS to impersonate it.

### Set Up Groups for Easy Administration

As you build the functional specification and use cases for your application (which will define how secure your application needs to be, as well as which access levels will be needed by various users or groups), you'll identify roles that users fall into. In most cases, these roles will map directly to groups of users in NT. Roles tend to be defined on the basis of what a particular user needs to do, such as backing up a database, preparing reports, or entering data. In the Rent-A-Prize application, we'll create groups for managers who manage inventory and generate reports via the Visual Basic application, and clerks who use the DHTML application to enter customer, reservation, and rental information. Clerks, who need only to be able to access and update reservations and rental invoices, would only have read-access to data on inventory or locations. Managers, by contrast, can update both inventory and location data, since they are the ones responsible for adding new vehicles to the inventory, and adding new locations as they are opened. Elsewhere in the company, there would be groups for accounting, human resources, service managers, and fleet program administrators, each with access only to the applications needed for their job functions.

## IIS Security Features

Internet Information Server (IIS), version 4.0, integrates tightly with the Windows NT security provider. It directly supports four different methods of authenticating users to the NT provider: *anonymous, basic/clear text, NTLM Challenge/Response*, and *client certificate mapping*. You can configure your entire server, a particular Web site, or an individual virtual directory, to use any combination of these solutions. See the section, "Authenticating Users," for a complete description of these methods and how to configure each of them. IIS also provides two levels of SSL encryption when you install a server certificate—both the highly secure version, which uses 128-bit keys, and the most secure version that the U.S. government currently allows for export, which uses 40-bit keys. The section, "Encrypting Communications," describes the merits of encryption and how to install SSL on your server.

## Certificate Server

To make use of the client certificate mapping features of IIS 4.0, each of your users must have their own certificate installed in their browser. These certificates are available from third-party trusted sources, called *certificate authorities* that verify that a user is who they say they are, and issues the encrypted certificate directly to them. Figure 10-1 shows the Secure Communications dialog box (accessible from the Microsoft Management Console Internet Information Server snap-in), which is used to configure client certificate use. If your organization is able to do this verification internally, you can issue your own client certificates, using Microsoft Certificate Server in conjunction with IIS. Certificate Server is an extremely flexible and extensible solution for issuing certificates and allows you to customize the process in several ways. As shown in Figure 10-2, the certificate request begins at the client and proceeds through four modules (*entry, certificate server, policy*, and *exit*) before the actual certificate is returned to the client. You can customize the process in any of the following ways:

- Customize the entry component and modify the client's request, adding additional standard fields if necessary.

■ Replace the standard policy component with a custom one, written in VB, J++, or C++. The policy component is responsible for verifying the request. You can customize it to enforce specific business rules, such as ensuring that the customer's account is in good standing. Certificate Server maintains a queue of pending requests, so your policy can include calls to asynchronous and manual offline processes using MSMQ or CDO. At this point, you can also set certificate extensions (such as a user's account number or access level) that will be encoded into the certificate.

■ Similarly, you can replace and customize the exit policy, which handles the server-side storage of the certificate, as well as handling automatic account mapping and updating other enterprise databases related to this customer. You can also use MSMQ to include asynchronous processes such as notifying an account representative for a follow-up call.

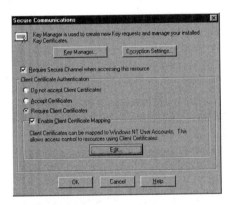

**Figure 10-1.**
*Options for requiring and mapping certificates.*

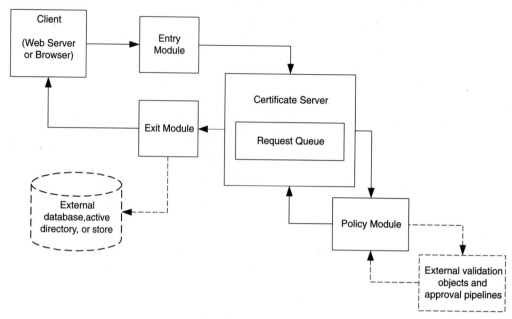

**Figure 10-2.**
*Certificate Server architecture.*

## Site Server

Microsoft Site Server provides a number of wizards, filters, and extensions that greatly extend the functionality of IIS. One such feature is the Membership Directory, which was originally part of the Microsoft Commercial Internet System (MCIS, formerly known as Normandy). The Membership Directory provides a framework for storing and maintaining user credentials and attributes in Microsoft SQL Server, Microsoft Access, and Active Directory store. Used together with Site Server's Personalization and Membership Services (P&M) and its Active User Object (AUO), it gives you great flexibility in maintaining credentials for a large number of Internet or extranet users. The section "Authenticating Users" provides more information on how P&M can help meet your security needs.

# Levels of Content Protection

Before we discuss the many options available for authenticating users and encrypting data, it's important to understand the security needs of the information in your application. Is the information in your pages sensitive? Would your company stand to lose money if someone other than authorized users got access to your application? Microsoft defines four different levels of content protection you can provide based on how sensitive (or nonsensitive) your data is (as used here, data includes the text content of your pages as well as data pulled from a database). As we proceed in this section, we'll use these levels to identify the needs of your application.

## Public Content

*Public content* is information that can be distributed broadly, such as a retailer's worldwide locations or a theater's performance schedule. The goal is to make this information as widely available as possible and allow anyone to access it, without opening your entire enterprise and its sensitive data to the Web. Public content is not protected by any authentication method. You identify one Windows NT account through which all application functions are performed. By default, IIS uses the <IUSR_MACHINENAME> account, where *MACHINENAME* is the name of the server on which IIS is installed. Once you've identified this account, you then limit its access to only the Web pages, Microsoft SQL stored procedures, and other resources that the application needs. See the sections on securing your application components, later in this chapter.

IIS 4.0, unlike IIS 3.0, allows you to define a different anonymous account for each application. This is recommended to increase the security of each individual application, especially if you have different teams creating and maintaining different applications.

## Restricted Content

*Restricted content* is online *quid pro quo*, in which you offer information to users in exchange for some information about them, perhaps to build mailing lists or marketing demographics. Restricted content is no more sensitive than public content, but it is valuable enough to your users that they'll be willing to fill out a form or questionnaire before they can gain access. In general, the user doesn't need to have an existing relationship with your organization. Web sites that offer free evaluation versions of software, for example, will often store them in restricted areas, requiring the user to give their name, e-mail address, and possibly phone number before downloading. This allows the site's owners to follow-up the download with sales offers for the full product. Microsoft's MSDN Online and the premium.microsoft.com site are also good examples of restricted content. To establish restricted content, you configure any authentication method (typically one of the methods that employ cookies, which will be described in the section "Authentication Methods"). You also use ASP code and Windows NT file security to limit access to certain parts of your application.

## Private Content

Access to *private content* is limited to registered users, whose identity you need to validate each time they connect to your site. This might include intranet sites limited to employees or sites set up especially for communication with business partners. To establish private content, you configure any of the authentication methods that implement strong security, such as NTLM, DPA, basic authorization, or client certificates. The authentication forces registered users to log on, and unregistered users to register, before they can access the protected content. By default, IIS presents an ugly "401..Not Authorized" message to the user if they fail to authenticate. To help you make this more user-friendly, IIS 4.0 lets you create your own ASP or HTML pages that appear when these errors occur, which give clearer explanations than the typical "HTTP 404—Not Found" variety. You can also use the custom error pages to tell users whom to contact when an error occurs, something that most people will appreciate. Once you create your custom page, you can map to it from the Custom Error tab of your virtual directory's property sheet (see Figure 10-3). You should configure all security-related options separately on each IIS virtual directory to allow you to control each application based on its specific requirements.

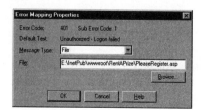

**Figure 10-3.**
*Mapping custom error pages in IIS 4.0.*

## Secure Content

*Secure content* is made available to only a subset of your registered users. This content is differentiated from less-secure content based on need-to-know, privilege, privacy, or payment of a premium fee. Microsoft's Web sites for Certified Professionals are a good example of this type of content. Only people who have passed a Microsoft certification can access these sites, and even then they can only access the site set up for their certification.

To establish secure content, you configure a secure authentication method, and you use Windows NT file security to set access controls on directories, individual files, and application and data resources. Again, see the section on securing application objects for details. Within each application, you'll need to rely on *application logic* to partition the data (i.e., prevent users from seeing each other's confidential information). For example, you can store a customer number as an extension in the user's client certificate, and then include that customer number in the WHERE clause of every SQL statement that returns confidential data. However you implement this kind of partitioning, put the logic in compiled components, where it is harder to compromise, and don't skimp on testing. Remember the *Wall Street Journal* test. You don't want to see your company's name on the front page of the *Journal* because a hacker managed to get past your security.

# Authenticating Users

An important step in securing your site is to take steps to identify who is trying to access your site, and control their access. *Authentication* is the process of identifying users (via a login ID and password or other methods described in this section), so that you can decide how much, if any, access to your content you want to give them. You'll need to decide two things: how the server will store each user's credentials; and how the browser and/or user will supply the credentials for authentication. In the Rent-A-Prize application's customer interface, authentication is required for a customer to make a reservation online, and is accomplished through a custom HTML form that lets the customer enter a customer ID and password. In this section, we'll discuss this and other methods of authenticating users.

## Security Provider (SSP) Options

*Security providers*, at a minimum, store the basic information needed to authenticate users and determine their access rights. Here, we present four options that can be used when building Web solutions on Internet Information Server (IIS).

### Windows NT Server Security Provider

This is the best solution for an intranet where you have a controlled and foreseeable number of users, especially if they already have Windows NT accounts for your internal network. Windows NT security gives you great flexibility and the ability to avoid coding security into your application. But there is a price for that flexibility and savings in code. Primary Domain Controllers (PDCs) and Backup Domain Controllers (BDCs) that keep track of user accounts require overhead for authentication; they do not scale well past 30,000 to 50,000 users, and users must be added and maintained manually. For these reasons, you should avoid using the Windows NT 4.0 security provider for Internet sites where users can self-register or for large-scale extranet applications.

### Membership Directory

Part of Microsoft Site Server's Personalization and Membership (P&M) services, the Membership Directory can be stored in MS Access, SQL Server, or an Active Directory store, and provides a COM interface for authenticating users and retrieving their preferences and other attributes. This interface, called *Active User Objects* (AUO), is straight-forward and well-documented, and supports more authentication methods than any other option listed here (see Table 10-1). AUO also supports online registration and profile maintenance, and provides Design-Time Controls for Microsoft FrontPage 98 and Visual InterDev 6.0, so you can easily customize registration and attribute access for your own needs.

### Existing Legacy Database

If your enterprise already maintains a security provider for your user base, such as a bank's ATM PIN database, you should consider authenticating against that database. Your customers will thank you for not making them remember yet another password, but will expect a rapid response to their login and data requests. Make sure that you have a fast, reliable connection between your Web server and the external database. Remember that authentication is a *synchronous process*, so asynchronous inter-application communication tools, such as MSMQ and MQSeries, will only complicate this process. In Chapter 13, "Accessing Legacy Data Sources," we'll cover several methods of accessing legacy data.

### Custom Credential Storage

If you do not have Site Server, you can create your own data model for storing users' IDs, passwords, attributes, and preferences in a SQL Server or other database, and then write your own routines for registration, authentication, and retrieving information. For a small application with simple security needs, such as our Rent-A-Prize example, this may be sufficient. For a large application, however, the potential time and expense incurred developing and testing these components could justify purchasing Site Server and using P&M. See the "Solutions" section at the end of this chapter for details on how implement custom security for Rent-A-Prize.

| Authentication Methods | Security Providers (SSPs) | | | |
| --- | --- | --- | --- | --- |
| | NT Server | P&M (AUO) | Legacy | Custom |
| Automatic Cookies | Yes | Yes | Yes | Yes |
| NTLM | Yes | No | No | No |
| Distributed Password (DPA) | No | Yes | No | No |
| Clear Text/Basic | Yes | Yes | Yes | Yes |
| HTML Forms | No | Yes | Yes | Yes |
| Client Certificates | Yes | Yes | Yes | Yes |

**Table 10-1.**
*Authentication and storage option support.*

## Authentication Methods

In this section, we'll discuss the six authentication methods that are most useful to ASP developers. Most of these are configured using the Microsoft Management Console (MMC) Internet Service Manager snap-in to configure the appropriate options, as shown in Figure 10-4. Not all of these methods are supported by all the security providers listed in the previous section. To see which providers support which authentication methods, see Table 10-1.

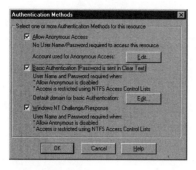

**Figure 10-4.**
*Configuring authentication methods in IIS 4.0.*

## Identification via Persistent Cookies

There are two types of cookies you can store on a user's browser:

- A *session cookie* lives as long as the user is connected to the site for one session and is used to hold information that is needed across pages. The ASP Session object is maintained by placing a session cookie in the browser. This cookie contains a unique key to IIS's session information, which it holds in memory on the server.

- A *persistent cookie*, by contrast, is stored permanently on the user's hard drive and is used to remember the user from one session to the next. In most cases, the application stores only a key to the user's entry in the database. See the section, "Securing Cookies," below for more information on how and why to do this.

Cookies provide no true security, and only a minimal amount of authentication, as they are stored in clear text on the client machine, and any user can view and modify their contents. Cookies are usually used in conjunction with IIS's anonymous user account, as we have already described under the sections on IIS and public content.

## Custom Authentication through HTML Forms

In implementing authentication through HTML forms, the server creates a login Web page that includes INPUT elements for the user's ID and password. When the user submits the page, their userID and password are validated and, if valid, the user is redirected to the application pages. To ensure that users don't bypass the login page by requesting a page inside the application (users will often bookmark the page or pages they use most), a session variable is used to keep track of whether the user is logged in. ASP code in each page checks the variable, redirecting them to the login page if they have not been authenticated. Like basic authentication, the password is sent in clear text. However, it is possible to require SSL on the login page only, allowing the rest of your application to enjoy higher performance.

This type of authentication is made especially easy in Visual InterDev 6.0, through the use of the data-bound Design-Time Controls (DTCs), which allow you to easily connect to your credential store, and the FormManager DTC, with which you can create event-driven forms that can be used for either login or registration, depending on the user's need.

### Windows NT Challenge/Response Authentication

Also known as NTLM authentication, Windows NT Challenge/Response authentication is extremely secure—it uses NT's security provider to find out which domain and account the user has logged into, and challenges the browser to validate that user. The challenge and the response messages are encrypted using an irreversible hash, so any nefarious persons snooping your network packets will not be able to obtain a user's password. Although NTLM authentication is extremely secure, it has two limitations:

- The user's browser must be able to receive the NTLM challenge and respond to it. Currently, only Microsoft Internet Explorer (version 2.x and higher) has this capability.

- The connection between the browser and server must allow RPC calls. Although this is usually the case in intranets, most proxy servers and firewalls are configured to block the RPC port—a good move for a security-minded enterprise. If you have field reps, telecommuters, or other users who need to access the intranet from outside your enterprise, you have several options: allow them to dial in using RAS; use a Virtual Private Network solution such as PPTP; or use a different authentication method such as DPA, clear text/ basic authentication, or client certificates.

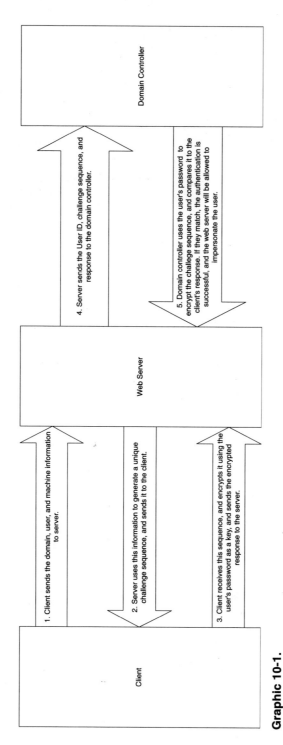

**Graphic 10-1.**
*The NTLM Challenge/Response process.*

1. Client sends the domain, user, and machine information to server.

2. Server uses this information to generate a unique challenge sequence, and sends it to the client.

3. Client receives this sequence, and encrypts it using the user's password as a key, and sends the encrypted response to the server.

4. Server sends the User ID, challenge sequence, and response to the domain controller.

5. Domain controller uses the user's password to encrypt the challenge sequence, and compares it to the client's response. If they match, the authentication is successful, and the web server will be allowed to impersonate the user.

Domain Controller

Web Server

Client

## Distributed Password Authentication (DPA)

DPA works the same way as NTLM authentication and has the same security benefits. The difference is that, while NTLM uses the Windows NT Server security provider, DPA uses Site Server's Personalization and Membership services Membership Directory. Multiple applications can share the same database, known as a *realm*, allowing users to authenticate once and move between any applications in your enterprise to which they have permission. DPA addresses both of NTLM's limitations. Microsoft has created a Netscape plug-in, called MAPN, that allows Windows 9x or Windows NT users running Netscape browsers to authenticate. DPA also has an HTTP option that lets it communicate through proxy servers, but that option requires a cookie, reducing DPA's otherwise high security benefits.

## Clear Text/Basic Authentication

In this standard feature of HTTP 1.0, the server requests credentials from the browser, and the user is presented with the browser's authentication box. Once the user types his user ID and password and submits them, the server completes the validation. The biggest risk with using basic authentication is that the password is transmitted to the server in clear text—subject to the packet sniffing that's far too common on the Web. This problem is alleviated if you encrypt your pages with SSL, but that may cause unnecessary performance reductions, especially if the password is the only piece of data that needs to be encrypted. (See the section on SSL later in this chapter.)

> NOTE: *Packet sniffing* is a process by which a person can use a network protocol analyzer or other monitoring tool to intercept the packets that make up messages sent across the Internet. Since messages traveling from computer to computer across the Internet must pass through many computers and network segments along the way, there are many opportunities for this kind of data snooping. The question you have to ask is whether it would be worth someone's time to snoop your data, and more important, what would it cost you if they did?

## Client Certificate Authentication

Client certificates provide the most broadly supported and highly secure solution for authenticating users and encrypting sensitive data in Web applications. Users request a *certificate*, created specifically for them, from a Certificate Authority (CA). The certificate contains five elements: details about its owner; details about the issuing CA; the owner's public encryption key; expiration dates; and an encrypted digest of the first four elements, used for ensuring that it hasn't been altered. Microsoft Certificate Server, part of the Windows NT 4.0 Option

Pack, allows you to become your own CA and tie certificates into your security provider. If third-party validation is important to you, commercial Certificate Authorities, including Verisign, Entrust, and GTE, can provide authorized certificates to your users. Both Microsoft Internet Explorer and Netscape Navigator support client certificates in their 3.0 and above versions.

# Securing your Application's Components

Independent of your authentication method, you need to look at every component in your system and determine how you need to protect it from unauthorized users. In multi-tier systems, you need to consider your Web pages, your business components, and your database, as well as the cookies you store in the user's environment. In this section we'll discuss the methods available for securing the various parts of your application, and the techniques used to implement them.

## Securing ASP and HTML Pages

In today's environment of automated Web crawlers that index even the most obscure sites, you can no longer rely on obscurity (not telling anyone your URL) to protect restricted and secure Web pages. You should secure your pages using NT file permissions, ASP code, or a combination of both.

### Setting File Permissions

For Windows NT to track file permissions on a file-by-file basis, you must be running on the NTFS file structure, not FAT or FAT32. By default, NT file permissions are granted to the Everyone group, which includes all users. While that may be acceptable on a department file server, the Internet requires greater security. Therefore, you should change your content's permission settings to only the users that need it. Users accessing files through IIS only need Read and Execute permissions, while authors in FrontPage or Visual InterDev need Read, Write, Execute, and Delete (RWXD) permissions. If you use NTLM authentication or certificate mapping, you can assign groups of users permissions to different files based on levels of access. If you use a custom authentication method, you'll need to give the anonymous user account Read and Execute permission on all files, and limit privileges within the ASP or component code.

## Using ASP Session Variables

Although it's recommended that you manage content security through file permissions, it is also possible, and simple, to do so within your ASP code. You may need to do this if, due to the structure of your organization, you have more access to the content of your pages than to the NT Access Control Lists (ACLs) of the files themselves. At login, store a session variable, or variables, describing the user's access level within the application. Then, on each page in which you restrict content, use a basic IF statement to determine if the user is eligible for the content. If they are not, either present a warning, or simply hide the content.

## • • • SOLUTION: Tracking Clerk Status with Session Variables

In implementing security for the Rent-A-Prize sample application, we considered a number of alternatives. While in the end the development team decided that the application should use Windows NT Challenge/Response Security (since we had already decided on IE 4 as a target browser for functional reasons), the application could also have been secured using ASP session variables. This method would be extremely useful in situations where the target browser could not be assured. For example, if Rent-A-Prize acquired another company with substantial IT assets whose hardware was incapable of running Internet Explorer 4, the use of session variables to secure the application would mean that those assets would not need to be replaced in order for the acquired locations to take advantage of the application (although the application servers might need to be upgraded depending on the number of locations added).

The following code calls the login method on the clerk component and stores the user's rights in a session variable. This code lives inside the page to which we post the login information. The *lRights* variable is a bitmask, allowing any combination of six different privileges. The 7th bit is reserved for forcing a password change. To make the right levels easier to keep track of, we use predefined constants. The different constants are added together to comprise the *lRights* variable. To test for a right level, we do a bitwise AND of *lRights* with the predefined constant.

```
' Define our RIGHTS constants

CONST RIGHT_LEVEL1 = 1

CONST RIGHT_LEVEL2 = 2

CONST RIGHT_LEVEL3 = 4

CONST RIGHT_LEVEL4 = 8

CONST RIGHT_LEVEL5 = 16
```

*(continued)*

```
CONST RIGHT_LEVEL6 = 32
CONST RIGHT_PASSWORD = 64
' Store the userid and password
Session("szUID") = request.form("txtUser")
Session("szPWD") = request.form("txtPWD")


Set oClerk = Server.CreateObject("RentaPrize.Clerk")
If oClerk is Nothing Then
    ' The szMessage session variable will be displayed to the user
    ' on the loginerror.asp page
    lErrCode = 32768
    szMessage = "Unable to instantiate clerk application."
    Session("szMessage") = szMessage
End If
' Call the login method. szUserName, szLocation, lRights, lErrCode,
' and szMessage are all by reference (output) parameters
iEmpID = oClerk.Login(Session("szUID"), Session("szPWD"), _
    szUserName, szLocation, lRights, lErrCode, szMessage)
If lErrCode <> 0 Then
    ' Check to see if any errors occurred in the component.
    If lErrCode = -2147467259 Then
        ' For recognized errors, display a friendly message
        Session("szMessage") = "Your user name or password '& _
            'was incorrect. please try again."
    Else
' For all other errors, szMessage contains Err.source,
'   Err.Number, and Err.Description
        Session("szMessage") = szMessage
    End If
Else
    ' If it was successful, save the user's information in the
    'session variable
    Session("iEmpID") = iEmpID
```

*(continued)*

```
      Session("szUserName")=szUserName
      Session("szLocation ")= szLocation
      Session("lRights")=lRights
End If
If (lErrCode = 0) AND ((lRights AND RIGHT_LEVEL2) = RIGHT_LEVEL2) Then
Session("aSpec2") = oClerk.GetSpecialInfo2(Session("szUID"), _
      Session("szPWD"), Session("iEmpID"), lSpec2Count, lErrCode, szMessage)
   If lErrCode <> 0 Then
      Session("szMessage") = szMessage
   Else
      Session("lSpec2Count") = lSpec2Count
   End If
End If
If (lErrCode = 0) AND ((lRights AND RIGHT_LEVEL3) = RIGHT_LEVEL3) Then
' ... Similar code for other rights levels 2  through 6.
End if
If lErrCode = 0 Then
   Session("bLoggedIn") = True
   ' Right level 7 of lRights tells us to force
   'the user to change their password.
   If (lRights AND RIGHT_PASSWORD) = RIGHT_PASSWORD) Then
      set oClerk = Nothing
      response.redirect "changepass.asp"
   Else
      set oClerk = Nothing
      response.redirect "mainmenu.asp"
   End If
End if
set oClerk = Nothing
response.redirect "loginerror.asp"


%>
```

The following code checks the user's rights to access this page, which in this example requires both the first and third rights levels. Again, we use a bitwise AND to make the comparison. This code should be placed at the top of the page, before any actual HTML text or tags.

```
If Not Session("bLoggedIn") = True Then

    Response.Redirect ("logintimeout.asp")

End If

    '== This is a bitwise AND, not a logical AND

If (Session("lRights") AND (RIGHT_LEVEL1 + RIGHT_LEVEL3)) = 0 Then

    Response.Redirect ("notauth.asp")

End if

%>

... Continuation of HTML and VBScript.
```

## • • • SOLUTION: Tracking Clerk Status Using Client Certificates

Another method we could have used to secure the Clerk interface of the sample application is *client certificates*, which would be installed on each clerk's machine. When using client certificates, we can either map certificates to NT accounts and control access with file permissions, or access the *request.certificate* method from within ASP.

Once you have an SSL certificate installed, certificate mapping is done from the property page of the Virtual Directory, using the Edit Secure Communications button of the Directory Security tab. You can map individual certificates on the Basic tab, or map groups of certificates to an NT account via rule-based mapping on the Advanced tab. Figure 10-5 shows the rule definition page of the Advanced Mapping Wizard. Once you define elements for your rule, you can map all certificates fitting those criteria elements to a specific NT account. This is also called *one-to-many mapping*.

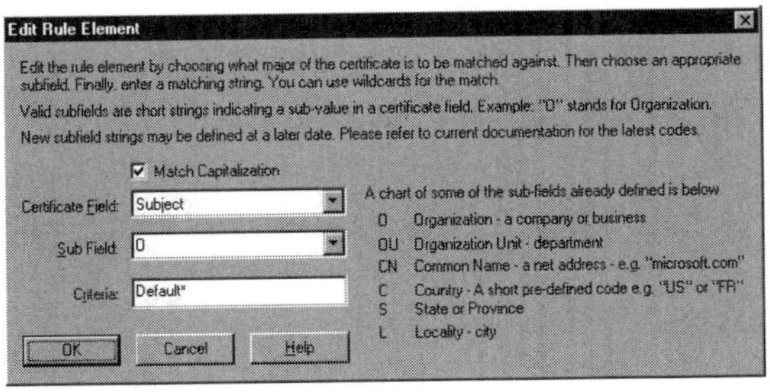

**Figure 10-5.**
*Rule-based mapping.*

Here is some simple code that enforces certificate-based security within your ASP code. Instead of storing the *lRights* attribute in a session variable, as we did in the previous example, we have encoded it into the certificate as a certificate extension which is part of our Certificate Server's custom policy module.

```
<% ' The following code checks the user's rights to access this page,
' which in this example requires both the first and third rights levels.
' This code should be placed at the top of the page, before any actual
' HTML text or tags.


' First, we check to make sure that the client certificate was issued by
' our own CA. If not, we redirect them to a page telling them their
' certificate is invalid
If Not Request.Certificate("ISSUER") = "RentAPrize" Then
    Response.Redirect ("InvalidCert.asp")
End If
' Next, we do a bitwise AND between the LRIGHTS variable, stored in the
' certificate, with the sum of the rights we are requiring. If that result
' equals zero, they do not have the rights and we redirect them to a page
' telling them so.


If (Request.Certificate("LRIGHTS") And _
    (RIGHTS_LEVEL1 + RIGHTS_LEVEL3)) = 0 Then
    Response.Redirect ("notauth.asp")
End if
%>
```

## Securing MTS Components

Microsoft Transaction Server (MTS) provides the ability to define roles for your application, and to make components available to only the roles that are entitled to use them. This gives you an additional way to abstract your security from your application code. See Chapter 8, "Enterprise Development Using Microsoft Transaction Server (MTS)," for more information on MTS roles.

## Securing Database Objects

Even if you define roles in MTS, it's still possible for people to bypass MTS and access your database directly. Here are two ways to protect your database from unauthorized access.

### Trusted Connections

If you use SQL Server for data storage, you should be using *mixed mode* or *integrated security* on the SQL server, and *trusted connections* in your ODBC DSN's. You could use standard security, but you would have to maintain login ID and password information in your application, either hard-coded or stored separately in the Registry. Whenever the password for that login is changed, as it should be periodically in a secure environment, you would have to change it in multiple locations. Under integrated security, groups of NT accounts are mapped to single SQL logins, so the only passwords that need to be changed are in the NT account directory and the Internet Service Manager. Use SQL Security Manager to map the accounts. Once you've done that, remove any unnecessary insert, update, and delete permissions from Internet user accounts. To make access as granular as possible, write your application to only use stored procedures, and then limit each group's permissions to just execute the stored procedures that group uses. In addition to added security, there are performance benefits to using stored procedures; they are covered in Chapter 14, "Optimizing Data Access."

> NOTE: In Microsoft SQL Server, there are three available security modes: *standard* (default), in which user IDs and passwords are managed by SQL Server; *Windows NT integrated*, in which SQL Server uses the network username or login ID to determine access using only trusted connections (authenticated connections between client and server); and *mixed mode*. In *mixed mode*, SQL Server attempts first to authenticate a user based on the integrated security

model, but looks to the standard mode user database if the first model fails. This allows greater security (for databases using integrated security) while clients that cannot use Integrated Security are able to use the standard mode.

In the example in Figure 10-6, we have just added all members of the Finance department to SQL Security, and given them access to the Staff database. We would then grant permissions to the Finance group for only the specific database objects they need for their job. To reduce administrative overhead in maintaining your application, simply add the Microsoft SQL Server Grant statements to the end of the SQL scripts you use to create your stored procedures.

**Figure 10-6.**
*Mapping NT groups to SQL logins.*

## Using Your Middle Tier as an Additional Firewall

Another way to provide security for your data in a multi-tier system is to use your application servers as a *firewall*. You do this by *dual-homing* each server, that is, giving it two network cards, each with its own network address. You connect one card to the network segment containing your Web servers via a router that allows only calls on restricted DCOM ports, and another to the network segment containing your data servers via a router that allows communication on only the SQL Server port. This way, the only access to your data servers is via DCOM calls to MTS components running on the applications servers. If you have implemented security on MTS correctly, this is an extremely secure method of protecting your network from outsiders.

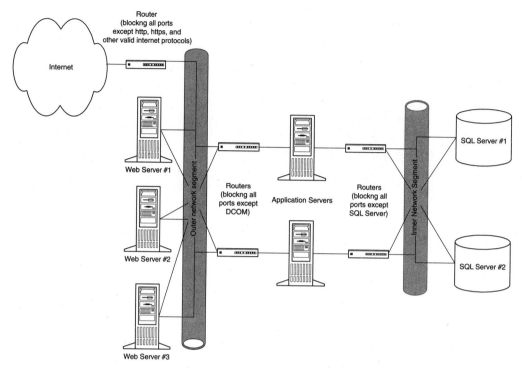

*Figure 10-7.*
*Secure segmented server architecture for a multi-tier Web application.*

## Securing Cookies

If you store persistent user information and preferences directly into a cookie, the browser will automatically send them up with each page request. To avoid sending this information repeatedly, store it in a SQL Server table, and place the table's primary key in the cookie. The primary key can be a userID, an identity column, or, as in Site Server, a generated GUID. When the user opens a new session in your restricted area, pull the information out of the table and place it in session variables, where your ASP code can access it easily. Here's an example of ASP code that does this, as part of the *Session_OnStart* event in GLOBAL.ASA:

```
szCookieID = Request.Cookie("RAPID")

Set oClerk = Server.CreateObject("RentaPrize.Customer")

' Call the get personal data method, which queries the database.

'  bSmokPref, szCarPref, lErrCode, and szMessage are all

'      by reference (output) paramaters

iEmpID = oClerk.GetPersonalData(szCookieID, bSmokPref, _

   szCarPref, lErrCode, szMessage)

If lErrCode = 0 Then

   Session("bSmokPref ") = bSmokPref

   Session("szCarPref ")= szCarPref

End If
```

This method has a number of advantages over storing the data in the cookie itself: it gives you greater control over the contents of the data; it keeps users from tweaking the cookie and possibly compromising your site; it cuts down on the size of page requests; and finally, it allows you to do demographic analysis of your users from the database.

# Encrypting Communications

As information moves over the Internet, it passes through any number of public routers and computers. At any of these hops, a hacker can easily copy information and read it, without anyone noticing. For most information sent over the Web, public and restricted content, this is not a big issue. But if your application uses private or secure content, you should consider encrypting it. *Encryption* is the process of scrambling data before it's transmitted over a network, then unscrambling it when it's received. Most encryption methods used on the Web fall in the category of *key-pair encryption*. Each server possesses both a private and public copy of a uniquely generated key. The first time a client requests encrypted content from a server, it also receives its public key in a separate packet. It uses that public key as a seed to generate and encrypt a random key, which only the server can decrypt. For the rest of the session, the browser and server use that random key to encrypt and decrypt the information they send. All of this encryption and decryption takes time, and applies to all elements of a page, including graphics, so it's important that you use encryption only when necessary. In this section, we'll discuss SSL encryption, as well as some of Microsoft's other encryption-related products.

## SSL Is the Most Common Solution

In all popular encryption schemes, the server only transmits its public key, not the algorithm for encryption and decryption. Therefore, whichever solution you choose must be supported by software on both the client and the server. Currently IIS supports only SSL for encryption. In fact, SSL is the most widely supported encryption method available. If you choose any other solution, you'll be faced with additional overhead of installing it onto your servers, and asking all of your users to install plug-ins into their browsers. SSL is supported by versions 3 and higher of Microsoft's and Netscape's browsers.

## • • • SOLUTION: Protecting Customer Data with SSL

Implementing SSL in IIS is a simple process, requiring only that you get a certificate (purchased from a Certificate Authority, or a test certificate generated for a development site), install it, and then configure your site to require SSL communications by following these steps:

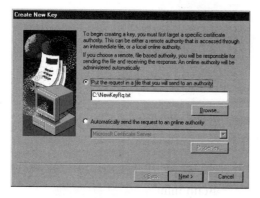

**Figure 10-8.**
*Creating a certificate-signing request.*

1. Use Key Manager to generate a certificate-signing request (CSR). Make sure you use a password that's eight characters or shorter, and doesn't contain any punctuation or other special characters. Don't lose this password, and remember that it is case sensitive.

2. Send the CSR to a Certificate Authority. They'll also need some information about your organization and, of course, your payment.

3. Once the CA has validated your request, they'll send you a signed certificate.

4. Return to Key Manager and install your key.

5. Stop and start the WWW service.

6. If you want to mandate encryption on a virtual directory, go to the Internet Service Manager and enable "Require Secure Channel" on the properties page of each Virtual Directory on which you want to require SSL. Figure 10-9 shows where this is done.

**Figure 10-9.**
*Installing a new key through Key Manager.*

Although this basic implementation is simple, there are other steps to integrating SSL into your application. Here are some rules to apply:

■ Encrypted pages should contain minimal graphics. As mentioned earlier, the images get encrypted along with the data, so the more graphical your site is, the longer it will take to encrypt.

■ To access a server over SSL, browsers must start their URL with the https: protocol instead of http:. Make sure your links are correct.

■ If, in the same application, you have public content and content that requires encryption, you'll need to use separate virtual directories.

Do not nest one virtual directory inside another, or session variables may be lost.

■ Even if you don't require SSL for a directory, users can still request encrypted content by starting their URL with https:, as long as you have a server certificate installed. If you allow users the choice of encrypting their secure content, use ASP or client-side JavaScript to give a warning if they are not secure. The following ASP code could be placed in an Include file that is referenced by all of your secure pages:

```
<!-- This SERVER_PORT_SECURE variable will be 1 for secure, 0
for non-secure -->

<% If Request.ServerVariables("SERVER_PORT_SECURE")=0 Then %>

    <P>WARNING: this page is not secure.

    <!-- This link redirects back to this same page in secure
mode. We use  variables here for the server name or path to this
page to allow this to be part of a generic include file -->

    <A href='https://<% =Request.ServerVariables("SERVER_NAME") _

        & Request.ServerVariables("PATH_INFO")%>'>

    Click here for a secure version.</A></P>

<% End if %>
```

## Can SSL Be Cracked?

A ring of hackers has been working to crack the 40-bit export-authorized version of SSL in an attempt to influence the American government to allow exports of the much safer 128-bit version. In the most recently reported success, a group of computers took eight days to decipher a single 40-bit encrypted message, at considerable expense in CPU time. In order to crack other messages, the entire process would have to be repeated for each message, even if from the same server. Damien Doligez, the French student who led this effort, when asked if he would use a product using 40-bit SSL himself, said, "It depends on what kind of information would go through this Web site. It has been pointed out that SSL is still quite safe for credit card numbers, but for really confidential information, like a password that gives access to a bank account, or a stock broker taking orders via the Web, I wouldn't." This sentiment is common among cryptographers. Although 40-bit SSL can be cracked in controlled situations, it is still quite secure. However, for seriously valuable data, it is best to use 128-

bit encryption, if it is legally available in your location and that of your users. (For more information see Doligez's Web site at http://pauillac.inria.fr/ ~doligez/ssl/press-conf.html.)

More recently, a researcher at Lucent Technologies discovered a brute-force method of deriving a server's public key by sending millions of challenges to the server and analyzing the responses. RSA, Microsoft, and Netscape immediately issued patches to prevent such an attack. What you should take from these attacks is not so much concern about the security of SSL, but an under-standing that security is *your* responsibility. This means making sure you have any and all security-related patches for your OS and other products installed, as well as being sure you understand the ramifications of the security decisions you make. Vendors cannot guarantee security, they can only provide the best tools they can, and respond promptly to reported holes or cracks. It is up to you to make sure you keep up-to-date on the products you use.

## Encryption-related products

One useful encryption-related product to take a look at is Microsoft Wallet. This is a client-side product that helps users organize their certificates and credit card numbers, and encrypts them for secure storage on the user's hard drive. Whenever a user wishes to make an online payment to a site that supports Wallet, they simply choose the appropriate card from the Wallet interface, type in their password to allow its use, and let the browser send the encrypted information to the server.

Originally developed specifically for credit card purchases using the SET protocol, Microsoft Wallet supports many payment options and protocols. Like the other Microsoft solutions discussed in this chapter, it provides a COM interface that lets developers write supporting components for additional payment methods, protocols, and specialty credit cards. Many third-party banks, financial services firms, and electronic commerce vendors are developing Wallet components, and it may yet become the standard for online commerce over the Internet.

Another useful product in the Microsoft encryption world is the CryptoAPI. CryptoAPI is an excellent technology that allows developers to create their own custom security solutions. It provides direct access to many common functions, including data encryption and decryption, key generation, key exchange, hashing, and digital signatures. It allows for abstraction of cryptography from your application, so that as new, more secure protocols are released, only the Cryptography Service Providers (CSPs) need to be updated, not your application.

Don't let the API part of its name scare you away. If you are using SSL, Certificate Server, or many of the solutions described in this chapter, you're already using CryptoAPI. In addition, many third-party vendors are building CSP's that support specific features such as *smart cards, encryption accelerators,* and *virtual private networks.* If that's not enough, you can use it to build solutions that meet the specific needs of your own organization.

# Suggested Solutions

In this section, we'll describe suggested solutions for a variety of situations, including intranet applications, Internet applications, and extranet applications. We'll then walk through an example that uses elements of all three for different parts of a single application.

## Intranet Applications

In considering intranet applications, ones that are used solely by employees and other closely held personnel such as contractors and temps, we start with a basic assumption: your internal network is sufficiently guarded from the outside by firewalls and other routers. Unfortunately, in today's enterprises, this assumption is as true as often as the basic assumptions of high-school physics ("frictionless surfaces") or free-market economics ("perfect competition without external forces"). In other words, it's rarely true at all. Although securing your internal network is extremely important, and more easily solved than defeating friction, it is beyond the scope of this book. Suffice to say, no matter how great your efforts, your application can ultimately only be as secure as your network.

NTLM Authentication is the preferred method for accessing secure content on an intranet. It is transparent to the user, and extremely secure. If your application needs to support non-Microsoft browsers, then clear-text/basic authentication against the NT user directory is an acceptable substitute, provided your internal network is shielded from the Internet and safe from packet snoopers.

## Internet Applications

Internet applications generally fall into the public and restricted classes of content protection. In either case, anonymous user access is generally adequate. For restricted information, you can store a user's ID in a persistent cookie, or ask them to login using an HTML form running. In either case, authenticate against Membership Directory or a custom database. Determining the line between public and restricted content requires a good sense of your customers' desires and what your competitors are offering. One way to gather this type of information is to offer an e-mail address for feedback about your site. Any content you decide to restrict must be valuable enough that the user will want to complete the registration process. You don't want to make someone complete a six-page questionnaire just to find out your company's address or phone number.

## Extranet Applications

Extranet applications provide private and/or secure content to users outside your enterprise. Examples include a manufacturer's network of dealers and service providers, a bank's account balance and transfer system, or an insurer's claim submittal and status application. These applications require high security and wide availability. They are good candidates for client certificates, or HTML forms authentication in conjunction with SSL.

## • • • SOLUTION: Combining Security Approaches to Secure the Rent-A-Prize Application

So far, we've discussed a number of options for authenticating users and encrypting their data, and seen what solutions Microsoft provides in their server products. To conclude this section, let's return to our Rent-A-Prize example application and show how we'll implement security at various levels of users: Web surfers, customers, and clerks.

We'll use anonymous access for Web surfers—people who want to look at our fleet of cars, search our locations database, or see marketing specials. This is public information that we want to make available to anyone. However, we'll tighten down the anonymous user's access to just the Web pages that represent public content, and to the MTS components that query the location and fleet information. In addition, we could use cookies to keep track of our users' preferences, such as the part of the country they were searching, or which level of car they were looking at, and then use Site Server's P&M to show marketing banners targeted for them based on that information.

Once a user decides to make a reservation, they change from a Web surfer to a customer, and enter restricted content. Here, we use HTML forms for authentication against a custom credential store. When an unauthenticated user hits any page in the reservations area, they are redirected to the login page, where they can type their customer ID and password. There's also a link on the login page that allows new customers to register. We'll use our existing customer database to store their standard requests, such as insurance requirements, car class and model, and smoking preference. If the customer chooses to guarantee or pre-pay their registration with a credit card, we collect the card number over an SSL-secured page to reduce the chance of fraud.

The clerk interface needs to be secure, but, since the clerks are located at airports around the country, we still want to take advantage of the Internet's infrastructure to communicate with them. We'll use client certificates, issued by our own internal Certificate Server and tied to NT security, to handle all of our security requirements: authentication, encryption, and transmission integrity. To do this, we don't need any additional code in our application. We use Certificate Server's default policies to issue certificates manually for all our clerks, and map those certificates to the clerks' NT domain accounts, which are members of the Clerks group in each domain. We then restrict access to the application by requiring client certificates on the virtual directory, and allowing only accounts in the Clerks group to access the ASP pages and MTS components that are part of the clerk application.

# Design-Time Security with Visual InterDev

Visual InterDev 6.0 uses FrontPage extensions to control design-time access to Web pages, maintaining author and administrator rights on each site. When combined with IIS's permission levels and NT file security, enabling access for your programming and design teams while blocking access to others can be a difficult exercise. In this section, we'll show you some things you need to watch for.

## File System

To use any of the benefits of NT File Security mentioned in this chapter, including design-time security, your server needs to be storing its Web files on an NTFS share. If you are running on a FAT or FAT32 system, stop reading here, and go reformat your server's hard drive to use NTFS. Otherwise, you won't be able to control file access on your Web site.

## Access Levels and Managing Permissions

The FrontPage Extensions defines three security levels:

- **Browse permission** These users can access files from a browser. Their ability to execute scripts or other application logic depends on the permission setting defined for the Web within IIS (Read, Execute, Script, and so on).

- **Author permission**   These users can open a Web in a tool such as Visual InterDev or FrontPage, and add, modify, and delete content.

- **Administer permission**   These users are able to create, delete, and copy entire Webs. They can also change permissions for other users, as well as browse and author content.

You can set Administer and Author permissions for entire Web sites, or different virtual directories. The Browse permission is more flexible—it can be set down to the file level.

## Setting Permissions

Setting Web permissions from Visual InterDev is simple. You bring up the Web Permissions dialog box (see Figure 10-10) by selecting Web Project | Web Permissions... from the Project menu. You then add NT users and/or groups to the permissions list, and assign an access level to each. From this dialog box, you can also revoke permissions and change access levels for existing users.

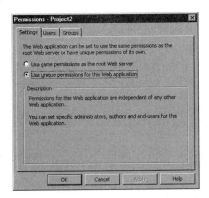

**Figure 10-10.**
*Web permissions dialog box in Visual InterDev 6.0.*

## Using Groups to Simplify Permission Management

In most cases, you will want to separate your team into groups of developers who each work on separate applications within your site. In the Rent-A-Prize example, we would have three different teams —one working on public content, one working on the customer reservation system, and one building the clerk application. Within each of those groups, we have *administrators* and *authors*. Within our development group, we took the easy approach to managing these permissions, and gave everyone Administer permission on all three sites. If you're in a large organization, you may not wish to be so free. You can simplify the process by creating six new local groups in the NT User Manager, giving each one appropriate permissions on the respective site.

- FP_ Admins_Inet
- FP_Authors_Inet
- FP_Admins_Clerk
- FP_Authors_Clerk
- FP_ Admins_Reserve
- FP_Authors_Reserve

Remember that in NT, unlike other enterprise operating systems, users can belong to more than one group. This is useful if you have overlap between your development teams.

## Permission Inheritance

When you create a new Web, it will always inherit the permissions from the server's root Web. Despite evidence or common-sense reasoning that would imply any other behavior, this is *always* true. It is true when you create a new Web project from Visual InterDev or FrontPage. It is true when you create a new Web site or virtual directory from the Internet Service Manager. Most important, it is true if you use Visual InterDev's Copy Web Application, Publish, or Deploy functions. In these cases, it does not copy any permissions from the source Web—the new Web will *always* inherit the permissions from the root Web on *its* server.

## How Administer and Author Permissions Are Enforced

When you create a new Web on a server containing FrontPage extensions, the server creates a directory called *_vti_bin* inside the Web's root directory. Within _vti_bin, the server creates two other directories, called *_vti_adm* and *_vti_aut*. These two directories contain ISAPI extensions that deliver the functionality for administrative and authoring features, respectively. When you change Administer or Author permissions for a user in Visual InterDev or FrontPage, the FrontPage extensions change the NT permissions on the _vti_aut and _vti_adm directories themselves. By preventing an unauthorized user from accessing the ISAPI extensions themselves, FP has prevented access. If you are troubleshooting problems with too much or too little access to those functions, start by going into the NT Explorer and checking the permissions on those directories.

## Visual SourceSafe Integration

As siblings in the Visual Studio family, Visual SourceSafe and Visual InterDev are designed to work seamlessly with each other. SourceSafe, however, maintains its own database of users and permissions that are separate from NT file security or FrontPage extensions. You must maintain these permissions separately in the SourceSafe admin program. To prevent users from having to log into the SourceSafe database, make sure their user names are the same as their NT logins.

In addition, there are differences in terminology between the two tools, as shown in the following table:

| InterDev Action | SourceSafe Action | Meaning |
| --- | --- | --- |
| Get Latest Version | Get | Create a local, read-only copy of the file. |
| Get Working Copy | Check Out | Create a writable local copy of the file; disallow any other users from checking it out. |
| Release Working Copy | Check In | Save changes to the server; allow other users to check it out and make changes. |
| Discard Changes | Undo Checkout | Discard any changes you have made to the file; allow other users to check it out and make changes. |

**Table 10-3.**
*Mapping Visual InterDev actions to Visual SourceSafe actions.*

Overall, Visual SourceSafe makes team programming less frustrating and more productive then using Visual InterDev 6.0 by itself. By understanding these two concepts, your team can become even more productive.

# Summary

In this chapter, we've discussed a wide variety of topics that will help you in securing your applications. These included:

- Authentication
- Content Restriction
- Windows NT Security Features
- Securing Application Components
- Security in Visual InterDev 6.0

Many of these topics are applicable to traditional client/server applications as well as Web applications. There is also a great deal more to be learned about security in Windows NT than can be taught in a single chapter, so you would be well served by picking up a good book or two on NT Security.

In the next chapter, we will begin our coverage of challenges and solutions of the data tier. We will begin by discussing the new features of Visual InterDev 6.0 for designing, modifying, and maintaining databases, and database objects in Chapter 11, "RAD Database Development and Data Access."

# PART IV

# SOLVING DATA TIER CHALLENGES

**C H A P T E R   E L E V E N**

# RAD Database Development and Data Access

• • • **GOAL: To Quickly Create and Easily Maintain Database Solutions for the Rent-A-Prize Application**

Data. It's one of the most important parts of any application. Why then is it that data always seems to be the most difficult part of an application to deal with? Why does data usually have only minimal support from your development tools? If you've found yourself asking these questions, you'll be happy to hear that the days of limited database support functionality are officially over.

Visual InterDev 6.0 provides a new set of database tools that allow you to do just about anything you need to do with your Oracle or Microsoft SQL Server databases—from creating and querying tables, to changing datatypes without moving your data—all without ever leaving the Visual InterDev IDE. In this chapter, we'll take a close look at the new Visual Database Tools, and see how they bring the advantages of rapid application development to the world of database development for the first time.

> NOTE: The Visual Database Tools are available with the Enterprise Edition of Microsoft Visual InterDev 6.0, Microsoft Visual J++ 6.0, Microsoft Visual C++ 6.0, and Microsoft Visual Basic 6.0. Certain functionality that was available in all versions of Visual InterDev 1.0, such as creating and modifying tables and views in Microsoft SQL Server 6.5 databases, will only be available with Visual Studio, Enterprise Edition. For the purposes of this chapter, we will be discussing the full Visual Database Tools feature set that is available with Visual Studio, Enterprise Edition.

# The Visual Database Tools

The Microsoft Visual Database Tools, first introduced with Visual Studio 97, provide a wide variety of features designed to make working with and querying databases easier and more convenient for both Web and client/server developers. The first version of the Visual Database Tools was limited to Microsoft SQL Server databases, and did not offer much in terms of schema management features. The latest release improves on this area, and also adds support for Oracle databases.

Accessing the Visual Database Tools is relatively simple: you open a Web project or a database project, then add a database connection to the project. Once the database connection has been established, you can access the four components that make up the Visual Database Tools. They are:

- Data View
- Database Designer
- Query Designer
- Source Code Editor

## Data View

The Data View is a visual interface to your database. It allows you to view and access your project's database connections and work with the objects associated with that database. The database objects accessible from the Data View, as seen in Figure 11-1, include:

- Database diagrams
- Tables
- Triggers
- Views
- Stored procedures

As we'll demonstrate in the section, "Using the Data View in Visual InterDev," the Data View is one of the primary tools you'll use in Visual InterDev to create, modify, and access data and database objects.

**Figure 11-1.**
*The Data View window.*

## Database Designer

The Database Designer provides a graphical interface with which you can create, modify, and delete database objects, such as tables, indexes, and triggers, in real time while you are connected to the database. To view and/or modify objects in your database you must first create a new database diagram (a process we'll describe in the section entitled "Using the Database Designer"). Once you've created a database diagram, you can drag existing tables from the Data View window into the diagram. The Database Designer displays the tables and their relationships as shown in Figure 11-2.

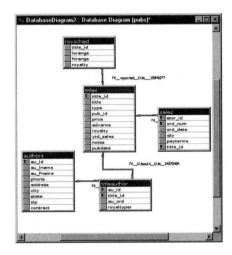

**Figure 11-2.**
*Tables and relationships in the Database Designer.*

Right-clicking on a table in the diagram gives you access to a host of possibilities, including changing how the table is viewed in the diagram, adding or removing columns from a table, and adding primary keys or indexes. The Database Designer also gives you the luxury of making changes freely without risk to the underlying database, since changes aren't made to the underlying database until you explicitly save the database diagram or the table you are working on. The best part of all this is that most of the changes you make using the Database Designer do not require you to write a single line of SQL code.

## Query Designer

With the Query Designer, you can efficiently design or modify queries either graphically or by typing in SQL commands. The Query Designer provides four panes, as shown in Figure 11-3, to help you design your queries, each of which may be turned on or off independently:

- The Diagram pane displays the tables or views you're querying (input sources), shown at the top of the center window in Figure 11-3.

- The Grid pane allows you to specify options for your queries, such as sort order or grouping, as well as which columns to display. This pane is second from the top in Figure 11-3.

- The SQL pane displays the SQL syntax representing the query you are building. This pane can also be used to type in SQL queries directly. This pane is the third from the top in Figure 11-3.

- The Results pane displays the results of the most recently executed SQL SELECT query. You can also use this pane to modify data resulting from a query. This is the bottom pane in Figure 11-3.

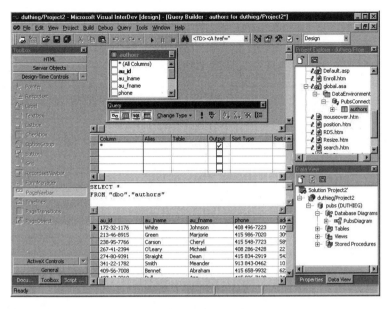

**Figure 11-3.**
*Using the Query Designer in Visual InterDev 6.0.*

When you make changes in any of the panes of the Query Designer, the other panes (with the exception of the results pane) are automatically updated. You can refresh the results pane by executing the current SELECT query.

## Source Code Editor (for Stored Procedures)

The Source Code editor is used for writing and editing stored procedures and triggers. It can also be used to execute stored procedures and view the results, as well as debug stored procedures (which requires either Visual C++ or Visual Studio, Enterprise Edition). The Source Code editor uses color-coding to identify SQL keywords, and like the other text editors in Visual InterDev, the properties of the editor (such as Tab width) can be specified on a per-language basis. For example, if you are using an Oracle data source and wish to change the Tab width to 5 (the default is 4). You'd simply follow these steps:

1. Select Tools | Options…, then expand the Text Editor node.

2. Expand the Tabs node and select the PL/SQL entry.

3. Change the setting for Tab size to 5, then click OK.

This kind of customization can make it easier for you to recognize the platform your SQL code was written for by using a different tab size and style for each language.

NOTE: All of the functionality described in this chapter is available in Visual InterDev database projects, as well as in the Web projects we are discussing. Database projects allow you perform the actions described in this chapter separate from the context of a Web application.

# Using the Data View in Visual InterDev

The Data View is one of the most useful tools you'll find in Visual InterDev. With it, you can open tables and edit their data, create new tables or modify the schema of existing tables, open and edit views and stored procedures, as well as using it in combination with the Data Environment for powerful drag-and-drop functionality.

## Creating and Modifying Database Objects

Perhaps the most powerful feature of the Data View is the ability to create and modify database objects. In this section, we'll look at the steps required for creating and modifying tables. The techniques demonstrated here are also applicable to other database objects.

### Creating a Table

Creating a new table in your database is fairly straightforward, and requires only a few simple steps:

1. With the Visual InterDev project you're working on open, add a database connection if one does not already exist by right-clicking on the GLOBAL.ASA file in the Project Explorer and selecting Add Data Connection....

2. Select the DSN for the desired data source (for more information on setting up ODBC DSNs, see Appendix B, "Installing the Rent-A-Prize Sample Application") and click OK. Once the connection has been made (you may be prompted for a user ID and password), the Data View window becomes available.

3. To create the new table, simply right-click the Tables node in the Data View window, and select New Table (see Figure 11-4). Enter a name for the table in the Choose name dialog box and click OK.

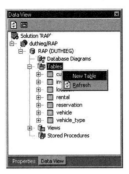

**Figure 11-4.**
*Creating a new table in the Data View window.*

4. Enter the parameters for your table (column names, datatypes, allow nulls, and so on), then click the Save button on the toolbar to save the new table. Note that when you save, Visual InterDev displays a dialog box asking if you want to save a change script for this action. Saving a change script is a good idea, since it can give you a written record of the modification that have been made to the database (although it would be nice if you could choose a meaningful name for the file instead of the default, *DBDGM1.SQL*).

## Modifying a Table

Modifying a table is just as easy. Having opened your project and created a database connection (or logged in to the existing connection):

1. In the Data View window, expand the database node to show the available database objects, then expand the Tables node to show the available tables.

2. Right-click the name of the table you wish to edit, and select Design. Visual InterDev will open the table in single-table design mode, as shown in Figure 11-5.

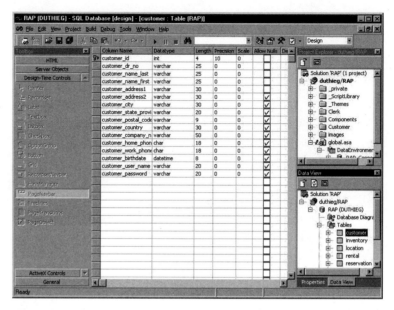

**Figure 11-5.**
*Rent-A-Prize Customer table in design mode.*

3. Make the desired modifications by adding or removing columns, changing datatypes, or setting defaults in the design grid. You can also right-click a column to set a primary key.

4. Once you have completed your modifications, click the Save button on the toolbar (or select File | Save *<tablename>*). Visual InterDev will notify you of other tables that will be changed as a result of your table modifications. When you click OK, Visual InterDev again prompts you to save the change script, which you should do.

The Data View window also allows you to open a table and edit its data, create a *trigger* (a special type of stored procedure that reacts to inserts, updates, or deletes on that table) on the table, or even delete the table (and its data), by simply right-clicking the table name and selecting the appropriate command. In addition, there is a command on the table's context menu called *Copy SQL Script*, which lets you copy the SQL required to create that table (or other database object) to the Windows Clipboard. You could then paste that code into an e-mail to a co-worker looking to reproduce the table, saving him or her valuable time.

One big benefit of using the Visual Database tools in Visual InterDev to modify tables is that with these tools, you do not need to worry about your existing data when modifying a table. Working directly with SQL Server 6.5, you are required to drop and re-create a table any time you want to change a column's datatype or remove a column. In Visual InterDev, you simply make the changes you want, and let the tools take care of the rest. Another benefit is that the Visual Database Tools also monitor the effects of your changes on other tables in the database. If you change a datatype of a column that is referenced by other tables, Visual InterDev will ask you to confirm that you want to change those tables as well. And of course, as described in the step-by-step examples, Visual InterDev allows you to save the change scripts, so you can keep track of all the changes you've made.

## Drag-and-Drop Functionality

The other area in which the Data View really shines is in providing drag-and-drop access to data and database objects. As we've seen in earlier chapters, creating a data command representing a table is exceedingly simple:

1. With a Visual InterDev project containing a valid database connection open in the IDE, select a table from the Data View window and drag it onto the database connection in the Project Explorer window (the connection should appear under the Data Environment, which is under GLOBAL.ASA). You can also drop tables (or stored procedures) onto the Data Environment.

2. Now you can use this new command by dragging it (or the fields exposed by it) onto a page. Dragging a command object to a page results in a Recordset Design-Time Control (DTC) being added to the page, while dragging fields results in label and textbox (or other as appropriate) data-bound DTCs being added.

NOTE: The use of the Visual Database Tools and the Data Environment does not necessitate the use of the data-bound DTCs and the Scripting Object Model. You can also access database connections and commands created in the Data Environment by scripting the DE object created by Visual InterDev when you set up the database connection. This will be covered in the section, "Custom Data Access Using the Data Environment," later in this chapter.

# Using the Database Designer

The Database Designer can be thought of as a sketch pad for your database. Within a database diagram, you can view some or all of tables in your database, complete with their relationships; create and modify tables, indexes, and relationships; and create printable schematics of your database. In this section, we'll show you how.

## Viewing Tables

Viewing tables in a database diagram is exceedingly simple, but as a tool for understanding and modifying the relationships between your tables, it offers a great deal of power. To view a table or tables from your database, open a Visual InterDev project with a valid database connection and follow these steps:

1. In the Data View window, right-click the Database Diagram node and select New Diagram. A new, empty database diagram is opened in the Database Designer.

2. Expand the Tables node.

3. Select the table or tables you wish to view and drag them into the database diagram. Note that the relationships between your tables are automatically represented in the diagram.

What you see initially may not be very useful, since the tables may be overlapping, making it harder to see the big picture. There are several things the Database Designer can do to help.

4. Right-click in an empty area of the database diagram and select Arrange Tables.

This arranges the tables so that they don't overlap, and so that the relationships can be seen clearly. Depending on how many tables you have, however, it may make it impossible to see all the tables on the screen at the same time, again hampering the "big picture" view.

5. Again, right-click in an empty area of the database diagram and select Zoom, then choose a zoom level between 10% and 200%. The Zoom command lets you view your database at the macro or micro level, allowing you to see the big picture or concentrate on the details of a particular table or group of tables as shown in Figure 11-6.

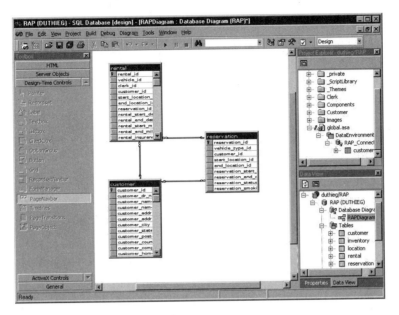

**Figure 11-6.**
*Viewing tables in the Database Designer.*

## Printing the Database Diagram

The Database Designer can also be used to print your database diagram, which can be particularly useful during prototyping, allowing you to show the prototype to supervisors or other design team members, without having to be at a computer. The Database Designer has a couple of features to assist with this process and to make your diagrams as readable and printer-friendly as possible. To prepare and print your database diagram, follow these steps:

1. Open or create a new database diagram and drag the tables you wish to view into the diagram (if they are not already in the diagram).

2. Right-click in an empty area of the database diagram and select Arrange Tables, which will give you a readable layout. At this point, however, if you print this layout, you may end up with tables that are half on one page and half on another.

3. To ready the layout for printing, right-click in an empty area of the diagram and select View Page Breaks. Now the Database Designer shows how the layout fits on the printed page.

4. Adjust the tables so that either no tables are on a page break, or all the tables are on a single page.

5. Select File | Print....

6. In addition to modifying the layout to facilitate printing, you can also change the page setup so that pages are printed at a smaller or larger scale by selecting File | Page Setup..., and changing the Print Scale attribute (see Figure 11-7).

**Figure 11-7.**
*Page Setup dialog box.*

## Creating and Modifying Tables and Indexes

Creating tables is one of the things for which the Database Designer can be most useful. In this solution, we'll see how to create a table in the database designer, and add an index to the new table (which can help reduce query time).

● ● ● **SOLUTION: Creating a Vehicle Table for Rent-A-Prize**

Among the many things that we need to be able to track in the Rent-A-Prize sample application are the vehicles being rented. To do so, we'll add a Vehicle table to the Rent-A-Prize database. Creating the table is as simple as most actions in the Database Designer. Simply follow these steps (note that in order for this solution to work, you must have installed the sample application according to the instructions in Appendix B, "Installing the Rent-A-Prize Sample Application"):

1. Open a new Web project and add a data connection to the Rent-A-Prize sample database.

2. Expand the database node in the Data View window. Create a new database diagram by right-clicking the Database Diagrams node, then selecting New Diagram.

3. Add a new table to the diagram by right-clicking in an empty area of the diagram, then selecting New Table. Since the Rent-A-Prize sample database actually already has a Vehicle table, name the table *Vehicle2*.

4. Add column information to the new table as shown in Table 11-1. For this exercise, you won't need to worry about the Precision, Scale, Default, Identity Seed, or Identity Increment columns. You can accept the defaults for these columns.

| Column Name | Datatype | Length | Allow Nulls | Identity |
|---|---|---|---|---|
| vehicle_id | int | 4 (default) | No | Yes |
| vehicle_type_id | int | 4(default) | No | No |
| vehicle_make | varchar | 30 | Yes | Yes |
| vehicle_model | varchar | 30 | Yes | Yes |
| vehicle_year | varchar | 4 | Yes | Yes |

**Table 11-1.**
*Column information for the Vehicle2 table.*

5. Once you've added all the columns, save the new table by selecting File | Save Selection. You can also simply save a change script representing the new table. Note that again, you'll be prompted to confirm that you want to save the new table to the database, and asked if you want to save a change script.

Since it's probably an accurate assumption that we'll have a lot of vehicles to keep track of in the Vehicle table, it's going to be a good idea to add an index to the table. We can also probably assume that most queries of the table will be done on the vehicle_make, vehicle_model, and vehicle_year columns, so we'll create a multi-column index on those columns, using the following steps:

1. With the Vehicle2 table open in the Database Designer, right-click the table, and select Property Pages.

2. In the Indexes/Keys tab of the Property Pages dialog box, add the vehicle_make, vehicle_model, and vehicle_year columns to the Column name list, as shown in Figure 11-8.

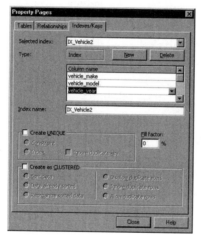

**Figure 11-8.**
*Indexes/Keys tab of the PropertyPages dialog box for Vehicle2.*

3. Click the Close button, then save the table by either selecting File | Save Selection, or by saving the database diagram (File | Save *<diagramname>*).

Now that you know how to create and add an index to a table using the Database Designer, let's look ahead to maintenance. What happens when somewhere down the road Rent-A-Prize buys some new vehicles and the model name of the new vehicles is longer than the thirty characters we've allotted to it? Assuming that abbreviating the name is not an option, the only choice is to modify the datatype of the vehicle_model column. In the past this was a somewhat arduous task that involved using the SQL Server bulk copy program (bcp) to copy the data in the table into a temporary location, dropping and re-creating the table, and copying the data back into the table using bcp. On tables like the vehicle table that have an *identity column* (a numeric column that automatically increments each time a row is added to the table in the vehicle table vehicle_id), the process is even more difficult because of the complexity of maintaining the existing identity values. Fortunately, the Database Designer makes this task simple, as we'll demonstrate in the following solution.

## • • • • SOLUTION: Changing the Datatype of the vehicle_model Column of the Vehicle Table

To change the datatype of the vehicle_model column, follow these steps:

1. If you do not already have one open, open a new database diagram by right-clicking the Database Diagrams node in the Data View window, and selecting New Diagram. Add the Vehicle2 table to the diagram.

2. In order to see the datatype column property, enable the table properties by right-clicking the table and selecting the Column Properties view.

3. Change the Length attribute of the vehicle_model from 30 to 40 to accommodate the lengthy name of our new vehicles.

4. Save the table by selecting File | Save Selection. Save the change script when prompted, if you wish.

As you may have noticed, when modifying tables in the Database Designer, it is not always necessary to save the database diagram you're using. In fact you can open a new database diagram solely as a place to work on your tables and delete it when you're done. Either way, what this solution demonstrates is just how much the Database Designer can simplify a developer's life. Now you've got time for that extra cup of coffee in the morning.

## Prototyping a Database

In the early stages of your project, you may want or need to spend some time playing around with the data storage structure for your application. This is an area in which the database designer excels. Because you can modify tables in the Database Designer without changing the underlying database (until you explicitly save the diagram or table), you can play with a variety of storage scenarios and options before you commit to a change. In addition, the ability to save change scripts allows you to keep track of all the changes you make, which makes rolling back a change that much easier, particularly in combination with the use of a source control tool, such as Visual SourceSafe.

# Using the Query Designer

Once you've created your tables and gotten them all modified to your heart's content, the next thing you'll want to do in all likelihood is query your data. Well, you're in luck, the Visual Database Tools has just the thing for you—the Query Designer (aka SQL Builder). If you've ever worked with Microsoft Query, you'll probably have no trouble with the Query Designer, since it is in some ways very similar. The Query Designer, however, offers a great deal more flexibility than Microsoft Query, while also offering the ability to create complex SQL queries (including grouping, ordering, and joins) quickly and easily, without writing a single line of SQL code (unless of course you want to).

## Creating SQL Queries in a GUI Environment

The key to this flexibility is in the four available panes of the Query Builder, which operate interactively and cooperatively to produce the query that you're working on. The first two panes, the *diagram* and *grid panes*, allow you to generate your queries visually, by dragging-and-dropping objects and by selecting or deselecting properties. The queries generated by this process are represented in the third pane, the *SQL pane*, which displays the SQL syntax of the current query. In addition to displaying the query, you can modify the query in the SQL pane, which gives you exceptional control over your queries. The fourth pane, the *results pane*, shows a real-time view of the results of the current query when it is executed.

> NOTE: In some cases, queries entered manually from the SQL pane may not be able to be represented visually by the diagram or grid panes. In this case, those panes may be grayed out to indicate this state. These panes, however, may still be used to modify the current query, despite being grayed out.

## Types of Queries Supported by Query Designer

Surprisingly enough, unlike many technologies that simplify development tasks, the Query Designer doesn't seem to ask you to give up functionality in order to achieve simplicity. The Query Designer supports a full range of query types, including:

- **Select query**  This is the default query type. This type of query retrieves data from one or more tables or views. Generates a SQL SELECT statement.

- **Insert query**  This type of query adds new rows to a table by copying existing rows from that table or another table. Generates a SQL INSERT...SELECT statement.

- **Insert Values query**  This type of query adds a new row to a table with values specified as a part of the query (parameters may be substituted for literal values). Generates a SQL INSERT INTO... VALUES statement.

- **Update query**  This type of query modifies the values of existing rows in a table. Which columns and rows are affected is determined by the specific query parameters. Generates a SQL UPDATE statement.

- **Delete query**  This type of query removes one or more rows from a table. Which rows are affected is determined by the specific query parameters. Generates a SQL DELETE statement.

- **Make Table query**  This type of query copies the results of a SELECT query into a new table. Generates a SQL SELECT INTO statement.

In this section, we'll concentrate on Select queries, but isn't it nice to know what a wide range of queries are available? So, without further ado, let's take a look at actually using the Query Designer.

## • • • SOLUTION: Creating and Testing SQL Queries for Customer Data Based on Selected Parameters

One common use for a data-enabled application is doing lookups of information based on different search criteria. In the Rent-A-Prize sample application, for example, the possibility was discussed of giving clerks and managers the ability to do lookups of customers based on a variety of criteria, including their city/state, country, company, or age (calculated from their birth date). These types of lookups could provide valuable insight into trends, such as whether more people renting cars lived locally or were from out of town, or whether a large number of people from the same company rented from Rent-A-Prize. This information could then be used in planning marketing campaigns or discount offers.

Now that we've determined what a good idea such queries would be, how do we go about creating them? For the purposes of this solution, we'll create a query in which we'll perform a lookup of all customers (name, address, and so on), ordered by city and state.

To create the query, follow these steps:

1. Open a Visual InterDev project with a valid connection to the Rent-A-Prize sample database (you can also follow this solution using another project and/or database if you choose. Just remember that you'll need to modify the table and column names as appropriate for the database you are using).

2. Expand the GLOBAL.ASA and DataEnvironment nodes to display the data connection. Right-click the data connection and select Add Data Command....

3. In the Command1 Properties dialog box, change the command name to *cmdCustCityState* (or another descriptive name).

4. Change the Source of Data attribute to SQL Statement, then click the SQL Builder button. The Query Designer will open. If you do not see the Query toolbar, open it by selecting View | Toolbars | Query.

5. Add the Customer table to the diagram pane of the Query Designer by dragging it from the Data View window and dropping it onto the diagram pane.

To return the customer information you want, select the appropriate columns from the table diagram.

6. In the customer table, check the boxes for customer_name_last, customer_name_first, customer_address1, customer_address2, customer_city, customer_state_province, and customer_postal_code. Note that the order in which you check the boxes determines the order of that column in the query (for example, if you check customer_name_first, then customer_name_last, they will appear in that order in the results of the query).

In order to make sure that the query syntax is correct, and the query is bringing back the data we want, we can use the Query toolbar (see Figure 11-9) to verify the SQL syntax, and run the query to view the results.

**Figure 11-9.**
*The Query toolbar.*

7. To verify the syntax of the current query, click the Verify SQL Syntax button on the Query toolbar. If the syntax is correct, you should see the dialog box shown in Figure 11-10.

**Figure 11-10.**
*SQL syntax verification dialog box.*

8. To check the results of the query in the results pane, click the Run Query button, located next to the Verify SQL Syntax button on the Query toolbar. The results are displayed in the results pane.

Assuming the results are as desired, all we need to do now is specify how we want the data ordered; that is, by city and state. Be aware, however, that how you state the query will affect how the results are ordered. In English, we state the query as "Give me all customer names and addresses, ordered by city and state." If we were to translate that directly into SQL syntax, our results would be ordered in such a way that customers who lived in the same state might not be listed together. In order for our query to be effective, we must actually order by state first, then by city, to get the ordering we want. To implement the ordering, we'll use the grid pane of the Query Designer.

9. In the grid pane, scroll down to the customer_city and customer_state column listings. In the Sort Type column, select Ascending, first for customer_state, then for customer_city. The Sort Order column should read 1 for customer_state, and 2 for customer_city.

10. Click the Run Query button to view the results. The customers should be listed by state and city.

11. Save the query either by clicking the Save button on the main toolbar, or by selecting File | Save cmdCustCityState.

Once you've defined this query, it is stored as a part of the Data Environment, where it can be used like any other command object (for example, you can drag the command or its exposed fields onto a page to bind them to DTCs). You can edit the query anytime you like by right-clicking on it, and selecting SQL Builder…. Keep in mind that although the queries you build with the Query Designer can be saved for later reuse, you can also simply use the Query Designer as a graphical editor for your SQL queries by defining your query as described above, copying the SQL code from the SQL pane, and pasting it into your page or component. Keep in mind that certain queries (including those that use parameters) may need some rewriting to work properly in other places (such as your Visual Basic components).

# Using the Source Code Editor

The Source Code Editor is the final Visual Database tool for us to talk about, and it's a dandy, because the Source Code Editor is the tool you use to create, test, and debug Microsoft SQL Server and Oracle stored procedures and triggers. A *stored procedure* is a precompiled batch of SQL code that can contain both SQL statements and control-of-flow language.

Stored procedures are important for enterprise applications because they serve two important purposes: they help abstract some of the work of accessing and updating data from the business tier, and they can improve performance by substantially reducing the amount of information that travels over the network in the form of SQL query strings. Abstraction helps the maintainability of your application by allowing you to make changes in data access logic without affecting components that call those stored procedures. If the same data access logic were in a compiled component, that component would need to be recompiled and reinstalled in order to make the change. Performance improvements come from the fact that stored procedures are precompiled on the database server, while the alternative, SQL query strings sent from your Active Server Pages (ASP) pages or components, must be parsed and compiled at the time they are run, which is substantially slower.

Stored procedures can use input and output parameters, return single or multiple recordsets and return values, and may offer other functionality specific to the DBMS (see the SQL Server or Oracle documentation for details on vendor-specific stored procedure features). As mentioned in the section on the data view, a *trigger* is a special type of stored procedure associated with a table that is executed in response to inserts, updates, or deletes performed against the table. Triggers are used to enforce business rules, and are also sometimes used to enforce or enhance data integrity (for example, by ensuring that when a record is deleted, all dependent records in other tables are deleted).

## • • • SOLUTION: Creating Stored Procedures for Frequently Used Tasks Such As Reservation Lookups

To demonstrate the use of the Source Code Editor, we'll develop a stored procedure for the Rent-A-Prize sample application that will retrieve all reservation information for a particular reservation ID. By using this procedure, a clerk can quickly look up a reservation for a customer by the number the customer is given at the time they make the reservation, so they can get the customer into their car as quickly as possible.

### Creating a Stored Procedure

To create the stored procedure, follow these steps:

1. Open a Visual InterDev project with a valid connection to the Rent-A-Prize sample database (you can also follow this solution using another project and/or database if you choose. Just remember that you will need to modify the stored procedure as appropriate for the database you are using).

2. In the Data View window, expand the database node to display the available database objects. Right-click the Stored Procedure node and select New Stored Procedure. The Source Code Editor will open with a skeleton stored procedure, as shown in Figure 11-11. The comments provided show the basic structure of using parameters with a stored procedure.

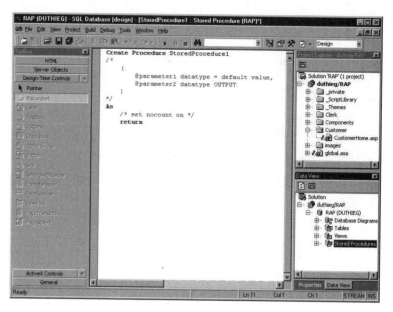

**Figure 11-11.**
*The Source Code Editor.*

3. Replace the default name of the stored procedure, *StoredProcedure1*, with a more descriptive name, *GetReservationByID*. Note that each stored procedure name must be unique within the database in which it resides. Also, try to use a consistent naming scheme with stored procedures, so that the purpose of a stored procedure (and perhaps its parameters) is apparent from its name.

4. Replace the code following the stored procedure name with the following code:

```
        @intReservationid        int
AS

SELECT   reservation_id,

      vehicle_type_id,

      customer_id,

      start_location_id,

      end_location_id,

      reservation_start_date,
```

*(continued)*

```
        reservation_end_date,

        reservation_status,

        reservation_smoking

    FROM reservation

    WHERE   reservation_id = @intReservationId
```

NOTE: The code above uses an input parameter, *@intreservationid*, to allow the caller to specify a reservation ID to search for. Note that the way we define the input parameter includes both the name (which we choose) and the datatype (which should match the datatype of the columns being used in the WHERE clause of the SELECT statement. The rest of the code is a simple multicolumn SELECT statement, retrieving a number of columns from the reservation table. For more information on the structure and syntax of stored procedures, see SQL Server Books Online, or refer to the Oracle documentation.

5. Save the stored procedure by either clicking the Save button on the toolbar, or selecting File | Save *<storedprocedurename>*.

## Executing and Viewing the Results of a Stored Procedure

Executing the stored procedure is actually quite simple. Just follow these steps:

1. Right-click in the Source Code Editor window and select Execute. Save the stored procedure if prompted. The Visual InterDev Output pane will appear.

2. Since the stored procedure has an input parameter, the Execute dialog box will appear. Enter *1* in the field labeled Value and click OK.

3. The results of the stored procedure appear in the Output pane. Note that if only a small portion of the screen is available for the Output pane, you may need to scroll up to see the results of the stored procedure.

NOTE: Remember that if you write stored procedures that update tables or delete rows, these actions will be performed against the database when you execute the stored procedure. For most situations, it is wise to have a development database against which you can develop your queries and stored procedures. While tools like the Database

Designer and Query Designer allow you to do a lot of work without explicitly affecting the underlying database, they cannot protect you from every mistake you may make. Working against a development database allows you to make the inevitable development mistakes without risk to data in the production environment. Once you have ensured that your stored procedures and queries work as desired, they can then be safely migrated to your production database.

Once you've written, saved, and tested your stored procedure, it is visible in the Stored Procedures node of the Data View window. You can edit the stored procedure at any time by either right-clicking it and selecting Open, or by simply double-clicking it. One piece of good news is that if you're stumped as to how to go beyond a simple SELECT statement in your stored procedure, the Source Code Editor lets you enlist the help of the Query Designer for your stored procedures. Simply right-click where you want your query to appear and select Insert SQL. Even better, highlight the existing SELECT query in the editor, right-click the highlighted text, and select Edit SQL. The Query Designer will open this time with the parameters for the current query already set. Now all you have to do is make the desired modifications and save the query. Now there is no excuse for not using stored procedures.

## Debugging Stored Procedures (Requires VC++ EE)

Another useful feature of the Source Code Editor that is available if you have either Visual Studio, Enterprise Edition, or Visual C++, Enterprise Edition installed, is the ability to debug stored procedures. Unlike debugging of client and server scripts, you don't debug stored procedures while they are running. Rather, you open them in the editor and debug them there by setting breakpoints and stepping into the stored procedure. There are some additional requirements for SQL debugging that you should be aware of:

- You must be running SQL Server 6.5 with Service Pack 2 or above.

- SQL Server must be running on Windows NT 4.0 or later.

- Your workstation must be running Windows 95 or Windows NT 4.0 or later.

- You must have installed SQL debugging components on your SQL server (see the Visual InterDev or Visual Studio documentation for installation instructions).

- You must have a Windows NT user account with administration privileges on the server computer where SQL Server is running.

- You must configure Distributed COM (DCOM) on the server for SQL debugging.

- You must ensure that the DCOM configuration on the client supports SQL debugging (Windows 95 workstations only).

Once you have ensured that all of the above requirements are met, debugging is as simple as right-clicking the stored procedure you wish to debug (in the Data View window), and selecting Debug. Once the stored procedure is open in the Source Code Editor in debug mode, you can set breakpoints, step through the procedure, and perform other typical debugging tasks. There are, however, a couple of differences between the SQL debugger and the debugger used for scripts:

- Neither the Auto nor the Immediate windows function with the SQL debugger.

- You cannot change the order in which your statements execute with the *Set Next Statement* command.

# Visual Database Tools Wrap-Up

In this section, we've discussed the four components of the Visual Database tools:

- The Data View
- The Database Designer
- The Query Designer
- The Source Code Editor

Although their functionality overlaps in some areas, these tools each have their own particular purpose, and they work together as an integrated package to help you create, use, and maintain the database objects necessary for your application. Whether you use Visual Database Tools to create queries for use from your ASP pages via drag and drop, or use the Source Code Editor to create stored procedures to be called from your components, this package has something to offer almost every developer.

# Moving Data Access to Components

While we're on the topic of components, one important issue we need to address is that of moving your data access into components. The Data Environment and the data-bound DTCs offer wonderful simplicity and a surprising amount of power. The truth is, however, that for high-performance data access in an enterprise application, you are better served by moving your data access code to components running on the business or data tier.

For enterprise applications there are two basic problems involved in performing data access from the client tier. First, if you are taking advantage of the data-bound DTCs, you are reliant on a large amount of script code, due to the necessity of using the Scripting Object Model. While the Scripting Object Model provides a great deal of power combined with attractive simplicity, it can't match the speed of compiled components. Second, data access code on the client tier must traverse an extra network layer in an n-tier application. So unless your Web server, component server, and database server are all the same machine (which they most certainly should *not* be in an enterprise application), the data access usually ends up making an extra hop on its way to the database server. In a multi-user application, this extra traffic will add up.

For these and other reasons, it is highly recommended for enterprise applications that you move your data access code to components. Moving this code to components has several advantages:

- **Speed**   Data access code in components is invariably faster than comparable script code.

- **Abstraction**   User interface developers don't need to worry about data access code. They can simply call the appropriate methods of the components you build, and pass the necessary values.

- **Maintainability**   By using components to call stored procedures on the database server, you can functionally compartmentalize you data access, while still allowing you to make changes, if necessary, without needing to recompile and reinstall your components.

- **Working from Strength**   Using the script calling component calling stored procedure architecture lets you make use of each tier's strengths, that is, the client tier's strength in displaying an attractive user interface, the business tier's strength in processing business logic, and the data tier's strength in performing data access. It is by taking advantage of these strengths that you can improve your application's performance and chances of success.

### • • • SOLUTION: Moving Data Access to Components

To demonstrate how easy it can be to move your data access into a component, we're going to build a simple Visual Basic COM component that will have one task: to call the stored procedure we wrote in the last solution. We'll use ActiveX Data Objects (ADO) to perform the data access by using the ADO Command object to call the stored procedure. This solution assumes that you've installed the Rent-A-Prize sample database. To create our data access component, use the following steps:

1. Open a new ActiveX DLL project in Visual Basic 5.0 (or later).

2. Use the Project properties window to change the name of the project to *MyDataAccess* and the name of the predefined class to *CDataAccess*, as shown in Figure 11-12.

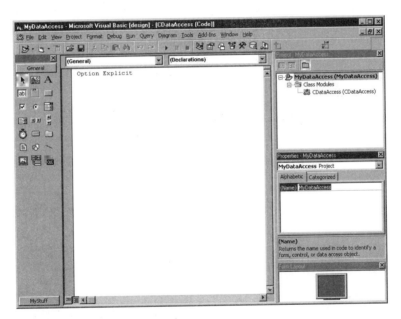

**Figure 11-12.**
*Changing the project name using the Properties window.*

3. Select Project | References... to bring up the References dialog box for the project. Scroll down in the list. Find and select the entry labeled Microsoft ActiveX Data Objects 2.0 Library (see Figure 11-13) and click OK. This will give us access to the ADO objects we need.

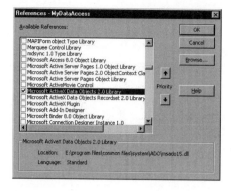

**Figure 11-13.**
*Setting a reference to the ADO library.*

4. Add a new Function to the CDataAccess class by selecting Tools | Add Procedure... (note that the code editor window must have focus in order for this to work). In the Add Procedure dialog box, select the Function and Public radio buttons, and name the procedure *vCallStoredProc*. We preface the procedure name with a *v* to denote that its return value will be a variant (actually a variant array). Click OK.

5. Change the first line of the procedure to the following:

```
Public Function vCallStoredProc() As Variant
```

6. Add the following code to the function:

```
'--------------------------------

' Purpose: Calls a Stored

'    Procedure and returns a

'    variant array containing

'    the results.

'--------------------------------

    'Declare required ADO objects

    Dim Conn As New ADODB.Connection

    Dim cmd As New ADODB.Command

    Dim rs As New ADODB.Recordset

    Dim pReservationID As New ADODB.Parameter
```

*(continued)*

416

```
'Declare array to hold reservation info
Dim vResDataArray() As Variant
ReDim vResIDArray(9, 25) 'Expand array if necessary to
                         'support more reservations


'Declare counter variables for looping
Dim iFieldCount As Integer
Dim iRowCount As Integer
iFieldCount = 0
iRowCount = 0


'Set query parameters
cmd.CommandType = adCmdStoredProc
cmd.CommandText = "GetReservationByID"


'Set and append pReservationID parameter
Set pReservationID = cmd.CreateParameter("@intreservationid", _
    adInteger, adParamInput, , iReservationID)
cmd.Parameters.Append pReservationID


'Open Connection
'NOTE: Replace connection string as
' appropriate for your machine and database
Conn.Open "DSN=RAP;UID=sa;PWD="


'Set Conn as Active Connection for command object
cmd.ActiveConnection = Conn
```

*(continued)*

```
'Execute command
Set rs = cmd.Execute


'Return value
If rs.EOF Then
    'Return value indicating no records
    vCallStoredProc = "0"
Else
    Do While Not rs.EOF
        iRowCount = iRowCount + 1
        For iFieldCount = 0 To rs.Fields.Count - 1
            vResIDArray(iFieldCount, iRowCount) = _
                rs(iFieldCount).Value
        Next
        rs.MoveNext
    Loop
    'Set first value in array to the row count
    vResIDArray(0, 0) = iRowCount
    ReDim Preserve vResIDArray(rs.Fields.Count, iRowCount + 1)
    vCallStoredProc = vResIDArray
End If


'Close Connection
Conn.Close


Set Conn = Nothing
Set cmd = Nothing
Set rs = Nothing
```

NOTE: The code above uses a variant array to store the results from the stored procedure called in the function and returns them back to the client. This illustrates just one of the many possible ways to transfer data between a component and its client. You could also use ADO recordsets, as mentioned in Chapter 8, to move the data between component and client. Or you could choose not to move the data to the client at all, but rather to use the *ScriptingContext* object provided by ASP to write the results of the stored procedure to the client browser as HTML (see the ASP documentation for more information on using the *ScriptingContext* object).

7. Save and compile the project (make sure you keep track of where your DLL is compiled for future reference).

In the code above, we declare our ADO *Connection, Command, Recordset,* and *Parameter* objects. Next we define the necessary properties: the *CommandType* and *CommandText* for the *Command* object, the various properties of the *Parameter* object, and of course the *ActiveConnection* property of the *Command* object. Note that the *ActiveConnection* property must be set using the *Set cmd.ActiveConnection* = syntax to work correctly. Also note that the connection string property necessary for the *Connection* object (which in this case is hard-coded) is passed as an argument to the *Open* method. This is not an uncommon way of doing things, but the connection string is often set up as a global or module-level variable that is populated from persistent storage (such as the Registry) at component initialization.

Once we've set all the necessary properties and opened the connection, we use the *Recordset* object, *rs,* to hold the results from the *Execute* method of the *Command* object, *cmd.* We then use the counter variables to keep track of the current record field and row as we loop through the fields and records and store them in a two-dimensional array. Once we're finished looping, we re-dimension the array to remove any empty space, and pass it to the calling procedure as the return value of the function.

Note that the code above does not implement any error handling. It is especially important to have proper error handlers in place when accessing databases from your components, since heavy network traffic, heavy database loads, or other problems can potentially cause timeouts when using the *Connection* or *Command* objects. If you have no error handling for these situations, your components will crash. See the ADO documentation for more information on handling errors with ADO.

To use our data access component, we simply use it as we would any other component in our Visual InterDev projects. Copy the component to our components project folder, register it either by using the regsvr32.exe utility (if the component will run on a component server) or by setting the component properties to register the component on the Web server, create an instance of the component using the ASP Server object's *CreateObject* method, and call the *vCallStoredProc* method, passing it a reservation ID to look up.

# Custom Data Access Using the Data Environment

Suppose your application lies somewhere in between the cases we've discussed already. The application requires too much scalability for using the DTCs and the Scripting Object Model, but you're not convinced that the scalability required justifies the development effort required to build data access components.

Fortunately, there is a middle ground that requires neither the use of the Scripting Object Model nor the use of components, but still allows you to take advantage of the drag-and-drop simplicity of the Data View and Data Environment, and make use of the Visual Database Tools. This middle ground involves using the DE object, which is exposed by Visual InterDev as a scriptable object for the Data Environment.

The DE object lets you access all the connections and commands that you've defined in the Data Environment of your project. Because the Data Environment is actually an abstraction of the ADO object model, working with the DE object is in many ways similar to working with ADO objects. To access the DE object, simply add the following lines of code to your page:

```
<%
Set DE = Server.CreateObject("DERuntime.DERuntime")
DE.Init(Application("DE"))
%>
```

To execute a query you've defined in the Data Environment, use the syntax, DE.*commandname*. For example to run a query called Reservations, use the following code:

```
<%
DE.Reservations
%>
```

If the command object requires parameters, you can supply them in this fashion:

```
<%
DE.Reservations(parameter1, parameter2)
%>
```

To access a return value from the *Command* object, you would use the following:

```
<%
intRetVal = DE.Reservation(intResID)
%>
```

Access to the contents of a recordset returned by a command is gained by prefixing *rs* to the name of the command, and setting an ADO recordset equal to the resultant DE call, as shown in the following code:

```
<%
Dim DE
Dim rs

    Set DE = Server.CreateObject("DERuntime.DERuntime")
    DE.Init(Application("DE"))

    DE.Reservations
    Set rs = DE.rsReservations
%>
```

Once you've got the recordset, moving through the records and fields is essentially the same as in ADO.

In many ways, using the DE object to script data access gives us the best of both worlds. Since we're not tied to the Scripting Object Model, we decide how much script to use in our application. Since the DE object gives us access to the command and connection objects we've defined in the Data Environment, we can use the rich feature set of the Visual Database Tools to define simple or complex queries that allow for easy reuse throughout our project. Remember though, that for the best performance in high-scalability situations, you will likely be best served by moving your data access code out of ASP script entirely and into components.

## Summary

In this chapter, we've discussed the Visual Database Tools, moving data access into components, and using the DE object to gain access to the rich command objects defined in the Data Environment without being bound (pun intended) to the data-bound DTCs and the Scripting Object Model.

Our discussion leads us to the conclusion that for small to medium applications, and for prototyping, coding your data access directly from Visual InterDev and using the data-bound DTCs may be an acceptable solution, but that for larger applications, it is probably wiser to consider either using the DE object to provide access to your predefined commands, or to move data access out of Visual InterDev entirely and into components.

Ultimately, the decision of which of the methods described in this chapter to use for data access will vary from application to application. Although it is generally better to move from data access in Visual InterDev to data access in components as an application grows, there is no hard-and-fast rule for where the dividing line is. It is your responsibility as a developer (or development team) to assess the needs of your application and decide what data access method will work for you.

In the next chapter, Chapter 12, "Accessing Legacy Data Sources," we'll discuss the thorny issues of getting to and integrating data from such sources as AS/400, MVS, and mainframe VSAM files, and demonstrate the solutions offered by SNA Server, which is provided as a part of Visual Studio 6.0, Enterprise Edition.

**C H A P T E R   T W E L V E**

# Interoperability with Legacy Systems

• • • **GOAL: To Integrate Data From Legacy Systems Transparently and Reliably**

American visitors to Japan usually find the trip a fascinating experience. For many tourists, one of the strangest things about Japan is the mixture of the exotic and the familiar. You can have your fortune told in a Buddhist temple, and then go to McDonalds for a Big Mac and Coke. You can watch a play at the Kabuki Theater, and then go to a department store and buy a Bruce Springsteen CD or a pair of jeans. Some parts of their national culture are uniquely Japanese. Some parts are familiar to any American tourist.

In this chapter, we will be travelers in a strange land. We will explore a world full of acronyms like SNA, CICS, MVS, and DRDA. Sometimes, we will encounter things that are very familiar, such as SQL databases and C programs. At other times, we will encounter exotic and unworldly creatures, such as SNA networks and CICS transactions.

You may be asking, "Why do I care? I just want to build Web applications." You care because we are working on enterprise-level systems, and enterprises store their data on mainframes. It has been estimated that 80 percent of the data on all the computers throughout the world is stored on IBM mainframes. The proportion decreases each time Oracle or Microsoft sell another database server, but staggering amounts of information cannot be accessed without connectivity to legacy systems. In the past, a typical solution to legacy system integration has been a nightly batch update, but this doesn't cut the mustard in today's enterprise, where executives demand answers now.

In this chapter, we'll look at access techniques for two types of legacy systems: mainframes and mid-range systems. Because we have heterogeneous systems, we'll have to deal with distributed applications. This means we'll need tools for building distributed systems such as transaction servers, DCOM, and message-oriented middleware. In this chapter we will explore a number of these tools and examine ways in which they can be used to provide access to legacy systems. We also will look at code solutions for two tools. One solution uses OLE DB Provider for AS/400 and VSAM, and the other uses COM Transaction Integrator.

# Legacy Systems

Before we look at the distributed systems tools, let's preview the computers we'll be working with. We'll look at IBM mainframes and mid-range computers, then we'll take a quick look at SNA, IBM's legacy networking architecture.

## Mainframes

In 1964, IBM bet the business on a new computer system, the IBM System/ 360. At that time, IBM produced fifteen incompatible computer systems for different classes of users. System/360 replaced these incompatible systems with a single architecture that could be used for a wide range of applications. IBM spent more than $1 billion to develop a set of five System/360 models, each of which was compatible with the others. IBM's bet has paid off handsomely over the years; System/360 and its descendants are the longest-lived line of computers the world has seen to date. In 1971, System/370 was launched, followed by 370/XA in 1981, and 370/ESA in 1988. S/390 was announced in 1990, bringing with it a new I/O model. That model is Enterprise System Connectivity (ESCON), a fiber optic I/O system that replaces the traditional "bus and tag" parallel I/O channels.

Since 1993, IBM has been busy rebuilding S/390 architecture. At the hardware level, the processors have moved from bipolar to CMOS technology. In 1997, S/390 Parallel Enterprise Server – Generation 4 delivered a CMOS system as powerful as the fastest bipolar systems. In 1998, S/390 Parallel Enterprise Server – Generation 5 produced another 80 percent improvement in performance. It also introduced another new I/O model. Fiber Channel Connectivity (FICON) supports 100 MB/sec bi-directional data transfer, as compared with ESCON's 17 MB/sec uni-directional throughput.

Also in 1998, IBM introduced S/390 Parallel Sysplex clustering technology, which provides massive scalability and very high levels of availability. A Parallel Sysplex cluster can link together up to thirty-two S/390 servers, each containing up to ten processors. IBM's GEOPLEX technology can spread a Sysplex cluster over two sites up to twenty-five miles apart for fault tolerance even after the complete loss of a site.

Although the modern S/390 is barely recognizable as a descendant of 1964's original System/360, the key to the success of the range has been evolution rather than revolution. Despite dramatic improvements in both power and performance, a high level of upward compatibility has encouraged organizations with an investment in IBM mainframe technology to continue to upgrade. Applications written for System/360 are still running today on S/390. Well over three decades after System/360 was launched, its S/390 descendant is still alive and thriving in many enterprises that need a high-performance computer platform. MVS has been able to support applications with hundreds of active users and terabytes of data for several years, whereas NT and UNIX systems still find this level of performance to be a stretch. For the last three years, S/390 shipments have seen double-digit growth.

Four operating systems are commonly found on S/390 computers: OS/390, MVS, VSE/ESA, and VM/ESA.

### OS/390 and MVS

The most powerful S/390 operating system is IBM OS/390, launched in 1995. OS/390 is a successor to the Multiple Virtual Storage (MVS) operating system. MVS was one of the earliest operating systems to support virtual storage, and has long been a preferred operating system in production facilities. OS/390 retains the classic strengths of MVS: security, scalability, and high availability. It adds compatibility with the X/Open UNIX 95 standard by providing over 1,100 UNIX API calls and many UNIX shell commands. This allows easy porting of UNIX programs to OS/390. In addition, OS/390 supports object-oriented programming through Component Broker for OS/390 and a Java virtual machine. Web development is enabled through the availability of Lotus Domino for OS/390. Interoperability features include TCP/IP and DCE support.

OS/390 is clearly IBM's choice for the S/390 operating system of the future.

OS/390 Security Server is an add-on for OS/390 that provides security for Internet applications. OS/390 Security Server provides support for X.509 certificates, LDAP directory service, an integrated firewall, DCE security, and Kerberos authentication.

### VSE/ESA

Virtual Storage Extended/Enterprise System Architecture (VSE/ESA) is a smaller operating system than MVS or OS/390, although it still seems to be a large and complex operating system when compared with Windows NT. It supports smaller S/390 installations, supporting systems with up to three processors. IBM continues to enhance VSE/ESA, for example by providing TCP/IP support and Y2K compliance, but OS/390 is the operating system that will take S/390 into the twenty-first century.

## VM/ESA

Virtual Machine/Enterprise System Architecture (VM/ESA) is often used in conjunction with VSE/ESA to provide extended services. VM is an operating system that can perform a really cool trick. It can run other operating systems inside itself. (Hence the name "Virtual Machine.") Each operating system is known as a "guest" operating system. As an example, imagine a software development company that owns a single mainframe, but wishes to develop for both MVS and VSE. By running VM, and then loading MVS and VSE as guest operating systems, the company can gain access to MVS and VSE simultaneously. VM can even run VM as a guest operating system, creating multiple instances of VM on a single system, where VM acts as a guest of itself. Other obvious uses of VM are to allow testing and production environments to run on a single system. One example that IBM recommends is to run a production and a test instance of VSE on the same system. The production instance can use live data while the date in the test instance is set forward to permit Y2K testing. VM/ESA V2R3 even supports multiple instances of OS/390 Parallel Sysplex to allow testing of clustered applications on a single computer.

VM/ESA supports POSIX 1003.1 and 1003.2 for UNIX compatibility, although it has not achieved the high level of UNIX certification of OS/390. Other compatibility features include a Java virtual machine, as well as TCP/IP, NFS, and DCE support.

# AS/400

Despite the success of System/360 and its successors, IBM did not ignore the small computer marketplace. In 1969, an IBM division based in Rochester, Minnesota, announced the System/3 mid-range system. This was followed by the System/32, System/34, System/38, and System/36. (Only IBM could count 32, 34, 38, 36!) The largest of these was System/38, which supported up to 256 workstations using a mere 32 MB of memory.

These computers proved that there was a demand for minicomputers that were easier to use than a mainframe and were more compatible with a small company budget. This led, in June 1988, to the launch of the AS/400.

Early AS/400 models had some architectural similarities to System/38. Since that time, AS/400 has seen the same type of evolutionary changes as the larger systems. The biggest change began in 1993, when IBM revamped the range to use reduced instruction set computer (RISC) processors instead of the older complex instruction set computer (CISC) architecture. In 1997, the range was renamed the AS/400e, to remind us of e-commerce, e-mail, and e-business.

The AS/400e range features ten models. Near the low end of AS/400 performance is the Model 150, which has a Power PC A10 RISC processor, 64 MB of RAM, and 4 GB of hard disk. A high-end system is the S40, which can support up to 20,480 MB of RAM, 1,546 GB of hard disk, and a 12-way SMP processor. (The minimum S40 configuration is 1,024 MB of RAM, 4.2 GB of hard disk, and 8-way SMP processor.)

To understand relative performance of the AS/400, we can look at database performance benchmarks from the Transaction Processing Performance Council (http://www.tpc.org). TPC's Web site has a benchmark for an AS/400e S40 Server that cost $3,217,385 and provided a throughput of 25,149.75 tpmC. This can be compared with a high-end Compaq 7000 server with four 400 MHz Pentium II CPUs that cost $473,203 and provided 18127.4 tpmC using Microsoft SQL Server 7.0. Although the Compaq server provided better performance in terms of dollars per tpmC, the AS/400 provided better overall performance.

The main operating system for the AS/400 is OS/400. (Older models of AS/400 also support an operating system called System Support Program (SSP) for backwards compatibility.) OS/400 provides the usual operating system capabilities; application development options include a Java Virtual Machine and support for Lotus Notes Domino, as well as more traditional languages such as RPG, COBOL, and C++.

An important feature of the AS/400 is DB2/400, the integrated database. When this appeared on the System/38, this was one of the world's first databases with relational properties. The database support has been a very successful aspect of the product, and is heavily used by almost every AS/400 installation. Every AS/400 ships with the database manager and the Data Description Specification (DDS) language. This provides a full database capability, but does not provide SQL support. The Query Manager and SQL development kit are an add-on that must be purchased separately. This means that DB2/400 without the SQL add-ons is, almost uniquely, a relational database that does not support SQL. Many AS/400 shops have avoided using SQL and built databases using DDS alone. This has created the requirement for a non-SQL interface to AS/400 databases that Microsoft has met with the OLE DB Provider for AS/400 and VSAM.

IBM also provides a product called Client Access. This runs on PCs with Windows 9x and Windows NT allowing them to use the AS/400 as a server. Another IBM product is the Integrated PC Server (IPCS). This is a Pentium Pro server that runs inside the AS/400 chassis, allowing Windows NT and OS/400 to co-exist in a single computer. The AS/400 computer runs OS/400, the IPCS runs Windows NT, and the two processors share access to the system's hard disk.

Future plans for the AS/400e line include disk compression, more RAM, new processors, and a clustering technology called OptiConnect that is conceptually similar to S/390 Parallel Sysplex.

## SNA

Systems Network Architecture (SNA) was the first widely deployed networking architecture. Unlike TCP/IP, which is defined by a standards committee, SNA is a proprietary system, controlled by IBM. SNA has developed through two distinct phases; it originated as a system for connecting terminals to mainframes and has evolved into a flexible networking solution that allows peer-to-peer networking.

### Host-based

IBM launched SNA in 1974. Back in those days, most organizations owned a single computer, stored in a room with glass walls. The room had glass walls so that every visitor to the organization could be walked past the computer room. SNA was developed to allow this single computer to be connected to dumb terminals scattered around the organization. These computers were fairly limited by modern standards, so a goal of SNA was offloading input and output to an array of devices that supported terminals. The most important categories of devices were cluster controllers and front-end processors. A front-end processor (FEP) typically sat in the data center next to the mainframe, connected to it by a fast link called a *channel*. The front-end processor was responsible for communicating with cluster controllers on behalf of the mainframe. Each group of 3270 terminals was connected to a *cluster controller*. Each cluster controller was responsible for communicating with the FEP across a leased telephone line.

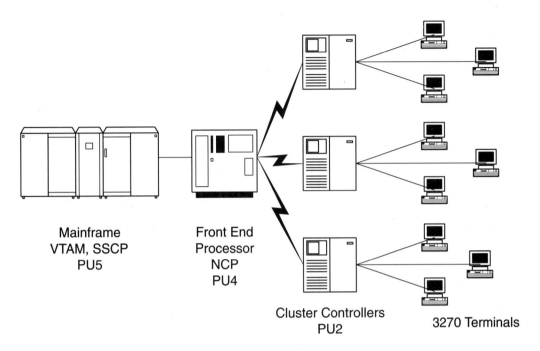

**Figure 12-1.**
*Typical SNA architecture.*

Each networking element in SNA was known as a *physical unit*. The physical units are not really hardware; they are the combination of a hardware device with a network program. The mainframe ran a software system called Virtual Telecommunications Access Method (VTAM). A module within VTAM called Systems Services Control Point (SSCP) controlled the complete SNA network. The SSCP module was referred to as a physical unit type 5 or PU5. The front-end processor or communications controller ran another software program called Network Control Program (NCP). This was referred to as PU4. The cluster controller was PU2. There were also *logical units*. These defined end points of communications across an SNA network. As an example, a 3270 terminal communicated with the mainframe as a logical unit 2 (LU2) data stream.

Unlike a typical TCP/IP network, a hierarchical SNA network was defined exhaustively by network definition tables loaded into VTAM. These tables describe every device on the network and provide work for systems administrators, who must regenerate the tables whenever a new device is added.

The 1974 version of SNA, known informally SNA-0, was quite limited in scope. It could support a single mainframe and FEP. Over the years, the number of configurations that SNA could support was increased. These new configurations included support for a variety of communications links, multiple FEPs, and multiple host computers. In 1983, IBM launched SNA Network Interconnection (SNI), which allowed interconnections between SNA networks. In 1984, IBM added support for SNA Distribution Services (SNADS), which allowed message distribution. Token ring support was introduced in 1986. The most important development, however, was the move toward a peer-to-peer SNA that gave rise to APPN. This included the development of a new logical unit type, LU 6.2. This LU allowed peer-to-peer communication between mainframes. Despite this introduction, the network was still ruled by its mainframe overlords and VTAM.

## APPN

In 1992, IBM launched advanced peer-to-peer networking (APPN). APPN is a fundamental re-working of the SNA architecture. In earlier versions of SNA, the mainframe was king and the other devices were subjects. In an organization with several mainframes, there could be several kings, but each of the other devices was owned by a specific mainframe that was its lord and master. Devices could only talk to each other if VTAM was aware of a route between them. APPN introduced democracy into the SNA world. In APPN, no single system is in control of the network; every system is a peer of every other system. New devices can be added to the network without the need to reconfigure the VTAM tables on a mainframe, and systems can talk to each other without anyone's permission.

APPN nodes can be divided into three types: LEN nodes, end nodes, and network nodes. Low entry-level networking (LEN) nodes were actually introduced in 1986. They provided a way to use SNA networking with the S/36 minicomputer. LEN nodes feature a scaled down SSCP that provides similar facilities to a mainframe SSCP, but more limited in capabilities and running in a minicomputer. LEN nodes were a new SNA physical unit type, known as PU2.1.

APPN End Nodes (EN), as the name implies, exist at the end of network links. They implement peer-to-peer networking, but not routing. APPN Network Nodes (NN), implement the complete set of peer-to-peer networking capabilities defined by APPN, and also provide routing services. NN can be used to connect up LEN nodes or end nodes to provide a complete peer-to-peer SNA network. In TCP/IP terms, the end node can be viewed as a server, whereas the network node is both a server and a router.

Both APPN end nodes and APPN network nodes are commonly implemented using AS/400 hardware. Other hardware that fits the model includes the IBM 3174 establishment controller, a product that can also be used as a mainframe FEP. When a 3174 is used with APPN, it is typically used as a network node to provide routing functions only.

# SNA Server

The most important tool we'll use to interface with legacy systems is Microsoft SNA Server. SNA Server provides a wide range of features that allow computers running Windows or Windows NT on a local area network (LAN) to connect to legacy systems. Early versions of SNA Server were focused on providing terminal emulation on the desktop. In SNA Server 3.0, Microsoft introduced tools for connecting to relational databases on mainframe systems and for using AS/400 folders as LAN file servers. In SNA Server 4.0, which became available in late 1997, several new tools were introduced that allow applications running in the NT environment to communicate with applications and databases on S/390 and AS/400. In the next section we'll look at some of these tools in more detail. First, we'll make a brief survey of SNA Server as a whole, before diving in to the specifics.

## Terminal Emulation and Host Print Services

SNA Server provides support for terminal emulation on both mainframe and AS/400 systems. Mainframe systems typically use 3270 terminals, whereas AS/400 systems use 5250 terminals. The details are outside the scope of this book, but SNA Server does a great job of providing connectivity for both 3270 and 5250 emulators. On Windows, Windows 9X, and Windows NT clients, installation of an SNA Server client allows use of full-featured terminal emulators from a wide variety of vendors. On UNIX, Apple Macintosh, and other client architectures, SNA Server supports the use of terminal emulators that comply with the TN3270, TN5250, and TN3287 Internet standards.

In a typical mainframe setup, an SNA Server computer will be connected to a mainframe system through either an SDLC or channel connection. The SNA Server computer will also have a standard Ethernet or token ring card that connects it to the LAN. Computers on the LAN will use a terminal emulation program to connect to the SNA Server computer. SNA Server will translate the LAN network protocol to an SNA-compliant protocol, and forward the LU2 data stream from the terminal to the mainframe. When the mainframe replies to the request from the terminal, SNA Server translates back from SNA protocol to LAN protocol and forwards the data stream back to the terminal emulator. SNA Server is said to act as a gateway between the LAN protocol and SNA.

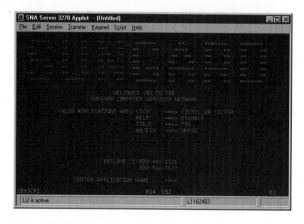

**Figure 12-2.**
*The 3270 Applet supplied with SNA Server can be used to test 3270 terminal emulation.*

The Host Print Service allows the AS/400 or mainframe to connect to a printer on the LAN as if it were attached to the host. Although this is a different service from terminal emulation, the two are often used together. When host print service is used with terminal emulation, a print job started by a terminal emulation user can be printed on their local LAN printer. This feature can provide a cost saving by allowing an installation to replace costly mainframe-compatible printers with low-cost laser printers.

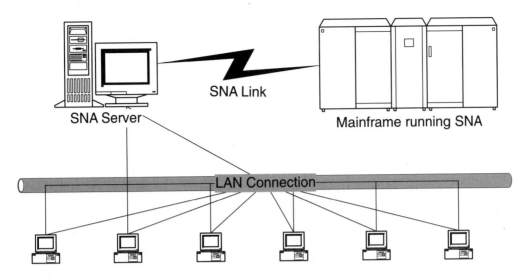

**Figure 12-3.**
*SNA Server acts as a gateway between the LAN and the SNA network.*

## Shared Folders

The Shared Folder service allows desktop systems to read AS/400 shared folders as if they were NT shares. (This service is discussed below in the section, "File Sharing.")

## File Transfer

SNA Server supports file transfer through APPC File Transfer Protocol (AFTP). It also acts as a gateway between FTP and AFTP, allowing LAN clients that can use FTP to transfer files to and from a host system running AFTP. In addition, the Virtual Storage Access Method (VSAM) File Transfer Utility supports transfer of files from VSAM on a host system to Windows NT. Finally, an add-on product to SNA Server called Host Data Replicator allows replication of DB2 data between IBM's DB2 product and Microsoft SQL Server. (These services are discussed below in the sections, "File Transfer" and "Snapshot Replication.")

## Security Integration

SNA Server security is tightly integrated with NT security, allowing the administrator to give specific users access to particular logical units. SNA Server permits a single sign-on to be used for both the Windows NT domain and the host. The Bulk Migration Tool for Host Security allows host accounts to be copied to SNA Server. With third-party add-ons, SNA Server provides support for password synchronization between Windows NT and host systems.

## OLE DB Provider

The OLE DB Provider for AS/400 and VSAM allows applications to use Active Data Objects (ADO) to retrieve data from AS/400 data files and mainframe VSAM files. (This service is discussed below in the section, "Database Access.")

## COMTI

The COM Transaction Integrator for CICS and IMS provides a wizard that creates COM objects that interface to either Customer Information Control System (CICS) or Information Management System (IMS). (This service is discussed below in the section, "Transaction Access.")

## ODBC/DRDA Gateway

The ODBC/DRDA Gateway for DB2 allows clients to use Open Database Connectivity (ODBC) to connect to IBM's DB2 database product on mainframe and AS/400 platforms. (This service is discussed below in the section, "Database Access.")

## Communications Features

SNA Server supports a wide variety of link services between the SNA Server computer and the SNA network. It also allows support of downstream physical units connected across the LAN. It provides compression and encryption of traffic passing between the client computer and SNA Server.

## Scalability

SNA Server can support up to 30,000 simultaneous sessions.

## Fault Tolerance

SNA Server provides fault tolerance and load balancing through the use of up to fifteen computers in a pool. If an SNA Server computer fails, another computer can take over.

## Administration

SNA Server 4.0 can be administered either by using the SNA Server Manager program or by using a set of Microsoft Management Console (MMC) snap-ins. There are several configuration wizards that help with common configuration tasks, such as setting up 3270 connections.

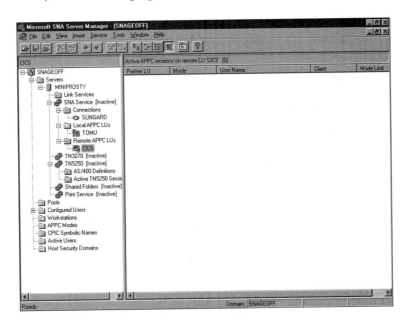

**Figure 12-4.**
*SNA Server Administrator.*

# Tools for Interoperability

In this section, we'll look at technologies for sharing data between our applications and legacy systems. We'll start with the simplest method, shared files, and move up the scale until we reach DCOM on the mainframe. Along the way, we'll look at solutions for access to AS/400 files, VSAM files, relational databases, and business logic implemented in mainframe transaction programs.

## File Sharing

The most basic method of sharing data between systems is to share files, but this approach can be very effective in some situations. There are two forms of file sharing: cross-platform file servers and file transfer.

## AS/400 Shared Folders

The AS/400 provides a feature that allows an area of AS/400 disk storage to be shared, in the same way as a computer running Windows NT Workstation can share a folder. This can be described as a *cross-platform file server solution*. The AS/400 acts as a file server that can support more than one platform.

The first step in using shared folders is to create the folders on the AS/400. You can create folders by selecting Work with Folders from the AS/400 menu systems, and then selecting option 1, create.

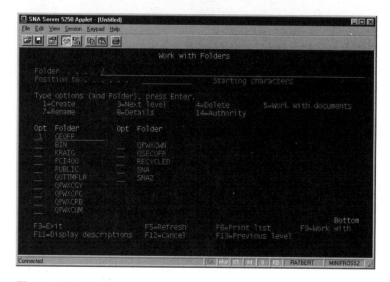

**Figure 12-5.**
*Administering shared folders on the AS/400.*

The next step is to use SNA Server Manager to create an AS/400 definition for the shared folder service. Once the AS/400 is defined, you can create a folder definition that specifies the AS/400 folder to share. Be sure to check the permanent drive box if you want to reconnect with this folder when you restart the server.

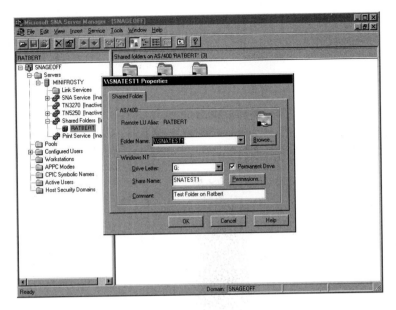

**Figure 12-6.**
*Administering shared folders on SNA Server.*

Once you've created the shared folder, NT will treat it as if it were a disk on the server. You can drag-and-drop files to and from the AS/400 using Windows NT Explorer, examine the folder's properties, and share the folder. If you share the folder, other desktop computers will be able to connect to it as if it were an NT shared folder, without using any special software. This allows a user with any Windows operating system, whether 16 or 32 bit, to copy files to the AS/400 by using standard Windows tools without any special software. Without SNA Server, IBM's Client Access Program is needed on each desktop computer to access these shared folders. With SNA Server, no additional client software is needed, and the same NT security permissions and access rights can be applied as with any other file.

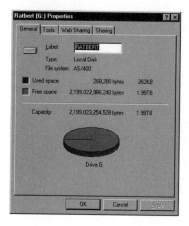

**Figure 12-7.**
*Examining the properties of a shared folder.*

### File Transfer Tools

The other approach to file sharing is *file transfer*. SNA Server provides a File Transfer Protocol (FTP) to APPC File Transfer Protocol (AFTP) gateway service for file transfer. AFTP is a file transfer protocol defined by SNA that resembles the FTP protocol used on the Internet. Although SNA Server supports direct use of AFTP from the desktop, the gateway can also translate between FTP commands originating at a desktop and the AFTP commands required by the host. This allows desktop computers, whether Windows, Macintosh, or UNIX, to use an existing FTP client to transfer files to and from the host computer.

Another tool supplied with SNA Server is the VSAM File Transfer Tool. This supports file transfer to and from Sequential Access Method (SAM) data sets, Partitioned Data Set (PDS), and Partitioned Data Set Extended (PDSE) members. The tool does not require additional software on the host; it communicates by using IBM's Distributed Data Management (DDM) facility. The tool uses a command line interface; enter *DDMFTP* at a command prompt to start it.

### File Sharing Limitations

There are two main limitations to file sharing solutions: time and data storage format. In solutions based on AFTP or other file transfer utilities, the file will be out of date as soon as it is transferred. When a user comes to a Web site to buy something, the user doesn't care if the item was in stock yesterday. They want to know if it is in stock today. An AFTP solution can't answer these questions.

A more compelling reason to stay away from file sharing is that it is simply inadequate for enterprise application development. We don't store data in flat files. We store data in relational databases. We encapsulate business logic in components and transaction programs. We need a more powerful approach to get the job done.

## Terminal Emulation, Screen-Scraping, and Surfing the Mainframe

Another obvious, simple technique to provide desktop access to legacy applications is to use a terminal emulator. This gets the job done but provides no integration with other client data.

If we are willing to write some software, there are several approaches that will allow a program to interact with "green screen" applications. All of them are based on the principle of "screen-scraping." *Screen-scraping* consists of using a terminal emulator that provides programmatic access to the data that would be displayed on the terminal.

A good example of screen-scraping is the High-Level Language API (HLLAPI). SNA Server doesn't implement HLLAPI, but a number of third-party terminal emulators such as products from Wall Data and Attachmate do. An application using HLLAPI would run a terminal emulator that supports HLLAPI and is connected to the legacy system. The terminal emulator wouldn't be used to display the legacy system's output. Instead, the application would read the contents of the screen using HLLAPI, and then supply input to the program using HLLAPI. By using this trick, the application can put a new front end on the legacy system. For example, a set of COM components could be created that use HLLAPI and provide an HTML interface to the legacy system. These COM components could then be run in an Active Server Page (ASP).

One of the interesting aspects of developing HLLAPI applications is timing. Often, the screen-scraping application will think the host is done reading data too early, and will read invalid data. Another timing effect is when the application sends data to the host before the host is ready. This can provide challenging debugging problems for developers using screen-scraping. In general, screen-scraping is more difficult and time-consuming to implement than the other approaches described in this chapter.

There are several flavors of HLLAPI. Extended HLLAPI (EHLLAPI) is a de facto standard developed by IBM. WinHLLAPPI is based on EHLLAPI, but includes additional features for the Windows platform. Most of the terminal emulation vendors have their own extended versions of HLLAPI. Most of the vendors also provide object interfaces to their products. These consist of a set of COM components that expose the product functionality. Examples are

EXTRA! Objects SDK from Attachmate (http://www.attachmate.com), and Rumba ObjectX Development Kit from Wall Data (http://www.walldata.com).

"Surfing the mainframe" is the name given to a set of techniques for connecting to host systems using Web technology. There are two main variants of surfing the mainframe: using a terminal emulator within a browser and using an HTML translator to convert the host's user interface to HTML. The main benefits of surfing the mainframe are support for both TCP/IP and SNA networks, and support for a wide variety of client platforms.

ActiveX terminal emulator controls are available from several terminal emulator vendors. To use these controls, you need to set up an HTML page that contains a reference to the control and sets its properties appropriately. When a user downloads the page, they will also download the control and start a mainframe session within their browser.

The other approach is to provide an ISAPI or ASP application that translates the 3270 data stream into HTML by screen-scraping. The user sees a user interface that looks very similar to the user interface of the original 3270 application, but is implemented entirely in HTML. Screens that require input are represented as HTML forms. When the user enters data, it is converted to a 3270 or 5250 data stream, and sent to the host. When the host responds with a display, it is converted on the fly to HTML. An example of a product that does this translation is Corridor from Teubner & Associates, Inc. (http://www.teubner.com/).

Both of these techniques were being heavily marketed during 1996-97, but seem to have been de-emphasized by the vendors. Perhaps they have realized that putting an ugly, green-screen application on the Web means exposing an ugly application to the world.

## SNA Server SDK and SNA APIs

SNA Server Client provides libraries that support several Application Programming Interfaces (APIs). You can use these APIs for low-level access to SNA Server facilities in your programs. Usually, it's much easier to use one of the higher-level facilities described in this chapter to get access to data or transactions. Each of these APIs will require you to do some C programming. However, if you want to do something outside the mainstream, these APIs may be the only way to achieve the effect you're looking for.

In this section, we'll provide a brief summary of each API. If you want more information, SNA Server supplies detailed online documentation for each API. If you need documentation, be sure that you perform a custom install of SNA Server and request online documentation. The documentation is very complete, but it's not in the printed version of the SNA Server manuals.

### AFTP API

The APPC File Transfer Protocol (AFTP) API provides support for the development of programs that use APPC file transfer.

### APPC API

The Advanced Program to Program Communications (APPC) API provides support for peer-to-peer communications in an SNA environment. APPC programming provides a general-purpose mechanism that allows programs to co-operate and share data. The interface provides a number of "verbs" that can be used to initiate and continue a conversation between applications.

In the Windows APPC API, a program that wishes to communicate through APPC will allocate a verb control block (VCB). IBM refers to an application communicating over APPC as a transaction program (TP). The VCB will be filled in with the identity of the verb, and the parameters required by the verb, and the void WINAPI APPC(long) function will be called. (The pointer to VCB should be cast to long.) This function will execute the verb, store a return code in the VCB, and return. A typical APPC conversation will include a number of verbs; for more information about APPC programming, check out the examples supplied in the \SDK\SAMPLES directory when SNA Server is installed.

### CPI-C API

The Common Programming Interface for Communications (CPI-C) API is another peer-to-peer SNA API. CPI-C is a more recent introduction than APPC,- and is compatible with IBM's Systems Applications Architecture.

### 3270 Emulator Interface

This API is used by third parties who develop 3270 emulators that support SNA Server.

### LUA Interface API

The Logical Unit Application (LUA) API allows the development of applications that use LU 0, LU 1, LU 2, or LU 3. Each of these LU types represents a protocol for communicating between mainframes and devices. For example, a 3270 terminal hooked to a mainframe through an SNA network will normally use the LU 2 data stream. The LUA Interface API will be used with mainframes running traditional host-based SNA.

### SNALink Interface

The SNALink Interface is used by device manufacturers to interface communication devices with SNA Server.

### SNANLS API

The SNA National Language Support API allows support for international languages in SNA applications.

### SNA Print Server Data Filter API

This API supports the creation of a DLL that provides banner pages or other special processing for the host print service.

## Database Access

Perhaps the most commonly used type of integration between Web applications and legacy systems is access to legacy databases. In this section, we'll take a look at several techniques for getting access to information on mainframes and AS/400s. They include Microsoft's Host Data Replicator, Microsoft's Data Transformation Services, IBM's DB2 Connect, Microsoft's OLE DB Provider for DDM, and StarQuest Software's StarSQL Pro.

### Snapshot Replication

Unlike the other solutions described in this chapter that access data when it is required by an application, the solutions in this subsection replicate a snapshot of the data at a particular point in time.

As an example, imagine a corporate address book on the intranet that provides access to employee phone numbers and office allocations. This data is maintained by an HR application that runs on a S/390 computer running OS/390, and uses DB2 to store employee information. The intranet application could be written to use a SQL Server database for the employee application. A *snapshot replication tool* could be used to transfer the employee information from DB2 to SQL Server each night. Obviously, this approach has the significant disadvantage that changes in the DB2 database will not be reflected on the intranet site until the following day. (This is one of the limitations we saw with some file sharing solutions.) However, if the S/390 computer is heavily loaded, or the network bandwidth between the mainframe and the intranet server is limited, snapshot replication could provide a significant performance boost. This is especially true in a corporation that has many offices that are geographically distributed. In this case, it is undesirable to burden the WAN links between sites each time somebody checks an address. The use of snapshot replication to perform data update outside the working day will free these links for more important uses.

Another example is a *data mining application*. If multiple operational systems exist within a corporation, some of which use legacy databases and some of which use Microsoft SQL Server, then snapshot replication can be used to combine data from both sources into a data warehouse for online analytical processing (OLAP). The snapshot replication could be performed on a daily basis, or on user request.

Microsoft Host Data Replicator (HDR) is an add-on to SNA Server that performs snapshot replication between IBM's DB2 and Microsoft SQL Server 6.5. It has been a successful product, but is likely to be made obsolete by the Data Transformation Services (DTS) in Microsoft SQL Server 7.0.

DTS is an OLE DB service that moves data between two OLE DB providers. One provider acts as the data source and the other acts as the destination. Both source and destination can be either native OLE DB sources, such as SQL Server or Access, ODBC sources, such as DB2 or Oracle, ASCII text files, supported by the SQL Server driver, or custom OLE DB sources. DTS provides facilities for transforming data. You can change data formats, restructure or map data, validate data, or improve data consistency. An Import Wizard and Export Wizard are provided to simplify administration. Both the data and the database schema can be moved, although DTS does not transfer triggers, stored procedures, rules, defaults, constraints, or user-defined data types between heterogeneous data sources.

The DTS Data Pump is an OLE DB service provider that moves and transforms OLE DB rowsets. A DTS package consists of one or more steps, each of which can execute a SQL statement, move data using the DTS Data Pump, execute a script, launch a program, or execute another DTS package. Administering DTS consists of defining packages, and then executing or scheduling packages. You can execute a DTS package by using the SQL Server 7.0 Enterprise Manager or the DTSRUN command line utility. You can schedule a package using the Import and Export Wizards or by creating a SQL Executive job that uses the DTSRUN utility.

## Real-Time Connectivity Tools for DB2

Tools that provide connectivity in real time, instead of transferring nightly snapshots, are likely to prove more useful in delivering enterprise applications. In this subsection, we'll look at tools for interoperation with the DB2 relational database.

SNA Server provides an evaluation copy of StarSQL Pro, an Open Database Connectivity (ODBC) driver that can connect to databases running Distributed Relational Database Access (DRDA). DRDA is an IBM protocol

443

that allows network access to relational databases; it is an element of IBM's Distributed Data Management (DDM) architecture. The ODBC driver for DRDA allows desktop applications that can use ODBC or OLE DB to connect to DB2 databases that support DRDA. As far as the application is concerned, it's dealing with a standard ODBC driver. As far as DB2 is concerned, it's dealing with a DRDA client. The driver acts as a gateway between the two, translating between ODBC and DRDA. SNA Server acts as a communications link between the ODBC driver and the SNA network.

The driver supplied with SNA Server is a version of StarSQL by StarQuest Software. A single client license is included with SNA Server. For information on licensing additional clients, or to get more information on StarSQL Pro, see http://www.starquest.com/. StarSQL Pro supports some additional connection options, such as TCP/IP, in addition to Microsoft SNA Server.

Competitors to StarSQL include IBM's DB2 Connect. This tool provides connectivity via DRDA to servers running DB2 for AS/400, DB2 for MVS/ESA, DB2 for OS/390, DB2 for VSE and VM, DB2 Common Server, DB2 Universal Database, and SQL/DS. DB2 Connect runs on AIX, HP-UX, 16- and 32-bit versions of the Windows operating system, OS/2, and Sun Solaris. An SNA connection to the host database uses the APPC protocol. On the client, ODBC and JDBC drivers allow desktop applications to access the host database. DB2 Connect supports MTS two-phase commit, allowing transactions to commit atomically between DB2 and other MTS-supported databases.

In addition to products from IBM and Microsoft, there are third-party middleware products that provide database connectivity. One example is Information Builders Inc.'s Enterprise Data Access (EDA) product (http://www.ibi.com/). EDA provides access to over seventy relational and nonrelational data sources on thirty-five different platforms. An EDA Server runs on each supported platform; EDA Hub Servers can provide location transparency to the client. Client tools include a set of ActiveX objects and IBI's Enterprise Component Broker that provides a CORBA ORB.

Other approaches to putting DB2 on the Web include IBM's DB2 WWW Connection product. This product uses macro files similar to the obsolete Internet Database Connector (IDC) files on IIS; the macros include SQL queries that are run when the macro file is requested by a user. This is a less powerful approach than ASP development, and would probably not provide the flexibility required for enterprise-class applications.

## OLE DB DDM Provider

The OLE DB DDM Provider is used with AS/400 data files, as well as mainframe SAM and VSAM files. As we noted in the "Legacy Systems" section, the AS/400's integrated database provides relational facilities but does not run SQL. (SQL is available as an add-on.) This means that a traditional ODBC driver cannot be used. On mainframe systems, large quantities of data are stored in files managed by the Data Facility Storage Management Subsystem (DFSMS). Examples of DFSMS files are Sequential Access Method (SAM) files, and Virtual Storage Access Method (VSAM) files. SAM files must be accessed sequentially. VSAM files support both keyed and sequential data, and may have multiple keys, such as employee number, name, and department. VSAM files may be accessed directly or relatively, and may be accessed as records or as a linear stream of bytes.

These files are accessible through IBM's Distributed Data Management (DDM) architecture. DDM access methods include stream I/O, DRDA, and Record Level I/O. DRDA was described in the previous section on DB2 Connectivity. Stream I/O provides bulk data transfer, and is used by the DDMFTP tool described in the earlier section entitled, "File Sharing." Record level I/O is used for record level access to data files that cannot support SQL.

OLE DB is the obvious tool for access to DDM Record Level I/O. Unlike ODBC, OLE DB can use SQL if it is available but does not require SQL. This flexibility allows OLE DB to access many nonrelational data stores. Examples are OLE DB providers that can read the Windows Registry or the Exchange directory. In this case, we'll use OLE DB to access legacy data files.

The OLE DB specification provides a set of COM interfaces for interactions between OLE DB providers and OLE DB consumers. Although it would be possible to use the SNAOLEDB provider through these interfaces, it is far easier to use Active Data Objects (ADO). In this solution, we'll look at an example of using the OLE DB DDM Provider with an AS/400 data file. The full range of supported file types is: AS/400 keyed and nonkeyed physical files; AS/400 logical files with external record descriptions; mainframe SAM data sets using BSAM and QSAM; mainframe VSAM data sets using ESDS, KSDS, RRDS, and VRRDS; basic partitioned access data sets using PDSE and PDS members. Read-only support is provided for PDSE and PDS directories.

Microsoft SQL Server provides a test database called PUBS. In this solution, we've copied the PUBS database to an AS/400 library called PUBS. The library contains physical files that correspond to the tables in the PUBS database, and logical files that correspond to indexes on the tables.

445

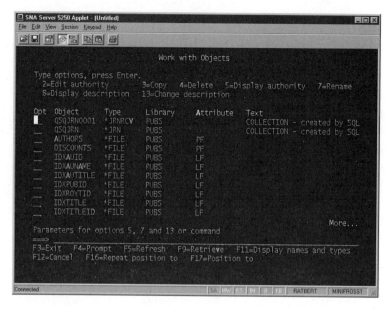

**Figure 12-8.**
*The contents of the PUBS library on the AS/400.*

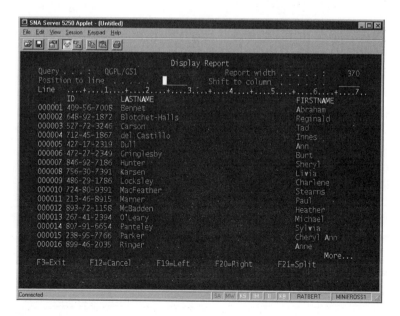

**Figure 12-9.**
*The contents of the Authors physical file.*

Let's assume SNA Server is installed, local and remote LUs have been set up to connect to the AS/400, and that we've installed ADO as provided with Visual InterDev 6.0. The next step is to run the SNA OLE DB Management MMC snap-in, and create a new data source. Right-click on the Data Sources folder, and select New, followed by Data Source. Once you've supplied a data source name, the Data Source Properties dialog box will be displayed. Select the local and remote LUs that provide APPC connectivity to the AS/400. All sessions with an AS/400 will use mode QPCSUPP. If you are setting up a VSAM data source, consult your local VTAM expert for mode information. Leave the RDB name the same as the remote LU alias, which is probably the same as the AS/400 name. Select the name of the AS/400 library that contains the data files, and pick a CCSID for your locale.

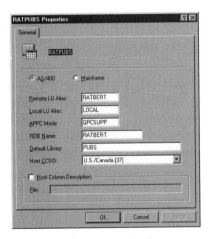

**Figure 12-10.**
*Creating a data source.*

Once the data source is installed, it's wise to test the source before using it in a program. You can test it using the OLE DB Rowset Viewer, which is installed with the ADO SDK. Open the Rowset Viewer, and select Full Connect from the File Menu. This will allow you to pick a data provider, which in this case is SNAOLEDB. Once you have selected a provider, the same dialog box should allow you to select the data source that you previously created. Click the OK button, and then select the physical file you wish to view. The file contents should be displayed in a grid.

447

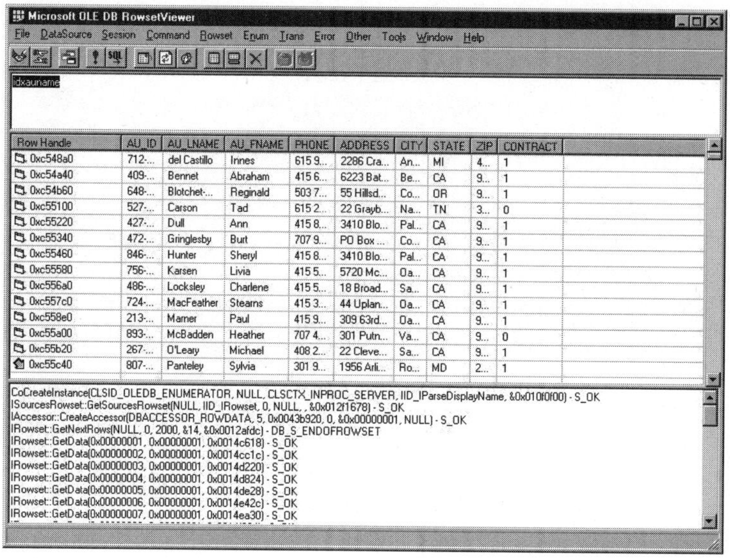

**Figure 12-11.**
*The IDXAUNAME logical file.*

Once we've got this far, the code to access the file is very simple.

```
Dim conAS400 As ADODB.Connection

Dim rsFirstName As ADODB.Recordset


Public Function GetFirst(strName As String) As String
    Set conAS400 = New ADODB.Connection
    Set rsFirstName = New ADODB.Recordset
    conAS400.Open "Provider=SNAOLEDB;Data Source=RATPUBS;" & _
        "User ID=GSUSER;Password=GSPASS"
    rsFirstName.Open "exec open PUBS/idxauname", _
        conAS400, adOpenForwardOnly, adLockOptimistic, adCmdText
    rsFirstName.MoveFirst
    rsFirstName.Find "AU_LNAME = '" & strName & "'", 1
    GetFirst = rsFirstName("AU_FNAME")
    Set rsFirstName = Nothing
    Set conAS400 = Nothing
End Function
```

This is the entire source code for a VB class that uses the OLE DB DDM Provider. It's a single routine that reads the AUTHORS data in PUBS, and gets the first name of an author whose last name we know. The class starts by defining variables to hold an ADO connection and ADO record set. Next, it opens a connection to OLE DB:

```
conAS400.Open "Provider=SNAOLEDB;Data Source=RATPUBS;" & _
    "User ID=GSUSER;Password=GSPASS"
```

This is very similar to code earlier in the book that opens ADO connections, but the provider is SNAOLEDB. In a real application, we would probably get the user ID and password from a Web form, but here we'll use a literal for simplicity. If we're running the code on a client machine, the OLE DB Provider can be used to pop up a request for the data source name, user ID, and password by using code like this:

```
Conn.Provider = "SNAOLEDB"
Conn.Properties("PROMPT") = adPromptAlways
Conn.Open
```

Obviously, this code won't work on a Web server because it would pop up a dialog box on the server, while the user was left staring at an unresponsive browser. The next step is to get a record set:

```
rsFirstName.Open "exec open PUBS/idxauname", _
    conAS400, adOpenForwardOnly, adLockOptimistic, adCmdText
```

The OLE DB DDM Provider defines two statements that can be used with the Open method. EXEC OPEN is used to open a record set. EXEC COMMAND executes a command in AS/400 Command Language, and is used with the ADO command object. In this case, we want to open a record set. In Figure 12-11, we can see the IDXAUNAME logical file. A *logical file* is roughly equivalent to a view in SQL Server. In this case, the logical file provides the same data as the underlying physical file, but ordered according to author name. Because we want to do a find command, we need to open the logical file, which is indexed, instead of the physical file that is unsorted. AS/400 data sets are opened using a LIBRARY/FILE syntax. VSAM data sets are opened using a DATASETNAME.FILENAME syntax, and partitioned data sets are opened using DATASETNAME.FILENAME(MEMBER). ConAS400 is the previously opened connection, and the other ADO options are standard.

Once we've opened the file, we can easily set the cursor to point to the correct record:

```
rsFirstName.Find "AU_LNAME = '" & strName & "'", 1
```

Finally, we read the author's first name, close the data connections, and return to the caller:

```
GetFirst = rsFirstName("AU_FNAME")
Set rsFirstName = Nothing
Set conAS400 = Nothing
```

There are a few gotchas to be aware of. If you want to update the data set, instead of just reading it, you have to use a connection object with CursorLocation set to ServerSide. To improve performance, try increasing the record set object's *CacheSize* property. By default, CacheSize is set to 1. Setting CacheSize to 20 or even 100 may improve performance. However, beware of locking issues if there is more than one client connected to the AS/400. If a large cache is used, the data cached in the local machine may be out of date from changes made by other users. Because the OLE DB DDM Provider only supports optimistic locking, you will have collisions if several users are updating simultaneously. In some Web applications, where all updates are made through the same IIS server, this may not be an issue. Performance testing to set the correct cache size is strongly recommended.

In addition to reading and updating data, you can use the OLE DB DDM Provider to execute AS/400 command language. The next subroutine executes an AS/400 command:

```
Dim conAS400 As ADODB.Connection
Dim cmdCL As ADODB.Command


Private Sub ExecuteCommand(strCommand as string)
    'This subroutine handles the execution of a command


    On Error GoTo Err


    ' Create objects
    Set conAS400 = New ADODB.Connection
    Set cmdCL = New ADODB.Command
```

*(continued)*

```
' Open Connection
conAS400.Open "Provider=SNAOLEDB;Data Source=RATPUBS;" & _
    "User ID=GSUSER;Password=GSPASS"
Set cmdCL.ActiveConnection = conAS400
cmdCL.CommandType = adCmdText


' Associate a parameter object with the command
Set Param = cmdCL.CreateParameter("Param1", adBSTR, adParamOutput)
cmdCL.Parameters.Append Param
cmdCL.CommandText = "Exec Command " & strCommand


' Execute the command
cmdCL.Execute adCmdText


' Display return message
If cmdCL.Parameters.Count > 0 Then
    MsgBox cmdCL.Parameters(0).Value, , "EXEC COMMAND Sample"
End If


Set cmdCL = Nothing
Set conAS400 = Nothing
Exit Sub


Err:
MsgBox Error, vbExclamation, "EXEC COMMAND Sample"
Set cmdCL = Nothing
Set conAS400 = Nothing
End Sub
```

This code will execute an AS/400 command language command on the AS/400 that is defined by the RATPUBS data source. This would allow you to create new libraries or databases from a Web application. In this example, we open the connection in the same manner as the previous example, set up a parameter to contain the result of the command, and the call the line:

```
cmdCL.Execute adCmdText
```

This line executes the actual command. After this, all we do is show a message box to display the response and then return to the caller.

If you prefer to move the entire database, instead of using the OLE DB DDM Provider, some third-party tools are available for AS/400 to SQL Server replication. One example is Symbiator from Vision Solutions (http://www.visionsolutions.com/). This product provides real-time or snapshot bi-directional replication between AS/400, SQL Server, or other ODBC sources.

## Transaction Access

COM Transaction Integrator (COMTI) allows us to use business logic implemented in CICS and IMS in our Web application, by building COM components that wrap CICS and IMS transactions without even having to write any code. In this section, we'll take a look at an example application that uses COMTI. Before that, however, we'll take a quick look at CICS and IMS for those who haven't worked with them before.

### CICS

Customer Information Control System (CICS) is IBM's transaction program monitor. According to IBM, 470 of the Fortune 500 run CICS somewhere within the organization. The CICS family of products is available for ESA (MVS and OS/390), VSE, AIX/6000, OS/400, and OS/2.

CICS acts as an application server, but provides many of the functions that are normally provided by an operating system. As an example, a transaction program (TP) running within CICS will use memory allocated by CICS instead of using the operating system's memory allocation facility. CICS features include transaction management, including two-phase commit and rollback capability, flat file and database support, terminal and screen handling, and many other distributed application services. One way to think of CICS is to consider it as an environment that runs on top of the operating system and supports applications, in the same way that Windows 3.1 ran on top of MS-DOS but supported applications that could not run on plain MS-DOS. The important difference is that unlike Windows 3.1, CICS supports huge transactional systems with thousands of simultaneous users.

Traditional CICS programming consists of developing screen maps and transaction programs. *Screen maps* define terminal displays using Basic Mapping Support (BMS); transaction programs are written in COBOL and define business logic. TPs callable from COMTI will consist of business logic only; COMTI cannot support CICS transactions that are intended to display data on the terminal.

Because CICS is available on Windows NT, a possible approach to integration with mainframe systems would be to run CICS on Windows NT, and use communication between the two CICS systems. We don't recommend this approach, simply because we prefer to use modern tools based on COM rather than write our Web-based applications in CICS.

## IMS

Information Management System (IMS) is a legacy IBM product for database and transactions. Although IBM continues to enhance IMS, any new development projects would be likely to use CICS in preference to IMS.

IMS runs on the MVS/ESA or OS/390 operating systems, and consists of two main modules. IMS Database Manager (IMS DB) provides database capabilities, and IMS Transaction Manager (IMS TM) provides data communications. IMS DB is a hierarchical rather than relational database, and it provides a proprietary language called DL/I for data manipulation. IMS TM adds support for interactive sessions with 3270 terminals, or calls to IMS transactions from other systems.

IMS version 5 had some limitations that affect COMTI. The most important was the lack of support for two-phase commit. This prevented COMTI components that use IMS from participating in MTS transactions, as COMTI transactions that use CICS do. IMS 6.0, introduced by IBM in December 1997, provides two-phase commit support. We expect that Microsoft will respond by announcing support for IMS two-phase commit in a future version of COMTI.

## COM Transaction Integrator

In this section, we'll take a detailed look at the Friendship Insurance tutorial that is distributed with SNA Server 4.0. This demonstrates two-phase commit using the COM Transaction Integrator (COMTI).

In the example, users enter insurance claims via a Visual Basic client or a browser interface. Both the VB and HTML versions use the same set of components to interface with VSAM, Microsoft SQL Server, and DB2. The VSAM and DB2 interactions use components created using CICS and COMTI. The SQL Server interaction uses components written in Visual Basic. Flow of control through the program is as follows:

1. Get information on the insurance claim from the Visual Basic client or HTML interface.

2. Get a claim ID number from a VSAM file on the mainframe.

3. Validate the claim against data stored in a SQL Server table.

4. Insert a claim summary record into SQL Server on Windows NT.

5. Insert a claim record into the DB2 database on the mainframe.

6. Provide a feedback message to the user.

All of the interactions take place in a single transaction, controlled by MTS. If any interaction fails, they all fail. As an example, imagine that the link to the mainframe goes down just as the claim record is being inserted into DB2. Because the DB2 component fails, all components in the interaction will fail and will be rolled back. This means that although the claim summary record was successfully inserted on Step 4, the record will be removed from the database, which is returned to the state it was in before the failed transaction took place.

Before we look at the source code, let's watch an insurance claim be inserted into the database. Figure 12-12 shows the screen used to create a new claim. Figure 12-13 shows the result of clicking the Submit button.

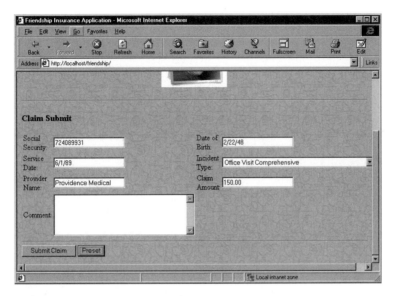

**Figure 12-12.**
*The HTML user interface for the Friendship Insurance demo.*

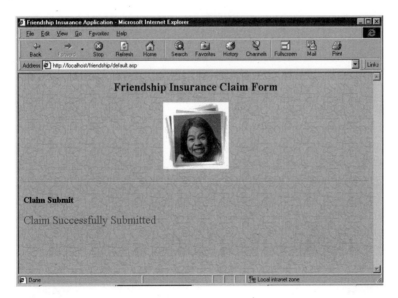

**Figure 12-13.**
*The claim was successfully submitted.*

Let's start our examination of the code by taking a detailed look at one of the COM components that interacts with CICS. Let's take a look at the source code for a component called CLAIMKEY. (Be prepared for a shock.) This component gets a claim ID number, which is just an integer that increases each time a new claim is reported.

```
*********************************************** CLAIMKEY
        IDENTIFICATION DIVISION.
        PROGRAM-ID. CLAIMKEY.


        ENVIRONMENT DIVISION.


        DATA DIVISION.


        WORKING-STORAGE SECTION.


        01   CLAIMKEY-AREA.
             02 FILLER                  PIC X(8) VALUE LOW-VALUES.
             02 CLAIM-KEY               PIC S9(9) COMP VALUE +0.


        01   CLAIMKEY-DD               PIC X(8) VALUE 'CLAIMKEY'.
        01   RESPONSE-CODE            PIC S9(9) VALUE +0.


        LINKAGE SECTION.


        01 DFHCOMMAREA.
           02   CLAIMKEY-COMMAREA.
                03   RVAL               PIC S9(9) COMP.
                03   CLAIM-NO           PIC S9(9) COMP.


        PROCEDURE DIVISION.


            EXEC CICS STARTBR
                 DATASET(CLAIMKEY-DD)
```

*(continued)*

```
                    RIDFLD(CLAIM-KEY)

                    GTEQ

                    END-EXEC.

        EXEC CICS ENDBR

                    DATASET(CLAIMKEY-DD)

                    END-EXEC.

        EXEC CICS READ UPDATE

                    DATASET(CLAIMKEY-DD)

                    INTO(CLAIMKEY-AREA)

                    LENGTH(LENGTH OF CLAIMKEY-AREA)

                    RIDFLD(CLAIM-KEY)

                    RESP(RESPONSE-CODE)

                    END-EXEC.

        ADD +1 TO CLAIM-KEY.

        EXEC CICS REWRITE

                    DATASET(CLAIMKEY-DD)

                    FROM(CLAIMKEY-AREA)

                    LENGTH(LENGTH OF CLAIMKEY-AREA)

                    RESP(RESPONSE-CODE)

                    END-EXEC.

        MOVE CLAIM-KEY TO CLAIM-NO.


        EXEC CICS RETURN

                    END-EXEC.
```

Yes, this really is the source code for a COM component. Yes, it really is written in COBOL, shocking as that might be. COMTI is a powerful technology because it allows us to take an existing CICS or IMS transaction program (TP) and make it available through COM.

COBOL programming may be as unfamiliar to some readers as Kabuki Theater is to many American tourists, so let's take a look at the program in detail. COBOL programs consist of four divisions: *identification, environment, data,* and *procedure.* The identification division specifies the PROGRAM-ID, and can also specify information about the author, version number, and so on. The environment division specifies how the computer should be set up to run the program. For example, if a specific magnetic tape needs to be mounted to run the program, that could be specified in the environment division. The data division allows us to define variables. The working-storage section defines working variables used by the program. The linkage section defines variables used to link the TP to other TPs. You can think of the linkage section as the TP's parameters. Finally, the procedure division consists of instructions that tell the TP what to do. This TP consists of five CICS commands and two COBOL instructions. The CICS commands are embedded in the COBOL, in the same way that some database programs embed SQL into a C or Pascal routine.

The first two CICS commands are STARTBR (start browse) and ENDBR (end browse). These commands open a dataset called CLAIMKEY and prepare the dataset for random access. The next CICS command is READ, which reads a record from the dataset. The UPDATE qualifier specifies that we will later update or delete the record. The INTO (CLAIMKEY-AREA) specifies that the contents of the record are loaded into the variable called CLAIMKEY-AREA. The next command is standard COBOL, and adds 1 to the variable called CLAIM-KEY. The next command is a CICS REWRITE command, which writes the record we just read. The final command is MOVE CLAIM-KEY TO CLAIM-NO, which moves the contents of the CLAIM-KEY variable to CLAIM-NO in the linkage field.

In summary, we read a record, added 1 to the last claim number we used, rewrote the record, and returned the new claim ID. Now that we understand the COBOL, how do we make it work with COM? We need to use the COMTI Component Builder's Cobol Wizard to create a component. This wizard will read the COBOL source code and create a COM component that can interface to it, without the need to write any code. Let's assume that somehow we've transferred a copy of the COBOL source code from the mainframe to our Windows NT system, and we've already used SNA Server Manager to set up some logical units and an APPC mode to allow us to communicate with the mainframe.

The process for using the wizard is fairly easy. Start by loading the Component Builder from the Start Menu. Select New from the File Menu, and the New Component Library dialog box will appear, as shown in Figure 12-14. At this stage, it's important to select the correct remote environment type. For this component, we will use CICS link.

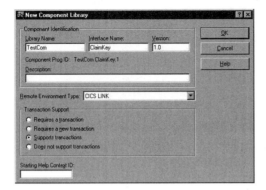

**Figure 12-14.**
*Creating a new component using the COMTI Component Builder.*

Once a component exists, we can add methods and recordsets. To use an existing COBOL file to add a method, select Import and then COBOL Wizard from the File Menu. After an introductory screen, the wizard will ask for the name of a COBOL source file. Select the source code for the CICS TP you wish to use, and click the Next Button.

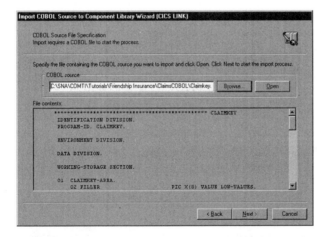

**Figure 12-15.**
*Selecting a source code file for the COBOL Wizard.*

The next step is to select a name for the new method, and the name of the corresponding TP.

459

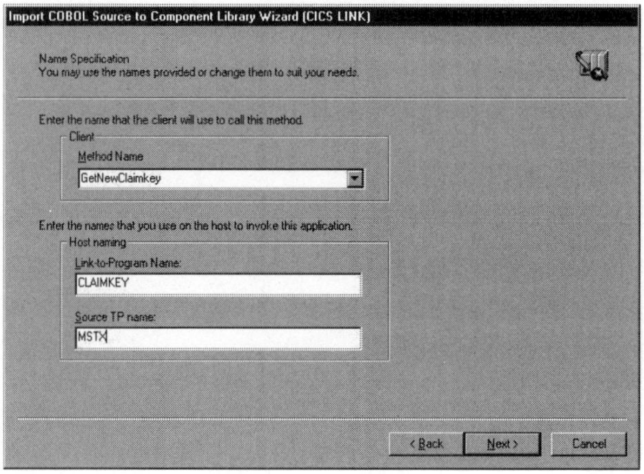

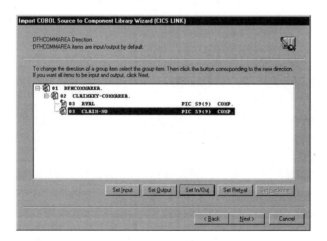

**Figure 12-16.**
*Selecting a method name.*

Once you've selected a method name, the wizard displays a series of screens that determine the component's linkage area, inputs, outputs, and return value. The wizard parses the COBOL to determine the contents of the data division, and provides simple point-and-click definition of the component. Once this task is completed, the wizard displays a final screen that lists any warnings or error messages.

**Figure 12-17.**
*Selecting the method's return value*

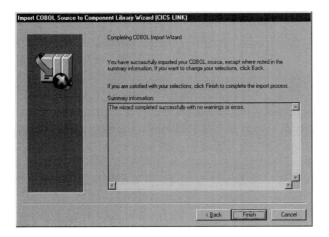

**Figure 12-18.**
*The final screen of the COBOL Wizard.*

Once the COBOL Wizard has completed, the method should be associated with the type library in the COMTI Component Builder. Once you've created as many methods and recordsets as you wish, select Save from the File Menu and save the information as a type library (.TLB) file.

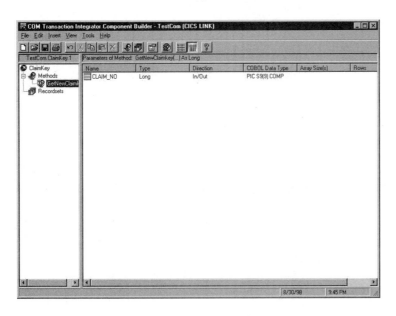

**Figure 12-19.**
*The COMTI Component Builder.*

The final step is creating the COM component is installation in Microsoft Transaction Server (MTS) and the COMTI run-time. Open the COMTI Management Console, which loads the COMTI and MTS snap-ins. If necessary, create a new MTS package to hold the component. Right-click the Components folder in the package and select New Component. Select the Install New Component button and then browse to the type library you saved in the Component Builder. This will install the new component into MTS.

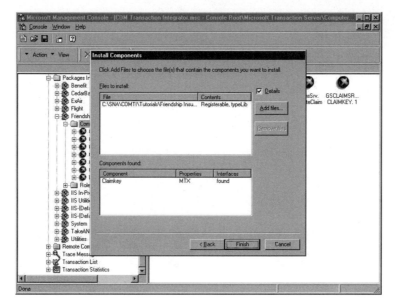

**Figure 12-20.**
*Installing the component into MTS.*

The next step is to create a new remote environment (RE) in the COMTI run-time. Go to the COMTI snap-in, and right-click the Remote Environments folder, then select a new RE. This will offer a choice of five remote environment types: diagnostic capture, diagnostic playback, IMS, CICS, and CICS link. Diagnostic capture and diagnostic playback are used for creating off-line demonstrations that do not require a mainframe. IMS is used with TPs that run in the IMS environment. The difference between CICS and CICS link is the communications mechanism on the mainframe side. When using CICS the TP must use APPC verbs to read parameters and write results. When using CICS link, the TP uses the COMMAREA as shown in the CLAIMKEY example. Because CICS link is an easier model for mainframe programmers to use, existing programs are more likely to use the CICS link model than the APPC verbs model. In this example, we will use CICS link. Once the RE type has been chosen, select the SNA parameters for the remote environment. The parameters involved are a local LU alias, remote LU alias, and mode name. (These should have been set up previously in SNA Server Manager.)

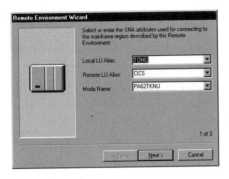

**Figure 12-21.**
*Setting the SNA parameters for a remote environment.*

The final step is to associate the component with the RE. If you only have one remote environment, the component will automatically associate with that RE. If you have multiple REs, you may need to move the component. Right-click the component in the COMTI snap-in and select Move, then select the correct RE.

Now let's look at some more familiar source code. We'll start by looking at the code that actually submits a claim. The ASP client consists of a single ASP page. It follows a popular pattern of providing both the form to enter input data and the code to process the data in a single file:

```
<html>

<head>

<meta http-equiv="Content-Type"

content="text/html; charset=iso-8859-1">

<meta name="GENERATOR"

content="Microsoft FrontPage (Internet Studio Edition) 2.0">

<title>Friendship Insurance Application</title>

</head>


<body background="images/coctail2.gif">

<p align="center"><font size="5"><strong>
```

*(continued)*

```
Friendship Insurance Claim Form
</strong></font></p>
<p align="center"><img src="Images/AnimLogo.gif" width="141"
height="139"></p>
<HR>
<h3>Claim Submit</h3>
<%
On Error Resume Next

If Request.Form("hname") = "" Then
' This part of the script allows a person
' to enter data on an HTML form.
%>

<FORM NAME="FORM"  METHOD=POST ACTION="default.asp">

<table>
<TR>
<TD>Social Security:</TD>
<TD><INPUT TYPE=TEXT NAME="SocSec"></TD>
<TD>Date of Birth:</TD>
        <TD><INPUT TYPE=TEXT NAME="DOB"></TD>
    </TR>
    <TR>
      <TD>Service Date:</TD>
      <TD><INPUT TYPE=TEXT NAME="SvcDt"></TD>
      <TD>Incident Type:</TD>
      <TD><SELECT SIZE=1 NAME="IncdntTyp">
        <option>
        <OPTION value ="92552">Audiometry
        <OPTION value ="16020">Burn Treatment
        <OPTION value ="85022">CBC
```

*(continued)*

```
<OPTION value ="93040">EKG Rhythm Strip
<OPTION value ="93000">EKG with Interpretation
<OPTION value ="92081">Eye Exam (Chart)
<OPTION value ="92082">Eye Exam (Machine)
<OPTION value ="82947">G.T.T. - 2 Hour
<OPTION value ="82953">G.T.T. - 3 Hour
<OPTION value ="82962">Glucose
<OPTION value ="85013">Hematocrit
<OPTION value ="82270">Hemoccult
<OPTION value ="10060">I & D Abscess
<OPTION value ="46083">I & D Hemorrhoid
<OPTION value ="11730">Ingrown Toenail Treatment
<OPTION value ="20610">Inject or Aspirate Knee/Hip/Shoulder
<OPTION value ="20550">Injection of Ligament/Tendon/Trigger
   Point/Small J
<OPTION value ="99075">Medical Testimony
<OPTION value ="99080">Medical Reports/Insurance Forms
<OPTION value ="99211">Office Visit Brief
<OPTION value ="99215">Office Visit Comprehensive
<OPTION value ="99214">Office Visit Extended
<OPTION value ="99213">Office Visit Intermediate
<OPTION value ="99212">Office Visit Limited
<OPTION value ="82996">Pregnancy Test(Blood)
<OPTION value ="81025">Pregnancy Test(Urine)
<OPTION value ="86280">Premarital Serology(Female)
<OPTION value ="86592">Premarital Serology(Male)
<OPTION value ="85610">Protime
<OPTION value ="85650">Sed Rate
<OPTION value ="80018">SMA 24
<OPTION value ="86403">Strep Test
<OPTION value ="12002">Suture Laceration 2.5cm - 7.5cm
<OPTION value ="12001">Suture Laceration 2.5cm or less
<OPTION value ="17499">Suture Removal
```

*(continued)*

```
                    <OPTION value ="92100">Tonometry
                    <OPTION value ="17110">Wart Remova
        </SELECT>
        </TD>
        </TR>
            <TR>
            <TD>Provider Name:</TD>
                <TD><INPUT TYPE=TEXT NAME="PrvdrNM"></TD>
                <TD>Claim Amount:</TD>
            <TD><INPUT TYPE=TEXT NAME="ClaimAmt"></TD>
        </TR>
        <TR>
                <TD>Comment:</TD>
            <TD><TEXTAREA ROWS=5 COLS=35 NAME="Cmmnt">
                </TEXTAREA></TD>
        </TR>
           </table>

           <INPUT TYPE=HIDDEN NAME="hname" VALUE="hvalue" >
        </TR>
        <HR>
           <TD><INPUT TYPE=SUBMIT VALUE="Submit Claim" NAME="btnSubmit"></TD>
           <TD><INPUT TYPE=BUTTON VALUE="Preset" NAME="btnPreset"></TD>
        </TR>
        </FORM>

        <SCRIPT LANGUAGE="VBScript">
        <!--
           dim mindex
           dim mClaimNbr
```

*(continued)*

```
Sub btnSubmit_OnClick
   call ValidateInput()
End Sub


Function ValidateInput
   mindex = document.Form.IncdntTyp.selectedIndex
   if mindex = 0 Then
      msgbox "Please select an Incident Type"
      exit function
   end if
End Function


Sub btnPreset_OnClick
   document.Form.SocSec.Value = "724089931"
   document.Form.DOB.Value = "2/22/48"
   document.Form.SvcDt.Value = "6/1/89"
   document.Form.PrvdrNM.Value = "Providence Medical"
   document.Form.ClaimAmt.Value = "150.00"
   document.Form.Cmmnt.Value = ""
End Sub
-->
</SCRIPT>


<% else

Set myobj = Server.CreateObject("PrcClaim.ProcessClaim")

msocsec = Trim(Request.Form("SocSec"))
mDOB = Trim(Request.Form("DOB"))
mincType = Trim(Request.Form("IncdntTyp"))
mSvcDt =  Trim(Request.Form("SvcDt"))
mPrvdrNM = Trim(Request.Form("PrvdrNM"))
```

*(continued)*

```
    mClaimAmt = Trim(Request.Form("ClaimAmt"))
    mCmmnt = Trim(Request.Form("Cmmnt"))


    mresult = myobj.ProcessClaim(CLng(msocsec),CStr(mSvcDt),Cstr(mDOB), _
        CLng(mincType),CStr(mPrvdrNM),CDbl(mClaimAmt),CStr(mCmmnt))


    Set myobj = Nothing


    If Err.Number = 0 Then
        'request submitted but transaction might have been aborted
        If mresult = -1 then %>


<p><font color="#FF0000" size="5" face="Times New Roman">Transaction
Rolled Back. Claim Not Submitted.</font></p>


    <%Else%>
        <%If mresult = 1 Then %>
<p><font color="#FF0000" size="5" face="Times New Roman">Invalid
Claim.  Rejection Logged.  Please Check Policy.</font></p>
        <%Else%>
<p><font color="#FF0000" size="5" face="Times New Roman">Claim
Successfully Submitted</font></p>
        <%End If
    End If
Else
    'Internal runtime error occurred%>
<p><font color="#FF0000" size="5" face="Times New Roman">
Your claim submission failed. Please contact your system
administrator.
</font></p>
```

*(continued)*

468

```
<p><font color="#FF0000" size="4" face="Times New Roman">
Description: <%=Err.Description%>
<br>
</font></p>
<INPUT TYPE=BUTTON NAME="Help" VALUE="Help...">


<script language="VBScript">
SUB Help_OnClick
   Dim desc, file, id

   desc = "<%=Left(Err.Description, Len(Err.Description)-2)%>"
   file = "<%=Err.HelpFile%>"
   id   = <%=Err.HelpContext%>

   MsgBox desc, 0, "Cedar detected a runtime error", file, id
END SUB
</script>
<%
   Err.Clear
End If
%>
<%End If%>
</CENTER>
</BODY>
</HTML>
```

The most important line in the script decides whether to display the form or
process the results:

```
If Request.Form("hname") = "" Then
```

If the *hname* field is blank, the page displays the input form. About half-way down the ASP file is an *else* statement:

```
<% else
Set myobj = Server.CreateObject("PrcClaim.ProcessClaim")
msocsec = Trim(Request.Form("SocSec"))
mDOB = Trim(Request.Form("DOB"))
mincType = Trim(Request.Form("IncdntTyp"))
mSvcDt = Trim(Request.Form("SvcDt"))
mPrvdrNM = Trim(Request.Form("PrvdrNM"))
mClaimAmt = Trim(Request.Form("ClaimAmt"))
mCmmnt = Trim(Request.Form("Cmmnt"))


mresult = myobj.ProcessClaim(CLng(msocsec),CStr(mSvcDt),Cstr(mDOB), _
    CLng(mincType),CStr(mPrvdrNM),CDbl(mClaimAmt),CStr(mCmmnt))


Set myobj = Nothing
```

This is the start of the code to process the data submitted on the form. The first step in processing is to create a ProcessClaim COM object. The ASP page then reads the data submitted on the HTML form, and calls the *ProcessClaim* method. Once the method returns, the page deallocates the object, and displays the results.

The line that does the actual processing is the call to the *ProcessClaim* method. Let's take a look at the method's source code. When you read this code, it's important to remember that it's in a separate COM object from the main program, so the only data that is available are the parameters to this routine.

```
' Name:
'     ProcessClaim
'
' Purpose:
' This is the mid-tier server component invoked by base clients
' (VB and ASP) to perform all claims processing.
```

*(continued)*

```
' Includes routines for creating all ClaimSrv objects (NT) and all COMTI
' objects (Mainframe), and for invoking the methods on these objects that
' perform the various database operations. Controls the outcome of
' transactions by using Set.Abort and Set.Complete within the transaction
' context.
'
' Includes ability to artificially force a transaction to abort so that
' true rollback can be demonstrated. This situation is triggered by the
' user entering "Chicago Hope" for the health service provider.
'
' Returns:
' 0 = Successful
' 1 = Claim rejected based on business rules, transaction succeeded
' -1 = Tranaction aborted
'
' Side Effects:
' Transaction modifies state of claims databases on DB2 and SQL Server
' and also updates VSAM data set containing the next claim number

Public Function ProcessClaim(lngCustSSN As Long, _
    dtmDateOfService As String, dtmDateOfBirth As String, _
    szIncident As Long, szProvider As String, _
    curAmount As Double, szComment As String) As Long

    'Get Object Context so can manage transaction outcome
    Set ctxObject = GetObjectContext()

    glngCustSSN = lngCustSSN
    gdtmDateOfService = CDate(dtmDateOfService)
    gdtmDateOfBirth = CDate(dtmDateOfBirth)
    gszIncCode = CStr(szIncident)
    gcurAmount = CCur(curAmount)
```

*(continued)*

471

```
gszProvider = szProvider
gszComment = szComment

'Initialize return value for success case
ProcessClaim = 0

'Allow all Automation Errors to take us to ErrorHandler
'(comment out if want errors to flow through)
'On Error GoTo ErrorHandler

'Convert Dates for use with DB2
gdtmMFDateProcessed = Format(Date, "yyyy-mm-dd-hh.mm.ss.sss")
gdtmMFDateOfService = Format(dtmDateOfService, _
   "yyyy-mm-dd-hh.mm.ss.sss")
gdtmMFDateOfBirth = Format(dtmDateOfBirth, _
   "yyyy-mm-dd-hh.mm.ss.sss")

' Assign a claim number via a CICS/VSAM mainframe program
If (AssignClaimNumber()) = False Then
   GoTo ErrorHandler
End If

' Check claim for validity against policy guidelines
If (ValidateClaimField()) = False Then
   gszStatus = "Claim Rejected"
   If (InsertClaimSummary()) = False Then
     GoTo ErrorHandler
   End If
   If (InsertRejectedClaim()) = False Then
     GoTo ErrorHandler
   End If
```

*(continued)*

```
      ' Claim is rejected for business reasons and recorded
      'as such, but all database actions succeeded.
      ProcessClaim = 1
  Else
      'claim is valid
      gszStatus = "Claim OK"
      ' Insert a claim summary record in SQL Server Claims database
      If (InsertClaimSummary()) = False Then
          GoTo ErrorHandler
      End If
      ' Insert a claim record in DB2 database under CICS
      If (InsertClaim()) = False Then
          GoTo ErrorHandler
      End If
  End If


  If Not ctxObject Is Nothing Then
      If gszProvider = "Chicago Hope" Then
      ' force a transaction abort on this condition (demo)
          GoTo ErrorHandler
      Else
      ' otherwise we are finished and happy
      ctxObject.SetComplete
      End If
      Set ctxObject = Nothing
  End If


  Exit Function


  ErrorHandler:
  If Not ctxObject Is Nothing Then
      ' we are unhappy with the outcome
```

*(continued)*

```
        ctxObject.SetAbort
        ' return value indicates transaction aborted
        ProcessClaim = -1
        Set ctxObject = Nothing
    End If


End Function
```

The function starts by setting global variables to avoid passing parameters to each routine it calls. The first of the mainframe interactions takes place in a routine called *AssignClaimNumber()*:

```
' Assign a claim number via a CICS/VSAM mainframe program
If (AssignClaimNumber()) = False Then
GoTo ErrorHandler
```

Let's take a look at the source code for *AssignClaimNumber()*:

```
' Name:
'  AssignClaimNumber
'
' Purpose:
'  This private function creates and uses an MTS/COMTI object to obtain a
'  unique claim number by using a VSAM file, under CICS, as a persistent
'  store.  This function is located on the mainframe because the assumption
'  is that it is used by other mainframe programs that are still 3270-
'  based, and must provide a shared service.
'
' Returns:
'  True =    Successful
'  False =   Failed
'
' Side Effects:
```

*(continued)*

```
' Assigns a claim number value to global variable glngClaimNo
' Creates and destroys an MTS object
'

Private Function AssignClaimNumber() As Boolean

    Dim lRet As Long

    AssignClaimNumber = True
    Dim obj As Object

    If Not ctxObject Is Nothing Then
        Set obj = ctxObject.CreateInstance("CLAIMSRV1.CLAIMKEY.1")
    Else
        Set obj = CreateObject("CLAIMSRV1.CLAIMKEY.1")
    End If

    If obj Is Nothing Then
        MsgBox "Create object ClaimsSrv.ClaimKey or " & _
            "CLAIMSRV1.CLAIMKEY.1 failed."
        AssignClaimNumber = False
        Exit Function
    End If

    glngClaimNo = 0
    lRet = obj.GetNewClaimKey(glngClaimNo)
    If lRet < 0 Then
        AssignClaimNumber = False
    End If

End Function
```

Again, the code is reasonably simple. It creates a CLAIMKEY object, and then calls the object's *GetNewClaimKey* method, passing a variable that is used to store the claim key number. We already saw how to create the CLAIMKEY component, so we've now seen the entire process for an interaction with CICS. The interaction started in ASP, called a middle tier component in VB, then called through SNA Server to a mainframe TP, and finally used data stored in a VSAM file on the mainframe.

There are actually a total of six components that are installed by the demonstration. The ProcessClaim component encapsulates the business logic for processing the claim. ClaimKey interacts with VSAM. InsertClaim and InsertRejectedClaim interact with DB2. ValidateClaim implements some business logic for validating a claim's details. InsertClaimSummary inserts a claim summary record in a Microsoft SQL Server database running on Windows NT. We won't take the space to go through each component in detail here. We recommend that you examine the sample if you want to see the complete code.

Let's take a look at another line from the *ProcessClaim()* method. This method interacts with MTS to provide the ACID transaction properties. If all goes well, the following line will commit the transaction:

```
Else
    ' otherwise we are finished and happy
    ctxObject.SetComplete
End If
```

To ensure transactional integrity, you will need to set the transactional properties of the components in the MTS Explorer. The ProcessClaim component is the first component called when a new claim is submitted, so it should be set to "Requires a New Transaction." The ValidateClaim component simply determines if the claim is valid but does not write to the database. It does not call SetComplete(), and should be set to "Does not Support Transactions." Each of the other components is called from within ProcessClaim() and interacts with a database on the mainframe or Windows NT. In each case, they should be set to "Requires a Transaction" to ensure that they can roll back if the transaction fails. Once these transactional properties are set, if any of the transactions fails, the entire transaction will fail.

Although it took several pages to describe the process of building a COMTI component, the process of running the wizards is fairly easy. However, don't assume that implementing COMTI will be trivial. We recommend that you should have four sets of skills on the team to implement this product:

- SNA and VTAM experience

- CICS or IMS application development experience

- SNA Server and Windows NT networking experience

- COM application development experience

You may find a mainframe expert who has both CICS and VTAM experience, and you may find a Windows NT expert who can handle Back Office and COM issues, but you are very unlikely to find a single person who can provide all four sets of skills. Legacy systems projects demand multi-disciplinary teams. You will want to ensure good communications between the application developers and the production team managing the mainframe.

Another issue you should consider when implementing COMTI is the requirement for well-structured code on the mainframe side. If you have spaghetti code on the mainframe, COMTI may be difficult to implement. Specifically, it is much easier to implement COMTI if there is a separation between business logic and display logic. IBM has been recommending this split for several years, but CICS programmers have not always heeded the call. If the same TP implements both business logic and display, you may have to be prepared for some modifications on the mainframe side. If these modifications are impossible, you may have to resort to screen-scraping.

## Message-Oriented Middleware

Chapter 9, Improving the Performance and Reliability of Enterprise Applications with Microsoft Message Queue Server (MSMQ)," introduced the Microsoft Message Queue Server (MSMQ). In this section, we'll take a brief look at using message-oriented middleware, known by the friendly acronym MOM, to link to legacy systems. We'll focus on two products, MQSeries from IBM and Falcon MQ from Level 8 Software. MQSeries can be used by itself to provide a link between Windows NT and legacy systems. Another approach is to run MSMQ on Windows NT, and use Falcon MQ to link to legacy systems.

This section is not a complete survey of the MOM marketplace. Important MOM products we don't mention include BEA MessageQ from BEA Systems, Inc., which provides interoperability between UNIX, Windows NT, OpenVMS, and mainframe systems. Other UNIX MOM products include Communications

477

Integrator from Covia Technologies and QuickSilver/MW from Data Research and Applications, Inc. For more MOM information, check out the Message-Oriented Middleware Association at http://www.moma-inc.org/.

### MQSeries

One of the most widely used MOM products is MQSeries from IBM. First shipped in 1994, MQSeries runs on a wide range of platforms. These include AIX, AT&T GIS UNIX, Digital Open VMS, DYNIX, HP-UX, Mac OS, MS-DOS, MVS/ESA, OS/2, OS/400, SINIX DC/OS, Sun Solaris, Tandem NonStop Kernel, UnixWare, VSE/ESA, Windows NT, Windows 95, and Windows 3.x. MQSeries provides many of the same advantages as MSMQ and other MOM products, including:

- **Guaranteed delivery and fault tolerance**   MQSeries guarantees message delivery. If a system or WAN link goes down, messages will wait in the queue until the recipient comes back up.

- **Decoupling**   A sending application can continue working even when the destination application is offline.

- **System independence**   Because MQSeries can support multiple systems, applications can communicate across platforms without modification for new destination systems.

- **Protocol independence**   MQSeries can support multiple network protocols with changing the application.

- **Simplified programming**   The MQI API allows program-to-program communication with relatively little application code.

MQSeries provides a common API across all platforms, the Message Queue Interface (MQI). This allows messaging routines to be transferred between platforms. An MQSeries application needs to connect to a queue manager before it can make any other MQI calls. When an application connects, it receives a connection handle. Because an application can connect to only one queue manager at a time, it can hold only one connection handle at a time. The queue manager an application connects to is referred to as the *local queue manager*.

Once a connection has been made to a queue manager, the application will open a queue. If the application will read a queue, it will open the queue for getting. If the application will write to a queue, it will open the queue for putting. If the application will do both, it may open the queue for both getting and putting. Opening a queue returns an object handle that acts as a reference to the queue.

Once the object handle is open, the application can call MQPUT() to put a message on the queue, or MQGET() to read a message from the queue. Typically, different applications connected to different queue managers will open the queue, and the queue managers will transfer messages between themselves. For example, an e-commerce Web application on Windows NT might communicate with a purchase order application on a mainframe or AS/400. Each program would open a queue manager on the local machine and the queue managers would communicate.

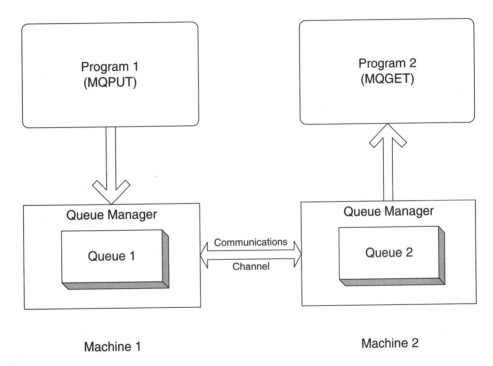

**Figure 12-22.**
*MQSeries Architecture.*

Because of its support for Windows NT, OS/400, and MVS/ESA, MQSeries provides a potential solution for integration between Web applications based on Windows NT and legacy systems. This solution is not appropriate for applications that require data lookup, such as providing information from a database table on an ASP page. However, for systems that need to update legacy systems, MQSeries could be a superb solution. As an example, consider an e-commerce system that accepts customer orders and needs to interact with purchase order software on a mainframe. If an MQSeries interface to the mainframe software is available or can be written, the e-commerce application can continue to accept orders irrespective of the status of the mainframe. Even if the mainframe goes down overnight for maintenance, the e-commerce application can keep rolling.

Although there are many other MOM products, IBM has been the main player in the creation of a market for MOM and MQSeries is currently the clear market leader. The battle between MQSeries and MSMQ will be a struggle of titans. Products like CICS, MQSeries, MTS, and MSMQ are at the heart of enterprise systems, and the winner of this battle will be the dominant power in enterprise applications in the early years of the twenty-first century.

## Level 8 Software

Microsoft recommends FalconMQ from Level 8 Systems (http://www.level8.com/) for interoperability of MSMQ with non-Windows platforms. There are two products in the FalconMQ suite: FalconMQ client and FalconMQ Bridge. FalconMQ Client provides access to MSMQ from non-Windows systems. FalconMQ Bridge allows applications using MSMQ to communicate with applications using IBM MQSeries.

FalconMQ Client provides an MSMQ dependent client on non-Windows platforms. It runs on UNIX, VMS, AS/400, MVS, and Unisys ClearPath HMP. The FalconMQ Client supports C, CICS, and COBOL. By providing an MSMQ API on non-Windows platforms, FalconMQ Client allows developers to extend their distributed applications to non-Windows platforms. As an example, an application written in Visual Basic on NT can use MSMQ to communicate with an application written in COBOL under MVS that uses FalconMQ Client. FalconMQ Client consists of two pieces: the client and the server. The client is installed on the non-Windows system. The server is installed on a Windows NT computer running MSMQ and listens for messages from the client.

FalconMQ Bridge communicates with all systems that support IBM MQSeries. It allows applications on Windows NT that use MSMQ to communicate with applications on other systems that use MQSeries. FalconMQ Bridge is installed on a Windows NT system running MSMQ. In addition, it requires IBM's MQSeries NT Client to be installed on the Windows NT system. Because the FalconMQ Bridge has both MSMQ and MQSeries available, it can translate messages from MSMQ to MQSeries and vice-versa. Because it uses MQSeries for communication with the non-Windows NT system, it can support any platform that is supported by MQSeries. FalconMQ Bridge has algorithms for ensuring transactional integrity between MSMQ and MQSeries. For example, it will not transmit messages to MQSeries until the MSMQ transaction is committed.

## DCOM on the Mainframe

Chapter 2, "Defining the Web Application Environment," introduced DCOM, Microsoft's technology for building distributed applications by distributing components. Although DCOM is seen by many as an "NT-only solution," that is an inaccurate perception. In fact, Microsoft has been encouraging vendors to implement DCOM on a wide variety of platforms, including UNIX and mainframes. A leading player in this arena is Software AG Americas (http://www.sagus.com/), whose DCOM For The Enterprise (DCOM FTE) product provides DCOM capabilities on OS/390 systems. (Support is also available for Sun Solaris, Digital UNIX, and Linux.)

SOFTWARE AG licensed the DCOM source code from Microsoft and ported it to OS/390. The port provides all the non-GUI portions of COM/OLE. This includes COM support for instantiating and using objects as well as structured storage, monikers, OLE automation, custom marshaling, connectable objects, and uniform data transfer. Drag and drop, in-place activation and other such functions require the GUI and are not provided. TCP/IP can be used as the network protocol, or the product can be combined with the Entire-NETWORK product from Software AG to support additional protocols.

Typically, a project that uses DCOM on the mainframe will involve the creation of objects that encapsulate business rules and data access as described in Chapter 7, "Addressing Performance and Scalability." These components will be created in either C++ or Java, and the COM sections will look very similar to COM components created on Windows NT. Other parts of the program will use OS/390 tools for data access and transactional integrity. Unlike COMTI, which did not require new code on the mainframe, components must be specially created in order to use DCOM. Typically, DCOM on the mainframe is most useful when additional programming is required to wrap mainframe transactions or when new business logic needs to be implemented.

Another difference between DCOM on the mainframe and COMTI is cost. Because COMTI does not require additional software on the mainframe, the only cost is a license for Microsoft SNA Server. In October 1997, the minimum cost for the Software AG product on OS/390 was $200,000.

DCOM has already been covered earlier in the book. We won't repeat the example code here, as the ASP code to create an object is independent of the machine where the object is created. As before, the CreateObject call in ASP will be handled on the client machine by the Service Control Manager (SCM). The client system SCM will determine from the class ID and Registry that the server is a RemoteServer32. The SCM will respond by making a remote procedure call (RPC) to the mainframe's SCM, requesting the creation of an object. The mainframe SCM creates the object, which calls CoInitialize to advertise its existence to DCOM. A proxy for the object is created on the client machine, and a pointer to the proxy is returned to the client application. Calls by the client will be marshaled to the mainframe, but will appear to the client to be simple calls to a local object.

The Software AG product is an important step along the road to bringing mainframe systems into the COM world. Their key to success will be to continue supporting new Microsoft technologies such as message queuing and transactions.

Other non-Windows NT implementations of DCOM include a COM to CORBA interoperability product from Iona Technologies (http://www.iona.com/). OrbixCOMet combines both the COM and CORBA distributed object models to provide bi-directional integration. This product can be integrated with Orbix for MVS to provide COM access to CORBA objects running in the MVS environment. Iona plans to link their OrbixOTM middleware with MTS to allow transactions that span MTS and OrbixOTM. Visual Edge (http://www.visualedge.com/) has also licensed the DCOM software and provides another interoperability solution between COM and CORBA. Compaq's Digital Products Division also provides a DCOM implementation for OpenVMS (http://www.openvms.digital.com/openvms/products/dcom/index.html/).

MainWin XDE 3.1 from Mainsoft (http://www.mainsoft.com/) provides a Win32 development environment on UNIX systems. By using the MainSoft product, you can develop applications for Win32 and then move them to UNIX simply by recompiling. This product provides yet another implementation of DCOM on a non-Microsoft platform.

## Summary

In this chapter we took a look at several ways to access legacy systems. We looked at examples of COMTI and OLE DB and discussed several other data access methods. When deciding which access method to use you need to answer some questions:

- What currently exists on the legacy system?
- Should real-time access or snapshot replication be used?
- Should new business logic be written on the legacy system, or should existing components be reused?

The answers will lead you to the correct technology. If you need to use CICS or IMS transactions, use COMTI. If you need real-time access to DB2, use StarSQL. If you need snapshot access to DB2, use Host Data Replicator. If you need real-time access to AS/400 or VSAM, use OLE DB DDM Provider. If you need replication from AS/400, use Symbiator. If you need replication from VSAM, use DDMFTP. If you need to interface to MQSeries, use Falcon MQ. Finally, if you need to create new code on MVS, OS/390, or any other platform, consider using DCOM. Although we have described many technologies, careful consideration of the requirements will usually lead to the correct tool.

Microsoft and the other vendors are not finished with their work in this area. Microsoft's SNA Server Group has recently been renamed the Enterprise Interoperability Group, and we expect some interesting announcements from Redmond after this book goes to press. The tools for creating heterogeneous applications continue to become easier to use, and the possibilities for access to legacy and other systems grow with each announcement. We are in an era of enterprise-wide information systems, and there are going to be some fascinating projects that combine Web technology with legacy systems.

## CHAPTER THIRTEEN

# Response Time

### • • • GOAL: Improve User Perception of Performance by Reducing User Wait Time, and Managing User Expectations

Response Time. Depending on the application, it can be cause for celebration or cause for mourning. The funny thing about response time is that the less attention it gets, the happier you'll be, because the only time you're likely to hear about it is when someone's complaining.

Don't be fooled by the fact that we've waited to cover response time until the second-to-last chapter. That's no reflection on its importance to your application. Response time—particularly when it's not particularly good—can be one of the single most important factors in how your users perceive the performance of your application.

Users don't know what's going on behind the scenes of your application, and what's more…*they don't care*. Your users want to know that when they fill out a form and click the submit button, the application's going to respond. Unfortunately, due to a number of factors, the application doesn't always respond as quickly as users expect. And if the application feels slow to the user, then it *is* slow, no matter how much work is going on behind the scenes. In this chapter, we'll discuss some of the primary causes of poor response time, which include:

- Poorly Optimized Queries
- Resource Contention
- Poor Component Implementation
- Hardware Issues

After which, we'll go on to suggest strategies and techniques for resolving the problems that can cause poor response time.

# Causes of Poor Response Time

Poor response time is caused by a number of factors. Your job, as a developer dealing with poor response time, is to discover which factors are behind the poor response time of your application, and take the appropriate steps to remedy the problem. In the next several sections, we'll discuss some of the more frequent culprits.

## Poorly Optimized or Inefficient Queries

The database is generally the first place people look when response time becomes an issue, and for very good reason. It is often the database that is responsible for response time problems. The challenge is identifying *where* in the database the problem resides. Many developers, when confronted with less than acceptable response time, immediately start looking at what indexes they can add to their tables to help the query processor speed up their queries. Unfortunately, what they often fail to take into account is that the problem may occur long before the query begins to execute.

### Dynamically Generated SQL Strings

One of the most common ways of accessing data from scripts or components is to generate SQL query strings dynamically based on user input. Why? Because it's easy, and because lots of people know how to do it. And because old habits die hard. Unfortunately, dynamic SQL strings are generally poor performers when compared to stored procedures. Whenever you perform a query with a dynamic SQL string, that string must be packaged up, sent over the network to the database, then parsed and compiled (SQL Server will also generate a query plan), and finally executed. The extra required steps of parsing and compiling the query can add up quickly, particularly in a multi-user application.

### Inefficient Stored Procedure Use

Just as one should avoid coarse-grained components as described in Chapter 8, "Enterprise Development Using Microsoft Transaction Server," the same guidelines should be applied to your stored procedures. Just because you *can* put a great deal of programmatic logic and control-of-flow coding into a stored procedure doesn't mean that you *should*. The more complex you make your stored procedures, and the more tasks you ask an individual stored procedure to perform, the longer those stored procedures will take to execute, which will result in poorer response time. Granted, the difference in a single execution of the stored procedure may not even be noticeable, but when you multiply it by the number of users you have to support, you may find that is makes a substantial difference.

Another common mistake is using ODBC call syntax when calling stored procedures from ADO, as shown in the following code:

```
"{call sp_get_Reservation_id (" & CStr(vReservationID) & ")}"
```

We ran into this issue in the sample application for the same reason that there are instances of the use of dynamically created SQL strings in the sample application: because it's what people know. Even though ADO has been out for more than a year now, it is still somewhat foreign to many developers. ADO offers a more efficient method of calling stored procedures, particularly when there are parameters involved. We'll discuss the preferred method of calling stored procedures from ADO in Chapter 14, "Optimizing Data Access."

## Resource Contention

Resource contention can be broken down into several areas:

- **Locking Issues**   When two or more users are attempting to access a row that has been locked by another query.

- **Database Connections**   When the maximum number of database connections has been reached and further connections are refused.

- **Memory Use**   When the maximum amount of memory allotted for use by the DBMS has been reached because of queries requiring substantial use of temporary tables or cursors.

- **Processor Time**   When the demands of the DBMS (and other software on the same machine) are greater than the processor can service efficiently.

Whether resource contention results from users or programs contending for limited resources, the result is usually a reduction in performance and response time.

## Locking Issues

Locking issues are caused when a query, particularly a long-running query, locks a substantial number of rows or pages in a table. As long as that query is running, other queries against that table will be limited depending on the type of lock. In Microsoft SQL Server there are three basic types of locks, *shared locks*, *update locks*, and *exclusive locks* (note that in SQL Server 6.5, the smallest lock available is a page lock).

Shared locks are generally used by SQL server during operations that do not update data, such as SELECT queries. Shared locks allow others to read the locked pages (and to establish shared locks or update locks), but do not allow updates (exclusive locks).

SQL Server uses update locks on pages it intends to modify during a query. Before the pages are actually modified, this type of lock will be upgraded to an exclusive lock. Update locks prevent others from establishing either an update lock or an exclusive lock on the affected pages. Others can still read the affected pages (and establish shared locks). An update lock cannot be upgraded to an exclusive lock until all shared locks on the affected pages have been released.

Exclusive locks are used by SQL Server to lock pages during modifications made by UPDATE, INSERT, and DELETE queries. Exclusive locks prevent others from establishing *any* lock on the affected pages.

Figure 13-1 illustrates two situations in which shared locks can cause blocking. In the upper half of the figure, User 1 establishes a shared lock on several pages containing rows from the rental table (1). Next, User 2 attempts to establish an update lock on the rental table (2). Since shared locks and update locks are compatible, this works fine. Finally, User 2 attempts to promote the update lock to an exclusive lock in order to perform the delete operation (3). Unfortunately, User 2 cannot do this, because User 1 is still holding a shared lock, which is incompatible with an exclusive lock.

In the lower half of Figure 13-1, User 1 establishes an update lock on the rental table (1). Next, User 2 attempts to establish a shared lock on the rental table (2). Since an update lock will allow a shared lock to be established, this works fine. Finally, User 1 attempts to promote the update lock to an exclusive lock (3). The attempt fails because User 2 is still holding a shared lock on the rental table, which will not allow an exclusive lock to be established.

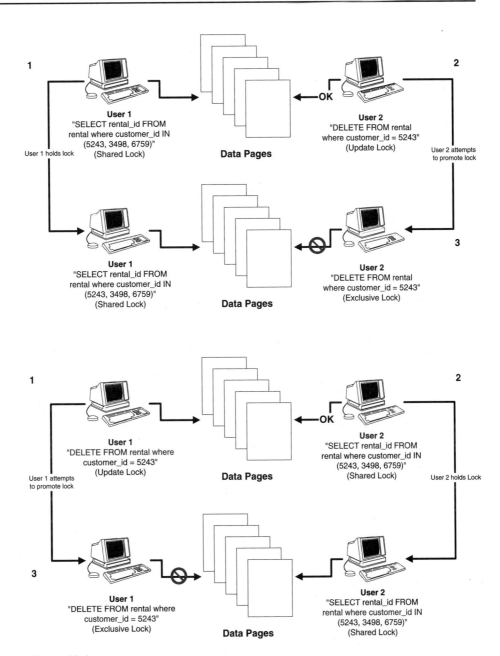

**Figure 13-1.**
*Locking in Microsoft SQL Server 6.5.*

489

What you will hopefully see from the above description is that even if you don't explicitly implement locks in your queries, SQL Server does it for you. Unfortunately, there are times when you may not need the level of locking SQL server provides. For example, let's say we want the Rent-A-Prize application to provide a count of all the reservations for a particular location in the next month. This query could potentially affect a large number of rows, which increases the likelihood that a locking conflict could occur if another user needs to update one of the affected rows. In this situation, it might be a good idea to weigh the necessity for absolutely up-to-date information against the cost of locking conflicts. If it is acceptable that updates may occur while the data is being read, the NOLOCK statement instructs SQL Server not to establish a lock during the query, reducing the potential for conflicts.

One piece of good news on the locking front is that while in SQL Server 6.5 you're stuck with page-level locking other than for inserts, in SQL Server 7.0, the smallest lock available will be a row-level lock. This will substantially reduce the impact of locking issues on applications using SQL Server 7.0.

## Database Connections

Most DBMSs, Microsoft SQL Server included, only allow a certain number of simultaneous connections to be established. Determining this number is a two-fold issue. First, you can only configure the number of connections for which you own licenses. The second, more practical issue is that you should only configure the number of connections that your server hardware can support (the memory overhead for each connection in Microsoft SQL Server is approximately 40K, in Oracle approximately 2MB).

It should be clear by now that for an application with a user base of thousands, or tens of thousands, and particularly for an application that is available over the Internet, it is neither practical nor in extreme cases possible to allot a database connection for each user of the application. Nor would this practice be efficient, since you would be spending a lot of money and using a lot of resources for database connections that would be underutilized except during peak use.

The problem is that if you don't have enough connections, some of your users are either going to have unacceptably long wait times, or may not be able to get into the application at all.

## Memory Allocation

In Microsoft SQL Server, the amount of memory allocated to SQL Server must be, at a minimum, sufficient for static memory needs (such as SQL kernel memory and connection overhead) and for the procedure cache and data cache. The *procedure cache* is used to store the most recently used stored procedures, while the *data cache* is used to store the most recently retrieved data pages. If the stored procedure being called or the data being queried cannot be found in the cache, it is read from disk.

As you probably already know, reading from disk is substantially slower than reading from memory, from which it follows that memory allocation can have a huge effect on the response time of your application.

### Processor Time

In Windows NT (and Windows 95 and 98, for that matter) processor time is allocated to all running programs in chunks called *time slices*. If we assume that all of these time slices are allocated evenly (a simplification for this example), then it is reasonable to assume that the more programs there are running on a given machine, the fewer time slices a given program will be allocated over a given period of time. This is an important concept to understand, because the upshot of it is that if your DBMS is running on a server with a number of other programs running on it, the DBMS has to compete with those other programs for processor time.

Competing for processor time may not be a major problem in smaller applications, but for scalable enterprise Web applications, it is definitely something to be aware of. Running your DBMS on the same machine as your Web server, for example, is asking for trouble.

## Poor Component Implementation

Components, as discussed in Chapter 8, "Enterprise Development Using Microsoft Transaction Server," should be fine-grained in order to be most efficient. If you write methods that perform multiple, complex tasks (a property of coarse-grained components), your response time will suffer (as will the reusability of your code). We'll talk about the role of components in improving response time in the section entitled, "Understand Component Issues."

## Hardware Issues

Three basic hardware issues can affect your response time:

- Processor Speed (and number of processors)
- Memory
- Disk Subsystem

All three of these issues should be addressed both when you are designing your application in the first place, and if you run into problems with performance and response time. We've already described some of the problems related to insufficient processor power and memory. The server's disk subsystem can also make a difference in the response time of your application, since whether you're talking about a database server or a Web server, the data and files used by your application are going to need to be read from (and written to) disk at some point during the application. How often this happens is in part a product of how much memory is installed on the system, but it's a good bet that if your disk subsystem is exceptionally slow, there will be a price to be paid in application performance (or lack thereof).

# Ways to Improve Response Time

As you can see, there are an awful lot of factors that can cause problems with response time. Fortunately for us, there are also a lot of ways to improve response time, which we'll discuss in the following sections.

## Optimize Database Queries

Poorly optimized (or not at all optimized) queries can be the bane of any application. And since the problem often exists within the application itself rather than the database, these queries are often overlooked by developers trying to improve the response time of their application. Suggested solutions for improving response time through query optimization include:

- **Use Stored Procedures** Stored procedures offer major performance gains, increased flexibility, and can also be used for increased security.

- **Use Batches Where Stored Procedures Aren't Possible** When it's not possible to use stored procedures, batching of SQL statements can offer substantial performance improvements.

- **Efficient Locking** Using the most efficient locking for your queries can help prevent deadlocks, which can kill your application.

- **Indexing** Although there are costs associated with overuse, the proper use of indexes can significantly reduce the time necessary to process certain queries.

All of the above optimization solutions are important and should be considered as a part of your overall data-access optimization strategy. We'll look at these solutions in greater detail in Chapter 14, "Optimizing Data Access."

## Use Resource Pooling

The obvious solution to the problem of contention for scarce resources such as database connections is for applications to open connections as late as possible and close them as early as possible. Modifying your application in this way can immediately reduce the number of concurrent database connections at any given time. Unfortunately, this method also has an inherent problem, which is that database connections tend to be very expensive to open. This means that some of the improvement in response time due to reducing contention for connections is eaten up by the cost of repeatedly opening the connection to the database.

Fortunately, there is also a solution for this problem: resource pooling. *Resource pooling* is a process by which a resource manager maintains scarce and/or expensive resources (such as database connections) in a pool for use by multiple users. When a user closes a resource, the resource manager intercepts the close request before the resource is closed and puts the resource into the pool instead of closing it. When a new resource request comes in, the resource manager looks in the pool to see if a resource with the properties requested exists in the pool. If one does, the resource manager fetches it out of the pool and hands it to the requester. If no matching resource exists, it is created in the normal fashion. Since the cost of getting a resource from the pool is substantially less than that of creating a new resource, the problem of getting resources late and releasing them early is effectively solved. Keep in mind that since resource pooling relies on the concept of finding resources in the pool whose properties match those being requested, you should make your use of pooled resources distinct connection strings used by your application(s), the less likely it is that your application will be able to use a connection from the pool.

## ODBC Connection Pooling

In ODBC connection pooling, which is provided by IIS 3.0 and 4.0, IIS acts as the resource manager. When an application requests a database connection, one of three things happens:

1. If the connection pool is empty, a new connection is created.

2. If there are connections in the connection pool and one of the available connection's properties (UserID, Password, Server, and so forth) match the request, then the connection from the pool will be used.

3. If there are connections in the pool, but none match the requested properties, a new connection with the appropriate properties is created.

ODBC connection pooling is enabled by default in IIS 4.0, but must be enabled manually in IIS 3.0. To enable connection pooling in IIS 3.0, change the setting *StartConnectionPool* in the registry key HKEY_LOCAL_MACHINE\ System\CurrentControlSet\Services\W3SVC\ (cont'd) ASP\ Parameters from 0 to 1.

NOTE: Editing the System Registry can cause serious system-wide problems. Before editing the Registry, make sure to make a backup using the utilities provided by Windows NT.

### Microsoft Transaction Server (MTS)

Microsoft Transaction Server is also capable of acting as a resource manager for ODBC connections for the components it serves, which means that components running under MTS can also take advantage of connection pooling. In addition to ODBC connection pooling, MTS uses a sort of faux resource pooling to provide less expensive access to components. In this method, when a user (or program) requests a component, MTS intercepts the request and instead provides an object that appears to the client to be the component, but is in fact a wrapper for the component. This wrapper allows the user to access all of the methods and properties exposed by the component. When the user signals that they are finished with the component, MTS is free to hand the component over to another user to fulfill their request. Because all the original user (or program) holds is a wrapper object, it can hold that object throughout its life.

This concept is important, since it is the exact opposite of database connections: In connection pooling, you should always open connections as late as possible and close them as early as possible. Using components with MTS, you should create components as early as possible and destroy them only when you are *completely* finished with them. For a more detailed discussion of MTS resource pooling issues, see Chapter 8, "Enterprise Development Using Microsoft Transaction Server (MTS)."

## Understand Component Issues

How you implement components (both off-the-shelf components such as ADO and custom components you create) in your application can have a major effect on response time. Three of the major areas that typically cause problems with component use are:

- Using the incorrect threading model for components called from ASP
- Component granularity
- Use of out-of-process components

494

## Know the Implication of Threading Models

As we discussed in Chapter 7, "Performance and Scalability," the ASP session and application objects impose certain restrictions on components stored within them. Components that are either single-threaded or apartment-threaded should not be stored as session- or application-level object variables. For better performance, it is recommended that you do not use single-threaded components within your ASP pages (unless you are running the component in MTS).

In addition to observing these restrictions for your custom-built components, you must also be aware of them in terms of components such as ADO. If for some reason you need to store an ADO object in a session- or application-level object variable, you must make sure the ADO components are marked as free-threaded in the Registry. When installed, ADO is marked as apartment-threaded by default, to allow you to work with Microsoft Access databases (if ADO is marked as free-threaded, ADO will not work with Microsoft Access databases). If you do not need to work with Access databases, you can change ADO's threading model using a Registry patch named ADOFre*XX*.reg (where *XX* is the version of ADO installed). Simply double-click the file, which is located in the ADO installation folder (by default *C:\Program files\Common files\ System\ADO*), then reboot the machine. If you later find that you *do* need to work with Microsoft Access, you can reverse the process with the patch named *ADOAptXX.reg*.

Keep in mind that this is another area where even though you *can* do something (in this case storing ADO objects in session or application variables), doesn't mean that you *should*. There are a couple of pitfalls to storing ADO objects in this way. The first is that passing an open connection around using session or application variables is usually less efficient than connection pooling (assuming of course that your database driver supports connection pooling). The second, and potentially more problematic if you are not expecting it is that if your connection gets dropped unexpectedly, it could cause hard-to-diagnose errors.

## Keep Components Fine-Grained

If it seems like we are over-emphasizing the importance of fine-grained components in this book, there's a very good reason for it. Fine-grained components can be key to some of the most important things you're looking for from your application: performance, scalability, and reusability.

Fine-grained components perform and scale better because they use simple methods that perform a single well-defined task (or as close to a single task as possible), then return control to the calling application. The more quickly and more frequently your components return control to the calling application, the better. The calling application can combine the available methods from all of the components that make up the application to perform more complex tasks without being tied to an execution sequence defined in (and controlled by) a component.

The same factor of using methods that perform a single task makes these components much more reusable. A component that deals with rental records for the Rent-A-Prize application could have an *Add* method, whose sole purpose is to accept the required information for a row in the rental table, and insert that information into the table. If that information needed to be validated before being inserted in the table, a fine-grained component would implement the validation as a separate method. This would allow clients that perform validation locally to make use of the Add method without having to waste time on validation logic they don't need (see Figure 13-2).

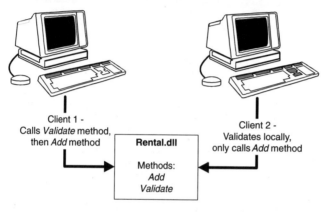

**Fine-grained component**

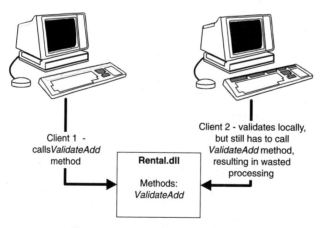

**Coarse-grained component**

**Figure 13-2.**
*Reusability in fine-grained components.*

### Use Out-of-Process Components Sparingly

Both IIS and MTS support the use of in-process (DLL) and out-of-process (EXE) components. The use of each, however, is not equivalent in terms of performance and your choice of which type of component to use will have an impact on the response time of your application.

An *in-process* component runs in the same process (or memory space) as the calling application (may be a client, IIS, or MTS). An *out-of-process* component runs in its own process separate from that of the calling application. The reason that this is an issue is that when you use an out-of-process component, all of the method calls and parameters passed to that component must be marshaled across the process boundary. *Cross-process marshaling*, which is the process of packaging up method calls and parameters into a neutral format, moving them across the process boundary, and repackaging them in a format understood by the client, is very expensive compared to in-process method calls, which do not require marshaling. This expense also applies to components called remotely via DCOM, which require marshaling across machine as well as process boundaries. Fortunately, for components running under MTS, this expense is more than compensated by the performance gains enabled by MTS.

## Optimize the Server Environment

"Optimize the Server Environment." Well that sounds obvious, doesn't it? Of course you'd want to do that, right? Surprisingly enough, the server environment is often neglected, if not completely ignored in attempting to improve response time. Often, this is because nobody really wants to think about adding the expense of a new server to the application's cost. Unfortunately, what this attitude fails to take into account is that a new server may not be necessary (even though in some cases it would help immensely). The following sections describe changes in the server environment that can help improve response time. These include both configuration changes *and* hardware additions or replacements.

### Have Sufficient Hardware Resources

An obvious area where attention should be paid, but often isn't, is in ensuring that your server(s) have sufficient hardware to support the application. Testing this can actually be relatively easy. By monitoring the hardware utilization on the server as described in the solution, "Monitoring the Hardware Utilization of the Rent-A-Prize Application with Performance Monitor," you can determine if the demands of your application (in combination with the demands of other applications on the server) are overtaxing the server's resources.

### Optimize Web Application Architecture

Optimizing the Web application architecture. Sounds pretty complicated, doesn't it? Well it's not. Optimizing the Web application architecture simply means avoiding the architectural choices that can impede performance and response time. Chief of these is the mistake of installing the Web server and database server on the same machine. The problem with this kind of configuration is that while you save money by only purchasing a single server (although one would hope that a single server purchased for this purpose would be more powerful than machines purchased to support the Web or database servers individually, and thus more expensive), and you save the expense of sending data across the network, such a configuration is inherently less scalable.

> NOTE: In smaller applications with fewer concurrent users, the necessity of avoiding resource starvation may not be as great, meaning that the expense of the extra hardware and of moving data over the network are larger, relatively speaking. In these situations, it may be appropriate to install the Web and database servers on the same machine. Just remember that as the number of users increases, this configuration will eventually negatively impact performance.

On a server that has to perform both the duties of Web server and database server, the point at which resources such as RAM and processor time become scarce comes twice as quickly (roughly). What's more, the times during which demand on the Web server and database server are at peak will often be the same (since the users using the Web application are all going to be accessing or updating data), which exacerbates the problem. The solution is clear. If you want to get the best responsiveness and performance out of your application, particularly as the numbers of users increase, install the Web server and database server on separate machines. In addition, make sure that for the absolute best performance you use dedicated machines, so that the Web server and database server do not need to contend with other applications for resources.

### • • • SOLUTION: Monitoring the Hardware Utilization of the Rent-A-Prize Application with Performance Monitor

In this solution, we'll demonstrate how you can use the Windows NT Performance Monitor utility to monitor the hardware utilization of your server(s), allowing you to determine areas of your hardware that need upgrading. We'll walk through the process of setting up a real-time chart with the following steps:

1. Open Performance Monitor by clicking the Windows NT Start button, and selecting Programs | Administrative Tools (Common) |

Performance Monitor. Performance Monitor will open with in chart view, as shown in Figure 13-3.

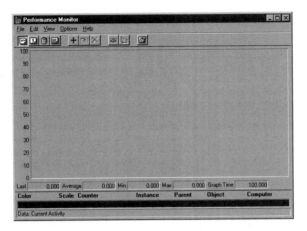

**Figure 13-3.**
*Windows NT Performance Monitor.*

2. Next, we'll add a counter to the chart by clicking the Add Counter button (which looks like a + sign) on the Performance Monitor toolbar.

Clicking the Add button brings up the Add to Chart dialog box (see Figure 13-4), which lets you select the object (processor, memory, SQL Server, Active Server Pages, and so on) and the specific counters that you wish to monitor. Each object has its own set of performance counters, some of which are installed with Windows NT (for example, processor and memory counters) and some by installed programs (for example, SQL Server and Active Server Pages counters). You can click the Explain>> button to display a brief description of the performance counter highlighted in the Counter list box. You can use the four drop-down list boxes at the bottom of the dialog box to change the color, scale, width, and style of the line representing the counter in the chart. Note that you can also use a single instance of Performance Monitor to monitor activity on multiple machines by using the Computer field to specify the remote machine to monitor (you must have the appropriate permissions to connect to the remote computer).

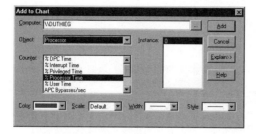

**Figure 13-4.**
*The Add to Chart dialog box.*

3. The Add To Chart dialog box has the Processor object and the % Processor Time counter selected by default. Click the Add button to add this counter to the chart. Click the Done button to close the dialog box, and observe the movement of the chart. Notice that certain activities, such as switching between running programs, can cause a brief spike in processor utilization.

4. Use the process above to add the following counters (note that depending on your system configuration, for processor and physical disk counters, you may need to use the Instance property to indicate which processor or disk you wish to monitor):

| Object | Counter |
| --- | --- |
| Memory | Available Bytes |
| | Page Faults/sec |
| Physical Disk | Avg. Disk Queue Length |

**Table 13-1.**
*Counters to monitor.*

5. As necessary, change the scale of a given counter to bring its values within the bounds of the chart. To do so, select the counter from the list below the chart, then click the Modify Selected Counter button on the Performance Monitor toolbar to open the Edit Chart Line dialog box. Use the drop-down list boxes at the bottom of the dialog box to alter the counter's display properties. You can also use

the Options button, or select Options | Chart... to change the display options for your chart, including the update interval.

The above process allows you to view the utilization of your system in real time, which can be useful. But what if you want to get a picture of utilization over time? In this case you would want to use Performance Monitor to create a log for the various objects you wish to monitor. To create a log with Performance Monitor follow these steps:

1. With Performance Monitor Open, click the Log status button, or select View | Log.

2. Set the location of the new log file by selecting Options | Log.... In the Log Options dialog box, Select the name and location for your log file and set the desired update interval, then click Save.

3. Click the Add Counter button to open the Add To Log dialog box (see Figure 13-5). The Add To Log dialog box lists only objects to be logged, so when you select an object, all the associated counters will be logged. Select the Processor object and click the Add button. Repeat for the Memory and Physical Disk objects, then click the Done button.

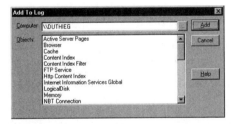

**Figure 13-5.**
*Add To Log dialog box.*

4. Once you've added all the objects that you wish to monitor, return to the Log Options dialog box and click the Start Log button. Leave Performance Monitor Running for as long as you want logging to continue. When you have collected all the data you want, return to the Log Options dialog box and click the Stop Log button (see Figure 13-6).

**Figure 13-6.**
*Log Options dialog box.*

NOTE: When setting up Performance Monitor log files, keep in mind that two factors determine the size of the log file: update interval and the number of objects monitored. The more often the log is updated, the faster the log file will grow. The same can be said of the number of objects monitored, the more you use, the larger the log file. If you choose to monitor all available objects, it would be wise to set the update interval as high as is feasible, unless you have a substantial amount of disk space available.

Once you've collected data in a Performance Monitor log, you can use the Chart and Report views to look at the data collected in the log. To do so only requires that you change the data source using the following steps:

1. Change to Chart or Report view.

2. From the Options menu, select Data From....

3. In the Data From... dialog box, select the Log File radio button and provide the location of the log file, then click OK. Note that to view current activity, you will need to reverse this setting.

4. Select objects and counters to display as described above.

Now that you know how to collect and view utilization statistics, let's talk briefly about how you can put this information to use. What we ultimately want to know is whether there are hardware areas that could benefit from upgrades. Three of the counters you should pay particular attention to are % Processor Time (Processor object), Page Faults/sec (Memory object), and Avg. Disk Queue Length (Physical Disk object).

If you find that the % Processor Time counter is consistently at 95% or above, that may be an indication that your processor is not up to the demands being made on it. In this case, your application could potentially benefit from a processor upgrade or from adding additional processors (if possible). On a Web server, high processing demands may be a product of numerous executing Active Server Pages scripts. On a database server, they may be caused by queries that require numerous values to be calculated, or which perform a great deal of data manipulation.

Although the Available Bytes counter of the Memory object is important in terms of indicating whether you are running out of memory completely, the Page Faults/sec counter is a better indicator of problems. When this counter is greater than 0, it indicates that information that the processor needs could not be found in the system RAM, and had to be read from disk. Given the phenomenal difference in performance between reading from disk and reading from memory, you can guess why this counter is important. If you find that this counter is consistently at or above 5, it's probably a good idea to think about adding more RAM. On a Web server, Additional RAM can provide IIS with more space to cache frequently requested pages, while on a database server, additional RAM can be used to expand the procedure and data caches, which can improve query performance dramatically.

Finally, the Avg. Disk Queue Length counter measures the average number of disk requests that were queued due to the disk controller not being able to fulfill them immediately. Generally speaking, the higher the value of this counter, the worse off you are. High numbers may indicate that your application would benefit from the use of a faster disk subsystem. Certainly, if you are currently using IDE disks, you could see a performance improvement by switching to a SCSI RAID system (RAID stands for Redundant Array of Inexpensive Disks). But before you spend a lot of money on switching to RAID or upgrading your RAID system, keep this in mind: One potential cause of disk queuing is insufficient RAM on the Web or database server, and as a consequence, insufficient cache space. This can result in applications reading a great deal more data from disk, which can increase the disk queue length.

As the disk queue length example shows, it is important when monitoring your application and/or your server utilization to be careful not to focus on one area only. Problems with response time are rarely caused by just one factor alone, and looking in one area only (such as disk queue length) may lead you to the wrong conclusions. By looking at a number of different counters, you can get a better-rounded picture of your server's performance.

### Increase Availability and Performance with Clustering

*Clustering* is the ability to group two or more machines together in such a way that either the servers appear to be a single machine, or one (or more) server(s) act as a hot failover machine for another. Microsoft Cluster Server (MSCS), available with Windows NT, Enterprise Edition, provides both failover support and scalability support (for cluster-aware applications).

Although clustering in the initial release of Cluster Server is limited to two machines, the Phase 2 release (which is expected to be in beta in 1998), will support larger clusters and better application scalability options. A full discussion of Cluster Server programming is beyond the scope of this book, but you will find that within the next year or two, Cluster Server will become as important to your largest applications as MTS or MSMQ. Find out more about Microsoft Cluster Server at the Windows NT Server Enterprise Web site (http://www.microsoft.com/ntserverenterprise).

# If Response Time Can't Be Further Improved

So you've reached the end of your rope. You've tweaked settings, added RAM, used stored procedures. In short, you've attempted every solution suggested in both this chapter and in Chapter 14, "Optimizing Data Access," and your response time is still not what you would like it to be. Don't panic. Unless your response time is measured in minutes instead of seconds (in which case you should probably re-read both this and the next chapter), you may be able to solve the problem by managing users' expectations.

Believe it or not, your users can actually be pretty reasonable. If you provide them with enough information about what is going on in your application and what they can expect, they will be much less likely to perceive your application as being slow, and thus much less likely to complain.

First of all, if you have queries or pages that you know take an especially long time to process, tell the users that. Put a notice or message on the page above a submit button that says "This request may require significant processing time. Please be patient and do not hit the *stop* or *back* buttons on your browser as this will only increase the time it takes for your request to be processed. Thank you for your patience." Users still won't like waiting very much, but at least they'll know what's going on, instead of wondering whether your application is broken.

If you know the peak usage times of your application, post a message on the login screen, "The peak usage times for this application are between 10am and 4pm, Eastern Time. During this time, you may experience longer than average processing time. For faster service, schedule application use outside of peak hours." Again, your users may still use the application at peak times to avoid the inconvenience of off-hours usage, but again, they'll know what to expect (and may even be pleasantly surprised to find the application is faster than they expected. In both cases, this can prevent users from using the stop or back button to repeatedly submit the same request, saving a lot of wasted processing time.

# Summary

In this chapter, we've discussed some of the primary causes of poor applications response time, which include:

- Poorly Optimized Database Queries
- Resource Contention
- Poor Component Implementation
- Hardware Issues

We also discussed solutions for these problems, including:

- Query Optimization
- Resource Pooling
- Component Optimization
- Hardware Optimization

In situations where the response time of an application is inadequate, a combination of the techniques described in this chapter should be sufficient to improve the situation. Remember, however, not to focus all your energy on one area of investigation. Only by looking at the parts of your application in the context of the whole will you be able to draw accurate conclusions about where performance problems originate.

In the next chapter, "Optimizing Data Access," we will delve deeper into subjects related to improving your database performance, including

- Profiling with SQL Trace
- Optimizing User Connections
- Optimizing Queries
- Optimizing Contention and Locking
- Optimizing Hardware Resources

Armed with the techniques described in these two chapters, you will be ready to ferret out and eradicate the performance problems that plague even the best developers.

## CHAPTER FOURTEEN

# Optimizing Data Access

● ● ● **GOAL: To Reduce Query Time and Increase Throughput for Greater Performance and Scalability**

In this chapter, we'll follow up on the previous chapter's discussion of improving your application's response time. We'll focus on the optimization of data access—often one of the most costly areas of an application. We'll begin by looking at how to pinpoint problem areas through the use of the SQL Trace utility. We'll then discuss some of the keys to optimal data access, and look at techniques that can make each of them possible.

# First Step—PROFILING!

*Profiling* is a word that's often bandied about in the context of improving the performance (and occasionally the readability) of your Visual Basic code, but not too many people apply it to SQL code. Given the profound effect that data access can have on an application, this is an unfortunate omission. In this section, we'll make a case for the necessity of profiling to improve your data access performance, and we'll show you how to use the SQL Trace utility, installed with Microsoft SQL Server, to perform that profiling.

## Before You Can Fix a Problem, You Must Find It

The central idea of application profiling is that in order to fix a problem, you have to know the *cause* of the problem. Too many people spend far too much time and effort trying blind fixes based on what they *think* the problem is, and while on occasion they get lucky and find the fix, the result is more often frustration.

So, if profiling is so important, why doesn't everybody do it? Because it can be difficult, and the perception is that a methodological approach *must* be harder than thrashing around in the dark. In Chapter 13, "Response Time," we described Performance Monitor, one of the tools Windows NT makes available to assist you in monitoring and profiling your applications. Right now, let's take a look at one of the tools available for profiling data access in your applications, SQL Trace.

### • • • SOLUTION: Profiling Rent-A-Prize Data Access with SQL Trace

*SQL Trace* is a graphical utility provided with Microsoft SQL Server 6.5 that captures all SQL and RPC calls to the database server that you are monitoring. In this solution, we'll show how you can use SQL Trace to capture data-access statistics for your application and then use SQL Server's bulk copy program (bcp) to transfer the captured data into a predefined table. Once you have the data in a table, you can query the table to learn about the performance characteristics of your application's data-access code.

NOTE: In order to complete this solution, you must have either Microsoft SQL Server 6.5, or the Microsoft SQL Server 6.5 client utilities installed on your workstation and you must have access to a SQL Server database in which you have CREATE permissions for tables.

## Running SQL Trace

Running SQL Trace on your database server allows you to determine which queries and operations are taking the most time. This information allows you to focus your optimization time, energy, and money on the areas that are most likely to produce dramatic results.

To get started, follow these steps:

1. Open SQL Trace by clicking the Windows NT Start button, then selecting Programs | Microsoft SQL Server 6.5 | SQL Trace. SQL Trace opens with the Connect Server dialog box displayed.

2. In the Connect Server dialog box (see Figure 14-1), enter the server name of the machine you wish to monitor, enter a valid Login ID and Password for that server (or choose trusted connection if your SQL Server is set up to use your NT user ID and password), and click the Connect button. If you do not know the exact server name, you can click the List Servers button to display a list of the servers registered on your workstation.

NOTE: In order to run SQL Trace against a remote SQL Server machine, you must first register that server on your local workstation using the SQL client configuration utility.

**Figure 14-1.**
*The Connect Server dialog box.*

3. If this is the first time you've run SQL Trace, the next thing you'll
   see once you've connected to the target server is a dialog box asking
   if you want to create a filter. For now, click the No button. We'll
   create a new filter in a bit. If you already have a filter or filters defined,
   you'll see a dialog box asking if you want to start a particular filter.
   Again, for now, click the No button.

The next step in profiling with SQL Trace is to create a filter. For this part
of the process, some definitions of filter options are in order. Figure 14-2 shows
the New Filter dialog box, from which these terms are drawn.

**Figure 14-2.**
*New Filter dialog box.*

- **Filter**  Used by SQL Trace to determine which events to keep and
  which to eliminate. Also used to define whether the results of the trace
  will be saved to a log file, saved to a script (.sql) file, or simply
  viewed on the screen. All three options may be selected at the
  same time.

- ■ **Login Name, Application, and Host Name** Filter properties that tell SQL Trace to record only events that match the specified property value.

- ■ **Capture Options Tab** Used to control how information captured is displayed or saved. Options include viewing data on screen, saving to a script file, and saving to a log file. Another option, Include Performance Information, is especially important when profiling, as it instructs SQL Trace to record the duration, CPU usage, and disk reads and writes for each event.

- ■ **Events Tab** Used to control which types of events are monitored. Includes connections, SQL statements, RPC (remote procedure calls), Attentions, and Disconnections. Both SQL statements and RPC have associated filter fields to limit the statements monitored.

Creating a filter is as simple as completing the fields in the New Filter dialog box. Fill out the fields as follows:

1. In the Filter Name field, enter a descriptive name for your filter, such as *MyFilter*.

2. In the Login Name, Application, and Host Name fields, enter the desired values. Separate multiple entries in a given field with semicolons (;). You can click the ellipsis button (…) to view a list of available choices. Only events matching the values entered in these fields will be monitored and/or recorded. For this example, accept the defaults (<all>).

3. On the Capture Options tab, choose how you wish the information captured by SQL Trace to be displayed or saved. For profiling purposes, you should always check the Include Performance Information check box. Note that you can view information onscreen, save to a script file, and save to a log file simultaneously. For this example, check the View on Screen, Include Performance Information, and Save as Log File check boxes, and select a filename and location for the log file (remember or write down the name and location, we'll need it later).

4. Now switch to the Events tab. On the Events tab, select the events to monitor. For this example, accept the defaults. Note that you can enter statements to be ignored in either the SQL Statement or RPC Filter fields.

5. Click the Add button to add your filter to SQL Trace. SQL Trace starts the filter and opens the filter display window. Note that you can run multiple SQL Trace filters simultaneously.

With your SQL Trace filter running, you should see events scrolling up the filter window, assuming that your application (or others accessing the SQL Server you're connected to) is running, as shown in Figure 14-3. If your application is still in development, round up some testers to run through the application, concentrating on those pages that perform database queries or store information from HTML forms.

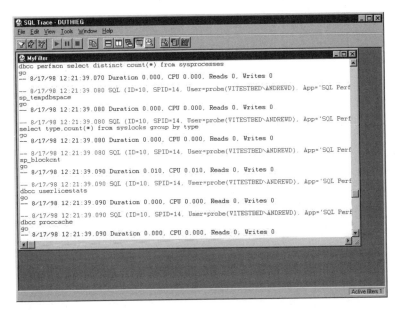

**Figure 14-3.**
*MyFilter window in SQL Trace.*

## Importing the SQL Trace Log to a SQL Server Table

In this next part of the solution, we'll show you how to set up a SQL Server table to accept data from the SQL Trace log and how to use bcp to import the data into the table. To set up the table you can use one of two methods, as indicated by these steps:

## Method 1—Using the Visual Database Tools

One way to set up the table is to use the Visual Database Tools. Follow these steps:

1. Open or create a Visual InterDev project with a database connection to the database where you wish to store the SQL Trace information (it's a good idea to store this in your application's database if the SQL Trace filter is specific to your application).

2. Expand the database node in the Data View window to display the Tables node. Right-click the Tables node and select New Table. Name the table *SQLTraceInfo*.

3. Enter the following column information for the table (as shown in Figure 14-4):

| Column Name | Datatype | Length | Nulls |
|-------------|----------|--------|-------|
| Event | Char | 12 | Yes |
| UserName | Char | 30 | Yes |
| ID | Int | n/a | Yes |
| SPID | Int | n/a | Yes |
| StartTime | Datetime | n/a | Yes |
| EndTime | Datetime | n/a | Yes |
| Application | Char | 30 | Yes |
| Data | VarChar | 255 | Yes |
| Duration | Int | n/a | Yes |
| CPU | Int | n/a | Yes |
| Reads | Int | n/a | Yes |
| Writes | Int | n/a | Yes |
| NT_Domain | VarChar | 30 | Yes |
| NT_User | VarChar | 30 | Yes |
| HostName | VarChar | 30 | Yes |
| HostProcess | VarChar | 13 | Yes |

**Table 14-1.**

*Column information for SQLTraceInfo table.*

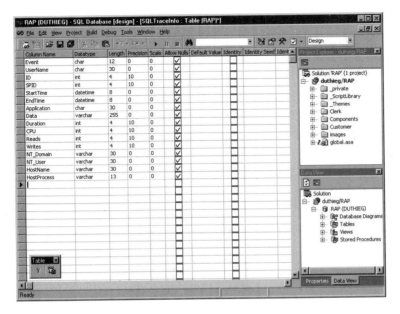

**Figure 14-4.**
*Table design window in Visual InterDev.*

4. Open the property pages for the table by right-clicking in the design window and selecting Property Pages. Switch to the Indexes/Keys tab.

5. Click the New button to create a new index. Set the Column Name to CPU and change the Index name to *cpu_index*.

6. Repeat step 5 to add the following indexes:

| Index Name | Column |
|---|---|
| duration_index | Duration |
| ntuser_index | NT_User |
| starttime_index | StartTime |

**Table 14-2.**
*Index parameters.*

7. Once you've entered all of the index information, click the Close button to return to the table design window.

8. Click the Save button on the Visual InterDev toolbar to save the new table and close the table design window.

## Method 2—Create the Table Using a SQL Script

Another way to set up the table is to use a SQL script. Follow these steps:

1. Open your preferred SQL Query environment (ISQL/w, Enterprise Manager, and so on).

2. Enter the following SQL Script in the query window:

```
/* CREATES TABLE TO RECEIVE SQL TRACE DATA VIA BCP */


CREATE TABLE SQLTraceInfo (

    Event char (12) NULL ,

    UserName char (30) NULL ,

    ID int NULL ,

    SPID int NULL ,

    StartTime datetime NULL,

    EndTime datetime NULL,

    Application char (30) NULL,

    Data varchar (255) NULL ,

    Duration int NULL,

    CPU int NULL ,

    Reads int NULL ,

    Writes int NULL ,

    NT_Domain varchar (30) NULL ,

    NT_User varchar (30) NULL ,
```

(continued)

```
    HostName varchar (30) NULL ,

    HostProcess varchar (13) NULL )
GO
CREATE INDEX cpu_index ON SQLTraceInfo(CPU)
GO
CREATE INDEX duration_index ON SQLTraceInfo(Duration)
GO
CREATE INDEX ntuser_index ON SQLTraceInfo(NT_User)
GO
CREATE INDEX starttime_index ON SQLTraceInfo(StartTime)
GO
```

3. Execute the script to create the table and indexes.

To import the SQL Trace data into the new table, we'll use bcp, as demonstrated in the following steps:

1. Open a Command Prompt window by clicking the Start button, then selecting Programs | Command Prompt.

2. At the command prompt, enter the following command. Change *tablename* to the name for the table you just created (*servername.owner.tablename*) and *path* to the full path to your SQL Trace log file):

```
bcp databasename in path -c -U sa
```

NOTE: See SQL Server Books Online for more information about bulk copy program command-line options.

3. In Visual InterDev, double-click the SQLTraceInfo table to verify that the log data has been successfully transferred into the table, as shown in Figure 14-5.

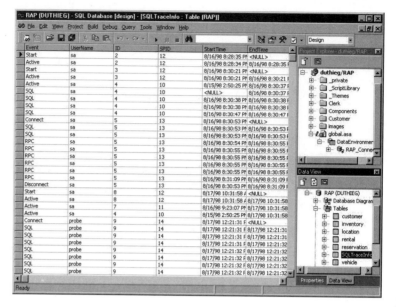

**Figure 14-5.**
*SQLTraceInfo table.*

## Querying the SQLTraceInfo Table

Now we come to the most interesting and useful part of the solution: Taking the data we've collected, and turning it into information. How do we do that? By running queries against the data to reveal performance trends. For example, you can use the following procedure to find out which events recorded by SQL Trace took the longest:

1. Open the Query Designer in Visual InterDev by expanding the Data Environment (under GLOBAL.ASA), adding a new data command, and in the Command1 Properties dialog box, selecting the SQL Statement radio button, then clicking the SQL Builder button.

2. Drag the SQLTraceInfo table from the Data View windows into the Diagram pane.

3. In the table diagram, select the Event, UserName, StartTime, Application, Data, Duration, and CPU check boxes to select these columns from the table.

4. In the Grid pane, click the first empty field (under *Column*) and select Duration from the drop-down list.

5. In the same row, clear the Output check box (if checked), and change the Sort Type to Descending.

6. Click the Run Query button (!) on the Query toolbar to execute the query and view the results in the Results pane (see Figure 14-6).

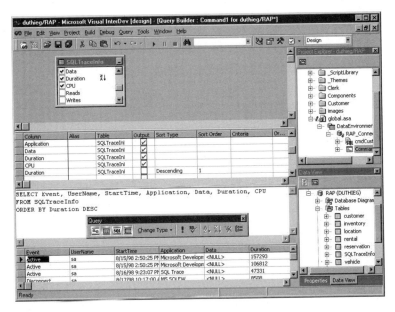

**Figure 14-6.**
*Querying the SQLTraceInfo table.*

The procedure described above lets you view which events in the SQLTraceInfo took the longest amount of time, which is a statistic that could be very helpful in prioritizing which queries to optimize. Another important measure, however, is the frequency with which a given query is called. By entering the following in the SQL pane:

```
SELECT COUNT(Data) FROM SQLTraceInfo

WHERE Data = SQLStatement
```

and replacing *SQLStatement* with the SQL statement (or stored procedure or RPC call) whose frequency you wish to measure, you can get a count of the number of times that SQL statement was executed. Other queries that can be helpful in determining which events are consuming the most resources include:

```
SELECT UserName, Data FROM SQLTraceInfo ORDER BY CPU DESC
SELECT UserName, Data FROM SQLTraceInfo ORDER BY Reads DESC
SELECT UserName, Data FROM SQLTraceInfo ORDER BY Writes DESC
```

All of the information above can be used to determine which applications and queries are the most expensive, and hence, which are likely to offer the best return on time invested in optimization. Remember that the expense of a query is based not only on its duration, but also on the frequency with which the query is executed.

## SQL 7.0 Improves Upon SQL Trace with the SQL Profiler

Now that we've gone through the process of learning to use SQL Trace in profiling your application's database use, there's some good news. In Microsoft SQL Server 7.0, SQL Trace is being replaced by SQL Profiler. SQL Profiler makes the process of profiling much simpler by eliminating the need to bcp data into your SQLTraceInfo table. SQL Profiler allows you to specify a table to insert data into at the same point as you would have specified a log file to record to in SQL Trace. This should make profiling a lot less tedious and complex, and more attractive.

## SQL Trace Wrap Up

In this section, we've demonstrated how you can use the SQL Trace utility program provided with Microsoft SQL Server 6.5 to profile your application's data access. Keep in mind, however, that SQL Trace only tells part of the story. SQL Trace only tells you about what information is being sent from your application to SQL Server, and how long that information took to process. SQL Trace won't tell you if your server is running out of RAM or if your disk subsystem is slowing down the process. This is why you should always combine SQL Trace profiling with a fair amount of monitoring with a utility such as Performance Monitor, as described in the previous chapter, as well as with a dollop of intuition and a healthy dose of common sense. Profiling is by nature a somewhat inexact science, since every application is different. But with practice, you'll learn what to look for, and your application profiling and tuning will become that much more effective.

# Keys to Optimal Data Access

Once you've used tools like SQL Trace and Performance Monitor to assess the current state of your application, you can begin to form a strategy to improve that state. Identifying the problems is half the battle. The other half is knowing what to do about them, knowledge that can also help you prevent these problems in the future.

To that end, the rest of this chapter will discuss some of the keys to optimal data access, providing techniques and strategies that will help you address the problems you face in your application's data access. These keys include:

- **User Connections**   In order to access data, users of your application must be able to connect to the database.

- **Query Optimization**   Optimizing queries can make the difference between an application that is a pleasure to use, and one that is barely tolerable.

- **Resource Contention and Locking**   If your application has to contend for resources such as processor time or RAM, or consistently runs into locked data due to incorrect use of locks, your users will surely voice their displeasure.

- **Hardware Usage**   Having the proper hardware resources may seem like a no-brainer, but when overlooked, this key can cause significant heartache for users and developers alike.

Understanding and following the techniques and suggestions outlined in these keys may not guarantee success, but it will almost certainly increase you chances of success.

# Optimizing User Connections

Given that the first step in accessing data is connecting to the database, whether the interface is your application, or a query interface such as ISQL/w, it seems appropriate to discuss first the issues related to maintaining an optimal number of database connections and making the most efficient use of these connections. The strategies you can use to ensure optimal performance and availability in your database connections fall into three areas:

- Using Connection Pooling
- Using Connections Efficiently
- Providing Sufficient Connections

Using these strategies, as described in the following sections, will reduce problems related to applications and users being unable to connect to your database due to lack of available connections.

## *Always* Use Connection Pooling

When you are building large, multi-user applications, regardless of whether or not they are available over the Internet, you should always use connection pooling if it is available. Connection pooling, whether implemented by Internet Information Server (IIS) or by Microsoft Transaction Server (MTS), can help you make tremendously more efficient use of your available database connections.

There are some guidelines you should use when programming with connection pooling in mind,

- ■ **Make your connection strings as generic as possible**  Since the efficiency of connection pooling relies on the ability to find connections in the pool that match the incoming request, the easiest way to increase the effectiveness of connection pooling is to use as few unique connection strings as possible. Set up a SQL Server login and password for run-time use by your application, and use it in all your connection strings. If you can use the same run-time login and password for other applications without compromising security, do so.

- ■ **Applications Should Connect Late and Release Early**  Since connection pooling reduces dramatically the cost of opening a connection each time one is needed, there is no longer a need for opening connections far in advance of when you'll use them. In fact, the later you open your connections and the earlier you close them, the more likely it is that there will be available connections in the pool for the next request. If everyone on your team gets in the habit of programming this way, you'll be much less likely to run out of connections.

## Use Connections Efficiently

Along the same lines as using connection pooling and connecting late and releasing early is the following advice. Don't store ADO connection objects in ASP session or application variables unless there is some overriding reason to do so. And performance isn't an adequate reason. With connection pooling enabled, storing ADO connection objects in session or application variables is more likely to reduce performance than it is to improve it, since a connection stored in a session or application variable is likely to have a considerable amount of idle time, which could be put to use if the connection were released to the connection pool. In addition, it is far too easy for connections (and recordsets) to be dropped or broken while stored in session or application variables, which can lead to hard-to-diagnose errors.

## Provide an Adequate Number of Connections

This one should be obvious, but we need to point out that whether or not you use connection pooling, and no matter how good you are about opening your connections late and closing them early, your efforts will amount to zilch if the number of database connections you have configured is insufficient for the number of users you are supporting. This is a problem that should be fairly easy to identify. If you have enabled connection pooling and ensured that all the applications hitting your database server are making efficient use of connections, and you're still getting "Cannot connect" errors due to the fact that the max number of connections is already in use, then it's a good bet that it's time to think about buying some more licenses and bumping up the number of configured connections. Figure 14-7 shows the use of the Configuration tab of the Server Configuration dialog box in SQL Server 6.5 to change the number of user connections. Note that the default is 15, which is rather low (an understatement) for an enterprise application.

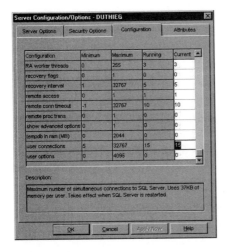

**Figure 14-7.**
*Server Configuration dialog box.*

# Optimizing Queries

One of the areas you'll rightly spend most of your optimization time on is in optimizing your queries. Thanks to your use of SQL Trace to profile your data access, you'll have a pretty good idea which queries you need to tackle. Now all you need to know is what you should be looking for to improve the situation. In this section we'll address that need, offering tips, guidelines, and suggestions based on common problems found in database queries (and sometimes perpetuated by the sample code we all learn from).

## Select *Only* the Data That the Application Requires

There is a direct correlation between how long your queries take and how much data your queries retrieve (or update). Given that, it should be obvious that one way to reduce the amount of time a query takes is to reduce the amount of data returned. If you have a SELECT query that returns 2,000 rows, of which only 50 are ever viewed or used, then it makes a great deal of sense to look at whether you can reduce the number of rows returned with a more restrictive WHERE clause.

### Never Use "SELECT * FROM" Syntax

For applications requiring high performance and scalability, there are few sins more grievous than using a SELECT * FROM query. There is rarely, if ever, a reason to use SELECT * that justifies the cost of returning every column and row in a table. This syntax gives you no control whatsoever over the expense of the query. Sure, this syntax allows you to access new columns if they are added, but if 5 new columns are added to the table at some later point, your query becomes that much more expensive, regardless of whether you need to use those columns or not.

If you need to be able to access columns that may be added in the future, you would be far better off using a more restrictive SELECT statement in a stored procedure. Then if, at some later date, columns are added that you wish to access, you can modify the stored procedure to include the new column(s).

### Other Syntax to Avoid

Other query syntax to avoid includes WHERE clauses like the following:

```
WHERE <column_name> != value
WHERE <column_name> <> value
```

What do these WHERE clauses have in common? They are both searching for the negative case. Why is this a problem? Because each of the above WHERE clauses, and any WHERE clause with NOT in it, will force SQL Server to do a table scan. Table scans (except for very small tables) are substantially slower than searching by indexes, so this SQL syntax should be avoided wherever possible. The bottom line here is that for the best performance, use only the rows and columns you know you'll need, and avoid queries that require a table scan.

## Avoid Joining Multiple Tables—Consider Views Instead

In any application that makes use of a database, particularly a normalized database, there will likely be times when a query will require retrieving values from more than one table. In most cases, this is accomplished by using SQL joins, in which the tables being queried are joined based on some shared value. The thing to keep in mind about using joins, however, is that certain joins make extensive use of temporary tables to accomplish the join. While this may not be a problem when joining two tables (especially if the tables are relatively small), as the number of tables in the join increases, the expense involved increases dramatically. It's important to remember here that the server's resources are limited. Though it may not be very likely, if 80 percent of your users all choose to execute a query that uses a multi-table join at the same time, you may find your server's resources sapped *very* quickly, as each execution of the query requires its own set of resources. By contrast, defining a view that includes the necessary columns can be much more efficient, since this method does not require the creation of temporary tables. In addition, multiple users can query a view without consuming as much of the server's resources.

## Consider Batching Statements

In an application that SQL Trace has shown to be sending the same query or queries over and over again, it makes sense to look at batching these queries where possible (a *batch* is a series of SQL commands followed by a "GO" command). The performance problem associated with statements that run over and over individually is referred to as the "teaspoon fire brigade." It's awfully hard to put out a fire when the only thing you've got to carry water in is a teaspoon.

The central problem is that a single statement, no matter how simple, requires a certain amount of overhead when it is transmitted to the server. For example, the SQL statement SELECT 1 will return the literal value 1. SQL statements don't come any simpler. As an experiment try, in your favorite SQL query interface, running the following code 1,000 times (cut and paste these two lines to make 1,000 copies):

```
SELECT 1
GO
```

Now compare this by running 1,000 SELECT 1 statements in a single batch (only one "GO"). The reason for the dramatic difference in performance is that although the overhead required for each trip is not that great, the cumulative overhead for 1,000 calls is huge. SQL batches, in essence, provide a bigger "bucket."

## Use Stored Procedures Where Possible

Stored procedures, as we observed in the previous chapter, are one of the most effective ways of improving the performance of a query. They are particularly effective at improving the performance of INSERT queries. Why? Because when you send SQL Queries to the server as text, that text must be parsed and compiled at the server, datatypes must be translated, and a query plan must be generated for the query. All of that overhead takes its toll, particularly for statements that are used repeatedly. Stored procedures execute much more quickly because they are precompiled, and after the first time they are run, they have a predefined query plan that saves even more overhead.

Other reasons to use stored procedures include security and reusability. If you have more than one application that makes use of the same database, it is possible with stored procedures to control access to the database on an application by application basis simply by granting or denying access to the stored procedures you have defined, without ever granting users or applications direct access to the underlying tables.

## • • • SOLUTION: Migrating Dynamic SQL Queries to Stored Procedures

So now that you're convinced of the wisdom of moving to stored procedures, let's take a look at how to actually accomplish it. Let's assume that you have a simple dynamically generated query in your ASP page or Visual Basic component that looks like the following:

```
strSQL = "SELECT customer_name_last, customer_name_first, " & _
    " customer_home_phone FROM customer " & _
    "WHERE customer_id = " & strSearchVal
```

Where the value of *strSearchVal* is provided at run-time via user input. You send the query to the server with the following code (this is what the code would look like in Visual Basic):

```
Dim Conn As New ADODB.Connection
Dim cmd As New ADODB.Command
Dim rs As New ADODB.Recordset

cmd.CommandType = adCmdText
cmd.CommandText = strSQL      'defined above

Conn.Open sConnectString     'connection string defined elsewhere

Set cmd.ActiveConnection = Conn

Set rs = cmd.Execute
```

The above code uses ActiveX Data Objects (ADO) to create a Connection, Command, and Recordset object, sets the command type as text (since that's what we're sending) sets the command text to the dynamic SQL string we defined earlier, opens the connection based on a predefined connection string, sets the active connection object property of the command object to the open connection (note that you must use the *Set cmd* = syntax, or the command will attempt to create and open a new connection when you execute it), and finally, the code executes the command and stores the results in a recordset object. This code will work just fine, until you try to scale it, at which point all of the overhead involved will start to impede performance.

Now let's take a look at the same query defined as a stored procedure. Instead of building a string dynamically in our VBScript or Visual Basic code, we create a parameterized stored procedure, and pass the required value as a parameter to the stored procedure. Because we're not limited to strings, we can pass the value as an integer, avoiding the need to convert the datatype (note that the range of numeric datatypes differs between Visual Basic and SQL. Make sure the variables you use have sufficient range for the values they'll need to hold). In Figure 14-8, we create a new stored procedure in Visual InterDev with the following code:

```
Create Procedure GetCustomer
        @custid     int
As


SELECT  customer_name_last,
        customer_name_first,
        customer_home_phone
FROM    customer
WHERE   customer_id = @custid
```

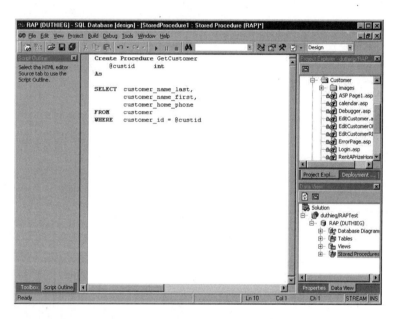

**Figure 14-8.**
*Creating a stored procedure in Visual InterDev.*

And here is what the code to call the stored procedure would look like:

```
Dim Conn As New ADODB.Connection
Dim cmd As New ADODB.Command
Dim rs As New ADODB.Recordset
Dim pCustID as New ADODB.Parameter
```

*(continued)*

```
cmd.CommandType = adCmdStoredProc
cmd.CommandText = "GetCustomer"        'stored procedure name
Set pCustID = cmd.CreateParameter("@custid", adInteger, adParamInput, _
    , , intCustID) 'intCustID is predefined or passed as an argument
cmd.Parameters.Append pCustID

Conn.Open sConnectString       'connection string defined elsewhere

Set cmd.ActiveConnection = Conn

Set rs = cmd.Execute
```

The code above differs from the earlier examples in two ways. First, it adds an ADO Parameter object, which is used to store the customer ID we're searching for and pass it to the stored procedure. Second, it sets the command type to *adCmdStoredProc*, which tells ADO that the command text property is the name of the stored procedure to execute. The code then creates a new parameter with the appropriate values (see the ADO documentation for the required arguments to the *CreateParameter* method of the command object) and appends that parameter to the command object's parameters collection. Now when we execute the command, the parameter and stored procedure name are packaged up and sent to SQL Server, which can quickly and efficiently unpack the name and parameter, execute the stored procedure, and return the recordset.

The above example is extremely simple, but it demonstrates some of what you can do with stored procedures. You can also try including parameters and control-of-flow logic in your stored procedures to determine which statements to execute, or using output parameters to return richly informative return values or messages. Stored procedures are very powerful and flexible, and they allow you to keep most of your data-access logic where it can run most efficiently—at the server.

## Understand ADO Usage

Another potentially major problem area in terms of query efficiency is the improper use of ADO. Lack of familiarity with ADO and old habits from DAO and RDO may be part of the reason. Some of the areas to be aware of include:

- **Understand the ADO defaults**  Don't assume that the defaults for ADO objects are necessarily the most efficient for your purpose.

For example, the default for the *CacheSize* property of the Recordset object is 1, meaning that when you initially open the recordset object, only 1 row is actually brought back from the server and cached locally. Each time you move past the last row in the cache, ADO retrieves the next set of rows (or in this case, row) according to the CacheSize. This can add an enormous amount of overhead to your data retrieval. Be sure you understand what the defaults are when you are using ADO objects.

■ **Use ADO objects the way they're designed to be used**   We highlighted an example of this in the previous chapter…stored procedure use. Calling a stored procedure with an ADO command object whose *CommandType* property is set to *adCmdText* using ODBC call syntax is contrary to the design of the command object. The command object has more than one command type for a reason. Use them.

■ **Set the appropriate lock type and cursor type (and location) for your needs**   ADO is very flexible when it comes to locks and cursors. But before you decide to start experimenting with dynamic cursors in your application, make sure you understand the expense involved. As a general rule, use the least expensive cursor type that will meet your needs. As for cursor location, keep in mind that server-side cursors use resources that are limited. The use of client-side cursors, where possible, can improve scalability. Keep in mind, however, that in a Web application, the client is often the Web server or component.

## Indexing

Indexes are used in Microsoft SQL Server to speed access to data in your tables. By creating indexes on frequently searched columns in your tables, you can substantially decrease the running time of your queries. In order to provide the best level of optimization, however, indexes must be used wisely. A full discussion of the proper use of Indexes is beyond the scope of this book, but here are some basic guidelines:

■ **Create indexes on columns that are frequently referenced in WHERE clauses**   Study the WHERE clauses of your queries, especially long-running queries, to see which columns you search the most frequently. Concentrate your indexing efforts on these columns.

- **Choose the right type of index for the job. Indexes may be clustered or nonclustered**   In clustered indexes, data is stored in the same order as the index keys that refer to the data. In nonclustered indexes the order of the keys does not match the data. Clustered indexes are appropriate for columns with a small (but not tiny) number of unique values. Nonclustered indexes should be used on columns with a large number of unique values.

- **Don't overdo it**   Indexes can provide a substantial amount of performance improvement, when used properly. Keep in mind that one consequence of adding indexes is an increase in the expense of INSERT queries. If you have a table that is searched only rarely, but into which new rows are inserted frequently, you should give serious thought to whether an index is worth the cost.

You can find more information about the use of indexes in SQL Server Books Online (installed with SQL Server), or in the MSDN documentation included with Visual InterDev.

# Optimizing Contention and Locking

Contention and locking conflicts can be major performance killers in your application. Depending on your error-handling, they can even be application killers. Understanding how to avoid the problems associated with multiple users attempting to update the same data, or users not being able to access data locked by other users (through your application) will help you make the entire process more efficient.

## Use the Most Optimistic Locking Option That Will Meet Your Needs

The concept of using the most optimistic locking option is pretty simple, yet many developers fail to realize that the most optimistic locking option is no lock at all. If your needs are such that it doesn't matter if another client alters data that you've retrieved (known as a "dirty read"), use the SQL Server optimizer hints to tell the optimizer not to lock the table, as shown in the following code:

```
SELECT  customer_name_last
FROM    customer(NOLOCK)
WHERE   customer_id = 1
```

You might use this in situations where your queries are bringing back data for statistical purposes, in which exact figures aren't as important as trends. Since these queries would likely affect large amounts of data, they could be particularly troublesome in terms of locking. The NOLOCK optimizer hint is one of several that you can use to control locking behavior in your queries. You can also use the *LockType* property of the ADO Recordset object to manipulate the lock type, but it will not allow you to specify no lock at all. Specifying NOLOCK, where possible, reduces the chances of other clients having to wait to update data until you are finished with your query, increasing concurrency.

## Use Connection and Command Timeouts Appropriately

The ADO Connection and Command objects both provide properties to allow you to specify the connection timeout and command timeout values, respectively (the Connection object has a *CommandTimeout* property in addition to its *ConnectionTimeout* property). One of the purposes of these properties is to let you tweak the behavior of these objects to compensate for network or database performance issues that might be making your queries time out before they are finished.

Unfortunately, it is very easy to abuse these properties and set their values far too high in an effort to avoid having to deal with timeouts at all. Unfortunately this can result in connections or commands that take up a great deal of server resources, when perhaps the solution should have been to optimize the query instead of increasing the timeout values. If you are having to set the connection and/or command timeouts in minutes rather than seconds, there is most likely a problem elsewhere that you need to address.

## Implement Error-Handling for Deadlocks and Timeouts

Inevitably, no matter how fast your queries, nor how reliable your network, you will run into occasions when your connections or commands will time out, or your application ends up in a deadlock with another process. Both of these circumstances results in errors that are easy to handle. Making sure that you implement proper error handling for these situations will allow your application to continue working, and give the user the opportunity to retry their query, instead of cursing the developers.

# Optimizing Hardware Resources

Optimizing hardware resources involves getting an accurate picture of hardware utilization over time. In the previous chapter, we discussed how you can use the Windows NT Performance Monitor utility to assess the utilization of your server. In addition to the counters we used in that example, Performance Monitor also has counters (installed by SQL Server) that allow you to monitor SQL Server activity. By combining counters for hardware utilization and SQL Server activity with the information gathered using SQL Trace, you should be able to get a very clear picture of what is happening on your database server, from the commands being sent from the client, to the resultant activity in SQL Server, to the response of the hardware. Armed with this knowledge, you can make decisions about how and when to configure and upgrade your hardware to better server your application's needs.

## Memory Usage and Allocation

Memory usage can be monitored using the Memory counters in Performance Monitor. The main thing to watch out for is excessive paging, indicated by high values for the page faults/sec counter. If you find that the system is paging a lot, you may want to increase the installed RAM. Over the past year or two, the price of RAM has dropped so much that there really is no excuse for starving your database server. The more RAM you can make available to SQL Server, the better your performance will be. A related area is the uses to which you database server is put. If your database server also performs other tasks, such as Web server or component server (or, heaven forbid, workstation), you need to make sure that the resources available can adequately support these tasks. You should also make sure that when you are monitoring the performance of your application, the conditions of the test include the additional tasks.

How you allocate memory in SQL Server can also make a difference in performance. Memory allocation in SQL Server is done either through the Enterprise Manager Server Configuration dialog box (see Figure 14-9), or using the sp_Configure system stored procedure with the appropriate parameters. There are two important settings, the memory to allocate to SQL Server, and the size of the procedure cache.

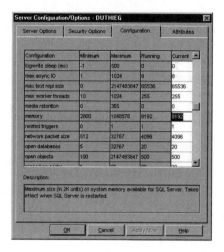

**Figure 14-9.**
*Setting the memory option in the Server Configuration dialog box.*

The memory setting specifies how much memory is allocated to SQL Server. In general, you should allocate as much memory to SQL Server as you can without choking Windows NT (and any other applications running on the server). The procedure cache setting specifies the size (in percent) of the SQL Server procedure cache (which stores stored procedures for reuse). The data cache (which stores the most recently used index and data pages) size is determined by the difference between the memory setting and the procedure cache setting (less the memory used by SQL Server overhead). On systems that use a lot of ad-hoc queries, it makes sense to reduce the size of the procedure cache (and thus increase the size of the data cache) while on systems that use a lot of stored procedures, the reverse is true. To determine whether the current procedure cache value is adequate, use the SQL Server Cache Hit Ratio and SQL Server—Procedure Cache counters to monitor the procedure and data cache usage.

## CPU Utilization

CPU utilization may also be monitored using Performance Monitor. High CPU utilization may be an indication that there are too many CPU-intensive operations being performed by your application. Examples might be stored procedures that make extensive use of server-side cursors, or tables or views that require a large number of computed columns. As the number of users being supported by your application increases, so too does the expense of these server-side tasks, which after all only have access to limited resources.

If such server-side tasks cannot be eliminated or reduced, the only option may be to upgrade the processor, or if possible, add more processors, to better handle the workload. CPU utilization is another area, like memory use, where additional tasks performed by the database server can have a substantial impact. If you cannot dedicate a machine solely to your database, make certain that the machine has sufficient hardware resources for the tasks it is asked to do.

## Minimize Disk I/O and/or Improve Disk Subsystem Performance

The disk subsystem is generally the slowest part of the hardware, and as such, it is also the one we want to have the least to do with our data. One way to accomplish this is to make sure that the system has sufficient RAM, and that the memory is allocated effectively. Unfortunately, no matter how much RAM you have, sooner or later, the data must be read from and written to the disk.

This being the case, you need to do everything in your power to ensure that your disk subsystem runs as efficiently as possible. Here are some guidelines that can help make this a reality:

- **Don't use IDE drives and use RAID if at all possible**  While IDE drives are still cheaper than SCSI, the performance difference can be substantial. For enterprise applications, RAID (Redundant Array of Inexpensive Disks) should be used to increase performance, as well as for its fault-tolerance features.

- **Don't put your data and log segments on the same physical device** Placing the data and log segments of your database on physically separate devices lets you divide the I/O requests for your database between the devices, which increases performance.

You can monitor the disk subsystem performance using the Logical Disk and Physical Disk Performance Monitor counters.

# There Is *No* Single Right Answer

In your quest for optimal performance from your database server, avoid the trap of tunnel vision. While it is important to focus in on individual areas, such as hardware utilization or query performance, it is equally important to keep a big picture view as well. Remember that each individual application is different and will have different needs. The techniques described in this chapter should be used as a starting point. Use them, but combine them with techniques from co-workers, from magazines, from SQL Server Books Online, and from anyplace else you can find database expertise. The quest for better database performance is a never-ending one.

In your pursuit of that quest, it's unlikely that you will find an application in which the sole cause of database problems is in just one area. The greatest gains in performance and optimization are almost always achieved by combining techniques of query optimization with hardware optimization, and with application optimization. High-performance database applications are made with good planning. But even poorly performing database applications can be substantially improved by profiling (with Performance Monitor and SQL Trace, as well as with other tools you may have available) and by discovering *where* the problems are. Once you know where the problems are, you can then use the techniques described in this chapter, as well as those of the previous chapter, to systematically eliminate those problems.

## Summary

In this chapter, we discussed ways to improve and optimize the data access portion of your application. The techniques and topics described included:

- Using SQL Trace to profile your data access
- Optimizing User Connections
- Optimizing Queries
- Optimizing Contention and Locking
- Optimizing Hardware Resources

Although they are only the beginning of a sound strategy for database optimization, the techniques described in this chapter will get you well on your way to the high-performance data access of your dreams.

# Debugging, Deployment, and Team-Based Development

Debugging, application deployment, and team-based development are features supported by Visual InterDev 6.0 that will help you polish and finish the implementation of your applications. We will take the opportunity in this appendix to familiarize developers with these features.

## Debugging Client and Server Scripts

*Debugging* is the process of locating and fixing errors or problems in your applications. Debugging environments, such as the one included with Visual InterDev 6.0, are designed to assist you in this task. Visual InterDev's integrated debugger allows you to perform standard debugging tasks, including:

- Setting breakpoints in your code
- Viewing and changing variable values
- Viewing the application's Call Stack (the list of active procedures)
- Setting values for variables that, when reached or exceeded, cause the application to enter break mode
- Stepping through code and procedures
- Altering the flow of application execution

In the next sections, we'll discuss the steps necessary to prepare for debugging your applications in Visual InterDev 6.0 and give an overview of the Visual InterDev debugging environment.

## Preparing for Debugging

In order to prepare for debugging your application in Visual InterDev there are several steps you must take. These are:

- Enabling debugging
- Setting a start page
- Setting a breakpoint

### Enabling Debugging

If you plan on debugging server-side ASP code (or client-side code in ASP pages), you'll need to enable debugging on your Web server. You can do this in one of two ways: automatically at debug time, or manually in advance. To set your project to automatically enable debugging, follow these steps:

1. In the Project Explorer window, right-click the project name and select Properties.

2. In the Launch tab of the project Properties dialog box, check the Automatically enable ASP server-side script debugging on launch check box, as shown in Figure A-1.

**Figure A-1.**
*Enabling server-side debugging.*

Now when you start a debugging session, Visual InterDev will take all the necessary steps to enable debugging on the server. If, however, you wish to debug by attaching to running processes or in response to run time errors, or you have problems with automatic debugging, you can manually configure the server for debugging with the following steps:

1. On the server, start the Internet Service Manager MMC snap-in by selecting Programs | Windows NT 4.0 Option Pack | Microsoft Internet Information Server | Internet Service Manager from the Start menu.

2. In the left-hand pane of the Internet Service Manager, expand the Web tree until your application's folder is visible, as shown in Figure A-2.

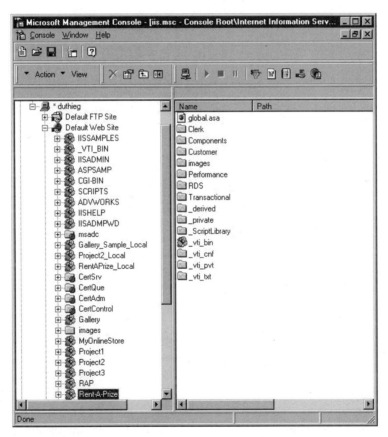

**Figure A-2.**
*Internet Service Manager MMC snap-in.*

3. Right-click the application folder and select Properties. In the application's Properties dialog box, check the Run in separate memory space (isolated process) check box.

4. Click the Configuration... button. In the App Debugging tab of the Application Configuration dialog box, check the Enable ASP server-side script debugging and Enable ASP client-side script debugging check boxes, and click OK (see Figure A-3).

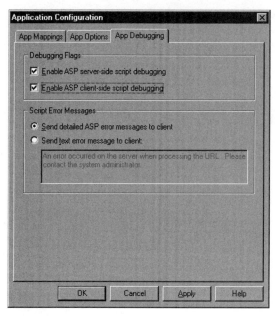

**Figure A-3.**
*App Debugging tab of the Application Configuration dialog box.*

5. Click OK or Apply in the application's Properties dialog box to apply your changes to the application. To disable debugging, reverse steps 3 through 5.

## Setting a Start Page

Setting a start page for debugging is quite simple. To set a start page for debugging in your project, simply right-click the file you wish to debug in the Project Explorer window, and select Set as Start Page. Alternately, you can set the *Start Page* parameter on the Launch tab of the projects' Properties dialog box to the name of the files you wish to debug.

## Setting a Breakpoint

Setting a breakpoint is also a simple process. To set a breakpoint in your page, simply open the page in the Source view, and click in the left margin next to the line at which execution should stop, as shown in Figure A-4. (Note that Visual InterDev displays a tooltip listing the line number at which you've set the breakpoint.)

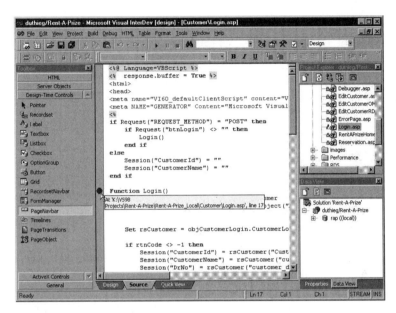

**Figure A-4.**
*Setting a breakpoint.*

Once you've set a breakpoint, you start debugging by either selecting the Start command from the Debug menu, or by clicking the Start button on the Debug toolbar (the raised button in Figure A-5).

While in Debug mode, you can use the Debug toolbar to step through your code, set and remove breakpoints, and display any of the debug windows (described in the section, "Debug Environment").

**Figure A-5.**
*The Debug toolbar.*

## Alternate Debugging Methods

In addition to setting a start page in your project, you can start a debugging session by connecting to running processes, or in response to a run-time error (just-in-time debugging).

### Connecting to Internet Explorer and IIS Processes

To debug by connecting to a running process:

1. Use the Debug toolbar to open the Processes dialog box.

2. Select a process to connect to, then click the Attach button, then click Close. The selected document process will appear in the Running Documents debug window.

### Just-in-Time Debugging

Just-in-time debugging invokes the Visual InterDev debugger in response to script errors in your pages. To enable just-in-time debugging:

1. Select Tools | Options....

2. In the Options dialog box, select Debugger.

3. Under Script, select the Just-in-Time debugging check box, and click OK.

When a script error occurs in a page running on a machine on which just-in-time debugging is enabled, a dialog box will be displayed asking if you wish to debug the page. Click Yes to open the page in the debugging environment.

## Debugging Environment

The debugging environment consists of the windows and commands used to debug your applications. These include:

- The **Debug toolbar** (see Figure A-5)   Provides access to frequently used debug commands and windows.

- The **Autos window**   Displays the values of variables within the scope of the line executing in the current procedure.

- The **Call Stack window**   Shows a list of all the active procedures for the currently executing thread.

- The **Immediate window**   Allows you to enter statements or expressions to be evaluated in the context of the currently executing thread.

- The **Locals window**   Shows a list of variables that are local to the currently executing procedure. The list changes as execution switches from one procedure to another.

- The **Running Documents window**   Shows a list of the documents loaded into the process you are debugging. You can open an editor window for a document by double-clicking it.

- The **Threads window**   Shows a list of threads for the current process and their properties.

- The **Watch window**   Allows you to monitor or change the values of selected variables. To add a variable to the Watch window, highlight the variable in the Source view window and drag it to the Watch window.

To make debugging more convenient, you may wish to set up some or all of the debug windows in a tabbed window, as shown in Figure A-6. To do so, simply open the first debug window and set its desired placement, then open and drag subsequent debug windows onto the title bar of the first window. (Note that this procedure works with any Visual InterDev window.) To view each debug window, simply select its tab.

**Figure A-6.**
*Tabbed window setup.*

NOTE: For performance reasons, it is recommended that you debug your Web applications against your local Web server. If you must debug your application remotely, you will need either to have Administrator rights to the remote machine, or you will need to be set up with debugging permissions for that server.

# Deploying Your Application

Once you've developed and debugged your application, the next thing you'll want to do, logically, is deploy it. Visual InterDev 6.0 makes deploying your Web applications quite easy. Before you deploy, however, you'll want to follow the advice found in the section, "Preparing for Deployment." Once you've determined that you're ready, just follow the steps outlined in the sections, "Deploying without Components," and "Deploying with Components," depending on whether or not your application uses components.

## Preparing for Deployment

Before you deploy your applications, there are a few things you should check to ensure successful deployment. They are:

- **Links**   Ensure that all links in your project will work when the project is deployed. All internal links should be specified as relative paths (for example, <A HREF="mypage.htm">). External links should use absolute paths (for example, <A HREF=http://myserver/mywebapp/mypage.htm >).

- **Files**   Ensure that all files used by the application, including components, are included in the Web project.

- **Updates**   Ensure that all files on the master Web server have been updated. Make sure you release all working copies or synchronize your local and master Web server files before deploying.

- **Data**   Ensure that your database connection will work on the production server. This can be accomplished either by using a File DSN, or if you are using a System DSN, by creating a matching System DSN on the production machine (Appendix B, "Installing the Rent-A-Prize Sample Application," describes the process of setting up a System DSN).

- **Components**   For applications that use components, ensure that the components are configured properly for installation on the target machine. Components in your application should be marked for client or server registration and/or installation in Microsoft Transaction Server (MTS) packages as required by your application (you will need the appropriate permissions to register components on the Web server).

Once you have verified all of the above information, you can move on to deployment.

## Deploying without Components

For the easiest method of deploying your application, your production server should have FrontPage server extensions installed. To deploy your application to a server with FrontPage extensions:

1. In the Project Explorer window, select the project you wish to deploy.

2. From the Project menu, select Web Project | Copy Web Application....

3. In the Copy Project dialog box (see Figure A-7), enter the name of the destination server, the folder name to deploy to (make sure to check or clear the Add to an existing Web project as appropriate), then click OK. Visual InterDev creates the application root on the target server (if necessary) and copies the Web application to the server. The application is now ready to use.

If you have trouble with your deployment, double-check the list in the section, "Preparing for Deployment," or check the Visual InterDev documentation under "Troubleshooting."

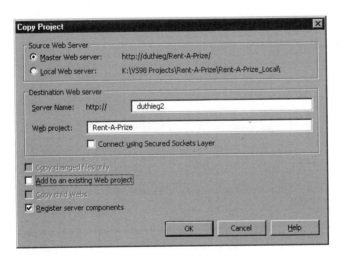

**Figure A-7.**
*The Copy Project dialog box.*

### Deploying with Components

There are three added steps to deploying an application that uses components from within Visual InterDev:

- **Adding components to your project**  Create a folder (or folders) in your application for your components, then drag the components from Windows Explorer into the project folders you defined.

- **Configuring component registration and packaging**  Use the Properties dialog box for each component to specify that the component should be registered on the client or server as appropriate. You can also use the Properties dialog box to specify that the component should be added to an MTS package, as well as to specify the package name, and the component's transactional attributes.

- **Register server components**  In the Copy Project dialog box, check the Register server components check box.

Once you have performed the additional steps listed above, the application can be deployed as shown above in "Deploying without Components."

NOTE: To install and register components on a remote Web server through Visual InterDev, the Web server must be running Internet Information Server and must have the Visual InterDev RAD Remote Deployment Support installed. For components to be used with Microsoft Transaction Server (MTS), MTS must be installed on the target machine.

# Using Team-Based Development Features

Visual InterDev provides a variety of features for supporting and enabling team-based development, which include the ability to work in local mode and integration with the Microsoft SourceSafe source code control system.

### Using Local Mode for Isolated Development and Testing

Local mode development allows developers to create and modify pages against a copy of the Web application that is running on their local machine. This allows developers to affect other developers with their changes and to avoid being affected by other developers' changes. After making changes and testing those changes against the local version of the application, the developer can either update the master Web application with the changes or discard the changes.

To work in local mode, right-click the project in the Project Explorer window and select Working Mode | Local. To return to master mode (which automatically saves any changes to the master Web project), select Working Mode | Master.

To update the master Web server with your changes, right-click the changed file and select Release Working Copy. To discard changes, right-click the changed file and select Discard Changes. If you create new pages while working in local mode, you can add those pages to the master Web application by right-clicking the new file(s) and selecting Add to Master Web.

## Integrating with Visual SourceSafe for Version Control

In addition to enabling developer isolation with local mode, Visual InterDev 6.0 allows developers to take advantage of the features of the Microsoft Visual SourceSafe source code control system to manage file access in a team-developed application. Putting your application's code under source control helps developers avoid overwriting one another's work, which can be a costly error.

Using Visual SourceSafe with Visual InterDev 6.0 requires that Visual SourceSafe be installed on the master Web server. At a minimum, you must install the SourceSafe database and administrative programs, and enable SourceSafe integration. See the Visual SourceSafe documentation for further information on installing SourceSafe. Because Visual InterDev is designed to integrate with Visual SourceSafe, you do not need to install the Visual SourceSafe client on each developer's machine.

There are three tasks you will typically perform with source code control:

- Enabling source control for a project
- Checking out a file
- Checking in a file

To enable source control for a project (note that you must have a SourceSafe login configured in order to add a project to source control):

1. From the Project menu, select Add to Source Control....

2. In the Initial Project Add dialog box, choose whether to add the entire solution or just the selected project(s) to source control.

3. Log in to the SourceSafe database (if necessary).

4. In the Add to SourceSafe Project dialog box, specify the project name and click the Create button. Click OK to add the project to SourceSafe.

NOTE: You may also need to set up a user account for the IUSR_*<machinename>* account in order to set up source code control for a project.

Once you have set up source code control for a project, you'll need to check files in and out in order to make changes and have those changes updated in the SourceSafe database (and the master Web application).

- To check a file out, simply right-click the file in the Project Explorer window and select Check Out *<filename>*... and click OK in the Check Out dialog box (if necessary).

- To check the file in, right click the file and select Check In *<filename>*... and click OK in the Check In dialog box.

- To release the file and discard any changes, right-click the file and select Undo Check Out of *<filename>*... and click OK in the Undo Check Out dialog box (if necessary).

It is also possible, if desired, to remove a project from source code control. To remove a project from source control:

1. In the Project Explorer window, select the project to remove from source code control.

2. From the Project menu, select Source Control | Disconnect Web Project. You'll be asked to confirm that you wish to remove the project from source control.

# Installing the Rent-A-Prize Sample Application

In order to install the sample application, there are a number of requirements you will need to meet and procedures you will need to follow. This appendix outlines what those requirements are and leads you through the procedures necessary to install the sample application.

> DISCLAIMER: The Rent-A-Prize sample application is supplied for educational purposes only. While you may feel free to use any and all of the code in the sample application in your own applications, we make no warranty as to its fitness for any such use. Please note also that the Rent-A-Prize sample application was developed using beta versions of Visual Studio, Enterprise Edition. As such, there may be changes from the beta to the released code that cause certain parts of the application to function incorrectly (or not at all). Please understand that while we have done our best to ensure that the procedures in this appendix will allow you to install the sample application in working order, differences in your system configuration from our test systems may also cause parts of the application to function incorrectly.

Now that we have that out of the way, we suggest that if you do find areas where the sample application does not function as you expect it to, that you take those areas as an opportunity to learn more about the application by troubleshooting. Troubleshooting and fixing application problems can be one of the most effective ways of learning how an application works.

# Requirements

In order to install and run the Rent-A-Prize sample application you must have installed the following on the Web server:

- Windows NT 4.0 (SP 3 or higher)
- Microsoft SQL Server 6.5 (SP 3 or higher)
- Microsoft Internet Information Server 4.0
- Microsoft Transaction Server 2.0
- FrontPage 98 Server Extensions
- Visual InterDev RAD Remote Deployment Support
- Microsoft Visual Basic 6.0 (or the VB6 runtime DLL, MSVBVM60.DLL, which can be found on the CD included with the book, in the RAP\COMPONENT\RUNTIME\ folder).

On the client, you should install the following:

- Microsoft Visual InterDev 6.0
- Microsoft Visual C++ 6.0 or Visual Studio 6.0, Enterprise Edition (optional for stored procedure debugging and additional Visual Database Tools functionality)

The easiest way to get all of the above installed (and more), is to install Visual Studio 6.0, Enterprise Edition. The Enterprise Edition not only includes all of the Visual Studio development tools, but also comes with Microsoft BackOffice Developer Edition, which includes Microsoft SQL Server 6.5 and SNA Server. For serious programmers developing enterprise-grade applications on Windows NT, the investment is well worth it.

# Installing the Project Files

Installing the files for the Web project is a three-step process. We'll install the Rent-A-Prize application by creating a new empty Web project, dragging and dropping the project files from the CD included with the book into the project, and setting up the necessary registration and packaging properties of the components.

## Creating a New Web Project

To start a new Web project, follow these steps:

1. Open Visual InterDev.

2. In the New Project dialog box, select the New Web Project icon, enter *Rent-A-Prize* in the Name field, and click the Open button.

3. In Step 1 of the Web Project Wizard, enter the name of the Web server on which you wish to install the sample application and make sure the Master mode radio button is selected, then click Next.

4. In Step 2 of the Web Project Wizard, select the option to create a new Web (the default). Since we won't be selecting Themes or Layouts, click Finish to bypass the last two pages of the wizard.

## Adding the Rent-A-Prize Files to the Project

To add the Rent-A-Prize files to your new project, follow these steps:

1. Open Windows Explorer.

2. Insert the CD included with this book into your CD-ROM drive, and use Windows Explorer to navigate to the folder D:\RAP\Project\, where *D* is the letter of your CD-ROM drive. The results should look similar to Figure B-1.

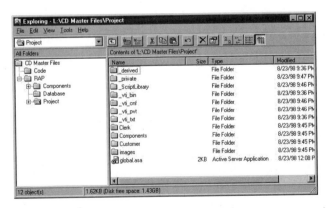

**Figure B-1.**
*Exploring the RAP\Project\ folder.*

3. In the Explorer window, select Edit | Select All to highlight all the files and folders in the Project folder.

4. Drag the highlighted files from Windows Explorer onto the Visual InterDev project in the Project Explorer window (you may need to rearrange the Visual InterDev and Explorer windows to make this possible). Make sure that you drop the files onto the project file, or the installation will not proceed correctly.

If you have followed all the steps correctly, the Merge Folders dialog box will appear. Each time it appears, check the Apply to all items check box and click Yes. The project files will be copied to the Web application's root folder, as well as to the local project folder. Save the project.

## Registering and Packaging Components

In order for the Rent-A-Prize application to work properly, the components provided in the \Components folder of the CD provided with this book must be properly registered on the Web server. For better performance, the components should also be added to a Microsoft Transaction Server (MTS) package.

To register the components, follow these steps:

1. In the Project Explorer window, right-click the first component in the \Components folder, then select Properties. Select the Component Installation tab.

2. On the Component Installation tab, check the Register on server check box and click Apply. Don't close the dialog box just yet.

3. Select the next component. The Properties dialog box will be updated to reflect the change in selection. Again, check the Register on server check box and click Apply.

4. Repeat Step 3 for the rest of the components. When you have registered the last component, click OK.

Installing the components into an MTS package can be done either through Visual InterDev or through the MTS Explorer snap-in for the Microsoft Management Console. We'll concentrate on the Visual InterDev method. To package the components from Visual InterDev, follow these steps:

1. Follow Steps 1 and 2 above, but don't click apply. When you check the Register on server check box, the Add to Microsoft Transaction Server package check box is enabled. Check this box.

2. In the Package name field, enter *RAP_Package*. All of the components may be installed in this package (note that this is not necessarily the way that you would want to do this in a production application).

3. Set the transaction support property for each component according to Table B-1 below (click Apply after setting the property for each component, as described above):

| Component | Setting |
| --- | --- |
| bsCreditCardAuth.dll | Requires a new transaction |
| bsCustomer.dll | Supports transactions |
| bsInventory.dll | Supports transactions |
| bsLocation.dll | Supports transactions |
| bsRental.dll | Supports transactions |
| bsReservation.dll | Supports transactions |
| bsVehicle.dll | Supports transactions |
| bsVehicleType.dll | Supports transactions |
| dsDataConnect.dll | Requires a transaction |

**Table B-1.**
*Transactional property settings for the Rent-A-Prize components.*

4. Once you have set the MTS properties for each component, click OK.

NOTE: Most of the Rent-A-Prize components have a class for fetching records and a class for updating records. If you were using the MTS Explorer to package these components, it might make some sense to set the update classes to require transactions, to decrease the likelihood of problems with data integrity. The MTS Explorer allows you to set properties at the class level, while Visual InterDev only allows you to set them on a DLL-by-DLL basis.

# Creating the Database

The database for the Rent-A-Prize sample application was created in Microsoft SQL Server 6.5. Creating the sample database requires four steps: creating the SQL Server database to host the data, creating the tables and stored procedures, importing the data into the tables, and setting up a DSN for the database.

## Creating the Rent-A-Prize Database

Creating the database requires two steps, creating the device on which the database will live, and creating the database itself. While both of these steps can be done in a number of ways with SQL Server 6.5, we are going to describe them as they would be performed using SQL Enterprise Manager, since it graphical interface is far easier to use than the alternatives. Note that for this part of the installation, we are assuming that you already have SQL Enterprise Manager available on your workstation, and that you have registered the server on which you wish to install the sample database. If you need assistance, contact your database administrator (DBA), or see the SQL Server Book Online topic, "Registering Servers."

> IMPORTANT: The login and password used when registering the server in Enterprise Manager must have permission to create devices, databases, tables, and stored procedures for the installation to proceed successfully. In addition, in order to run the scripts that import the sample data into the tables, your login account must have execute permission on the xp_cmdshell extended stored procedure. If you register the server using the built-in sa (system administrator) account, all of the above will be true.

1. Open SQL Enterprise Manager from the Start menu by selecting Programs | Microsoft SQL Server 6.5 | SQL Enterprise Manager.

2. Expand the server tree so that you can see the Database Devices and Databases folders. Right-click the Database Devices folder and select New Device.... If this option is disabled, then you do not have sufficient rights to create a device. See your DBA to get the necessary rights.

3. In the New Database Device dialog box (see Figure B-2), enter *RAP* in the Name field, select a location (use the default if possible), and enter *3* for the Size field (use a larger number if you expect to add substantially to the sample data). To create the device, click Create Now.

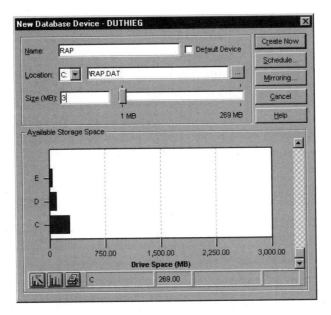

**Figure B-2.**
*New Database Device dialog box.*

4. Right-click the Databases folder and select New Database.... If this option is disabled, then you do not have sufficient rights to create a database. See your DBA to get the necessary rights.

5. In the New Database dialog box (see Figure B-3), enter *RAP* in the Name field, select the RAP device created in Step 3 for the Data Device field and for the Log Device field, enter *2* for the Data Device Size, and enter *1* for the Log Device size. To create the database, click Create Now.

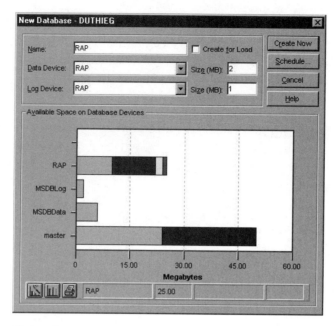

**Figure B-3.**
*New Database dialog box.*

NOTE: If we were creating a database for a normal application, we would want to create separate devices for the data and log segments of the database. In fact, for the best performance, those devices ideally want to be located on physically separate storage devices.

Now that the device and database have been created, it's time to move on to creating the tables that will store the data and the stored procedures that will manipulate it.

## Creating the Tables and Stored Procedures

We'll use SQL scripts to create the tables and stored procedure, to make the process as simple as possible. Follow these steps:

1. Open a query window in SQL Enterprise Manager by selecting the RAP database from the Server Manager window, and then selecting SQL Query Tool... from the Tools menu.

2. In the Query window, use the Load SQL Script button (see Figure B-4) to load the RAP_DB.sql script from the \RAP\Database\Scripts folder on the CD-ROM.

**Figure B-4.**
*Load SQL Script button.*

3. Execute the script either by clicking the Execute Query button (which looks like the play button on a tape player) or by using the Ctrl + E keyboard shortcut. The script should return the following response:

```
This command did not return data, and it did not return any
rows
```

The tables and stored procedures should now be installed.

## Importing the Data

Importing the data into the newly created tables is accomplished by the following steps:

1. In the already open Query window, use the Load SQL Script button to load the DataImport.SQL script from the \RAP\Database\Scripts folder on the CD-ROM.

    For each table (with the exception of the Rental and Credit tables), there is a command in the script that uses the SQL Server's bulk copy program (bcp) to import data into the table. In order for this to work properly, you may need to change the path and userID and password parameters that the script passes to bcp.

2. If you are installing the database on your local machine, make sure that the path parameter points to your CD-ROM drive. For example, the default path for the customer data in the script is:

```
D:\RAP\Database\Data\customer.bcp
```

    If your CD-ROM drive letter is F, you would change the path parameter to:

```
F:\RAP\Database\Data\customer.bcp
```

NOTE: If you are installing to a remote SQL Server, copy all the files in the \RAP\Database\Data folder to a temporary location on the SQL Server machine, then change the path parameter of each command to point to that path.

3. If you are using a userID and password other than sa and blank for your SQL Server database, change the –U and –P parameters to match your userID and password (remember that the account you use must have execute permission on the xp_cmdshell extended stored procedure in order to successfully import the data). For example, if your userID is *SQL* and your password is *server*, the command line for the customer table would look like this:

```
EXEC master..xp_cmdshell 'bcp rap.dbo.customer in
F:\RAP\Database\Data\customer.bcp -c -E -USQL -Pserver'
```

4. Once you have made the appropriate changes in the command for each table, execute the script by clicking the Execute Query button (or using Ctrl + E). Close the Query window when the script has finished executing.

## Setting Up the DSN

The final step in installing the Rent-A-Prize database is setting up the Data Source Name (DSN). The DSN tells Visual InterDev where to find your data. To set up the DSN for the Rent-A-Prize database, follow these steps:

1. Open the Rent-A-Prize project in Visual InterDev. When you first open the project, the Data Connection for the RAP database already exists, but it will not function without a DSN.

To add the DSN, we'll fool Visual InterDev into thinking we want to add a new Data Connection in order to get access to the command to create the DSN.

2. In the Project Explorer window, right-click GLOBAL.ASA and select Add Data Connection....

3. In the Select Data Source dialog box, switch to the Machine Data Source tab, and click the New... button.

4. Select System Data Source, then click Next.

5. Select the SQL Server driver and click Next, then click Finish. The SQL Server driver will now ask you to complete several more steps.

6. In the first step, enter *RAP* for the Name field, Rent-A-Prize sample database for the Description field, and use the drop-down box to select the appropriate server, then click Next.

7. In the second step, select the SQL Server Authentication option, then enter the Login ID and password with which you will be connecting to SQL Server. Make certain that the account you specify has sufficient rights (create, update, and so on) to perform all the actions you will need to perform in Visual InterDev. Click Next.

8. In the third step, check the Change the default database to: check box, and select the RAP database from the drop-down list and clear the check box for creating temporary stored procedures, then click Next.

9. In the fourth step, click Next to accept the defaults.

10. In the fifth step, click Finish. In the ODBC Microsoft SQL Server Setup dialog box, use the Test Data Source... button to make sure the DSN works, then click OK to close both dialog boxes.

11. Finally, click Cancel to close the Select Data Source dialog box.

You should now be able to connect to the sample database (you may be prompted for a password if you did not supply one in the DSN setup process).

# Viewing the Component Source Code

The Visual Basic source code for the Rent-A-Prize components is located in the folder D:\RAP\Component\ on the CD-ROM, where *D* is the letter of your CD-ROM drive. The folders containing the component source code are structured as follows:

- Components\Business Services\. Contains code for the business-tier components. Each component has a separate folder. This folder also contains a Visual Basic group file with which you can open all the business service components at once.

- Components\Common\. Contains code common to all of the components.

- Components\Data Service\. Contains code for the data service component.

- Components\DLLs\. Contains the components compiled as DLLs. Separated into business service DLLs and data service DLLs.

■ Components\Test\. Contains Visual Basic EXE projects built as test projects for the components. Note that these projects are for utility purposes only, and may not be as up-to-date as the rest of the code.

NOTE: Remember that the Rent-A-Prize application was designed primarily as a sample application and as a tool for learning. Although we endeavored to use the best practices in its construction, it is in the nature of sample applications that they rarely enjoy the same resources as the applications we design and build for clients (who are, after all, paying for the application). There may be areas where corners were cut to save time, or implementation was simplified to illustrate a point. This should not be construed as an endorsement of these practices. Readers should use what they've learned from this book to analyze the Rent-A-Prize sample application, find its weaknesses, and think about how they might be overcome.

# INDEX

# Spectrum Technology Group

## About Spectrum

Spectrum Technology Group provides IT management consulting and solutions delivery services that apply advanced methods and technologies to solve complex business problems.

Over the last 20 years, Spectrum has delivered over 600 successful information technology solutions for an impressive roster of clients. Today, Spectrum employs over 450 professionals at locations in 13 cities across the United States and as part of its National Practice of full-time traveling consultants. We're part of the CIBER Corporation (NYSE: CBR), which employs over 5,000 professionals in 80 locations.

Spectrum is a leader in delivering solutions and services in these areas:

- Enterprise IT Planning

- Project Management

- Data Warehousing

- Distributed Business Applications

- Web Solutions
- Technical Training

Visit our Web site at www.spectrumtech.com to learn more about Spectrum's services and solutions.

## Our Team

Spectrum's greatest strength is our team of information systems professionals. Spectrum is more than an individual branch office or consultant; it is an organized collection of people, experiences, and processes that offers more value than any one individual or group. To join our team of professionals, contact us at 1-800-486-5201 or visit the career section of our Web site: www.spectrumtech.com.

# About the Authors

**G. Andrew Duthie**   is a Microsoft Certified Solution Developer and a consultant for Spectrum Technology Group, Inc., in McLean, Virginia, where he specializes in Web development. Andrew's interest in programming began at the precocious age of ten, when he learned to write and modify programs in BASIC on his school's Commodore PET. After several years' hiatus, including a six-year stint working in technical theater, Andrew returned to the development world just in time for the release of Visual Studio 97, and in particular, Visual InterDev 1.0, which enabled him to leverage his knowledge of BASIC to move into Web development. In addition to consulting and writing (including articles for *SQL Server* magazine), Andrew has also spoken on Web development issues for the Internet Developer SIG of the Association of Windows NT Professionals, at the Microsoft Explorer 98 Technology & Business Conference and Exposition, and also gave the Visual InterDev 6.0 presentations at the Washington, DC/ Baltimore 1998 Developer Days conference. Andrew can be reached at AndrewD@SpectrumTech.com.

**Susie Adams** is a Manager at Spectrum Technologies, a client-server and Internet solutions consulting firm in McLean, Virginia. Susie is an experienced developer with over 12 years of experience in the Windows development arena. She currently focuses her attention on the design and development of active content Web applications and multi-tier component-based MTS enterprise solutions. Susie is the contributing editor for the *Cobb's Active Server Journal* and a frequent speaker at industry conferences. Susie can be reached at sadams@spectrumtech.com.

**Paul H. Parry** has served as chief architect and lead developer on key projects for clients in the telecommunications, financial services, and travel industries, specializing in enterprise intranets and extranets. He has spoken at several conferences, including VBITS Interactive, and his articles have appeared in *Visual Basic Programmers' Journal* and Ziff Davis's *Active Server Developers' Journal*. Paul has a degree in Engineering and Economics from Brown University, and lives with his wife, Robin, in Arlington, Virginia.

Paul is the Director of Product Development at Rocketworks in Bethesda, Maryland, where he is building an interactive online production service. He can be reached at paulp@rocketworks.com.

**Chris Dellinger** is a consultant with Spectrum Technology Group specializing in the architecture and development of distributed, n-tier systems for both the Internet and Windows platforms. He has been tinkering with computers since the age of twelve, when his father, believing that computer experience "might actually be valuable in the future," had the foresight to enroll Chris and himself in a BASIC class. Not too long thereafter, Chris's parents bought the family its first computer, a Commodore 64, and Chris was hooked. Since that time, he has been constantly playing with new technologies and programming with one language after another. Over the past few years, he has concentrated his efforts on developing client/server and Web-based systems with Microsoft technologies. Chris is a frequent writer for *Microsoft Interactive Developer* (MIND) magazine and has also spoken at several developer conferences.

Chris lives in Raleigh, North Carolina, with his wife, Ginny, and their two troublesome Siberian Huskies, Thor and Hokie. When not in front of a computer, Chris, Ginny, and "the boys" can be found running, backpacking, kayaking, or just enjoying life away from computers. This year has been a very busy year for the Dellingers, with the purchase of their first home, contributing to this book, the training for and completion of their first marathon (Big Sur), along with keeping up a busy work schedule. Chris can be reached at cdellinger@rubicontechnologies.com.

**Geoff Snowman** is a manager with Spectrum Technology Group, where he specializes in Windows DNA, Microsoft's distributed application architecture. He spends the majority of his time designing and developing client-server and Internet applications, using tools like Visual C++, Visual Basic, Active Server Pages, and SQL Server. One of Spectrum's practice areas is distributed applications, and Geoff especially enjoys working on enterprise-class projects that combine multiple data sources or multiple platforms.

Geoff is a regular speaker at seminars and conferences. He has spoken in North America, Japan, and Europe on topics ranging from COM component design and data modeling to interoperability with legacy systems. He is also active in Spectrum's Training Division, where he teaches classes in both distributed application design and Internet development.

Geoff has also been active in the multimedia community, where he was a member of several standards committees. He was a major contributor to Department of Defense Standard MIL-STD-1379D, an API for controlling MS-DOS based multimedia systems.

Geoff is a Microsoft Certified Systems Engineer, Microsoft Certified Solution Developer, and a Microsoft Certified Trainer. He is a British exile living in Maryland, and holds an M.A. degree in Computer Science from Cambridge University. Geoff's hobbies include taking MCP examinations, and his motto is "We don't need no stinking Netware."

The Manuscript for this book was prepared and submitted to Microsoft Press in electronic form. Text files were prepared using Microsoft Word 97. Pages were composed by WebSmith, Inc., using Adobe Pagemaker 6.52 for MAC, with text in Galliard and displaly type in Helvetica. Composed pages were delivered to the printer as electronic prepress files.

*Cover Graphic Designer*
Tim Girvin Design, Inc.

*Cover Illustrator*
Glenn Mitsui

*Project Manager*
Robert Kern

*Technical Editor*
Russ Mullen

*Development Editor*
Marty Minner

*Principal Compositor*
Manny Rosa

*Copy Editor*
Jessica Ryan

*Principal Proofreader*
Adam Newton

*Indexer*
Tim Griffin

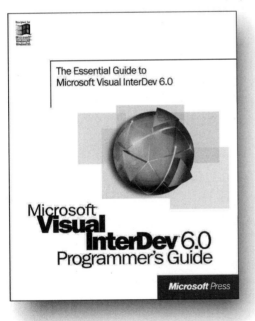

# mspress.microsoft.com

**Microsoft Press Online** is your road map to the best available print and multimedia materials—resources that will help you maximize the effectiveness of Microsoft® software products. Our goal is making it easy and convenient for you to find exactly the Microsoft Press® book or interactive product you need, as well as bringing you the latest in training and certification materials from Microsoft Press.

**Where do you want to go today?®**

# MICROSOFT LICENSE AGREEMENT

(Book Companion CD)

## SOFTWARE PRODUCT LICENSE

The SOFTWARE PRODUCT is protected by United States copyright laws and international copyright treaties, as well as other intellectual property laws and treaties. The SOFTWARE PRODUCT is licensed, not sold.

1. **GRANT OF LICENSE.** This EULA grants you the following rights:

    a. **Software Product.** You may install and use one copy of the SOFTWARE PRODUCT on a single computer. The primary user of the computer on which the SOFTWARE PRODUCT is installed may make a second copy for his or her exclusive use on a portable computer.

    b. **Storage/Network Use.** You may also store or install a copy of the SOFTWARE PRODUCT on a storage device, such as a network server, used only to install or run the SOFTWARE PRODUCT on your other computers over an internal network; however, you must acquire and dedicate a license for each separate computer on which the SOFTWARE PRODUCT is installed or run from the storage device. A license for the SOFTWARE PRODUCT may not be shared or used concurrently on different computers.

    c. **License Pak.** If you have acquired this EULA in a Microsoft License Pak, you may make the number of additional copies of the computer software portion of the SOFTWARE PRODUCT authorized on the printed copy of this EULA, and you may use each copy in the manner specified above. You are also entitled to make a corresponding number of secondary copies for portable computer use as specified above.

    d. **Sample Code.** Solely with respect to portions, if any, of the SOFTWARE PRODUCT that are identified within the SOFTWARE PRODUCT as sample code (the "SAMPLE CODE"):

        i. **Use and Modification.** Microsoft grants you the right to use and modify the source code version of the SAMPLE CODE, *provided* you comply with subsection (d)(iii) below. You may not distribute the SAMPLE CODE, or any modified version of the SAMPLE CODE, in source code form.

        ii. **Redistributable Files.** Provided you comply with subsection (d)(iii) below, Microsoft grants you a nonexclusive, royalty-free right to reproduce and distribute the object code version of the SAMPLE CODE and of any modified SAMPLE CODE, other than SAMPLE CODE (or any modified version thereof) designated as not redistributable in the Readme file that forms a part of the SOFTWARE PRODUCT (the "Non-Redistributable Sample Code"). All SAMPLE CODE other than the Non-Redistributable Sample Code is collectively referred to as the "REDISTRIBUTABLES."

        iii. **Redistribution Requirements.** If you redistribute the REDISTRIBUTABLES, you agree to: (i) distribute the REDISTRIBUTABLES in object code form only in conjunction with and as a part of your software application product; (ii) not use Microsoft's name, logo, or trademarks to market your software application product; (iii) include a valid copyright notice on your software application product; (iv) indemnify, hold harmless, and defend Microsoft from and against any claims or lawsuits, including attorney's fees, that arise or result from the use or distribution of your software application product; and (v) not permit further distribution of the REDISTRIBUTABLES by your end user. Contact Microsoft for the applicable royalties due and other licensing terms for all other uses and/or distribution of the REDISTRIBUTABLES.

2. **DESCRIPTION OF OTHER RIGHTS AND LIMITATIONS.**

    - **Limitations on Reverse Engineering, Decompilation, and Disassembly.** You may not reverse engineer, decompile, or disassemble the SOFTWARE PRODUCT, except and only to the extent that such activity is expressly permitted by applicable law notwithstanding this limitation.

    - **Separation of Components.** The SOFTWARE PRODUCT is licensed as a single product. Its component parts may not be separated for use on more than one computer.

    - **Rental.** You may not rent, lease, or lend the SOFTWARE PRODUCT.

    - **Support Services.** Microsoft may, but is not obligated to, provide you with support services related to the SOFTWARE PRODUCT ("Support Services"). Use of Support Services is governed by the Microsoft policies and programs described in the user manual, in "on-line" documentation, and/or in other Microsoft-provided materials. Any supplemental software code provided to you as part of the Support Services shall be considered part of the SOFTWARE PRODUCT and subject to the terms and conditions of this EULA. With respect to technical information you provide to Microsoft as part of the Support Services, Microsoft may use such information for its business purposes, including for product support and development. Microsoft will not utilize such technical information in a form that personally identifies you.

- **Software Transfer.** You may permanently transfer all of your rights under this EULA, provided you retain no copies, you transfer all of the SOFTWARE PRODUCT (including all component parts, the media and printed materials, any upgrades, this EULA, and, if applicable, the Certificate of Authenticity), **and** the recipient agrees to the terms of this EULA.

- **Termination.** Without prejudice to any other rights, Microsoft may terminate this EULA if you fail to comply with the terms and conditions of this EULA. In such event, you must destroy all copies of the SOFTWARE PRODUCT and all of its component parts.

3. **COPYRIGHT.** All title and copyrights in and to the SOFTWARE PRODUCT (including but not limited to any images, photographs, animations, video, audio, music, text, SAMPLE CODE, REDISTRIBUTABLES, and "applets" incorporated into the SOFTWARE PRODUCT) and any copies of the SOFTWARE PRODUCT are owned by Microsoft or its suppliers. The SOFTWARE PRODUCT is protected by copyright laws and international treaty provisions. Therefore, you must treat the SOFTWARE PRODUCT like any other copyrighted material **except** that you may install the SOFTWARE PRODUCT on a single computer provided you keep the original solely for backup or archival purposes. You may not copy the printed materials accompanying the SOFTWARE PRODUCT.

4. **U.S. GOVERNMENT RESTRICTED RIGHTS.** The SOFTWARE PRODUCT and documentation are provided with RESTRICTED RIGHTS. Use, duplication, or disclosure by the Government is subject to restrictions as set forth in subparagraph (c)(1)(ii) of the Rights in Technical Data and Computer Software clause at DFARS 252.227-7013 or subparagraphs (c)(1) and (2) of the Commercial Computer Software—Restricted Rights at 48 CFR 52.227-19, as applicable. Manufacturer is Microsoft Corporation/One Microsoft Way/Redmond, WA 98052-6399.

5. **EXPORT RESTRICTIONS.** You agree that you will not export or re-export the SOFTWARE PRODUCT, any part thereof, or any process or service that is the direct product of the SOFTWARE PRODUCT (the foregoing collectively referred to as the "Restricted Components"), to any country, person, entity, or end user subject to U.S. export restrictions. You specifically agree not to export or re-export any of the Restricted Components (i) to any country to which the U.S. has embargoed or restricted the export of goods or services, which currently include, but are not necessarily limited to, Cuba, Iran, Iraq, Libya, North Korea, Sudan, and Syria, or to any national of any such country, wherever located, who intends to transmit or transport the Restricted Components back to such country; (ii) to any end user who you know or have reason to know will utilize the Restricted Components in the design, development, or production of nuclear, chemical, or biological weapons; or (iii) to any end user who has been prohibited from participating in U.S. export transactions by any federal agency of the U.S. government. You warrant and represent that neither the BXA nor any other U.S. federal agency has suspended, revoked, or denied your export privileges.

## DISCLAIMER OF WARRANTY

**NO WARRANTIES OR CONDITIONS.** MICROSOFT EXPRESSLY DISCLAIMS ANY WARRANTY OR CONDITION FOR THE SOFTWARE PRODUCT. THE SOFTWARE PRODUCT AND ANY RELATED DOCUMENTATION IS PROVIDED "AS IS" WITHOUT WARRANTY OR CONDITION OF ANY KIND, EITHER EXPRESS OR IMPLIED, INCLUDING, WITHOUT LIMITATION, THE IMPLIED WARRANTIES OF MERCHANTABILITY, FITNESS FOR A PARTICULAR PURPOSE, OR NONINFRINGEMENT. THE ENTIRE RISK ARISING OUT OF USE OR PERFORMANCE OF THE SOFTWARE PRODUCT REMAINS WITH YOU.

**LIMITATION OF LIABILITY.** TO THE MAXIMUM EXTENT PERMITTED BY APPLICABLE LAW, IN NO EVENT SHALL MICROSOFT OR ITS SUPPLIERS BE LIABLE FOR ANY SPECIAL, INCIDENTAL, INDIRECT, OR CONSEQUENTIAL DAMAGES WHATSOEVER (INCLUDING, WITHOUT LIMITATION, DAMAGES FOR LOSS OF BUSINESS PROFITS, BUSINESS INTERRUP-TION, LOSS OF BUSINESS INFORMATION, OR ANY OTHER PECUNIARY LOSS) ARISING OUT OF THE USE OF OR INABIL-ITY TO USE THE SOFTWARE PRODUCT OR THE PROVISION OF OR FAILURE TO PROVIDE SUPPORT SERVICES, EVEN IF MICROSOFT HAS BEEN ADVISED OF THE POSSIBILITY OF SUCH DAMAGES. IN ANY CASE, MICROSOFT'S ENTIRE LIABILITY UNDER ANY PROVISION OF THIS EULA SHALL BE LIMITED TO THE GREATER OF THE AMOUNT ACTUALLY PAID BY YOU FOR THE SOFTWARE PRODUCT OR US$5.00; PROVIDED, HOWEVER, IF YOU HAVE ENTERED INTO A MICROSOFT SUPPORT SERVICES AGREEMENT, MICROSOFT'S ENTIRE LIABILITY REGARDING SUPPORT SERVICES SHALL BE GOVERNED BY THE TERMS OF THAT AGREEMENT. BECAUSE SOME STATES AND JURISDICTIONS DO NOT ALLOW THE EXCLUSION OR LIMITATION OF LIABILITY, THE ABOVE LIMITATION MAY NOT APPLY TO YOU.

## MISCELLANEOUS

This EULA is governed by the laws of the State of Washington USA, except and only to the extent that applicable law mandates governing law of a different jurisdiction.

Should you have any questions concerning this EULA, or if you desire to contact Microsoft for any reason, please contact the Microsoft subsidiary serving your country, or write: Microsoft Sales Information Center/One Microsoft Way/Redmond, WA 98052-6399.

# Register Today!

Return this
*Microsoft® Visual InterDev™ 6.0 Enterprise Developer's Workshop*
registration card today

## Microsoft®Press
**mspress.microsoft.com**

**OWNER REGISTRATION CARD**                                    0-7356-0568-8

## Microsoft® Visual InterDev™ 6.0 Enterprise Developer's Workshop

FIRST NAME            MIDDLE INITIAL        LAST NAME

INSTITUTION OR COMPANY NAME

ADDRESS

CITY                                      STATE        ZIP

                                          (    )
E-MAIL ADDRESS                            PHONE NUMBER

U.S. and Canada addresses only. Fill in information above and mail postage-free.
Please mail only the bottom half of this page.

**For information about Microsoft Press®
products, visit our Web site at
mspress.microsoft.com**

**Microsoft®** *Press*

Ill..l..l.l.lll..l..l.ll.l.l.l.l.l..ll.ll....ll.l